Self-Determination and Humanitarian Secession in International Law of a Globalized World

Juan Francisco Escudero Espinosa

Self-Determination and Humanitarian Secession in International Law of a Globalized World

Kosovo v. Crimea

Springer

Juan Francisco Escudero Espinosa
Faculty of Law
University of Leon
Leon, Spain

ISBN 978-3-030-10237-1 ISBN 978-3-319-72622-9 (eBook)
https://doi.org/10.1007/978-3-319-72622-9

Printed on acid-free paper

This Springer imprint is published by the registered company Springer International Publishing AG part of Springer Nature.
The registered company address is: Gewerbestrasse 11, 6330 Cham, Switzerland

To the memory of my parents,
Juan Antonio and Paula,
who laid the foundations for all I am

Preface

One of the great challenges facing an internationalist is the attempt to provide guidelines for behaviour in new situations arising within an international community in constant flux. Among the numerous and varied ranges of circumstances demanding attention, processes of fragmentation running counter to the trends for integration and globalization so characteristic of early twenty-first-century international society have proved an especially hard nut to crack. The cases of Kosovo and Crimea are two outstanding instances that have attracted attention from the international community over the last two decades. As events developed, basic principles of international law such as self-determination, territorial integrity of States, non-intervention, prohibitions on the threat or use of force by States, or notions like secession, statehood, or recognition were all brought under the microscope. The closeness of these cases, occurring in the continent of Europe, together with similar centrifugal movements of some virulence in Spain itself, was the trigger for this analysis of such trends in the light of international law and most recent international practice.

In many of these instances, claims were made that a supposed right to self-determination gave legitimate grounds for secession. In contraposition to this idea of the exercise of an entitlement to self-determination recognized in international law, the principle of territorial integrity has been invoked to defend continuity of unaltered boundaries for States. Recent cases of unilateral declarations of independence, those of Kosovo in 2008 and Crimea and its later annexation by the Russian Federation in 2014, are clear examples of the situation described. Even though Kosovo was deemed a 'unique case', it was cited by the Russian Federation in its attempts to justify the independence of Crimea. Nevertheless, reactions by the international community were totally distinct in these two instances, and the extent of recognition of the two new entities has been completely different.

With this as a starting point, the aim is to investigate the two cases so as to shed light on the international legal regime affecting entities smaller than a sovereign State. To this end, an analysis will be undertaken of the principles of international law brought into play in this matter, the intention being to determine their scope and review them in the light of the most recent practice and developments in international law. Thereafter, the events of relevance for international law that occurred in the changing situations in Kosovo and Crimea will be examined and explained. Finally, on the basis of these legal considerations, the question will be addressed of possible reactions by the international community when faced with situations that may go against international law, together with the effectiveness of measures that might be taken. Whether certain situations might be legitimate will also be discussed, despite running counter to international law, because a concept could be emerging that unilateral secession may be justified in specific circumstances, such as serious and large-scale violations of basic human rights.

This task dovetails with the last case considered in the author's doctoral thesis, which was entitled 'La intervención humanitaria y el Derecho internacional' [Humanitarian Intervention and International Law], which was the North Atlantic Treaty Organization (NATO) intervention in Kosovo in March 1999. This research was suggested by and carried out under the supervision of Professor Romualdo Bermejo García, who himself has recently published a study under the title 'La vuelta de Crimea a la madre-patria: Algunas reflexiones a la luz del Derecho Internacional' [The Return of Crimea to the Motherland: Reflections in the Light of International Law]. One of the aims of this monograph is to pay homage and tribute to him as his academic career gradually approaches its close after 25 years of sharing the ups and downs of the Section of International Public Law and International Relations of the University of Leon.

The paper is divided into three parts. The first part, entitled 'Self-Determination and Secession Versus Territorial Integrity in International Law', strives to determine the scope of the principles of international law related to the topic under study. With this aim, the section is subdivided into two chapters. Chapter 2 concentrates on establishing the boundaries of the right to self-determination in contemporary international law. Chapter 3 attempts to delimit the scope of unilateral declarations of independence in international law on the basis of diverse postures adopted which finally leads to the view that international law is neutral with regard to them. However, there are certain circumstances in which secession has been claimed to violate peremptory norms such that it would be illicit according to international law.

The second part, with the title 'The Independence of Kosovo and Crimea in the Light of Contemporary International Law', provides an exposition of the facts seen as relevant for an assessment of the declarations of independence made by the entities Kosovo and Crimea. This section comprises three chapters. The first of these involves an explanation of the changes in claims to autonomy made by the Albanian-Kosovar population in Kosovo, the humanitarian crisis caused by government repression of these, NATO intervention and later administration by the United Nations Interim Administration Mission in Kosovo (UNMIK). Investigation of the instance of Crimea is undertaken in Chap. 5 of the paper. Particular attention is paid to commitments to respect the territorial integrity of Ukraine, the holding of a referendum in Crimea under Russian auspices and the later annexation of Crimea to the Russian Federation. This part ends with Chap. 6 of the paper, which performs an evaluation of the unilateral declarations of independence of Kosovo and Crimea in the light of international law and of the Kosovo Advisory Opinion of the

International Court of Justice (ICJ) from 2010, the attention being paid to any possible violation of peremptory norms of international law.

The third part, 'The Emergence of Humanitarian Secession as a Response to Humanitarian Crises', is the boldest and attempts to provide lines of argument for the possible response of the international community to such situations. Chapter 7 offers an analysis of reactions to supposed illicitness and the scope of the stance of non-recognition from the viewpoint of its legal content and of international practice in such matters. Chapter 8 considers the possibilities of actions that in certain situations might be deemed legitimate. These would involve infringement of some rules of international law, but would require acceptance of secession as a last resort for protecting populations having the nature of a people when they are faced with grave, massive violations of basic human rights. The case of Kosovo, while it cannot be claimed to set a precedent, does lay the foundations for humanitarian, rather than remedial, secession as an emerging concept in international law.

I should like to record my thanks to Professor Miguel Díaz y García-Conlledo, head of the Department of Public Law. He was lead researcher for the project 'Las garantías penales como límite y guía en la solución de problemas penales complejos: La necesidad de evitar atajos', reference DER2013-47511-R, funded by the Ministry of Economy and Competitiveness of the Government of Spain. I wish to thank him for all his unselfish help, as this study was undertaken with his assistance.

I am also particularly grateful to Oliver Jütersonke, head of research, and Sandra Reimann, senior coordinator, of the Centre on Conflict, Development and Peacebuilding at the Graduate Institute of International and Development Studies in Geneva. They made me very welcome during my research visit as a scholar in residence funded by the University of Leon, which allowed me to gather all the necessary documentation and bibliography.

Finally, I should like to express my gratitude to Steven Dodd, translator and translator-trainer, who carried out the tasks needed to ensure that the English in this piece of work to be published would be correct, and to Piedad Luna Tovar for her patient management of the University of Leon's translating and interpreting service.

Leon, Spain — Juan Francisco Escudero Espinosa
12 October 2017

Contents

Abbreviations

ADI	*Anuario de Derecho Internacional*
AFDI	*Annuaire français de droit international*
AFRI	*Annuaire français de rélations internationales*
AHLADI	*Anuario Hispano-Luso-Americano de Derecho Internacional*
AJIL	*American Journal of International Law*
AJICL/RADIC	*African Journal of International and Comparative Law/Revue africaine de droit international et comparé*
APSR	*American Political Science Review*
ARIEL	*Austrian Review of International and European Law*
ASIL Proceedings	*Proceedings of the Annual Meeting of the American Society of International Law*
AVR	*Archiv des Völkerrechts*
Brook. J. Int'l L.	*Brooklyn Journal of International Law*
Brown JWA	*Brown Journal of World Affairs*
B.U. Int'l L.J.	*Boston University International Law Journal*
BYIL	*British Yearbook of International Law*
Cambridge LJ	*Cambridge Law Journal*
Cambridge RIA	*Cambridge Review of International Affairs*
Canadian YIL	*Canadian Yearbook of International Law*
Case W.Res.J. Int'l L.	*Case Western Reserve Journal of International Law*
Chicago JIL	*Chicago Journal of International Law*
Chinese JIL	*Chinese Journal of International Law*
CIS	Commonwealth of Independent States
COE	Council of Europe
Columbia JTL	*Columbia Journal of Transnational Law*

CSCE	Conference on Security and Co-operation in Europe
CWILJ	*California Western International Law Journal*
Déf. Nat.	*Revue Défense Nationale*
DJILP	*Denver Journal of International Law and Policy*
DUDI	*Diritti umani e diritto internazionale*
ECHR	European Court of Human Rights
EFAR	*European Foreign Affairs Review*
EILR	*Emory International Law Review*
EJIL	*European Journal of International Law*
Ethics & Int'l A.	*Ethics & International Affairs*
EU	European Union
FARK	Forcat e Armatosura të Republikës së Kosovës (Armed Forces of the Republic of Kosovo)
Finnish YIL	*Finnish Yearbook of International Law*
Fordham Int'l L.J.	*Fordham International Law Journal*
FRY	Federal Republic of Yugoslavia
Ga.J. Int'l & Comp. L.	*Georgia Journal of International and Comparative Law*
German LJ	*German Law Journal*
GoJIL	*Goettingen Journal of International Law*
HRLJ	*Human Rights Law Journal*
HRQ	*Human Rights Quarterly*
ICFY	International Conference of the Former Yugoslavia
ICJ	International Court of Justice
ICLQ	*International and Comparative Law Quarterly*
ICLR	*International Community Law Review*
IICK	Independent International Commission on Kosovo
IJGR	*International Journal on Minority and Group Rights*
IJHR	*International Journal of Human Rights*
ILC	International Law Commission
ILM	*International Legal Materials*
ILSA JICL	*ILSA Journal of International and Comparative Law*
Indian JIL	*Indian Journal of International Law*
Italian YIL	*Italian Yearbook of International Law*
IYHR	*Israel Yearbook on Human Rights*
JDI	*Journal du Droit International*
JILIR	*The Journal of International Law and International Relations*
JRMP	*Jugoslovenska Revija za Međunarodno Pravo*

JUFIL	*Journal on the Use of Force and International Law*
KFOR	Kosovo International Security Force
KVM	OSCE Kosovo Verification Mission
LBD	Lëvizja e Bashkuar Demokratike (United Democratic Movement)
LDK	Lidhja Demokratike te Kosovës (Democratic League of Kosovo)
LJIL	*Leiden Journal of International Law*
LNTS	*League of Nations Treaty Series*
Max Planck YUNL	*Max Planck Yearbook of United Nations Law*
MLR	*Military Law Review*
ML & LWR	*Military Law and Law of War Review*
NATO	North Atlantic Treaty Organization
N & EP	*Nationalism and Ethnic Politic*
NILR	*Netherlands International Law Review*
Nordic JIL	*Nordic Journal of International Law*
N.Y. Law Sch.J. Hum. Rights	*New York Law School Journal of Human Rights*
NYUJILP	*New York University Journal of International Law and Politics*
OJEU	*Official Journal of the European Union*
OSCE	Organization for Security and Co-operation in Europe
Oxford JLS	*Oxford Journal of Legal Studies*
para.	Paragraph
RBDI	*Revue belge de droit international*
RCEEL	*Review of Central and East European Law*
RDI	*Rivista di diritto internazionale*
Rev. dr. Int. et comp.	*Revue de droit international et de droit comparé*
Recueil des cours	*Recueil des cours de l'Académie de droit international de La Haye*
REDI	*Revista Española de Derecho Internacional*
REEI	*Revista Electrónica de Estudios Internacionales*
RGDIP	*Revue générale de droit international public*
RHDI	*Revue hellénique de droit international*
RICR/IRRC	*Revue internationale de la Croix-Rouge / International Review of the Red Cross*
Romanian JEA	*Romanian Journal of European Affairs*
RSPI	*Rivista di Studi Politici Internazionali*
Russian LJ	*Russian Law Journal*
SACEUR	Supreme Allied Commander in Europe
SFRY	Socialist Federal Republic of Yugoslavia
SJIL	*Stanford Journal of International Law*
Soviet YIL	*Soviet Yearbook of International Law*

Survival	*Survival: Global Politics and Strategy*
SZIER/RSDIE	*Schweizerische Zeitschrift für internationales und europäisches Recht/Revue suisse de droit international et de droit européen*
TLCP	*Transnational Law & Contemporary Problems*
Tul. J. Int'l & Comp. L.	*Tulane Journal of International and Comparative Law*
UCLR	*The University of Chicago Law Review*
UN	United Nations
UNHCHR	United Nations High Commissioner for Human Rights
UNHCR	United Nations High Commissioner for Refugees
UNHRC	United Nations Human Rights Council
UN Doc.	Document of the United Nations
UN Charter	Charter of the United Nations
UNIMIK	United Nations Interim Administration Mission in Kosovo
UNTS	*United Nations Treaty Series*
UÇK	Ushtria Çlirimtare e Kosovës (Kosovo Liberation Army)
US	United States of America
USSR	Union of Soviet Socialist Republics
U.St.Thomas J.L & Pub. Pol'y	*University of St. Thomas Journal of Law and Public Policy*
Vand. J. Transnat'l L.	*Vanderbildt Journal of Transnational Law*
VJ	Vojska Jugoslavije (Yugoslav Forces)
VJIL	*Virginia Journal of International Law*
WTO	World Trade Organization
YJIL	*Yale Journal of International Law*
ZaöRV/HJIL	*Zeitschrift für ausländisches öffentliches Recht und Völkerrecht/Heidelberg Journal of International Law*

Table of Case Law

International Court of Justice

Regional Courts of Human Rights

National Courts

Table of Documents of International Organizations and Associations

Conference on Security and Co-operation in Europe / Organization for Security and Co-operation in Europe

Council of Europe

North Atlantic Treaty Organization

European Union

General Assembly

Security Council

International Law Commission

Expert Reports

Table of National Laws

National Laws

Table of Treaties and International Texts

Treaties and International Texts

Chapter 1
Introduction

In a speech given before the Members of the highest institutions of the Russian Federation and the Representatives of the Republic of Crimea and Sebastopol, Vladimir Putin spoke out against his colleagues in Western Europe and North America for their incongruous assessments as contrary to international law of the actions and events that led to the independence and later annexation of Crimea.[1] He argued that the circumstances of Crimea, 'was legitimate and did not require any permission from the country's central authorities', because it was a situation similar to that of Kosovo, 'a precedent our western colleagues created with their own hands'.[2]

The very Declaration of Independence by the Crimean authorities on 17 March 2014 referred to the 'well-known Kosovo precedent', as Vladimir Putin called it. The status of this appeared to have been confirmed by the ICJ in its Advisory Opinion of 22 July 2010 in the formula: 'general international law contains no applicable prohibition of declarations of independence'.[3]

The historical circumstances present at the start in Kosovo and Crimea do show some parallels. In respect of Kosovo, the territory is considered by the Serbs as one of their heartlands as a nation. Forming part of the Republic of Serbia, it was incorporated in Yugoslavia from 1946 onwards. Its population of nearly two million is made up for the most part of Albanians living alongside minorities of diverse origins. It is one of the poorest regions in Europe, with the majority of the population working in agriculture. Politically, the province enjoyed a statute of autonomy for

[1] 'Address by President of the Russian Federation on March 18, 2014', The Kremlin, Moscow, at para. 26. http://en.kremlin.ru/events/president/news/20603.

[2] Id., at para. 29.

[3] *Accordance with the International Law of the Unilateral Declaration of Independence in Respect of Kosovo, Advisory Opinion, I.C.J. Reports 2010*, 403–626, p. 438, para. 84. http://www.icj-cij.org/files/case-related/141/141-20100722-ADV-01-00-BI.pdf.

J. F. Escudero Espinosa, *Self-Determination and Humanitarian Secession in International Law of a Globalized World*,
https://doi.org/10.1007/978-3-319-72622-9_1

decades until this was unilaterally rescinded by the Slobodan Milošević regime in 1989.

As for Crimea, Ukrainian historians see its past as linked to the State of Kiev, meaning that the peninsula was part of the first Ukrainian State. Ukrainians were to be found in the peninsula long before the arrival of Russians in the eighteenth century.[4] However, Russian historians see the State of Kiev as the origin of the first Russian State. The debate finally concentrated on the ethnic origin, Russian or Ukrainian, of one of the protagonists of these events, Prince Vladimir the Great of Kiev.[5] The population is in its majority of Russian origin, but is a real mix of cultures and traditions, with a variety of ethnic groups, like Russia itself, as Vladimir Putin put it,[6] in accordance with the perception of Russians as the core part of the Russian nation.[7] In the decades following the disintegration of the Soviet Union, aspirations in the peninsula were aimed at achieving greater autonomy to satisfy the desires for sovereignty that had been latent since its incorporation into the Ukraine in 1954.

It can be stated that the aspirations to extend existing autonomy in these two regions led to crises of very different types, even though in both cases they culminated in a declaration of independence intended to attain secession and the creation of a new State. In Kosovo, stances became ever more extreme until they led to a bloody internal conflict in which massive violations of basic human rights caused a grave humanitarian crisis. The desperate situation triggered resort to the use of force by NATO, the so-called 'Operation Allied Force', in March 1999. This was a controversial intervention, deemed by some contrary to international law because it did not enjoy the necessary authorization from the Security Council, specifically because of opposition from the Russian Federation.[8] A large group of analysts did see reconstruction of internal self-determination in Kosovo as a needful step after the abolition of autonomy by Slobodan Milošević in 1989.[9]

The magnitude of human rights infringements and the exhausting of negotiations aimed at achieving a definitive status led to the bringing into play of possible external self-determination, the right to create a new State, going beyond the principle of internal self-determination, as the sole remaining alternative.[10] This proposal was made by the Special Envoy of the Secretary-General, Martti Ahtisaari, as a *sui generis* case, not a solution that could be taken as a precedent for similar situations.[11] Independence was suggested as the last resort for achieving respect for

[4]Cfr. Knysh (1993), pp. 294–317.

[5]Cfr. Armandon (2013), p. 137.

[6]Cfr. 'Address by President of the Russian Federation on March 18, 2014', supra, this chapter, note 1, at para. 6.

[7]Cfr. Kappeler (1997), pp. 21–22.

[8]Cfr. Intervention of Mr. Martynov (Russian Federation), UN Doc. S/PV.3988, of 24 March 1999, 20, p. 15.

[9]Cfr. Vidmar (2009), p. 787. Weller (2009), p. 35.

[10]Cfr. Oeter (2012), p. 117.

[11]Cfr. 'Report of the Special Envoy of the Secretary-General on Kosovo's future status', UN Doc. S/2007/168, of 26 March 2007, 9, p. 2, para. 5.

the rule of law and effective protection for minorities, the best guarantee for ensuring the peace and stability that were under threat in Kosovo.[12] Finally, on 17 February 2008, the Assembly of Kosovo's Provisional Institutions of Self-Government declared independence.[13]

In Crimea the course of events immediately preceding the declaration of independence was essentially different from what had happened in the so-called 'Kosovo precedent'. It is true that the various legislative reforms of differing trends according to the more or less Russian-speaking central government, tensions between Russia and the Ukraine, the Ukrainian crisis constituted the chief causes for Russian intervention. While at first the Russian authorities stated that they were not involved in any way, they later justified the use of force in order to protect the lives of Russian citizens and to respond to the invitation of the man they considered the legitimate Ukrainian President, Viktor Yanukovych.[14] This intervention renders questionable the validity of the referendum intended to legitimize the independence of Crimea. This referendum opened the door to secession and subsequent annexation to the Russian Federation on 18 March 2014. Prior infringements of international law by certain western countries in the NATO intervention in Kosovo did not give authority to the Russian Federation to undertake actions that also ran counter to international law.[15]

Reactions by the international community in the two cases were also very different. As for Kosovo, it currently enjoys considerable effectiveness as a State. The new status of the territory has been recognized by 113 States, including 111 (57%) of the 193 United Nations Member States, among them three permanent members of the Security Council (France, the United Kingdom and the US).[16] In contrast, the situation of Crimea is barely recognized outside the Russian Federation, no more than ten States and no permanent member of the Security Council other than the Russian Federation having granted it recognition.

The views of some prominent internationalists are such as to allow arguments that double standards have been applied by the international community. In the case of Crimea, most western countries complained that the Russian Federation had violated international law.[17] These same countries, as pointed out by Vladimir Putin, had justified intervention and supported independence in Kosovo, as well as backing the secession of South Sudan. This stance has been criticized from several angles as lacking coherence.[18] If the declaration of independence by Kosovo was not contrary

[12]Cfr. Id., p. 4, para. 10.

[13]See 'Kosova Declaration of Independence' 17 February 2008. http://www.assembly-kosova.org/?cid=2,128,1635.

[14]Cfr. Intervention of Mr. Vitaly Churkin (Russian Federation), UN Doc. S/PV.7125, of 3 March 2014, pp. 3–4.

[15]Cfr. Christakis (2014), p. 736.

[16]Cfr. 'International Recognitions of the Republic of Kosovo', http://www.mfa-ks.net/?page=2,224.

[17]Cfr. Kohen (2014), at para. 2, https://www.letemps.ch/opinions/2014/03/12/ukraine-respect-droit-international.

[18]Cfr. Id., para. 2.

to international law, as declared by the ICJ in its Advisory Opinion, it would not seem consistent to argue now that the declaration of independence by the Parliament of the Autonomous Republic of Crimea constituted a violation of international law. In order to provide an explanation for this diversity of treatment, it would be necessary to address the question of whether these are really similar situations so that the Kosovo case is a true precedent or whether, on the contrary, these are differing events demanding individualized responses.

An answer to this question requires in-depth study in the light of international law and the most recent international practice. In particular, attention must be paid to the Advisory Opinion of the ICJ on Kosovo's declaration of independence, which concluded that general international law has no prohibition on unilateral declarations of independence. From this viewpoint, various legal aspects must be taken into account for analysis in the light of international law.

Firstly, there is the regime relating to the principle of self-determination envisaged in the Charter of the United Nations (UN Charter) and Resolution 2625 (XXV) 'Declaration on Principles of International Law Concerning Friendly Relations and Co-operation among States in Accordance with the Charter of the United Nations'.[19] Its two aspects, internal and external, must be considered in any study of possible recognition of a right to secede in international law outside the context of decolonization. Closely linked is the problem of reconciling self-determination with an interpretation of the principle of the territorial integrity of states recognized in the UN Charter and its applicability to secessions by sub-state units according to international law.[20]

Secondly, there is the impact of the threat or use of force in international relations, which infringes a norm of international *jus cogens*, and its occurrence in processes of secession. Whilst international law remains neutral relative to the occurrence of secession, intervention by NATO in Kosovo and the Russian Federation in Crimea have highlighted the fact that not all secession processes are in conformity with international law.

Thirdly, there are standards for holding referenda and the scope of their results as a possible basis for secession. So-called 'sovereignty referenda' affect essentials notions like the concept of statehood, territorial changes, or mergers of territories and states. Because of their scope, they are of particular interest for the international community. Their crucial nature in an international context has led to the setting of certain basic rules for holding them, in the light of which it is necessary to examine the procedures followed in Crimea.

Fourthly and finally, there are the criteria for, and possible consequences of, the recognition of bodies that have made proclamations of independence, together with

---

[19]'Declaration on Principles of International Law Concerning Friendly Relations and Co-operation among States in Accordance with the Charter of the United Nations' UN Doc. A/RES/2625 (XXV), of 24 October 1970, at Annex, 'The Principle of Equal Rights and Self-Determination of Peoples', para. 1.

[20]Cfr. Van den Driest (2015), p. 468.

the effectiveness of non-recognition. Here, there must be an examination of the options for reaction by the international community when faced with a secession, especially if there has been an infringement of international law. Both the premature declarations of recognition made in the case of Kosovo and those of non-recognition of the situation in Crimea have re-opened debates on the part these measure play with regard to secession and the consolidation of statehood.

To sum up, the cases of Kosovo and Crimea raise the question whether the inhabitants of a given territory can decide to split off from the State in which it is included and create a new State.[21] It is a matter of the extent to which such new entities can become consolidated on the basis of effectiveness as against an infringement of international law that would overthrow the long-established principle that *ex injuria jus non oritur*.

The differences between the two cases are relevant, but in the final analysis the recognition of Kosovo by a large majority of States for Kosovo raises the question of whether there is any right that certain groups might enjoy to lay claim to secession in certain circumstances. As a number of academics have seen it, this recognition was the culmination of a process the foundation for which was laid by Resolution 1244 (1999) of the Security Council establishing UNMIK.[22] At this point it is inevitable that the validity of the controversial theory of 'remedial secession' will be raised. On the basis of the principles inspiring it, the case of Kosovan secession might be seen as a 'precedent' for future situations in which serious, systematic violations of fundamental human rights take place.

The secession of Crimean peninsula is seen as a move unacceptable not just for the Ukrainian authorities but also for a large majority of the international community. Matters relating to control of this territory and of Sebastopol, together with the Black Sea Fleet have always been seen by the Ukrainian authorities as a test of respect for the sovereignty and independence of the Ukraine.[23] The declaration of independence and later annexation to the Russian Federation imply a considerable challenge both to Ukrainian domestic law and to international law, but it is hard to see what action the international community might take when it appears impossible to return to the *status quo ante*.

References

Armandon, E. 2013. *La Crimée entre la Russie et Ukraine. Un conflit qui n'a pas eu lieu*. Bruxelles: Bruylant.

Christakis, T. 2014. Les conflits de sécession en Crimée et dans l'Est de l'Ukraine et le droit international (The Conflicts of Secession in Crimea and Eastern Ukraine and International Law). *JDI* 141: 733–764.

[21] Cfr. Cfr. Wilson (2009), p. 463.

[22] UN Doc. S/RES/1244 (1999), of 10 June 1999, at para. 5.

[23] Cfr. Armandon (2013), p. 149.

Kappeler, A. 1997. *Petite histoire de l'Ukraine*. Paris: Institut d'études slaves.

Knysh, G. 1993. The Crimean Roots of Ancient Ukrainian Statehood. *The Ukrainian Quarterly* 49: 294–317.

Kohen, M.G. 2014. L'Ukraine et le respect du droit international, *Le Temps* 12 mars 2014. https://www.letemps.ch/opinions/2014/03/12/ukraine-respect-droit-international.

Oeter, S. 2012. Secession, Territorial Integrity and the Role of the Security Council. In *Kosovo and International Law: The ICJ Advisory Opinion of 22 July 2010*, ed. P. Hilpold, 109–138. Leiden; Boston: M. Nijhoff Publishers.

Van den Driest, S.F. 2015. From Kosovo to Crimea and Beyond: On Territorial Integrity, Unilateral Secession and Legal Neutrality in International Law. *IJGR* 22: 467–485.

Vidmar, J. 2009. International Legal Responses to Kosovo's Declaration of Independence. *Vand. J. Transnatl L.* 42: 779–851.

Weller, M. 2009. *Contested Statehood: Kosovo's Struggle for Independence*. Oxford: Oxford University Press.

Wilson, G. 2009. Self-Determination, Recognition and the Problem of Kosovo. *NILR* 56: 455–481.

Part I
Self-Determination and Secession Versus Territorial Integrity in International Law

Chapter 2
The Recognition of the Right to Self-Determination in International Law

The concept of self-determination has classically been linked to the idea of self-government.[1] At the present day, a rough definition could be given for self-determination as the right of peoples to decide their own political status. However, at the beginning of the Modern Era the notion was associated rather more with concepts like national or popular sovereignty as understood during the French Revolutionary Period and opposed to the absolute power of a monarchical sovereign.[2]

The principles proclaimed during the French Revolution were widely known in the United States. Thus, the man who drew up the Declaration of Independence in 1776, Thomas Jefferson, had been steeped in revolutionary ideas in Paris between 1785 and 1789, long before he became President in 1801. In his instructions to American ambassadors regarding the recognition of governments, he stressed that nations had a right to govern themselves in both internal and foreign affairs (self-government) as the principle inspiring American policy.[3] The later blossoming of

[1]Cfr. Przetacznik (1990), p. 51.

[2]Cfr. Anaya (1993), p. 134. Calogeropoulos-Stratis (1973), p. 18.

[3]The text of one of the passages in his many letters that address the idea of internal and external self-government runs as follows:

> We certainly cannot deny to other nations that principle whereon our own government is founded, that every nation has a right to govern itself internally under what forms it pleases, and to change these forms at it's [sic] own will: and externally to transact business with other nations thro' [sic] whatever organ it chuses [sic], whether that be a king, convention, assembly, committee, president, or whatever it be. The only thing essential is the will of the nation.

From Thomas Jefferson to Thomas Pinckney, 30 December 1792. Cfr. *From Thomas Jefferson to Gouverneur* [sic] *Morris, 7 November 1792*. The text may be consulted in Boyd et al. (1950), Vol. XXIV, pp. 802 and 593.

On Thomas Jefferson's views, see Falkowski (1991).

J. F. Escudero Espinosa, *Self-Determination and Humanitarian Secession in International Law of a Globalized World*,
https://doi.org/10.1007/978-3-319-72622-9_2

nationalism in Europe over the course of the nineteenth century gave rise to a linkage between this concept and state-building. According to these new presuppositions, each nation had the right to create its own State, and each State should be made up of one nation.[4]

One of the first political and social thinkers to refer to the idea of self-determination was Mikhail Alexandrovich Bakunin, when in 1866 he stated that society should be re-organized so that ‘every individual, every association, every commune, every region, every nation’ would have ‘the absolute right to self-determination, to associate or not to associate, to ally themselves with whomever they wish’.[5] Bakunin also felt that they had the right to determine in which State they wished to live and the form of government that they wished installed.[6]

It was President Woodrow Wilson who in 1919 and 1920 enunciated the principles on which the free determination of peoples should be based.[7] He even used the expression ‘self-determination’ as a replacement for ‘self-government’.[8] The newer term incorporated the right of a people to choose its own form of government in a continuing process that would be synonymous with a democratic type of regime.[9] Wilson’s ideas were expressed as an amalgam of the concepts of internal self-determination, universal democracy and a guardianship over primitive peoples as they moved towards the ultimate goal of full autonomy.[10] Moreover, Woodrow Wilson went further in his concepts, as he understood democracy to be not merely an ally of the idea of self-determination, but fused with it to form a notion of ‘free option of peoples’ and ‘self-government’.[11] As he saw it, the governments of nations, controlled by the will and the votes of their peoples, were a guarantee of the preservation of peace in the world.[12]

---

[4]Cfr. Lauwers and Smis (2000), p. 43.

[5]Bakunin (1972), at IX.G.

[6]Cfr. Przetacznik (1990), p. 51.

[7]The Presidential speeches in which Woodrow Wilson’s views on self-determination of peoples were laid out may be consulted in Baker and Dodd (1927), 2 Vol.

[8]Cfr. Calogeropoulos-Stratis (1973), p. 39. Whelan (1994), p. 100.

An analysis of Wilson’s views on the ideas of self-determination and self-government may be found in Pomerance (1976), pp. 1–27. Woodrow Wilson preferred the term ‘self-government’, which in his thinking implied the right to elect one’s own democratic government.

[9]Cfr. Notter (1937), 695, pp. 68 and 69.

[10]Cfr. Pomerance (1976), p. 17.

[11]Cfr. Jaber (2011), p. 928.

[12]Cfr. Baker and Dodd (1927), p. 84.

2.1 Self-Determination Under the Charter of the United Nations

2.1.1 Origins of the Idea of Self-Determination

The principle of self-determination of peoples was proclaimed in the Atlantic Charter during the Second World War as a principle of respect for the forms of regime chosen by different peoples.[13] At the end of the war, the emergence of the UN provided an occasion to achieve what President Woodrow Wilson had been unsuccessful in attaining through his proposals in the 'Fourteen Points', which involved a commitment to guarantee the political independence and territorial integrity of nations.[14] Now, the international community accepted the principle of self-determination as one of the fundamental rules on which the new world order would be based.[15] Nonetheless, the principle was not seen by those drawing up the UN Charter as a legal principle that should be ratified by practice in order to become a legally binding obligation.[16]

Basically, the so-called right to self-determination granted peoples the freedom to determine their own destinies.[17] It might be exercised in many ways, although it was usual to differentiate between internal and external self-determination.[18] According to this distinction, the internal aspect of self-determination could be described as 'the right of all peoples to freely pursue their economic, social, and cultural development

---

[13]On the contents and scope of the Atlantic Charter in this respect, see Kiss (1986), p. 166. Laing (1989), 113-; and, by the same author Laing (1991), p. 250.

The third paragraph of the Atlantic Charter, the text of which may be found in 35:Supplement *AJIL* (1941), p. 191, referred to the right to self-government in the following terms:

> Third, they respect the right of all peoples to choose the form of government under which they will live; and they wish to see sovereign rights and self-government restored to those who have been forcibly deprived of them;

[14]The programme presented to the United States Congress on 8 January 1918 envisaged a need to create a 'League of Nations', which would provide mutual guarantees of political independence and territorial integrity. Cfr. Point XIV of the 'Fourteen Points', Scott (1918), pp. 359–362. Finch (1919), pp. 161–163.

On the attempts to establish a right to self-determination before the UN Charter, see Cassese (1995), at this chapter. Crawford (2007), pp. 107–131.

[15]Cfr. Lauwers and Smis (2000), p. 44. Wilson (2009), p. 463.

[16]Cfr. Higgins (1963), pp. 101–102. Lauwers and Smis (2000), p. 44.

[17]Cfr. Expert opinion by Franck et al. (2000), p. 248.

[18]Cfr. Cassese (1981), p. 96. Pomerance (1982), p. 37. Przetacznik (1990), p. 54. Ryngaert and Griffioen (2009), p. 574. General Recommendation XXI (48), adopted on 8 March 1996, in 'Report of the Committee on the Elimination of Racial Discrimination', UN Doc. A/51/18, 30 September 1996, 129, p. 125, para. 9.

without outside interference',[19] and within their existing borders.[20] This tried to find a compromise between the idea of sovereignty and the idea of the general will,[21] such as to grant all citizens the right to take part in the decision-making processes in the State in which they resided,[22] and to determine the system of government under which they wished to live.[23] This internal aspect, as Antonio Cassese pointed out, presupposed that individuals enjoyed a set of rights such as the freedom of opinion and expression mentioned in Art. 19, the right of peaceful assembly cited in Art. 21, that to freedom of association of Art. 22 and the right to vote quoted in Art. 25.b) of the 'International Covenant on Civil and Political Rights', and a general 'right to take part in the conduct of public affairs' (Art. 25.a)).[24]

For its part, the external aspect implies that all peoples 'have the right to determine freely their political status and their place in the international community based upon the principle of equal rights and exemplified by the liberation of peoples from colonialism and by the prohibition to subject peoples to alien subjugation, domination and exploitation'.[25] This was an external feature that referred exclusively to the establishment of the status of a people and the determination of its relations with other peoples in the ambit of the international community.[26] It implied freedom from any foreign interference that might affect its international status, as also from any violation of its independence.[27] According to some authors, it would even include questions relative to a people's belonging to a State,[28] either through the formation of a new State, or through incorporation into an existing State.[29]

Overall, the idea of self-determination should be broadly defined, including both aspects, as the right of peoples to decide about their own internal affairs and about their relations with other States, and to determine their equality of status with other States in the international community.[30]

---

[19]General Recommendation XXI (48), adopted on 8 March 1996, in 'Report of the Committee on the Elimination of Racial Discrimination', UN Doc. A/51/18, 30 September 1996, 129, p. 125, para. 9.

[20]Cfr. Cirkovic (2010), p. 908.

[21]Cfr. Tolstykh (2015), p. 125.

[22]Cfr. Cirkovic (2010), p. 908. Raič (2002), p. 237.

[23]Cfr. Wilson (2009), p. 463.

[24]Cassese (1981), p. 97.

On the 'International Covenant on Civil and Political Rights', *infra*, this chapter, note 51.

[25]General Recommendation XXI (48), adopted on 8 March 1996, in 'Report of the Committee on the Elimination of Racial Discrimination', UN Doc. A/51/18, 30 September 1996, 129, p. 125, para. 9.

[26]Cfr. Cirkovic (2010), p. 909.

[27]Cassese (1981), p. 100.

[28]Cfr. Wilson (2009), p. 463.

[29]Cassese (1981), p. 98.

[30]Cfr. Cirkovic (2010), p. 910.

2.1.2 *The Principle of Self-Determination in the Charter of the United Nations*

The idea of the existence of a right to self-determination in the sense described above is generally accepted in international law. Starting from this premise, a range of questions must be addressed relative to its recognition in international law. With regard to its legal content, these include ownership of the right (who is the 'self' involved?) and the scope of 'determine'.[31] A search for answers to these questions has made the idea of self-determination into a real *cause célèbre* in international law.[32] Moreover, the absence of a specific set of guidelines implies that such studies must be carried out within the framework of general international law.[33]

The UN Charter constitutes the first document with legal force to proclaim the principle of the self-determination of peoples, although the formulation adopted saw the principle as something to be aimed at, not a definite obligation.[34] The wording used was the result of compromises between colonial powers and those who presented themselves as anti-colonialist.[35] It did manage to ensure the development of friendly relationships and strengthen world peace, but is was far from recognizing a real right to choose one's own government.[36]

The expression 'self-determination' appears twice in the UN Charter: in Art. 1(2), in relation to the purposes listed in Chap. I 'Purposes and Principles', and in Art. 55 of Chap. IX 'International Economic and Social Co-operation', considered a sort of 'second preamble.[37] In the first of the appearances it is described as a means to develop friendly relations among nations in order to strengthen universal peace,[38] whilst in the second there is a listing of the actions that the United Nations (UN) should promote to ensure 'peaceful and friendly relations among nations based on respect for the principle of equal rights and self-determination of peoples'.[39] This Article is of particular importance specifically because of the full and

---

[31]Cfr. Pomerance (1982), pp. 14–28.

[32]Cfr. Wengler (1957), p. 26.

[33]Cfr. Ryngaert (2010), p. 488.

[34]Cfr. Cassese (1979), p. 138.

[35]Cfr. Russell (1958), p. 811.

[36]Cfr. Cfr. Cassese (1979), p. 138.

[37]Cfr. Pellet (1991), p. 841.

[38]Cfr. Article 1(2) of the UN Charter.

[39]Cfr. Article 55 of the UN Charter.
Cfr. Lauwers and Smis (2000), p. 44.

unconditional recognition of the principle that the international community laid down in the UN Charter.[40]

Both articles in the Charter refer to the 'principle of self-determination', which Ian Brownlie sees as making it a real legal principle or constituent.[41] However, the wording gives no idea of the scope of the principle.[42] It must be added that, against expectations, it is not listed among the 'principles' in Art. 2, which were intended to govern the actions of the UN. The conclusion, as highlighted by Yehuda Zvi Blum, is that 'self-determination, in contrast to sovereignty and all that flows from it, was not originally perceived as an operative principle of the Charter; ... it was one of the desiderata of the Charter rather than a legal right that could be invoked as such'.[43]

In the whole of the rest of the text of the UN Charter there are no further references to the principle of self-determination. It would have been logical for it to be cited in Chap. XI 'Declaration Regarding Non-Self-Governing Territories', and in Chap. XII 'International Trusteeship System', which are of particular importance in establishing the scope of the notion of self-determination in the context of the UN Charter.[44]

2.1.3 *The Right to Self-Determination in the Era of Decolonization*

The 1950s and 1960s were characterized by a striking increase in the number of new independent States resulting from decolonization processes.[45] The principle of self-determination gradually took shape as an international custom, thanks to the adoption of various resolutions by the General Assembly that provided guidelines of international practice.[46] The UN managed to get the political premise and the

[40]Cfr. Goodrich et al. (1969), p. 29. Levin (1962), p. 46.

Olga Shukovich affirms that Soviet doctrine was unanimous in considering that the principle of self-determination was a generally recognized principle of international law that found its confirmation in Art. 1 and 55 of the Charter. Among the authorities she cites are D.B. Levin, G.B. Starushenko, Sharmanzvashili, and G.I. Tunkin. Cfr. Shukovich (1964), p. 179, note 14.

[41]Cfr. Brownlie (1990), p. 575. Bokor-Szegö (1970), pp. 51–52. Magaraševič (1956), p. 32.

[42]Cfr. Pomerance (1982), p. 9.

[43]Blum (1975), p. 511.

[44]Cfr. Lauwers and Smis (2000), p. 45.

[45]Up to 1955, only 9 States were admitted, a consequence of the attitude of the Soviet Union within the Security Council. Gradual detente between the two superpowers led to the incorporation of 16 new States, 9 of them European, during the tenth period of sessions of the General Assembly. In 1960, 18 further States were incorporated, of which 16 were African. Thus, over this period the original 51 member States became 100 in 1960, and 127 in 1970, with an ensuing more than doubling of the number of members.

[46]Cfr. Lauterpacht (1965), p. 271. Lauwers and Smis (2000), p. 45. McCorquodale (1992), p. 594.

An analysis of the principle of self-determination of peoples in the shape of an international custom may be found in Johnson (1973), p. 153. Emerson (1971), pp. 459–475. Laing (1991).

pragmatic norm incorporating it, Art. 1(2), to become little by little one of the fundamental principles given the legal force typical of *jus cogens*.[47]

The most important step in the development of Art. 1(2) and 55 of the Charter was the adoption of Resolution 1514 (XV) of the General Assembly of the UN, the 'Declaration on the Granting of Independence to Colonial Countries and Peoples' of 14 December 1960.[48] In its content there was a re-iteration of the right of all colonial peoples to self-determination, measures were taken to make this effective, what it consisted of was made explicit 'by virtue of that right they freely determine their political status and freely pursue their economic, social and cultural development'.[49]

Some years later, in 1966, the 'International Covenant on Civil and Political Rights' and the 'International Covenant on Economic, Social and Cultural Rights', likewise proclaimed the right to self-determination in a more general and binding way.[50] Both these covenants defined the right identically in their first Art., 'By virtue of that right they freely determine their political status and freely pursue their economic, social and cultural development'.[51]

It should be added that Art. 1(3) established that 'the States Party to the present Covenant, including those having responsibility for the administration of Non-Self-Governing and Trust Territories, shall promote the realization of the right of self-determination, and shall respect the right, in conformity with the provisions of the

---

[47]Cfr. Brownlie (1990), p. 513. Cassese (1991), p. 45. Cirkovic (2010), p. 907. Crawford (1988), p. 166. Gros Espiell (1979), *passim*. Gros Espiell (1976), p. 68. Hannum (1990), p. 45. Kiss (1986), p. 174. Orakhelashvili (2006), pp. 51–53. Oeter (2014), p. 52.

Nonetheless, there are those who deny that this is a norm in *jus cogens*, simply because they do not see it as a '*jus*'. Cfr. *The Right of Self-Determination: Historic and Current Development on the Basis of United Nations Instruments.* Study prepared by Aureliu Cristescu, Special Rapporteur of the Sub-Commission on Prevention of Discrimination and Protection of Minorities (1981), UN Doc. E/CN.4/Sub.2/404/Rev.1, 125, p. 23, para. 154. Blum (1975), p. 511. Pomerance (1982), pp. 70–71.

[48]Cfr. Kelsen (1964), pp. 840 and 852.

Resolution 1514 (XV) was adopted by 89 votes to 0, with 9 abstentions (Australia, Belgium, Dominican Republic, France, Portugal, Spain, Union of South Africa, United Kingdom and US).

[49]'Declaration on the granting of independence to colonial countries and peoples', UN Doc. A/RES/ 1514 (XV), of 14 December 1960, at para. 2.

[50]Cfr. Cassese (1981), p. 93.

[51]'International Covenant on Civil and Political Rights' and 'International Covenant on Economic, Social and Cultural Rights', of 16 December 1966, at Art. 1(1).

The two International Covenants were adopted by Resolution UN Doc. A/RES/2200 (XXI), of 16 December 1966, 999 *UNTS* (1976), No. 14669, 171–281; and 993 *UNTS* (1976), No. 14531, 3–12, respectively. Also 6:2 *ILM* (1967), 360–385. The 'International Covenant on Civil and Political Rights' came into force from 23 March 1976, in accordance with Art. 49, except for Art. 41, which applied from 28 March 1979. The 'International Covenant on Economic, Social and Cultural Rights' entered into force from 3 January 1976, in accordance with its Art. 27(1).

Charter'.[52] Through this, all the States Party committed themselves to take steps to put it into operation,[53] so that it was given an authentic *erga omnes* character.[54]

At the end of the 1960s, the General Assembly approved Resolution 2625 (XXV) 'Declaration on Principles of International Law Concerning Friendly Relations and Co-operation among States in Accordance with the Charter of the United Nations' which constituted a real landmark in the United Nations' commitment to the right of self-determination.[55] In its section on 'The Principle of Equal Rights and Self-Determination of Peoples' it is stated that: 'By virtue of the principle of equal rights and self-determination of peoples enshrined in the UN Charter, all peoples have the right freely to determine, without external interference, their political status and to pursue their economic, social and cultural development, and every State has the duty to respect this right in accordance with the provisions of the Charter'.[56]

It must be highlighted that Resolution 2625 (XXV) contains a 'safeguard clause' in which it is stressed that exercise of the right to self-determination is limited so as to prevent threats to the territorial integrity of States[57]:

> Nothing in the foregoing paragraphs shall be construed as authorizing or encouraging any action which would dismember or impair, totally or in part, the territorial integrity or political unity of sovereign and independent States conducting themselves in compliance with the principle of equal rights and self-determination of peoples as described above and thus possessed of a government representing the whole people belonging to the territory without distinction as to race, creed or colour.[58]

The merit of the document lay in the fact that it achieved agreement on a consensus text between Western States and the Socialist Bloc.[59] The result was that the right to self-determination gained a legal status, becoming a right conferred on all peoples. Its application was extended to a much broader range of cases.[60]

---

[52]Id., at Art. 1(3).

[53]Cfr. 'Centre for Civil and Political Rights General Comment No. 12: Article 1 (Right to Self-Determination) The Right to Self-Determination of Peoples', Adopted at the Twenty-first Session of the Human Rights Committee, on 13 March 1984', in 'Compilation of General Comments and General Recommendations Adopted by Human Rights Treaty Bodies, Note by the Secretariat', UN Doc. HRI/GEN/Rev.1, 29 July 1994, 107, p. 13, para. 6.

[54]Cfr. Milano (2014), p. 43, http://www.qil-qdi.org/wp-content/uploads/2014/05/CRIMEA_Enrico-Milano_FINAL.pdf. Van den Driest (2015), p. 337.

[55]Cfr. Lauwers and Smis (2000), p. 45.

On Resolution 2625 (XXV) see also Arangio-Ruiz (1979), Johnson (1973), Rosenstock (1971).

[56]'Declaration on Principles of International Law Concerning Friendly Relations and Co-operation among States in Accordance with the UN Charter' UN Doc. A/RES/2625 (XXV), Annex, 24 October 1970, at 'The Principle of Equal Rights and Self-Determination of Peoples', para. 1.

[57]Cfr. Van den Driest (2015), p. 338. Vidmar (2011), p. 367; and, by the same author Vidmar (2015), p. 369.

[58]'Declaration on Principles of International Law Concerning Friendly Relations and Co-operation among States in Accordance with the UN Charter' UN Doc. A/RES/2625 (XXV), Annex, 24 October 1970, at 'The Principle of Equal Rights and Self-Determination of Peoples', para. 7.

[59]Cfr. Johnson (1973), p. 155. Lauwers and Smis (2000), p. 46.

[60]Cfr. Chowdhury (1977), p. 73. Johnson (1973), p. 148. White (1981), p. 148.

2.2 The Right to Self-Determination After the End of Decolonization

2.2.1 *The Right to Self-Determination as a Norm of* jus cogens

The new scope of the principle was incorporated in other soft law instruments such as the 'Helsinki Final Act', of 1975,[61] the 'Charter of Paris for a New Europe',[62] of 1990, in the framework for the Conference on Security and Co-operation in Europe, and the 'Vienna Declaration and Programme of Action',[63] approved by the United Nations World Conference on Human Rights of 1993.[64] In Principle VIII of the 'Helsinki Final Act' it was declared that the right to self-determination was recognized for the peoples of European States and consequently was no longer bonded exclusively to occupied or colonized territories.[65] Still, it must be highlighted that in all these instances there was the so-called 'safeguard clause', with the right to self-determination limited by any threat it might pose to the territorial integrity of States.[66]

In an African context, the 'African Charter on Human and People's Rights' also clearly stated in its Art. 20(1) that there was an inalienable right of all peoples to self-determination. This meant they should be free to determine their political status and pursue their economic and social in conformity with freely chosen policies.[67]

---

[61]'Conference on Security and Co-operation in Europe Final Act', Helsinki, 1 August 1975. This is available from http://www.osce.org/helsinki-final-act?download=true. 14:5 *ILM* (1975), 1292–1325, p. 1293.

More specifically on the right to self-determination in the 'Helsinki Final Act' the following may be consulted: Arangio-Ruiz (1983), pp. 523–552. Cassese (1977), pp. 83–110. Salo (1991), pp. 307–321.

[62]Conference on Security and Co-operation in Europe, 'Charter of Paris for a New Europe', Paris, 21 November 1990, at 'Friendly Relations among Participating States', para. 7. http://www.osce.org/mc/39516?download=true. 30:1 *ILM* (1991), 193–208.

[63]World Conference on Human Rights, 'Vienna Declaration and Programme of Action', 25 June 1993, UN Doc. A/CONF.157/24, 53, p. 20, Part I, para. 2. 32:6 *ILM* (1993), 1661–1687.

[64]Cfr. Van den Driest (2015), p. 337. Kapustin (2015), p. 102.

[65]Cfr. 'Conference on Security and Co-operation in Europe Final Act', Helsinki, 1 August 1975, supra, this chapter, note 61, at Sect. 1(a) 'Declaration on Principles Guiding Relations between Participating States', Principle VIII 'Equal rights and self-determination of peoples'.

Cfr. Cassese (1995), p. 285. Jia (2009), p. 33.

[66]Cfr. Van den Driest (2015), p. 338.

[67]The text of Art. 20(1) is as follows:

> All peoples shall have the right to existence. They shall have the unquestionable and inalienable right to self-determination. They shall freely determine their political status and shall pursue their economic and social development according to the policy they have freely chosen.

The 'African Charter on Human and People's Rights' was adopted on 27 June 1981 and entered into force on 21 October 1981, OAU Doc. CAB/LEG/67/3 rev.5, http://www.au.int/en/sites/default/files/treaties/7770-file-banjul_charter.pdf. It may also be seen in 21:1 *ILM* (1982), 58–68.

These texts adopted by very diverse groups of States, do not all possess the same legal force, nor do all bind the same States. However, as stated by Elihu Lauterpacht, the right of peoples may be considered an integral part of positive law and not simply a political principle.[68] The difficulty arising is the need to reconcile the rights of States with those of peoples, when these rights are often incompatible in practice.[69]

The existence of a right to self-determination in International law has been recognized by the ICJ.[70] The same is true of the Supreme Court of Canada in its noteworthy *Reference re Secession of Quebec* in a case from 1998 in which it stated:

> The existence of the right of a people to self-determination is now so widely recognized in international conventions that the principle has acquired a status beyond 'convention' and is considered a general principle of international law.[71]

It might be concluded that in the field of International law there is a right to self-determination equal to other rights enshrined in covenants on human rights, considered a fundamental and guiding principle of international law, and an integral part of *jus cogens.*[72] The principle of self-determination would have evolved from a philosophical into a political concept in international relations and then into a fundamental principle of positive international law.[73] However, although there is a broad consensus on internal self-determination, there are particular difficulties with regard to external self-determination outside any decolonization process.[74] On these lines, it would be possible to hold that the practice of the UN sees the principle of self-determination as fundamentally a 'vehicle for decolonization', and not a route to secession.[75] It would be circumscribed to processes of decolonization.[76]

---

[68]Cfr. Scelle (1957), pp. 385–391. Virally (1983), p. 60.

[69]Cfr. Lauterpacht (1965), p. 270. Virally (1983), p. 60.

[70]Cfr. Kapustin (2015), p. 104. Wilson (2009), p. 465.

Legal Consequences for States of the Continued Presence of South Africa in Namibia (South West Africa) notwithstanding Security Council Resolution 276 (1970), Advisory Opinion, I.C.J. Reports 1971, 16-66. *Western Sahara, Advisory Opinion, I.C.J. Reports 1975*, 12-176. *East Timor (Portugal v. Australia), Judgment, I.C.J. Reports 1995*, 90–277.

[71]Supreme Court of Canada, *Reference re Secession of Quebec* [1998] 2 SCR 217. 115 *International Law Reports* (1999), 536, p. 278, para. 114. http://scc-csc.lexum.com/scc-csc/scc-csc/en/item/1643/index.do. 37:6 *ILM* (1998), 1342–1377.

[72]Cfr. Przetacznik (1990), p. 95.

[73]Cfr. Umozurike (1972), p. 198.

[74]Cfr. Charney (2001), p. 457. Wilson (2015), p. 465.

[75]Cfr. Buchheit (1978), p. 87. Gros Espiell (1976), p. 55.

[76]Cfr. Berndtsson and Johansson (2015), p. 451. Carrillo Salcedo (1976), p. 33. Cassese (1995), p. 332. Christakis (2014), pp. 736 and 739. Van den Driest (2015), p. 351. Gros Espiell (1976), p. 56. Hilpold (2015), p. 251. By the same author Hilpold (2006), pp. 247–288; and Hilpold (2009), pp. 47–61. Jia (2009), p. 32. Ker-Lindsay (2013), p. 841. Marxsen (2014), p. 385. Oeter (2014), p. 53. Röben (2010), p. 1071. Vidmar (2015), p. 370. Wilson (2009), p. 466. Yee (2010), p. 777.

2.2.2 The Scope of the Right and the Notion of a People

Establishing the degree of recognition and the scope of a right to external self-determination outside any decolonization process has been a matter of controversy for a number of decades.[77] International practice shows that from 1945 down to the declaration of independence by Kosovo in 2008 there were numerous attempts at unilateral secession by groups or territories in independent States not within any colonial setting.[78] Nonetheless, the sole new State successfully arising from a process of unilateral secession that received broad recognition from the international community was Bangladesh when it broke free from Pakistan in 1971.[79] States in practice may be said to show resistance to recognizing any right to self-determination other than in a colonial context.[80]

For its part, case law on this topic established during the postcolonial period amounts to no more than two questions referred to the ICJ. These were the decisions on the *Legal Consequences of the Construction of a Wall in the Occupied Palestinian Territory* of 2004, and on the *Accordance with the International Law of the Unilateral Declaration of Independence in Respect of Kosovo* of 2010, which were not enough to provide a precise determination of its scope.[81]

It may be stated that in the postcolonial period emphasis has been laid on characterizing the principle of self-determination as a right to self-administration or self-government within the framework of a given State and subordinate to the principle of territorial integrity.[82] This aspect of internal self-determination has become a current customary norm for the international community.[83]

The UN Charter, in referring to the principle of self-determination as the self-determination of peoples, defines it as a legal reality with different nuances from the right to self-determination in the strict sense.[84] Just like other principles of international law, the principle of self-determination gives rise to rights and obligations, but in this particular case these affect not just State, but also peoples.[85] The man who

---

[77]Cfr. Castellino (2014), p. 30. Wilde (2011), p. 152.

[78]Cfr. Crawford (1998), p. 107.

[79]Cfr. Id., pp. 114–115. Ker-Lindsay (2013), p. 841. Nanda (1979), p. 72. Wilson (2009), p. 466.

[80]Cfr. Cassese (1995), pp. 118–124. Crawford (2007), pp. 107–131. Wilson (2009), pp. 465 and 480.

[81]See *Legal Consequences of the Construction of a Wall in the Occupied Palestinian Territory, Advisory Opinion, I.C.J. Reports 2004*, 136–271. *Accordance with the International Law of the Unilateral Declaration of Independence in Respect of Kosovo, Advisory Opinion,* supra, Chap. 1, note 3.

Cfr. Peters (2011), p. 108. Yee (2010), p. 778.

[82]Cfr. Crawford (2000), p. 32. Hilpold (2009), p. 55. Ker-Lindsay (2013), p. 841. Müllerson (2009), pp. 18–19. Ryngaert and Griffioen (2009), p. 575.

[83]Cfr. Cassese (1995), pp. 311 and 347.

[84]Cfr. Kapustin (2015), pp. 101–103. Johnson (1973), p. 157. Röben (2010), p. 1074. Ryngaert and Griffioen (2009), p. 575.

[85]Cfr. Kapustin (2015), pp. 102–103.

was Special Rapporteur of the Sub-Commission on Prevention of Discrimination and Protection of Minorities, Héctor Gros Espiell, summed it up as being a fundamental principle of an imperative nature in international law that constitutes a right of individuals and of peoples subject to colonial domination.[86]

Whilst recognition had been granted, the establishment and development of the right of peoples to self-determination came later and may be seen as taking shape after the 1960s.[87] However, the conceptions of its meaning and content are highly varied and divergent, as also instances of its being put into place.[88]

The main problems relating to the interpretation of the right of peoples to self-determination in the post-colonial era centre on the problem of delimiting the scope and content of external self-determination. In particular, crucial aspects are the definition of a 'people' and the question whether the right to self-determination implies a right to secede from a state.[89]

Whilst the principle of self-determination has been recognized as a central principle in International law, as noted above, the problem that arises is the setting of limits to its scope. This may be summed up as its intermeshing with other principles that are the basis for the idea of a State in the international community: the principle of equal sovereignty and the principle of territorial integrity.[90] Hence, it is not surprising that a supposed right to secession has been seen by many as illegitimate, non-existent or, in brief, as incompatible the principles, also recognized in the UN Charter, of sovereignty and territorial integrity.[91]

The starting point must be the idea that in the current state of international law the right to self-determination, in conformity with the UN Charter, is not circumscribed exclusively to non-self-governing territories, but constitutes a right *erga omnes*.[92] It is a right characterized by some authors as a universal right that needs to be defined as broadly as possible in both its internal and its external features.[93] Nonetheless, it must in turn not be understood as an absolute right, but one that normally does not give rise to changes in international frontiers, even if this is not absolutely prohibited by international law.[94]

---

[86]Cfr. Gros Espiell (1976), p. 55; and, by the same author, *Study on Implementation of United Nations Resolutions Relating to the Right of Peoples under Colonial and Alien Domination to Self-Determination*, UN Doc. E/CN.4/Sub.2/377, 1976.

[87]Cfr. Berndtsson and Johansson (2015), p. 450.

[88]Cfr. Kirgis (1994), p. 307.

[89]Cfr. Berndtsson and Johansson (2015), p. 450.

[90]Cfr. Id., p. 451. Kirgis (1994), p. 308. McFarlane and Sabanadze (2013), pp. 624–625.

[91]Cfr. Berndtsson and Johansson (2015), p. 451.

[92]Cfr. *East Timor (Portugal v. Australia), Judgment*, supra, this chapter, note 70, p. 102, para. 29. *Legal Consequences of the Construction of a Wall in the Occupied Palestinian Territory, Advisory Opinion*, supra, this chapter, note 104, p. 81, para. 88.

[93]Cfr. Binder (1993), p. 236. Jaber (2011), p. 929. Johnson (1973), p. 148. Ryngaert and Griffioen (2009), p. 575.

[94]Cfr. Shany (2014), p. 234. Vidmar (2015), p. 366.

The ownership of the right to self-determination is generally accepted as lying with 'peoples'.[95] In practice, the beneficiaries of an external right to self-determination are identified as a 'people', understood as 'the entire population living in the territory subject to illegal domination.[96] This attribution of the ownership of the right to self-determination finds support in various resolutions of the General Assembly and a number of legal decisions.[97] This view implies that the idea of a people is based on geographical considerations, and only the entirety of the population residing within the frontiers of an internationally recognized territory can be the owner of a right to self-determination in accordance with the *uti possidetis* principle.[98] Article 1 of the 'International Covenant on Civil and Political Rights' states that the right to self-determination constitutes a human right of 'all peoples'.[99] The wording of the Article stresses its universal nature and extends it beyond just colonial peoples.[100]

Determining the notion of a people has generated an extensive literature. As noted above, it has been one of the main debates on which the interpretation of the right to self-determination has centred in the post-colonial era.[101]

Some States expressly took the line that the right belonged to sub-groups existing within the structure of an independent State. Others proposed that the definition should include 'large compact national groups', 'members of a group inhabiting a compact territory to which they belong, ethnically, culturally, historically, or otherwise', 'racial units inhabiting well-defined territories', and also 'ethnic, religious and linguistic minorities'.[102]

The result was that no agreement was reached on the definition of a people. The establishing of the characteristics defining a group that could invoke the right to self-determination turned out to be an unanswered question, since there was no agreement on how a people should be defined.[103] To conclude, the idea of a people should be taken in its broadest sense, because no precise, detailed definition could be found.[104]

In 1981, the Special Rapporteur of the United Nations Sub-Commission on the Prevention of Discrimination and the Protection of Minorities, Aureliu Cristescu,

---

[95]Cfr. Supreme Court of Canada, *Reference re Secession of Quebec*, supra, this chapter, note 71, p. 281, para. 123.

[96]Cfr. Tancredi (2012), p. 91.

[97]Cfr. Jaber (2011), p. 930.

[98]Cfr. Shany (2014), p. 236.

[99]Cfr. Gros Espiell (1976), p. 52.

[100]This conclusion is also supported by the debates that preceded adoption of the 'International Covenant on Civil and Political Rights' in which States managed to agree on the universal nature of the principle and its application to all peoples, not just colonial peoples. Cfr. Bossuyt (1987), p. 32. Cassese (1981), p. 94.

[101]Cfr. Ryngaert and Griffioen (2009), p. 576.

[102]Cfr. Bossuyt (1987), pp. 32 and 33.

[103]Cfr. Jaber (2011), p. 930.

[104]Cfr. Id., p. 929.

presented a study which concluded with a proposal for a synthesis of the features defining what constitutes a people fit to enjoy and exercise the right of self-determination:

> (a) The term 'people' denotes a social entity possessing a clear identity, and its own characteristics;
> (b) It implies a relationship with a territory, even if the people in question has been wrongfully expelled from it and artificially replaced by another population;
> (c) A people should not be confused with ethnic, religious or linguistic minorities, whose existence and rights are recognized in article 27 of the International Covenant on Civil and Political Rights.[105]

In agreement with these statements, most authors coincide in seeing the idea of a people as involving at least two elements: one sociological and one geographical. The first, worded as a 'social entity possessing a clear identity', implies a coincidence of an objective and of a subjective aspect.[106] The objective aspect centres on the existence of joint features such as race, ethnicity, nationality, culture, history, religion, language, or a common economic base, with a sufficiently large number of members.[107] The subjective aspect refers to the existence of an idea of shared identity held by the group.[108] According to this view, individuals feel themselves to be members of the group and express a desire to preserve the group's signs of identity.

The second elements is oriented towards the relationship with a territory, and is a determining factor in demands for self-determination.[109] It lies in the existence of a link of an ethnic, cultural, historical or some other kind between a group and a territory in respect of which the right to self-determination is invoked.[110] Establishing with what territory the group concerned has this link poses many questions.[111] Indeed, a strict territorial linkage for the idea of a people, as owner

---

[105] *The Right of Self-Determination: Historic and Current Development on the Basis of United Nations Instruments.* Study prepared by Aureliu Cristescu, UN Doc. E/CN.4/Sub.2/404/Rev.1, supra, this chapter, note 47, p. 41.

[106] Cfr. Lauwers and Smis (2000), p. 55. Raič (2002), p. 262.

[107] Cfr. Hannum (1993), p. 35. Raič (2002), p. 262. *The Events in East Pakistan, 1971. A Legal Study by the Secretariat of the International Commission of Jurists* (Geneva: International Commission of Jurists, 1972), 98, p. 70. http://icj.wpengine.netdna-cdn.com/wp-content/uploads/1972/06/Bangladesh-events-East-Pakistan-1971-thematic-report-1972-eng.pdf. *Final Report and Recommendations. International Meeting of Experts on Further Study of the Concept of the Rights of Peoples, UNESCO, Paris, 27-30 November 1989*, UNESCO Doc. SHS-89/CONF.602/7, 22 February 1990, 18, p. 7, para. 22. Oeter (2012), p. 115; and, by the same author Oeter (2014), p. 53.

[108] Hannum (1993), p. 35. Ryngaert and Griffioen (2009), p. 575.

[109] Cfr. *The Right of Self-Determination: Historic and Current Development on the Basis of United Nations Instruments.* Study prepared by Aureliu Cristescu, UN Doc. E/CN.4/Sub.2/404/Rev.1, supra, this chapter, note 47, p. 41. Hannum (1993), p. 35.

[110] Cfr. Lauwers and Smis (2000), p. 56.

[111] Cfr. Jaber (2011), p. 931.

of the right to self-determination, is itself not accepted by a considerable number of authors.[112] This is because they feel that the right to self-determination should be seen as a right of 'peoples', rather than of territories.[113]

In his study, Aureliu Cristescu stressed that the idea of a people was different from that of an ethnic, linguistic or religious minority as covered by Art. 27 of the 'International Covenant on Civil and Political Rights'.[114] The same view has been held by the majority of States and by legal theory.[115] Although it is not at all easy to distinguish between a people and a minority, it can be stated that having long-standing roots in a given territory provides a sufficient criterion for noting the presence of a people.[116]

To conclude, the idea of a people evokes a social entity with a clear relationship with a territory, but not to be confused with ethnic, religious or linguistic minorities.[117] This notion ultimately corresponds to a conception of a State in conformity with the model adopted after the Peace of Westphalia of spheres comprising one territory, one population or community, and one authority. This conception has long since become outdated because of the superposition of populations and authorities, and the interdependence present in the present-day international community.[118] Thus, the international community is made up of a complex visible intertwining of categories of statehood in which the exercise of the human right to self-determination, understood as external self-determination, has become diluted in a world less and less centred on individual States.[119]

2.3 The Extent and Limitations of the Principle of Territorial Integrity

In the process of decolonization, the principle of self-determination preceded the principle of territorial integrity.[120] Nonetheless, during the debate arising in the post-colonial period States declared that the right to self-determination was subordinate to

---

[112]Cfr. Ryngaert and Griffioen (2009), p. 576.

[113]Cfr. Van den Driest (2015), p. 351. Vidmar (2011), p. 364.

[114]Cfr. *The Right of Self-Determination: Historic and Current Development on the Basis of United Nations Instruments.* Study prepared by Aureliu Cristescu, UN Doc. E/CN.4/Sub.2/404/Rev.1, supra, this chapter, note 47, p. 41.

[115]Cfr. Cassese (1981), p. 101. Jaber (2011), p. 932. Lauwers and Smis (2000), p. 56.

[116]Cfr. Jaber (2011), p. 933. Lauwers and Smis (2000), p. 57.

[117]Cfr. *The Right of Self-Determination: Historic and Current Development on the Basis of United Nations Instruments.* Study prepared by Aureliu Cristescu, UN Doc. E/CN.4/Sub.2/404/Rev.1, supra, this chapter, note 47, p. 41.

[118]Cfr. Anaya (1993), p. 140.

[119]Cfr. Id., p. 140.

[120]Cfr. Blay (1986), p. 443.

the principle of territorial integrity.[121] One American lawyer commented that 'the Charter [of the United Nations], which affirmed the principle of self-determination, also recognized the legitimacy of the 'territorial integrity' of nations (Art. 2(4))'.[122] These words sum up the approach which saw the principle of self-determination as in conflict with the principle of territorial integrity, and the conclusion that the UN Charter excluded secession in putting into practice the right to self-determination.[123]

The principle of territorial integrity contemplated in Art. 2(4) of the UN Charter is referred to in relation with the prohibition of the threat, or actual use, of force between States in their international relations. It was also referred to in Resolution 2625 (XXV) 'Declaration on Principles of International Law Concerning Friendly Relations and Co-operation among States in Accordance with the UN Charter' as a requirement for States to abstain from any type of action that might damage or decrease the territorial integrity of another State.[124]

Other agreements of a regional nature, such as the 'Helsinki Final Act' of 1975, saw the principle of territorial integrity as a fundamental support.[125] However, the 'Helsinki Final Act' does not give the principle of territorial integrity an absolute status, but accepts that 'frontiers can be changed, in accordance with international law, by peaceful means and by agreement'.[126] The framework within which the idea of territorial integrity appears is closely linked to the question of the external use of force between participating States.[127]

In effect, the principle of territorial integrity has been construed as linked to the fundamental rule prohibiting the threat or use of force that governs international relations.[128] As such, the territorial integrity of a State can be harmed only by another State.[129] Thus, the ICJ concluded in its Kosovo Advisory Opinion that 'the scope of the principle of territorial integrity is confined to the sphere of relations

[121]See supra, Sect. 2.2.2., note 82.

[122]Cfr. Perkins (1981), p. 75.

[123]Cfr. Przetacznik (1990), p. 101.

[124]Cfr. 'Declaration on Principles of International Law Concerning Friendly Relations and Co-operation among States in Accordance with the UN Charter' UN Doc. A/RES/2625 (XXV), Annex, 24 October 1970, at 'The Principle of Equal Rights and Self-Determination of Peoples', para. 8.

Cfr. Ker-Lindsay (2013), p. 839. Muharremi (2010), p. 879.

[125]Cfr. 'Conference on Security and Co-operation in Europe Final Act', Helsinki, 1 August 1975, supra, this chapter, note 61, 'Questions relating to Security in Europe' 1. (a) Declaration on Principles Guiding Relations between Participating States, at IV.

The participating States will respect the territorial integrity of each of the participating States.

Cfr. Ker-Lindsay (2013), p. 839. Urrutia Libarona (2012), p. 109.

[126]'Conference on Security and Co-operation in Europe Final Act', Helsinki, 1 August 1975, supra, this chapter, note 61, 'Questions relating to Security in Europe' 1. (a) Declaration on Principles Guiding Relations between Participating States, at I.

[127]Cfr. Ibid.

[128]Cfr. Van den Driest (2015), p. 353. Peters (2011), p. 106.

[129]Cfr. Van den Driest (2015), p. 353. Walter (2014), p. 19.

between States'.[130] This is the sense in which territorial integrity principle has been understood by a wide group of scholars who consider it a horizontal rule 'confined to the sphere of relations between States', not applicable to non-sovereign groups.[131] It is true that the UN Charter admits two exceptions to the prohibition on the threat or use of force, so that it may be inferred that the principle of territorial integrity is certainly not absolute.[132]

The interpretation adopted by another group of authors leads them to understand that the prohibition on the threat or use of force also applies to non-State actors.[133] They feel that the interpretation restricting the prohibition to the sphere of States would run against Principle 5 of Resolution 2625 (XXV).[134] The principle of territorial integrity is thus invested with and inter-State character, as stressed by the ICJ, but it cannot be said that the prohibition on the use of force is similarly limited to the inter-State sphere.[135]

In the past, the right to self-determination has proved to be in conflict with the principle of territorial integrity, and has had to be exercised by peoples within the framework of States, without harming their territorial integrity.[136] In practice there was a tendency to 'place the territorial sovereignty above external self-determination in the hierarchy of values'.[137] This was the line taken by the Supreme Court of Canada in its *Reference re Secession of Quebec*: 'accordingly, the general state of international law with respect to the right to self-determination is that the right operates within the overriding protection granted to the territorial integrity of 'parent' states'.[138]

---

[130]Cfr. *Accordance with the International Law of the Unilateral Declaration of Independence in Respect of Kosovo*, *Advisory Opinion,* supra, Chap. 1, note 3, 403–626, p. 437, para. 80. Walter (2014), p. 19.

[131]Cfr. Christakis (2011), p. 84. Corten (2011), p. 90. Falkowski (1991), p. 229. Ingravallo (2012), p. 228. Lauwers and Smis (2000), p. 62. Marxsen (2015), p. 13. Muharremi (2010), p. 879. Röben (2010), pp. 1068 and 1079. Walter (2014), p. 22.

[132]Cfr. Vidmar (2012), p. 161.

[133]Cfr. Peters (2011), p. 106. Vashakmadze and Lippold (2010), p. 632.

[134]Cfr. Vidmar (2011), p. 369.

[135]Cfr. Walter (2014), at 21 and 23.

[136]Cfr. Crawford (1998), p. 85. Ker-Lindsay (2013), p. 840. Tamayo Álvarez (2014), p. 102.

Russian doctrine also takes this line, as may be seen from various authors such as I.P. Blischenko, S.V. Chernichenko, the Russian Association of International Law, and N.V. Ostroukhov. Cfr. Merezhko (2015), pp. 176–182.

[137]Dugard and Raič (2006), p. 134.

[138]Cfr. Supreme Court of Canada, *Reference re Secession of Quebec*, supra, this chapter, note 71, p. 284, para. 131.

With a similar stance, Judge Abdul Gadire Koroma gave a dissenting opinion saying that the 'Declaration on Principles of International Law Concerning Friendly Relations and Co-operation among States in Accordance with the UN Charter', 'leaves no doubt that the principles of the sovereignty and territorial integrity of States prevail over the principle of self-determination'. 'Dissenting Opinion of Judge Koroma', *Accordance with International Law of the Unilateral*

The consequence arising from this premise was that because the principle of territorial integrity prevailed over the right to self-determination, the possibility of secession was incompatible and hence excluded.[139] In the terms of Valerii I. Kuznetsov and Bakhtiiar R. Tuzmukhamedov in their textbook on international law published under the aegis of the Russian Association of International Law, 'self-determination should not be realized from the separatist stance to the detriment of the territorial integrity and political unity of the state'.[140]

The opinion of another major sector of doctrine, in accord with the reasoning of the ICJ in the Kosovo Advisory Opinion, held that the principle of territorial integrity could not be invoked at the level internal to States.[141] It could be said to have a horizontal application only, not vertical.[142] In conclusion, the principle of territorial integrity remains one governing relations between territorial sovereigns,[143] and a unilateral secession within the framework of a sovereign State would not run counter to the principle of the territorial integrity of States.[144]

2.4 Towards a Definition of the Right to Self-Determination

The statement on self-determination contained in the 'Declaration on Principles of International Law Concerning Friendly Relations and Co-operation among States in Accordance with the Charter of the United Nations' of Resolution 2625 (XXV) of 1970 constitutes the starting point for providing a definition in accord with the present-day international community.[145] To cite the wordings of other authors, it could be summed up that the right to self-determination comprises the right giving to peoples the freedom to choose in determining their own destiny, and constitutes a genuine human right.[146] Similarly, it could be expressed as the right to govern oneself on the basis of a free and genuine expression of the will of the governed.[147] As seen by Ian Brownlie, it would be 'the right to cohesive national groups

---

Declaration of Independence in Respect of Kosovo, Advisory Opinion, supra, Chap. 1, note 3, p. 476, para. 22. http://www.icj-cij.org/files/case-related/141/141-20100722-ADV-01-02-BI.pdf. Cfr. Jia (2009), pp. 40 and 41. Van den Driest (2015), p. 354.

[139]Cfr. Van den Driest (2015), p. 352. Merezhko (2015), p. 181. Ryngaert and Griffioen (2009), p. 491.

[140]Cfr. Kuznetsov and Tuzmukhamedov (2009), p. 214.

[141]Cfr. Corten (2011), p. 94. Walter (2014), p. 25. Wilde (2011), p. 152.

[142]Cfr. Röben (2010), p. 1079.

[143]Cfr. Ibid.

[144]Cfr. Vidmar (2012), p. 163. See also, by the same author Vidmar (2015), p. 367; and Vidmar (2011), p. 370.

[145]Cfr. Kaikobad (2011), p. 57.

[146]Cfr. Expert opinion by Franck et al. (2000), p. 248.

[147]Cfr. Lauwers and Smis (2000), p. 58.

('peoples') to choose for themselves a form of political organization and their relation to other groups'.[148]

In view of these ideas, three essential elements may be identified as shaping the right to self-determination. First, the owner of this right to self-determination are peoples, groups of individuals having some social cohesion, with a clear identity and their own characteristics, and an implicit a relationship with a territory.[149]

Secondly, the material content extends both to all aspects of political status and to the economic, social and cultural system. With reference to its formal content, the right to self-determination is centred on the exercise of the people's sovereignty through democratic governance manifested through channels that imply a free and genuine expression of their will in the internal context and in the externa dimension.[150]

Thirdly, the legal status of the right to self-determination formed by these elements would also be shaped by a further four aspects which have been gradually identified by legal doctrine. It is a principle applicable to all non-self-governing territories and trust territories, and not merely a policy guiding the behaviour of member States of the UN in their relations with these.[151] Despite the clear distinction maintained in the UN Charter between classes of colonial peoples, developments after the Namibia Advisory Opinion determined that the principle of self-determination should apply to all territories.[152] From Resolution 1514 (XV), the 'Declaration on the Granting of Independence to Colonial Countries and Peoples', onwards, it became clear that self-determination was not so much a lawful policy and goal of governments as a legal right of peoples of non-self-governing territories.[153]

The right to self-determination constitutes one of the most basic of all human rights.[154] This is the expression used in Art. 1 of the 'International Covenant on Civil and Political Rights' and of the 'International Covenant on Economic, Social and

[148]Brownlie (1990), p. 599.

[149]Cfr. *The Right of Self-Determination: Historic and Current Development on the Basis of United Nations Instruments.* Study prepared by Aureliu Cristescu, UN Doc. E/CN.4/Sub.2/404/Rev.1, supra, this chapter, note 47, p. 41.

[150]Cfr. Cassese (1981), p. 101. Nawaz (1965), p. 84. Wambaugh (1920), p. 2.

[151]Cfr. Kaikobad (2011), p. 63.

[152]Cfr. *Legal Consequences for States of the Continued Presence of South Africa in Namibia (South West Africa) notwithstanding Security Council Resolution 276 (1970), Advisory Opinion*, supra, this chapter, note 70, p. 31, para. 52.

Cfr. Crawford (2007), p. 101. Ofuatey-Kodjoe (1977), p. 150.

[153]Cfr. UN Doc. A/RES/1514 (XV), of 14 December 1960, at para. 5.

Cfr. Shaw (1997), pp. 481–482.

[154]Cfr. McCorquodale (1994), p. 872. Tolstykh (2015), p. 126.

The first author to refer to considering self-determination as linked to human rights was Higgins (1963), p. 105. For later views, see also Chen (1981), pp. 88–94. *The Right of Self-Determination: Historic and Current Development on the Basis of United Nations Instruments.* Study prepared by Aureliu Cristescu, UN Doc. E/CN.4/Sub.2/404/Rev.1, supra, this chapter, note 47, p. 4, para. 27. *The Right of Self-Determination: Implementation of the United Nations Resolutions.* Study prepared by Héctor Gros Espiell, Special Rapporteur of the Sub-Commission on Prevention of

Cultural Rights' of 1966.[155] The Human Rights Committee saw as fundamental its status as a human right because 'its realization is an essential condition for the effective guarantee and observance of individual human rights and for the promotion and strengthening of those rights'.[156] To sum up, it may be considered a human right because of its purpose of protecting communities and groups from oppression, since individuals form part of these. A second reason is its integration with the protection of individual rights, for if peoples are subjected individuals' rights will not be fully protected.[157]

Self-determination is a right *erga omnes*, and guaranteeing it concerns all members of the international community. This view was supported by the ICJ in the matters of *East Timor* and the *Palestinian Wall* Advisory Opinion.[158] The idea that questions referring to self-determination are limited to the relationship between a metropolitan power and an entity demanding its independence has been set aside.[159] Similarly, the UN now have legitimate cause to intervene in such matters, which are now no longer restricted exclusively to the domestic jurisdiction of member states.

Finally, as noted, the right of self-determination is a norm of *jus cogens* such that no derogations from it would be permitted.[160] This claim implies that all peoples have the right to self-determination and may exercise all aspects it brings with it as a peremptory right from which no exceptions are allowed. However, there are certain aspects involved in the right to self-determination about which there is no general recognition of their integration into its content such as to enjoy the nature of a peremptory norm from which the basic right benefits.[161]

References

Anaya, S.J. 1993. A Contemporary Definition of the International Norm of Self-Determination. *TLCP* 3: 131–164.

Arangio-Ruiz, G. 1979. *The United Nations Declaration on Friendly Relations and the System of the Sources of International Law*. Alphen aan den Rijn: Sijthoff & Noordhoff.

Discrimination and Protection of Minorities (1980), UN Doc. E/CN.4/Sub.2/405/Rev.1, 86, p. 2, para. 10. Dinstein (1976), pp. 106–107.

[155]See supra, Sect. 2.1.3.

[156]Cfr. 'Centre for Civil and Political Rights General Comment No. 12: Article 1 (Right to Self-Determination) The Right to Self-Determination of Peoples', Adopted at the Twenty-first Session of the Human Rights Committee, on 13 March 1984', in 'Compilation of General Comments and General Recommendations Adopted by Human Rights Treaty Bodies, Note by the Secretariat', UN Doc. HRI/GEN/Rev.1, 29 July 1994, 107, p. 12, para. 1.

[157]Cfr. McCorquodale (1994), p. 872. Peters (2009), p. 543.

[158]See supra, Sect. 2.2.2, note 92.

[159]Cfr. Kaikobad (2011), p. 61.

[160]See supra, Sect. 2.1.3, note 47.

[161]Cfr. Kaikobad (2011), p. 64.

———. 1983. Autodeterminazione dei popoli e diritto internazionale. Dalla Carta delle Nazioni Unite allAtto di Helsinki (CSCE). *RSPI* 50: 523–552.

Baker, R.S., and W.E. Dodd, eds. 1927. *War and Peace: Presidential Messages, Addresses, and Public Papers (1917–1924)*. New York: Harper & Bros.

Bakunin, M.A. 1972. Revolutionary Catechism. In *Bakunin on Anarchy: Selected Works by the Activist-Founder of World Anarchism*, ed. S. Dolgoff, 76–97. New York: Vintage Books.

Berndtsson, J., and P. Johansson. 2015. Principles on a Collision Course? State Sovereignty Meets Peoples Right of Self-Determination in the Case of Kosovo. *Cambridge RIA* 28: 445–461.

Binder, G. 1993. The Case for Self-Determination. The Kaplan Lecture on Human Rights. *SJIL* 29: 223–270.

Blay, S.K.N. 1986. Self-Determination versus Territorial Integrity in Decolonization. *NYUJILP* 18: 441–472.

Blum, Y.Z. 1975. Reflections on the Changing Concept of Self-Determination. *Israel LR* 10: 509–514.

Bokor-Szegö, H. 1970. *New States and International Law*. Budapest: Akadémiai kiadó.

Bossuyt, M. 1987. *Guide to the 'travaux préparatoires' of the International Covenant on Civil and Political Rights*. Dordrecht, Boston: Martinus Nijhoff.

Boyd, J.P., et al., eds. 1950. *The Papers of Thomas Jefferson*. Princeton, NJ: Princeton University Press.

Brownlie, I. 1990. *Principles of Public International Law*. 4th ed. Oxford: Oxford University Press.

Buchheit, L.C. 1978. *Secession: The Legitimacy of Self-Determination*. New Haven: Yale University Press.

Calogeropoulos-Stratis, S. 1973. *Le droit des peuples à disposer d'eux-mêmes*. Bruxelles: E. Bruylant.

Carrillo Salcedo, J.A. 1976. Libre determinación de los pueblos e integridad territorial de los Estados en el dictamen del Tribunal Internacional de Justicia sobre el Sahara Occidental. *REDI* 29: 33–49.

Cassese, A. 1977. The Helsinki Declaration and Self-Determination. In *Human Rights, International Law & The Helsinki Accord*, ed. T. Buergenthal and J.R. Hall, 83–110. Montclair; New York: Allanheld, Osmun & Co.; Universe Books.

———. 1979. Political Self-Determination – Old Concepts and New Development. In *UN Law Fundamental Rights – Two Topics in International Law*, ed. A. Cassese, 137–165. Sijthoff & Noordhoff: Alphen aan den Rijn.

———. 1981. The Self-Determination of Peoples. In *The International Bill of Rights: The Covenant on Civil and Political Rights*, ed. L. Henkin, 95–113. New York: Columbia University Press.

———. 1991. Article 1, paragraphe 2. In *La Charte des Nations Unies. Commentaire article par article*, ed. J.P. Cot and A. Pellet, 2nd ed., 39–45. Paris/Brussels: Economica/Bruylant.

———. 1995. *Self-Determination of Peoples: A Legal Reappraisal*. Cambridge: Cambridge University Press.

Castellino, J. 2014. International Law and Self-Determination. In *Self-Determination and Secession in International Law* ed. C. Walter, et al. 27–45. Oxford: Oxford University Press.

Charney, J.I. 2001. Self-Determination: Chechnya, Kosovo, and East Timor. *Vand. J. Transnat'l L.* 34: 455–446.

Chen, L. 1981. Self-Determination: An Important Dimension of the Demand for Freedom. *ASIL Proceedings* 75: 88–94.

Chowdhury, S.R. 1977. The Status and Norms of Self-Determination in Contemporary International Law. *NILR* 24: 72–84.

Christakis, T. 2011. The ICJ Advisory Opinion on Kosovo: Has International Law Something to Say about Secession? *LJIL* 24: 73–86.

———. 2014. Les conflits de sécession en Crimée et dans l'Est de l'Ukraine et le droit international (The Conflicts of Secession in Crimea and Eastern Ukraine and International Law). *JDI* 141: 733–764.

Cirkovic, E. 2010. An Analysis of the ICJ Advisory Opinion on Kosovo's Unilateral Declaration of Independence. *German LJ* 11: 895–912.
Corten, O. 2011. Territorial Integrity Narrowly Interpreted: Reasserting the Classical Inter-State Paradigm of International Law. *LJIL* 24: 87–94.
Crawford, J., ed. 1988. *The Rights of Peoples*. Oxford: Clarendon Press.
———. 1998. State Practice and International Law in Relation to Secession. *BYIL* 69: 85–117.
———. 2000. State Practice and International Law in Relation to Unilateral Secession. In *Self-Determination in International Law: Quebec and Lessons Learned*, ed. A.F. Bayefsky, 31–62. The Hague: Kluwer Law International.
———. 2007. *The Creation of States in International Law*. 2nd ed. Oxford: Clarendon Press.
Dinstein, Y. 1976. Collective Human Rights of Peoples and Minorities. *ICLQ* 25: 102–120.
Dugard, J., and D. Raič. 2006. The Role of Recognition in the Law and Practice of Secession. In *Secession: International Law Perspectives*, ed. M.G. Kohen, 94–137. Cambridge: Cambridge University Press.
Emerson, R. 1971. Self-Determination. *AJIL* 65: 459–475.
Falkowski, J.E. 1991. Secessionary Self-Determination: A Jeffersonian Perspective. *B.U. Intl L.J* 9: 209–242.
Finch, G.A. 1919. The Peace Conference of Paris, 1919. *AJIL* 13: 159–186.
Franck, T.M., R. Higgins, A. Pellet, M.N. Shaw, and C. Tomuschat. 2000. The Territorial Integrity of Québec in the Event of the Attainment of Sovereignty – Experts Report. In *Self-Determination in International Law: Quebec and Lessons Learned*, ed. A.F. Bayefski, 333–342. The Hague: Kluwer Law International.
Goodrich, L.M., E. Hambro, and A.P. Simons, eds. 1969. *Charter of the United Nations: Commentary and Documents*. 3rd revised ed. New York; London: Columbia University Press.
Gros Espiell, H. 1976. En torno al derecho de la libre determinación de los pueblos. *ADI* 3: 49–74.
———. 1979. Self-Determination and Ius Cogens. In *UN Law Fundamental Rights – Two Topics in International Law*, ed. A. Cassese, 167–173. Sijthoff & Noordhoff: Alphen aan den Rijn.
Hannum, H. 1990. *Autonomy, Sovereignty, and Self-Determination: The Accommodation of Conflicting Rights*. Philadelphia: University of Pennsylvania Press.
———. 1993. Rethinking Self-Determination. *VJIL* 34: 1–69.
Higgins, R. 1963. *The Development of International Law Through the Political Organs of the United Nations*. London, New York: Oxford University Press.
Hilpold, P. 2006. Self-Determination in the 21st Century – Modern Perspectives for an Old Concept. *IYHR* 36: 247–288.
———. 2009. The Kosovo Case and International Law: Looking for Applicable Theories. *Chinese JIL* 8: 47–61.
———. 2015. Ukraine, Crimea and New International Law: Balancing International Law with Arguments Drawn from History. *Chinese JIL* 14: 237–270.
Ingravallo, I. 2012. Kosovo after the ICJ Advisory Opinion: Towards a European Perspective? *ICLR* 14: 219–241.
Jaber, T. 2011. A Case for Kosovo? Self-determination and Secession in the 21st Century. *IJHR* 15: 926–947.
Jia, B.B. 2009. The Independence of Kosovo: A Unique Case of Secession? *Chinese JIL* 8: 27–46.
Johnson, C.D. 1973. Toward Self-Determination – A Reappraisal As Reflected in the Declaration on Friendly Relations. *Ga.J. Intl & Comp L.* 3: 145–163.
Kaikobad, K.H. 2011. Another Frozen Conflict: Kosovo's Unilateral Declaration of Independence and International Law. In *Kosovo: A Precedent?: The Declaration of Independence, the Advisory Opinion and Implications for Statehood, Self-Determination and Minority Rights*, ed. J. Summers, 55–85. Leiden, Boston: Martinus Nijhoff Publishers.
Kapustin, A. 2015. Crimea's Self-Determination in the Light of Contemporary International Law. *ZaöRV/HJIL* 75: 101–118.
Kelsen, H. 1964. *The Law of the United Nations: A Critical Analysis of its Fundamental Problems* (4th printing). London: Stevens & Sons Ltd.

Ker-Lindsay, J. 2013. Preventing the Emergence of Self-determination as a Norm of Secession: An Assessment of Kosovo Unique Case Argument. *Europe-Asia Studies* 65: 837–856.

Kirgis, F.L., Jr. 1994. The Degrees of Self-Determination in the United Nations Era. *AJIL* 88: 304–310.

Kiss, A. 1986. The Peoples' Right to Self-Determination. *HRLJ* 7: 165–175.

Kuznetsov, V.I., and B.R. Tuzmukhamedov, eds. 2009. *International Law: A Russian Introduction*. Utrecht/Portland, OR: Eleven International Publishing/International Specialized Services.

Laing, E.A. 1989. The Contribution of the Atlantic Charter to Human Rights Law and Humanitarian Universalism. *Villamette Law Review* 26: 113.

———. 1991. The Norm of Self-Determination, 1941-1991. *CWILJ* 22: 209–308.

Lauterpacht, E. 1965. Some Concepts of Human Rights. *Howard Law Journal* 11: 264–274.

Lauwers, G., and S. Smis. 2000. New Dimensions of the Right to Self-determination: A Study of the International Response to the Kosovo Crisis. *N & EP* 6: 43–70.

Levin, D.B. 1962. The Principle of Self-Determination in International Law. *Soviet YIL*: 45–48.

Magarašević, A. 1956. A View on the Right to Self-determination in International Law. *JRMP* 3.

Marxsen, C. 2014. The Crimea Crisis - An International Law Perspective. *ZaöRV/HJIL* 74: 367–391.

———. 2015. Territorial Integrity in International Law – Its Concept and Implications for Crimea. *ZaöRV/HJIL* 75: 7–26.

McCorquodale, R. 1992. Self-Determination Beyond the Colonial Context and its Potential Impact on Africa. *AJICL/RADIC* 4: 592–608.

———. 1994. Self-Determination: A Human Rights Approach. *ICLQ* 43: 857–885.

McFarlane, N., and N. Sabanadze. 2013. Sovereignty and Self-Determination: Where are We? *International Journal* 68: 609–627.

Merezhko, O. 2015. Crimea's Annexation by Russia – Contradictions of the New Russian Doctrine of International Law. *ZaöRV/HJIL* 75: 167–194.

Milano, E. 2014. The Non-Recognition of Russia's Annexation of Crimea: Three Different Legal Approaches and One Unanswered Question. *Questions of International Law*, *Zoom Out* I 35–55. www.qil-qdi.org.

Muharremi, R. 2010. A Note on the ICJ Advisory Opinion on Kosovo. *German LJ* 11: 867–880.

Müllerson, R.A. 2009. Precedents in the Mountains: On the Parallels and Uniqueness of the Cases of Kosovo, South Ossetia and Abkhazia. *Chinese JIL* 8: 2–25.

Nanda, V.P. 1979. Self-Determination Outside the Colonial Context: The Birth of Bangladesh in Retrospect. *Houston Journal of International Law* 1: 71.

Nawaz, M.K. 1965. The Meaning and Range of the Principle of Self-Determination. *Duke Law Journal* 82: 82–101.

Notter, H. 1937). *The Origins of the Foreign Policy of Woodrow Wilson* Baltimore: The Johns Hopkins Press, 695, pp. 68 and 69

Oeter, S. 2012. Secession, Territorial Integrity and the Role of the Security Council. In *Kosovo and International Law: The ICJ Advisory Opinion of 22 July 2010*, ed. P. Hilpold, 109–138. Leiden, Boston: Martinus Nijhoff.

———. 2014. The Role of Recognition and Non-Recognition with Regard to Secession. In *Self-Determination and Secession in International Law*, ed. C. Walter, et al., 45–67. Oxford: Oxford University Press.

Ofuatey-Kodjoe, W. 1977. *The Principle of Self-Determination in International Law*. New York: Nellen.

Orakhelashvili, A. 2006. *Peremptory Norms in International Law*. Oxford: Oxford University Press.

Pellet, A. 1991. Chapitre IX: 'Cooperation économique et sociale internationale'. Article 55, alinéas (a) et (b). In *La Charte des Nations Unies. Commentaire article par article*, ed. J.P. Cot and A. Pellet, 2nd ed., 841–861. Paris/Brussels: Economica/Bruylant.

Perkins, J.A. 1981. *The Prudent Peace: Law as Foreign Policy*. Chicago, London: University of Chicago Press.

Peters, A. 2009. Humanity as the A and Ω of Sovereignty. *EJIL* 20: 513–544.
———. 2011. Does Kosovo Lie in the Lotus-Land of Freedom? *LJIL* 24: 95–108.
Pomerance, M. 1976. The United States and Self-Determination: Perspectives on the Wilsonian Conception. *AJIL* 70: 1–27.
———. 1982. *Self-Determination in Law and Practice. The New Doctrine in the United Nations*. The Hague: Martinus Nijhoff.
Przetacznik, T. 1990. The Basic Collective Human Right to Self-Determination of Peoples and Nations As a Prerequisite for Peace. *N.Y. Law Sch. J. Hum. Rights* 7: 49–109.
Raič, D. 2002. *Statehood and the Law of Self-Determination*. The Hague: Martinus Nijhoff Publishers.
Röben, V. 2010. The ICJ Advisory Opinion on the Unilateral Declaration of Independence in Respect of Kosovo: Rules or Principles? *GoJIL* 2: 1063–1086.
Rosenstock, R. 1971. The Declaration of Principles of International Concerning Friendly Relations. A Survey. *AJIL* 65: 713–735.
Russell, R.B. 1958. *A History of the United Nations Charter. The Role of the United States 1940–1945*. Washington: The Brookings Institution.
Ryngaert, C. 2010. The ICJs Advisory Opinion on Kosovo's Declaration of Independence: A Mixed Opportunity?: International Court of Justice, Accordance with International Law of the Unilateral Declaration of Independence in Respect of Kosovo, Advisory Opinion of 22 July 2010. *NILR* 57: 481–494.
Ryngaert, C., and C. Griffioen. 2009. The Relevance of the Right to Self-determination in the Kosovo Matter: In Partial Response to the Agora Papers. *Chinese JIL* 8: 573–587.
Salo, J. 1991. Self-Determination: An Overview of History and Present State with Emphasis on the CSCE Process. *Finnish YIL* 2: 307–321.
Scelle, G. 1957. Quelques réflexions sur le droit des peuples à disposer deux-mêmes. In *Grundprobleme Des Internationalen Rechts: Festschrift Für Jean Spiropoulos = Foundamental Problems of International Law = Problèmes fondamentaux du droit international*, ed. J.C.T. Eustathiades, C.N. Fragistas Spiropoulos, and D.S. Constantopoulos. Bonn: Schimmelbusch.
Scott, J.B., ed. 1918. *President Wilson's Foreign Policy – Messages, Addresses, Papers*. New York: Oxford University Press. https://archive.org/stream/presidentwilson03wilsgoog#page/n388/mode/2up.
Shany, Y. 2014. Does International Law Grant the People of Crimea and Donetsk a Right to Secede? Revisiting Self-Determination in Light of the 2014 Events in Ukraine. *Brown JWA* 21: 233–244.
Shaw, M.N. 1997. Peoples, Territorialism and Boundaries. *EJIL* 8: 478–507.
Shukovich, O. 1964. Self-Determination as a Principle of Coexistence. *Annuaire d'anciens auditeurs de l'Academie de Droit International de La Haye* 34: 175–183.
Tamayo Álvarez, R. 2014. La secesión unilateral de Crimea y el derecho internacional. *Revista Análisis Internacional* 5: 97–113.
Tancredi, A. 2012. Some Remarks on the Relationship Between Secession and General International Law in the Light of the ICJs Kosovo Advisory Opinion. In *Kosovo and International Law: The ICJ Advisory Opinion of 22 July 2010*, ed. P. Hilpold, 79–108. Leiden, Boston: Martinus Nijhoff Publishers.
Tolstykh, V. 2015. Three Ideas of Self-Determination in International Law and the Reunification of Crimea with Russia. *ZaöRV/HJIL* 75: 119–139.
Umozurike, U.O. 1972. *Self-Determination in International Law*. Hamden, CT: Archon Books.
Urrutia Libarona, I. 2012. Territorial Integrity and Self-Determination: The Approach of International Court of Justice in the Advisory Opinion on Kosovo. *Revista destudis autonòmics i federals* 16: 107–140.
Van den Driest, S.F. 2015. Crimea's Separation from Ukraine: An Analysis of the Right to Self-Determination and (Remedial) Secession in International Law. *NILR* 62: 329–363.

Vashakmadze, M., and M. Lippold. 2010. Nothing But a Road Towards Secession? The International Court of Justices Advisory Opinion on Accordance with International Law of the Unilateral Declaration of Independence in Respect of Kosovo. *GoJIL* 2: 619–647.
Vidmar, J. 2011. The Kosovo Advisory Opinion Scrutinized. *LJIL* 24: 355–383.
———. 2012. Conceptualizing Declarations of Independence in International Law. *Oxford JLS* 32: 153–177.
———. 2015. The Annexation of Crimea and the Boundaries of the Will of the People. *German LJ* 16: 365–383.
Virally, M. 1983. Panorama de droit international contemporain (Cours général de droit international public). *Recueil des cours* 183: 9–382.
Walter, C. 2014. The Kosovo Advisory Opinion: What It Says and What It Does Not Say. In *Self-Determination and Secession in International Law*, ed. C. Walter, et al. 13–26. Oxford: Oxford University Press.
Wambaugh, S. 1920. *A Monograph on Plebiscites, with a Collection of Official Documents.* New York: Oxford University Press.
Wengler, W. 1957. Le droit de la libre disposition des peuples comme principe du droit international. *RHDI* 10: 26–39.
Whelan, A. 1994. Wilsonian Self-Determination and the Versailles Settlement. *ICLQ* 43: 99–115.
White, R.C.A. 1981. Self-Determination: Time for a Re-Assessment? *NILR* 28: 147–170.
Wilde, R. 2011. Self-Determination, Secession, and Dispute Settlement after the Kosovo Advisory Opinion. *LJIL* 24: 149–154.
Wilson, G. 2009. Self-Determination, Recognition and the Problem of Kosovo. *NILR* 56: 455–481.
———. 2015. Crimea: Some Observations on Secession and Intervention in Partial Response to Müllerson and Tolstykh. *Chinese JIL* 14: 217–223.
Yee, S. 2010. Notes on the International Court of Justice (Part 4): The Kosovo Advisory Opinion. *Chinese JIL* 9: 763–782.

Chapter 3
The Right to Self-Determination and Unilateral Secession

The decades following the adoption of the UN Charter were marked by the process of decolonization in which the right to self-determination was invoked, implying as an inherent presumption a demand for independence.[1] Going beyond decolonization in contemporary international law, the question posed is that of the possibility of recognizing a right to secede that is consubstantial to putting self-determination into practice.

The idea of secession has been seen in different ways in the theory of international lay. It has generally been understood as 'the separation of part of the territory of a State carried out by the resident population with the aim of creating a new independent State or acceding to another existing State'.[2] Current majority opinion holds that this separation takes place in the absence of consent of the previous State.[3] When this consent has been given, it is understood that there is a 'devolution',[4] also called 'consensual secession', rather than 'secession'.[5] According to these views, to quote Professor of the Graduate Institute Marcelo Kohen, it may be defined as:

> [. . .] the creation of a new independent entity through the separation of part of the territory and population of an existing State, without the consent of the latter.[6]

There is no regulation of secession in International law, although it is possible to find certain indirect references in the regulation of state succession, requirements for statehood and recognition by third states.

---

[1]Cfr. Jaber (2011), p. 934.

[2]Haverland (2000), p. 354.

[3]Cfr. Van den Driest (2015), p. 334. Haverland (2000), p. 354. Kohen (2006), p. 3.

[4]Cfr. Kohen (2006), p. 3.

[5]Cfr. Buchanan (2007), http://plato.stanford.edu/archives/spr2007/entries/secession.

[6]Kohen (2006), p. 3.

J. F. Escudero Espinosa, *Self-Determination and Humanitarian Secession in International Law of a Globalized World*,
https://doi.org/10.1007/978-3-319-72622-9_3

It is clear that determining whether the right to self-determination implies a right to secession constitutes a complex question for International law.[7] The principal international texts and documents would appear to consider the right to secede as a legitimate means of exercising the right to self-determination. On these lines, reference may be made to Resolution 2625 (XXV), the section of which on 'The Principle of Equal Rights and Self-Determination of Peoples' proclaims that:

> The establishment of a sovereign and independent State, the free association or integration with an independent State or the emergence into any other political status freely determined by a people constitute modes of implementing the right of self-determination by that people.[8]

In contrast, international practice shows that when a group or entity seeks to secede from a State, alleging its right to unilateral secession as a way of exercising its right to self-determination, its applicability is usually challenged by the State concerned, which opposes the breaking away of a part of its territory.[9] In effect, as pointed out by Professor James Crawford of the University of Cambridge, since 1945 States have systematically opposed any right to unilateral secession,[10] only Bangladesh and Kosovo having been recognized, as against some twenty failed attempts at unilateral secession.[11]

In view of the disagreement between standards and actual practice, an extensive debate has taken place between those international legal scholars who recognize a right to secede derived from the right to self-determination and those who hold that it is not contemplated in International law, seeing it as admissible only in exceptional circumstances.[12] On each side of these different arguments a host of authors are to be found, with as many different reasonings put forward to uphold or challenge the legitimacy and legality of a right to secede in International law.[13] If there is any first premise, this must be that the exercise of the right to self-determination is not equivalent to a right to secession, as was concluded by the International Fact-Finding Mission on the Conflict in Georgia in 2009.[14]

---

[7] Cfr. Kapustin (2015), p. 105.

[8] 'Declaration on Principles of International Law Concerning Friendly Relations and Co-operation among States in Accordance with the UN Charter' UN Doc. A/RES/2625 (XXV), Annex, 24 October 1970, at 'The Principle of Equal Rights and Self-Determination of Peoples', para. 4.

Other international documents, such as the 'Helsinki Final Act' of 1975 and the 'Vienna Declaration and Programme of Action' of 1993, refer to Resolution 2625 (XXV) when contemplating the right to self-determination. Cfr. 'Conference on Security and Co-operation in Europe Final Act', Helsinki, 1 August 1975, supra, Chap. 2, note 61. World Conference on Human Rights, 'Vienna Declaration and Programme of Action', 25 June 1993, supra, Chap. 2, note 63, p. 20.

[9] Cfr. Van den Driest (2015), p. 334.

[10] Cfr. Crawford (2007), pp. 388–402. Vashakmadze and Lippold (2010), p. 634.

[11] Cfr. See supra, Sect. 2.2.2.

[12] Cfr. Kapustin (2015), p. 106.

[13] Cfr. Id., p. 105.

[14] The comment of the Independent International Fact-Finding Mission was that 'Abkhazia was not allowed to secede from Georgia under international law, because the right to self-determination does not entail a right to secession'. *Report of the Independent International Fact-Finding Mission*

3.1 The Absence of a Prohibition on Unilateral Secession in International Law

The majority of jurists start from the fact that there is no recognition of a right to secede in International law.[15] Among these, many consider that exercise of an external right to self-determination is confined to processes of decolonization.[16] In fact, although it was debated during the preparatory sessions preceding adoption during the San Francisco Conference, the term 'secession' in the end did not figure in the text of the UN Charter as a clear expression of the decision taken by the drafters.[17] The later Art. 1 shared by the two Covenants may be seen as relevant, but it is not possible to conclude that the right to seceded is reflected in the text of the original precept.[18]

Indeed, some authors also take into account arguments of a non-legal nature in not admitting any right to secession.[19] As they reason, recognition of a wide right to secede would be a dangerous pretext that might be alleged in any State with racial, linguistic, political or religious minorities.[20] Furthermore, it would lead to a progressive fragmentation of the international community through the creation of numerous unviable mini-states.[21] Moreover, each new State might incorporate a minority that would in its turn seek a new secession.[22] Similarly, such authors claim, there would be a negative effect for democratic States in which any minorities would always have the opportunity of blackmailing the majority by threatening to secede if its wishes were not satisfied.[23]

As noted, while 28 new States have emerged outside any decolonization process since 1945, cases such as Senegal (1960), Singapore (1965), Eritrea (1993) and South Sudan (2011) involved consent between the parties concerned prior to

---

on the Conflict in Georgia, of 30 September 2009, Vol. II, 441, p. 147. http://www.mpil.de/files/pdf4/IIFFMCG_Volume_II1.pdf.

Cfr. Lauwers and Smis (2000), p. 65. Tancredi (2014), p. 80.

[15]Cfr. Christakis (2011), p. 77. See also, by the same author Christakis (2014), p. 743. Jaber (2011), p. 934. Lauwers and Smis (2000), p. 64. Tomuschat (2006), p. 26.

[16]Cfr. Tancredi (2014), p. 80.

See supra, Sect. 2.2.2.

[17]Cfr. Buchheit (1978), p. 73. Cassese (1995), pp. 39–40. Lauwers and Smis (2000), p. 62.

[18]Cfr. Tomuschat (2006), p. 26.

[19]Cfr. Buchanan (1991), at ch. 3. Buchheit (1978), pp. 28–30. Heraclides (1991), p. 28. Burke-White (2014), p. 71. Wilson (2009), p. 474.

[20]Cfr. Buchheit (1978), p. 14.

[21]Cfr. Ibid.

[22]Cfr. Higgins (1993), p. 35.

[23]Cfr. Heraclides (1991), p. 28.

independence. In other instances, for example the Baltic States Latvia, Lithuania and Estonia (1991), it was a question more of the re-emergence of States, since they recovered the independence that had earlier been seized from them.[24] In yet other cases there were states that came into being as a consequence of the collapse of Communism: Armenia, Azerbaijan, Belarus, Georgia, Kazakhstan, Kirgizstan, Moldova, Tajikistan, Turkmenistan, the Ukraine and Uzbekistan emerging from the former Soviet Union in 1991; Slovenia, Macedonia, Croatia, Bosnia-Herzegovina, Federal Republic of Yugoslavia (FRY), that arose from the former Yugoslavia in 1991 and 1992, followed in 2006 by Montenegro; and the former Czechoslovakia, which split into the Czech Republic and Slovakia in 1993.[25] In reality, in international practice there are only the cases of Bangladesh (1971) and Kosovo (2008) that are new States arising as the result of a process of unilateral secession.[26] In view of this, recognition of a right to secession in international law by the international community would hence not appear to find the necessary and sufficient precedents in reality.[27]

Moreover, this view would be reinforced by the occurrence of cases like those also cited by James Crawford: Tibet (China, 1959), Katanga (Congo, 1960), Biafra (Nigeria, 1967), Kashmir (India, 1987), East Punjab (India, 1970), the Karen and Shan States (Burma, 1949 and 1960), the Turkish Federated State of Cyprus (Cyprus, 1975), Tamil Eelam (Sri Lanka, 1983), Bougainville (Papua New Guinea, 1990), Somaliland (Somalia, 1991), Kosovo (FRY, 1991), Chechnya (Russia, 1991), Nagorno-Karabakh (Azerbaijan, 1991), Kurdistan (Iraq/Turkey, 1992), Republika Srpska (Bosnia-Herzegovina, 1992), Abkhazia (Georgia, 1992), South Ossetia (Georgia, 1992), the Democratic Republic of Yemen (Yemen, 1994), and more recently Crimea. In all these the attempts at secession by groups or territories within an independent State failed to gain recognition as new States from the international community.[28]

In view of the lack of any recognition of a right to secede, the conclusion reached by some of these authors is that it is impossible to invoke the right to self-determination in order for a territory to break away from an existing State.[29] Some would go even further, making the claim that if there is no recognition for a right to secede, then secession is not permitted, in other words, it is prohibited by international law. Some comment, in addition, that this is so because there is a presumption in favour of stability, rather than an acceptance of secession.[30]

---

[24]Cfr. Crawford (1998), p. 115.

[25]Cfr. Id., pp. 93 and 115. Wildhaber (1995), pp. 53–54.

[26]Cfr. Shany (2014), p. 237. Vidmar (2015), p. 370. Wilson (2015), p. 218.

[27]Cfr. Crawford (1998), p. 114. Jaber (2011), p. 937. Vidmar (2015), p. 370.

[28]Cfr. Crawford (1998), pp. 107 and 108. Shany (2014), p. 237. With regard to the cases of Kosovo, Chechnya, Republika Srpska and Katanga, among others, see Vashakmadze and Lippold (2010), pp. 634–636.

[29]Cfr. Burke-White (2014), p. 71. Christakis (2014), p. 741. Marxsen (2014), p. 385. Ryngaert (2010), p. 491. Tancredi (2014), p. 80.

[30]Cfr. Peters (2011), p. 99.

3.1.1 The Neutrality of International Law Toward Unilateral Secession

However, another interpretation of this same reality would state that the absence of a right to secede does not necessarily imply that secession is prohibited in international law.[31] As Professor Thomas Martin Franck of New York University noted, 'it is wrong to say there is no right of secession if by that one seeks to convey the impression that any secession is prohibited by international law'.[32] In other words, secession is not recognized as a right by international law, but neither does international law prohibit secession.[33]

From this second premise, it is possible to follow the dictum *permissum videtur in omne quod non prohibetur*. This view was adopted by the Permanent Court of International Justice in the Lotus affair of 1927, and is known as the 'Lotus freedom principle'.[34] It may be held that the absence of any prohibition would confirm the legitimacy of exercising a right to secede.[35]

This proposal does not seem to be fully correct, and criticisms of it have been made from various standpoints.[36] The first objection raised against such a claim was to note that the principle should apply to relations among States and in one way or another processes of self-determination take place between non-State entities and States from which they aim to secede.[37] Indeed, the 'Lotus principle' was understood as a safeguard of State sovereignty rather than a general norm of international law.[38] It would be a contradiction to hold that this 'principle' gives backing for secession against the sovereignty of States such that 'state sovereignty may be weakened' if the line is taken that with secession not prohibited, there is an actual right to declare independence.[39]

[31]Cfr. Christakis (2014), p. 743. Wilson (2015), p. 217.

[32]Franck et al. (eds.) (2000), p. 335.

[33]Cfr. Abi-Saab (2006), p. 474. Christakis (2011), p. 83. Hilpold (2008), p. 117. Lauwers and Smis (2000), p. 64. Muharremi (2010), p. 875. Vidmar (2012), p. 164.

A similar view emerges in *Accordance with the International Law of the Unilateral Declaration of Independence in Respect of Kosovo, Advisory Opinion,* supra, Chap. 1, note 3, pp. 26–27, para. 56.

[34]*The Case of the S.S. 'Lotus', Judgment of 7 September 1927, Series A – No. 10,* 33, p. 18. http://www.icj-cij.org/files/permanent-court-of-international-justice/serie_A/A_10/30_Lotus_Arret.pdf.

> The rules of law binding upon States therefore emanate from their own free will [. . .] and established in order to regulate the relations between these co-existing independent communities or with a view to the achievement of common aims. Restrictions upon the independence of States cannot therefore be presumed.

[35]Cfr. Wilde (2011), p. 152.

[36]Cfr. Jacobs (2011), p. 804. Sciso (2014), p. 1009.

[37]Cfr. Christakis (2011), p. 79. Ingravallo (2012), p. 228. Orakhelashvili (2011), p. 77.

[38]Cfr. Jacobs (2011), p. 804.

[39]Cfr. Peters (2011), p. 100. Walter (2014), p. 24.

Cfr. Christakis (2011), p. 79.

Secondly, it is not possible either to affirm identity between those things that are not prohibited and those which are permitted or are in conformity with international law.[40] Rather, the claim should be limited to saying that international law neither prohibits nor authorizes secession,[41] leaving a 'law-free zone'.[42] Faced with what seems a 'deliberate silence', Judge Bruno Simma stated that it implied that certain actions were not illegal, but not necessarily thus legal.[43]

A third line would be taken by those who maintain there is simply no regulation: 'Secession thus remains basically a phenomenon not regulated by international law'.[44] In this way, it may be said that international law remains 'neutral' on this subject.[45] In accordance with this reasoning, Malcolm Shaw, a former Professor at the University of Leicester, made a clear-cut claim that: 'as a matter of law the international system neither authorises nor condemns such attempts, but rather stands neutral. Secession, as such, therefore, is not contrary to international law'.[46] However, it must be noted that the neutrality of international law is circumscribed to a unilateral act of secession, and does not extend to new realities arising at an international level.[47]

3.1.2 Unilateral Secession as a Fact and Presumptions in Favour of the State

The idea of 'neutrality' relative to secession has been challenged by those who maintain that international law is significantly favourable towards States.[48] This would be the stance held by Serbia during the development of the Kosovo Advisory

---

[40]Cfr. Orakhelashvili (2011), p. 81. Tancredi (2012), p. 85. See also, by the same author Tancredi (2011), p. 223.

[41]Cfr. Van den Driest (2015), p. 354. Oeter (2012), p. 114. Vidmar (2015), p. 367.

[42]Peters (2011), p. 99.

[43]Cfr. 'Declaration of Judge Simma', *Accordance with the International Law of the Unilateral Declaration of Independence in Respect of Kosovo, Advisory Opinion,* supra, Chap. 1, note 3, p. 480, para. 9. http://www.icj-cij.org/files/case-related/141/141-20100722-ADV-01-03-BI.pdf.

[44]Abi-Saab (2006), p. 474.

Cfr. Corten (2011), p. 88. See also, by the same author Corten (2006), p. 232. Christakis (1999), p. 74. Crawford (2007), p. 374. Kohen (2006), p. 5. Oeter (2012), p. 112. Walter (2014), p. 24.

[45]Cfr. Orakhelashvili (2011), p. 79. Sciso (2014), p. 1009. Tancredi (2014), p. 68.

[46]Shaw (2000), p. 136.

Cfr. Jia (2009), p. 39.

[47]Cfr. Orakhelashvili (2011), p. 81. Vidmar (2012), p. 177.

[48]Cfr. Corten (2006), p. 254. Tancredi (2014), p. 94.

This argument was put forwards by Professor Concepción Escobar Hernández in her intervention on behalf of Spain: 'Accordingly, from the legal point of view it is impossible to accept that international law can remain 'neutral' in respect of an act (the Unilateral Declaration of Independence) which has serious international consequences', I.C.J. CR 2009/30, of 8 December 2009, *Accordance with the International Law of the Unilateral Declaration of Independence in Respect of*

Opinion 'Thus, not only does international law not remain 'neutral' in the case of secession, it governs the issue and imposes as a condition for the existence of a new State the legality of its creation. In this regard, the maxim *ex injuria non oritur jus* is plainly applicable'.[49]

It should be kept in mind that international law has no regulations relating to the processes that might lead to secession. These are aspects which until the existence of a new State is recognized fall into the category 'matters which are essentially within the domestic jurisdiction of any state',[50] internal sovereignty, preserved by one of the structural principles of international law, that of non-intervention.[51] Together with the principle of the sovereign equality of States and the ban on the threat or use of force by States, this constitutes the basis for maintaining international peace and security.[52] This is the root of what may be seen as a presumption in favour of the existence of States, which can be rebutted only through recognition of the necessary effectiveness of the statehood of any new entity split off from the original State.

In view of this, the set of events that would result in secession are acts occurring within the framework of the internal jurisdiction of a State according to international law: 'Secession is a matter of fact, not a matter of law',[53] a 'historical occurrence'.[54] It is the final outcome of a 'continuous spectrum of activities',[55] considered an internal matter belonging to the domestic jurisdiction of a State and outside the sphere of inter-state relations.[56]

It is necessary to look to the internal context of each State to see if the process leading to the creation of a new State is licit or illicit according to its internal structures. Without expressly using the term 'secession', most constitutions include provisions that prohibit this type of process, referring to the indivisibility of the state, to state or national unity or both, or, most often, to territorial integrity.[57] Alongside this group, there is a minority of constitutions which have no such provision, but which when interpreted by their highest legal or political organs have been seen as

---

Kosovo, (Request for an Advisory Opinion), of 15 April 2009, 63, p. 15, para. 55. http://www.icj-cij.org/files/case-related/141/141-20091208-ORA-01-01-BI.pdf.

[49]'Written Statement of the Government of the Republic of Serbia', *Accordance with the International Law of the Unilateral Declaration of Independence in Respect of Kosovo, (Request for an Advisory Opinion),* of 15 April 2009, 371, p. 356, para. 1033. http://www.icj-cij.org/files/case-related/141/15642.pdf.

[50]Art. 2(7) of the UN Charter.

[51]Cfr. Oeter (2012), p. 114.

[52]Cfr. Article 2(1), 2(4), and 1(1) of the UN Charter.
Cfr. Peters (2011), p. 99. Tancredi (2014), p. 94.

[53]Cfr. Borgen (2009), p. 8. Christakis (2006), p. 155. Musgrave (2000), p. 192. Oeter (2015), p. 56.

[54]Cfr. Tancredi (2008), p. 37.

[55]Norman (2003), p. 203.

[56]Cfr. Orakhelashvili (2011), p. 81. Ryngaert (2010), p. 491.

[57]Cfr. Ioannidis (2015), pp. 175–177. Jovanović (2009), p. 63. Sunstein (1991), pp. 633–670.

excluding any right to secession.[58] Finally, there are four constitutions in which the possibility of secession is contemplated, these being those of Liechtenstein, from 1921, of Saint Kitts and Nevis, from 1938, of the Slovak Republic, from 1992, and of the Federal Republic of Ethiopia, from 1994. Together with these, it is also possible to cite the provisions of the 'Northern Ireland Act', of 1998, which included a right for this Province to become united with the Republic of Ireland.[59]

3.2 The Scope of Unilateral Declarations of Independence and Their Effectiveness

The formulation of a unilateral declaration of independence in the context of a process of secession lacks any legal regulation in international law.[60] As stated above, a unilateral declaration of independence may be illicit in accordance with

---

[58]Professor Théodore Christakis emphasized the famous *Texas versus White* case argued before the United States Supreme Court of 1869 https://www.law.cornell.edu/supremecourt/text/74/700, and *Reference re Secession of Quebec* case de 1998 before the Supreme Court of Canada Supreme Court of Canada, *Reference re Secession of Quebec*, supra, Chap. 2, note 71. Cfr. Christakis (2014), p. 743, note 46.

[59]Among those constitutions contemplating secession clauses is the 'Constitution of the Principality of Liechtenstein' of 5 October 1921 (Art. 4(2)) http://www.wipo.int/wipolex/en/text.jsp?file_id=234654, together with the 'Constitution of St. Kitts and Nevis' of 22 June 1983 (Art. 113 (1) and 115 on secession of Nevis) http://www.wipo.int/wipolex/en/text.jsp?file_id=235246, the 'Constitution of the Slovak Republic' of 1 September 1992 (Art. 93(1)) http://www.wipo.int/wipolex/en/text.jsp?file_id=416332, the 'Constitution of the Federal Democratic Republic of Ethiopia' of 8 December 1994 (Art. 39) http://www.wipo.int/wipolex/en/text.jsp?file_id=193667, and the provisions of the 'Northern Ireland Act' of 1998 (Art. 1) http://www.legislation.gov.uk/ukpga/1998/47/contents.

Article 39 of the 1994 Constitution of The Federal Democratic Republic of Ethiopia lays down the following:

> Article 39 Rights of Nations, Nationalities, and Peoples.
>
> (1) Every Nation, Nationality and People in Ethiopia has an unconditional right to self-determination, including the right to secession.
>
> [...]
>
> (4) The right to self-determination, including secession, of every Nation, Nationality and People shall come into effect:
>
> [...]
>
> (5) A 'Nation, Nationality or People' for the purpose of this Constitution, is a group of people who have or share large measure of a common culture or similar customs, mutual intelligibility of language, belief in a common or related identities, a common psychological make-up, and who inhabit an identifiable, predominantly contiguous territory.

Cfr. Christakis (2014), p. 743, note 46. Jovanović (2009), pp. 64–65. Oeter (2012), p. 113.

[60]Cfr. Bothe (2010), p. 837. Oeter (2012), p. 112. Orakhelashvili (2011), p. 79. 'Written Statement of the Kingdom of Norway', *Accordance with the International Law of the Unilateral Declaration of Independence in Respect of Kosovo, (Request for an Advisory Opinion),* of 16 April 2009, 27, p. 5, para. 10. http://www.icj-cij.org/files/case-related/141/15650.pdf.

internal law, but it cannot be claimed that it violates general international law.[61] It is just another act like all those making up the 'continuous spectrum' that may lead to the creation of a new State.[62] On these lines, it would be necessary to distinguish between a unilateral declaration of independence, as the manifestation of a desire to break away from a State, and secession.[63]

This does not mean that unilateral declarations of independence do not generate certain consequences from a legal standpoint.[64] It would not be fully correct to state that they lie out of the reach of international law.[65] Rather, they should be seen as a step in progressing towards independence in which competence relative to international society is claimed.[66] However, the declaration can be accepted, challenged, or even ignored by the community of States, including the State from which it is intended there should be secession.[67]

Unilateral declarations of independence do not create a new State, nor do they constitute a manifestation of the elements of statehood contemplated by the 'Convention on Rights and Duties of States' (Montevideo Convention) de 26 December 1933.[68] Whilst there have been some instances of new States arising from a unilateral declaration of independence,[69] as the ICJ stated in the Kosovo Advisory Opinion 'the existence or disappearance of the State is a question of fact'.[70] For the

---

[61]Cfr. *Accordance with the International Law of the Unilateral Declaration of Independence in Respect of Kosovo, Advisory Opinion,* supra, Chap. 1, note 3, p. 438, para. 84.

Cfr. Tancredi (2008), p. 55.

[62]Cf. Vidmar (2011), p. 368.

[63]Cfr. Peters (2011), p. 96. Tancredi (2008), p. 55. Vidmar (2011), p. 368.

[64]Cfr. Röben (2010), p. 1082.

[65]Cfr. Ibid.

[66]Cfr. Ibid.

[67]Cfr. Ibid.

[68]Cfr. Orakhelashvili (2011), p. 79. Wilson (2009), p. 459.

Article 1 of the Montevideo Convention stated:

> State as a person of international law should possess the following qualifications: a) a permanent population; b) a defined territory; c) government; and d) capacity to enter into relations with the other States.

'Convention on Rights and Duties of States' adopted by the Seventh International Conference of American States. Signed at Montevideo, 26 December 1933. 165 *LNTS* (1936), No. 3802, 19–43. https://treaties.un.org/doc/Publication/UNTS/LON/Volume%20165/v165.pdf.

Consideration is given to the 'doctrine of the three elements' laid down by Georg Jellinek at the end of the nineteenth century. See Jellinek (1905). See also Cohen (1961), pp. 1127–1171.

[69]Cfr. *Accordance with the International Law of the Unilateral Declaration of Independence in Respect of Kosovo, Advisory Opinion,* supra, Chap. 1, note 3, p. 438, para. 79.

[70]Arbitration Commission of the Conference on Yugoslavia, 'Opinion No. 1', of 29 November 1992, at para. 1).a). 31:6 *ILM* (1992), 1488–1526, pp. 1494–1497.

Cfr. Tancredi (2012), p. 94.

creation of a new State, the definitive point is the coming together of elements of statehood and effectiveness in exercising statehood.[71]

In international legal opinion, the features seen as manifestations of efficacious statehood include the existence of an effective government, a capacity to keep up relationships within the international community in an independent way,[72] establishment of the entity, which Théodore Christakis stresses should be 'beyond all reasonable doubt', and exercise of control 'beyond all hope of return'.[73]

Hence effectiveness is assigned a review or action function, as noted by Jean Touscoz, in relation to certain legal titles for which, as in this instance, it is a necessary but not a sufficient condition.[74] Statehood would be a legal title, attributed by international law on the basis of the principle of effectiveness, which would grant sovereignty over a given territory.[75] It is true that in cases of secession the effectiveness of statehood may be challenged, and it is here that the concept of recognition takes on particular relevance, so that statehood, effectiveness and recognition constitute concepts of the utmost significance.[76]

The function of the idea of recognition in international law was broadly delimited by Sir Hersch Lauterpacht, who held that it is unnecessary and irrelevant when the licit nature of an act giving rise to a claimed legal title appears clear and unchallengeable.[77] In contrast, recognition takes on more importance when the legality of the act or the existence of the legal title on which it is based is appears to be dubious or debatable.[78]

As against what might be maintained by jurists such was Hans Kelsen,[79] the principle of effectiveness is fully valid in the framework of international law only within the limits established by international law itself.[80] This is a principle according to which acts running counter to law can create only *de facto* situations, which may become seen as legal by virtue of the passage of time or of other circumstances.[81] Hence, effectiveness is not the exclusive condition for recognition to be licit, but, as pointed out by Gabriele Salvioli, it is necessary to bring the

---

[71]Cfr. Ibid. Vidmar (2011), p. 370. Wilson (2009), p. 459.

[72]Cfr. Crawford (2007), pp. 62–89.

[73]Cfr. Christakis (2014), p. 747, quoting Lauterpacht (1947), p. 8. Nguyên et al. (2009), p. 585. Vidmar (2012), p. 159.

[74]Cfr. Miaja de la Muela (1958), pp. 12–13.

Cfr. Chemillier-Gendreau (1975), p. 42. De Visscher (1958), pp. 601–609. Salvioli (1953), pp. 274–275. Touscoz (1964), p. 256. Tucker (1953), pp. 31–48.

[75]Cfr. Tancredi (2012), p. 93.

[76]Cfr. Salvioli (1953), p. 275. Wilson (2009), p. 459.

[77]Cfr. Lauterpacht (1947), pp. 411–412. Menon (1990), pp. 247–273.

[78]Cfr. Lauterpacht (1947), pp. 411–412.

[79]Cfr. Kelsen (1964), p. 114.

[80]Cfr. Miaja de la Muela (1958), p. 49.

[81]Cfr. Id., p. 50.

principle of effectiveness into harmony with other fundamental principles of international law.[82]

3.3 The Wrongfulness of Secession Under Certain Circumstances

Secession is not prohibited by international law. However, an attempt at independence from a State may be considered illicit because it runs counter to general international law in certain circumstances.[83] Secession must necessarily be in accordance with international law, so that any attempt at secession that implies clear violation of the norms of general international law[84] or of any *lex specialis* of international law will be illegal.[85]

The emergence of a new State is no longer simply 'a question of fact'; it also demands legitimacy in its creation.[86] Following the reasoning of the authors termed 'legalists' by Professor Antonello Tancredi of the University of Palermo, as opposed to 'realists', statehood is a legal status granted or denied by international law, as has been seen. Hence, it is not possible to accept the emergence of a new entity merely on grounds of effectiveness; rather *ex injuria non oritur jus*.[87]

This opinion is based on the practice adopted with regard to matters such as the creation of Northern Cyprus, unilateral declarations of independence by Southern Rhodesia and the South African Homelands, and South Africa's illegal presence in Namibia.[88] All these unilateral declarations of independence, to which must be added that claimed by the Republika Srpska, were noted by the ICJ in its Kosovo Advisory Opinion to have been condemned as illegal by the Security Council.[89] Illegality in all these cases was rooted in the fact that the attempt to set up new entities in the international community was through the use of force, through violation of the right to self-determination, or by virtue of apartheid[90]:

---

[82]Cfr. Salvioli (1933), pp. 51–54.

[83]Cfr. Van den Driest (2015), p. 332. Vidmar (2015), p. 374.

[84]Cfr. Van den Driest (2015), p. 335, note 28.

[85]Cfr. Vidmar (2012), p. 169.

[86]Cfr. Tancredi (2008), pp. 37–38.

[87]Cfr. Christakis (2011), p. 82. Tancredi (2008), p. 38.

[88]Cfr. Christakis (2011), p. 82; and, by the same author Christakis (2014), p. 749. Tancredi (2012), p. 87. Vidmar (2012), pp. 171–175. See also, by the same author Vidmar (2015), p. 375.

[89]Cfr. *Accordance with the International Law of the Unilateral Declaration of Independence in Respect of Kosovo, Advisory Opinion,* supra, Chap. 1, note 3, p. 437, para. 81.

Cfr. Christakis (2011), p. 82. Van den Driest (2015), p. 356. Yee (2010), p. 781.

[90]Crawford (2007), pp. 107–157. Vidmar (2011), p. 371. Vidmar (2015), p. 375.

> [...] in all of those instances the Security Council was making a determination as regards to concrete situation existing at the time that those declarations of independence were made; not from the unilateral character of these declarations as such, but from the fact that they were, or would have been, connected with the unlawful use of force or other egregious violations of norms of general international law, in particular those of a peremptory character (*jus cogens*).[91]

All secessions involving the violation of norms considered to be of a peremptory character, that is, forming *jus cogens*,[92] would be illegal. For its part, illegality as a consequence of violation of a *lex specialis* is also seen by the ICJ in those instances where the Security Council sought to 'establish restrictive conditions for the permanent status of a territory'[93] or where a treaty prevented a change in the legal status of that territory.[94]

The distinction between proposition and action, and the means for achieving it, is one of the merits of the Kosovo Advisory Opinion.[95] International law contains no provisions relating to the aim or to the unilateral nature of a secession, but it does condemn situations constituting infringements of the norms of *jus cogens*, which bring with them the illegality of the declaration of independence.[96] Interpretation of circumstances, to which the ICJ refers widely as 'in connection with'[97] an event, must be understood in a broad sense as the consolidation of an effective situation arising from violation of the peremptory norms of international law.[98]

In conclusion, the most striking point is that not all means to achieve independence are allowed. International law remains neutral with regard to secession, but condemns those processes occurring by means of the use of force in international relations or constituting an infringement of human rights.[99] To sum up, international law recognizes, in accordance with the UN Charter, a higher value for peace and international security than for the exercise of the right to self-determination or any process of secession.[100]

---

[91] *Accordance with the International Law of the Unilateral Declaration of Independence in Respect of Kosovo, Advisory Opinion*, supra, Chap. 1, note 3, p. 437, para. 81.

[92] Cfr. Orakhelashvili (2011), p. 82. Tancredi (2012), p. 87. Vidmar (2012), p. 169; and, by the same author Vidmar (2015), p. 375.

[93] *Accordance with the International Law of the Unilateral Declaration of Independence in Respect of Kosovo, Advisory Opinion*, supra, Chap. 1, note 3, p. 438, para. 83.

[94] Cfr. Vidmar (2012), p. 169.

[95] Cfr. Peters (2011), p. 105.

[96] Cfr. Van den Driest (2015), p. 356.

[97] *Accordance with the International Law of the Unilateral Declaration of Independence in Respect of Kosovo, Advisory Opinion*, supra, Chap. 1, note 3, p. 437, para. 81.

[98] Cfr. Vidmar (2012), p. 171.

[99] Cfr. Peters (2011), p. 108. Vidmar (2012), p. 177.

[100] Cfr. Kaikobad (2011), p. 64.

References

Abi-Saab, G. 2006. Conclusion. In *Secession. International Law Perspectives*, ed. M.G. Kohen, 470–476. Cambridge and New York: Cambridge University Press.

Borgen, C.J. 2009. The Language of Law and the Practice of Politics: Great Powers and the Rhetoric of Self-Determination in the Cases of Kosovo and South Ossetia. *Chicago JIL* 10: 1–33.

Bothe, M. 2010. Kosovo – So What? The Holding of the International Court of Justice Is Not the Last Word on Kosovo's Independence. *German LJ* 11: 837–840.

Buchanan, A.E. 1991. *Secession: The Morality of Political Divorce from Fort Sumter to Lithuania and Quebec*. Boulder: Westview Press.

———. 2007. Secession. In *The Stanford Encyclopaedia of Philosophy*, ed. E.N. Zalta. http://plato.stanford.edu/archives/spr2007/entries/secession.

Buchheit, L.C. 1978. *Secession: The Legitimacy of Self-Determination*. New Haven: Yale University Press.

Burke-White, W.W. 2014. Crimea and the International Legal Order. *Survival* 56: 65–80.

Cassese, A. 1995. *Self-Determination of Peoples: A Legal Reappraisal*. Cambridge: Cambridge University Press.

Chemillier-Gendreau, M. 1975. À propos de l'effectivité en droit international. *RBDI* 11: 38–46.

Christakis, T. 1999. *Le droit à l'autodétermination en dehors des situations de décolonisation*. Paris: La Documentation française.

———. 2006. L'état en tant que 'fait primaire': réflexions fur la portée du principe d'effectivité. In *Secession: International Law Perspectives*, ed. M.G. Kohen, 138–170. Cambridge: Cambridge University Press.

———. 2011. The ICJ Advisory Opinion on Kosovo: Has International Law Something to Say About Secession? *LJIL* 24: 73–86.

———. 2014. Les conflits de sécession en Crimée et dans l'Est de l'Ukraine et le droit international (The Conflicts of Secession in Crimea and Eastern Ukraine and International Law). *JDI* 141: 733–764.

Cohen, R. 1961. The Concept of Statehood in United Nations Practice. *University of Pennsylvania Law Review* 109: 1127–1171.

Corten, O. 2006. Are There Gaps in the International Law of Secession? In *Secession. International Law Perspectives*, ed. M.G. Kohen, 231–254. Cambridge and New York: Cambridge University Press.

———. 2011. Territorial Integrity Narrowly Interpreted: Reasserting the Classical Inter-State Paradigm of International Law. *LJIL* 24: 87–94.

Crawford, J. 1998. State Practice and International Law in Relation to Secession. *BYIL* 69: 85–117.

———. 2007. *The Creation of States in International Law*. 2nd ed. Oxford: Clarendon Press.

De Visscher, Ch. 1958. Observations sur l'effectivité en droit international public. *RGDIP* 62: 601–609.

Franck, T.M., R. Higgins, A. Pellet, M.N. Shaw, and C. Tomuschat. 2000. The Territorial Integrity of Québec in the Event of the Attainment of Sovereignty – Experts Report. In *Self-Determination in International Law: Quebec and Lessons Learned*, ed. A.F. Bayefski, 333–342. The Hague: Kluwer Law International.

Haverland, C. 2000. Secession. In *Encyclopedia of Public International Law*, ed. R. Bernhardt, vol. IV, 354–359. Amsterdam: North Holland Publishing.

Heraclides, A. 1991. *Self-Determination of Minorities in International Politics*. London: Frank Cass.

Higgins, R. 1993. Postmodern Tribalism and the Right to Secession. In *Peoples and Minorities in International Law*, ed. C. Brolmann, R. Lefeber, and M. Zieck, 29–35. Dordrecht: Martinus Nijhoff.

Hilpold, P. 2008. Die Sezession – zum Versuch der Verrechtlichung eines faktischen Phänomens. *ZaöRV/HJIL* 63: 117–141.
Ingravallo, I. 2012. Kosovo After the ICJ Advisory Opinion: Towards a European Perspective? *ICLR* 14: 219–241.
Ioannidis, N.A. 2015. Constitutional Prohibition of Secession Under the Prism of International Law: The Cases of Kosovo, Crimea and Cyprus. *Edimburgh Student Law Review* 2: 169–180.
Jaber, T. 2011. A Case for Kosovo? Self-Determination and Secession in the 21st Century. *IJHR* 15: 926–947.
Jacobs, D. 2011. International Court of Justice. Accordance with International Law of the Unilateral Declaration of Independence in Respect of Kosovo, Advisory Opinion of 22 July 2010. *ICLQ* 60: 799–810.
Jellinek, G. 1905. *Allgemeine Staatslehre*. Berlin: O. Häring.
Jia, B.B. 2009. The Independence of Kosovo: A Unique Case of Secession? *Chinese JIL* 8: 27–46.
Jovanović, M.A. 2009. Can Constitutions Be of Use in the Resolution of Secessionist Conflicts? *JILIR* 5: 59–87.
Kaikobad, K.H. 2011. Another Frozen Conflict: Kosovo's Unilateral Declaration of Independence and International Law. In *Kosovo: A Precedent?: The Declaration of Independence, the Advisory Opinion and Implications for Statehood, Self-Determination and Minority Rights*, ed. J. Summers, 55–85. Leiden; Boston: Martinus Nijhoff Publishers.
Kapustin, A. 2015. Crimea's Self-Determination in the Light of Contemporary International Law. *ZaöRV/HJIL* 75: 101–118.
Kelsen, H. 1964. *The Law of the United Nations: A Critical Analysis of Its Fundamental Problems (4th Printing)*. London: Stevens & Sons Ltd.
Kohen, M.G. 2006. Introduction. In *Secession. International Law Perspectives*, ed. M. Kohen, 1–20. Cambridge and New York: Cambridge University Press.
Lauterpacht, H. 1947. *Recognition in International Law*. Cambridge: Cambridge University Press.
Lauwers, G., and S. Smis. 2000. New Dimensions of the Right to Self-Determination: A Study of the International Response to the Kosovo Crisis. *N & EP* 6: 43–70.
Marxsen, C. 2014. The Crimea Crisis – An International Law Perspective. *ZaöRV/HJIL* 74: 367–391.
Menon, P.K. 1990. The Problem of Recognition in International Law: Some Thoughts on Community Interest. *Nordic JIL* 59: 247–273.
Miaja de la Muela, A. 1958. *El principio de efectividad en Derecho internacional*. Valladolid: Universidad.
Muharremi, R. 2010. A Note on the ICJ Advisory Opinion on Kosovo. *German LJ* 11: 867–880.
Musgrave, T.D. 2000. *Self-Determination and National Minorities*. Oxford: Oxford University Press.
Nguyên, Quôc Dinh, et al. 2009. *Droit international public*. 8th ed. Paris: Librairie générale de droit et de jurisprudence.
Norman, W. 2003. Domesticating Secession. In *Secession and Self-Determination*, ed. S. Macedo and A. Buchanan, 193–237. New York; London: New York University Press.
Oeter, S. 2012. Secession, Territorial Integrity and the Role of the Security Council. In *Kosovo and International Law: The ICJ Advisory Opinion of 22 July 2010*, ed. P. Hilpold, 109–138. Leiden; Boston: M. Nijhoff Publishers.
———. 2015. The *Kosovo Case* – An Unfortunate Precedent. *ZaöRV/HJIL* 75: 51–74.
Orakhelashvili, A. 2011. The International Courts Advisory Opinion on the UDI in Respect of Kosovo: Washing Away the Foam on the Tide of Time. *Max Planck YUNL* 15: 65–104.
Peters, A. 2011. Does Kosovo Lie in the Lotus-Land of Freedom? *LJIL* 24: 95–108.
Röben, V. 2010. The ICJ Advisory Opinion on the Unilateral Declaration of Independence in Respect of Kosovo: Rules or Principles? *GoJIL* 2: 1063–1086.

Ryngaert, C. 2010. The ICJs Advisory Opinion on Kosovo's Declaration of Independence: A Mixed Opportunity?: International Court of Justice, Accordance with International Law of the Unilateral Declaration of Independence in Respect of Kosovo, Advisory Opinion of 22 July 2010. *NILR* 57: 481–494.

Salvioli, G. 1933. Les régles générales de la paix. *Recueil des cours* 46: 5–163.

———. 1953. L''effettività' in diritto internazionale. *Rivista trimestrale di diritto pubblico* 3: 271–280.

Sciso, E. 2014. La crisi ucraina e lintervento russo: profile di diritto internazionale. *RDI* 97: 992–1031.

Shany, Y. 2014. Does International Law Grant the People of Crimea and Donetsk a Right to Secede? Revisiting Self-Determination in Light of the 2014 Events in Ukraine. *Brown JWA* 21: 233–244.

Shaw, M.N. 2000. Re: Order in Council P.C. 1996-1497 of 30 September 1996'. In *Self-Determination in International Law: Quebec and Lessons Learned*, ed. A.F. Bayefsky, 125–152. The Hague: Kluwer Law International.

Sunstein, C.R. 1991. Constitutionalism and Secession. *UCLR* 58: 633–670.

Tancredi, A. 2008. Neither Authorized nor Prohibited? Secession and International Law after Kosovo, South Ossetia and Abkhazia. *Italian YIL* 18: 37–62.

———. 2011. The ICJ's Kosovo Advisory Opinion as an Exercise in Pre-Understanding. In *Questions de droit international autour de l'avis consultatif de la Cour Internationale de Justice sur le Kosovo*, ed. M. Arcari and L. Balmond, 217–236. Milan: Giuffrè.

———. 2012. Some Remarks on the Relationship Between Secession and General International Law in the Light of the ICJs Kosovo Advisory Opinion. In *Kosovo and International Law: The ICJ Advisory Opinion of 22 July 2010*, ed. P. Hilpold, 79–108. Leiden; Boston: M. Nijhoff Publishers.

———. 2014. Secession and the Use of Force. In *Self-Determination and Secession in International Law*, ed. C. Walter et al., 68–94. Oxford: Oxford University Press.

Tomuschat, C. 2006. Secession and Self-Determination. In *Secession. International Law Perspectives*, ed. M. Kohen, 23–45. Cambridge: Cambridge University Press.

Touscoz, J. 1964. *Le principe d'effectivité dans l'ordre international*. Paris: Librairie générale de droit et de jurisprudence.

Tucker, R.W. 1953. The Principle of Effectiveness in International Law. In *Law and Politics in the World Community: Essays on Hans Kelsen's Pure Theory and Related Problems in International Law*, ed. G.A. Lipsky, 31–48. Berkeley, CA: University of California Press.

Van den Driest, S.F. 2015. Crimea's Separation from Ukraine: An Analysis of the Right to Self-Determination and (Remedial) Secession in International Law. *NILR* 62: 329–363.

Vashakmadze, M., and M. Lippold. 2010. Nothing But a Road Towards Secession? The International Court of Justices Advisory Opinion on Accordance with International Law of the Unilateral Declaration of Independence in Respect of Kosovo. *GoJIL* 2: 619–647.

Vidmar, J. 2011. The Kosovo Advisory Opinion Scrutinized. *LJIL* 24: 355–383.

———. 2012. Conceptualizing Declarations of Independence in International Law. *Oxford JLS* 32: 153–177.

———. 2015. The Annexation of Crimea and the Boundaries of the Will of the People. *German LJ* 16: 365–383.

Walter, C. 2014. The Kosovo Advisory Opinion: What It Says and What It Does Not Say. In *Self-Determination and Secession in International Law*, ed. C. Walter et al., 13–26. Oxford: Oxford University Press.

Wilde, R. 2011. Self-Determination, Secession, and Dispute Settlement After the Kosovo Advisory Opinion. *LJIL* 24: 149–154.

Wildhaber, L. 1995. Territorial Modifications and Breakups in Federal States. *Canadian YIL* 33: 41–74.

Wilson, G. 2009. Self-Determination, Recognition and the Problem of Kosovo. *NILR* 56: 455–481.
———. 2015. Crimea: Some Observations on Secession and Intervention in Partial Response to Müllerson and Tolstykh. *Chinese JIL* 14: 217–223.
Yee, S. 2010. Notes on the International Court of Justice (Part 4): The Kosovo Advisory Opinion. *Chinese JIL* 9: 763–782.

Part II
The Independence of Kosovo and Crimea in the Light of Contemporary International Law

Chapter 4
Kosovo's Long Road to Independence in 2008

The tumultuous recent history of Kosovo has been the subject of studies constituting a large body of literature.[1] It falls within the context of the Socialist Federal Republic of Yugoslavia (SFRY), which for a long time constituted a model of integration of nationalities and minorities in a multi-ethnic federal State.[2]

The Kosovo territory, considered by the Serbs as one of their lands of origin as a nation, was incorporated into the Republic of Serbia within Yugoslavia in 1946, although over time its population had become largely Albanian. From 1946 until 1989 it enjoyed a state of autonomy. The Yugoslav Federal Constitution of 1974 gave Kosovo the status of an autonomous province, like the Vojvodina.[3] This autonomy permitted management of internal affairs without control by Serbia, thanks to an administration with its own legislative and judicial bodies, making it equal to the six republics in the federation.[4]

From the demographic angle, the population make-up of the province of Kosovo, which had 1,954,000 inhabitants in 1991, had 82.2% of Albanian origin, 10% of Serbian origin, 2.9% Moslem Slav, 2.2% Roma, 1% Montenegrin, 0.6% of Turkish origin, and 0.4% Croat.[5] These proportion changed over time until the population of Albanian origin reached 90% as an outcome of a high birth rate and the movement of the other inhabitants to various regions of the former Yugoslavia. The total

[1]For a brief overview, see: Hilpold (2008), pp. 779–801. See also, by the same author Hilpold (2009b), Malcolm (1998), Weller (2009).

[2]Cfr. Hilpold (2009a), p. 262.

[3]Cfr. Article 2 of the Constitution of 21 February 1974 (Šturanović and Jelinčić (1989), 248 pp.). Muharremi (2008), p. 406. Vidmar (2011), p. 145.

[4]Cfr. Independent International Commission on Kosovo, *The Kosovo Report: Conflict, International Response, Lessons Learned* (New York: Oxford University Press, 2000), 372, pp. 35–36. Ghebali (1999), p. 63. Schmidt (1993), p. 22.

[5]Cfr. Troebst (1999a), p. 47; and, by the same author Troebst (1999c), pp. 85–116.
On the origins of the population of Kosovo, see: Velebit (1999).

J. F. Escudero Espinosa, *Self-Determination and Humanitarian Secession in International Law of a Globalized World*,
https://doi.org/10.1007/978-3-319-72622-9_4

population had dropped to 1,747,000 inhabitants by the date of the declaration of Independence in 2008.[6]

The region's economic situation was characterized by being one of the poorest zones in Yugoslavia. There had been a major increase in the population working in agriculture, an unusual phenomenon in Europe, and there had also been considerable emigration to other States.[7]

4.1 The Disintegration of the Yugoslav State and Demands for Autonomy

4.1.1 Albano-Kosovar Reactions to Repression

The situation in Kosovo went largely unnoticed by the international community during the dramatic events occurring in Bosnia and Herzegovina in the process of disintegration of the Yugoslav State. Although its problems went back a long way in time,[8] as noted by the High Representative of the International Community in Bosnia-Herzegovina, Carlos Westendorp, they may be seen as becoming more obvious between the suppression of the political institutions of the province of Kosovo, whose autonomy had been withdrawn in 1989, and the subsequent proclamation of the Republic of Kosova on 7 September 1991,[9] and the first attacks by the Kosovo Liberation Army (*Ushtria Çlirimtare e Kosovës*, UÇK) in February 1996.[10]

The regime of autonomy was suppressed unilaterally by the Slobodan Milošević government in 1989.[11] The Kosovans' reaction to Serbian repression was peaceful and measured in the context of the process of dissolution of the SFRY.[12] The leader

---

[6]Cfr. Baggett (1999), p. 59. Malcolm (1998), pp. 352 and 353.

[7]Cfr. Lauwers and Smis (2000), p. 48. Roux (1992), p. 322. Velebit (1999), p. 194.

[8]On the origins and development over time of the Kosovo question, see: Dogo (1992), Malcolm (1998), Navarro Nijssen (1999), Vickers (1998), Roux (1992). By the same author Roux (1999). Schubert (1997), Sundhaussen (1999), Troebst (1997).

[9]Cfr. Schmidt (1993), p. 23.

[10]Cfr. Westendorp (1999), p. 45. Also Montaz (2000), p. 89. Perritt (2008), 264 pp. Pettifer (2012), 379 pp.

[11]Cfr. Hughes (2013), p. 995. Lauwers and Smis (2000), p. 49. Malcolm (1998), at Chap. 17. Muharremi (2008), p. 407. Rrecaj (2011), p. 116. Weller (2009), p. 36. Williams (2003), p. 397. Yee (2010), p. 765.

On the development of the conflict, see: Duijzings et al. (1996), Lukic et al. (1996).

[12]Cfr. Jaber (2011), p. 927.

Among measures adopted by the Assembly of the Republic of Serbia, there were the establishment of 'Serb only' municipalities, the closure of newspapers published in Albanian, the shutting-down of the Kosovo Academy of Sciences, and the dismissal of thousands of Kosovar Albanian state employees, a total of 80,000 in 1990 (Cfr. Malcolm (1998), p. 346. Lauwers and Smis (2000), at 53). 'Situation of Human Rights in the Territory of the Former Yugoslavia. Report on the situation of human rights in the territory of the former Yugoslavia submitted by Mr. Tadeusz

of the Democratic League of Kosovo (*Lidhja Demokratike te Kosovës*, LDK), Ibrahim Rugova, managed to rally the Albanian population around the idea of peacefully creating a State through generalized civil disobedience.[13] Once the clandestine Republic of Kosova had been declared a sovereign State by its Parliament in September 1991, he was elected President in the ballot in May 1992, with support amounting to 99.56% of votes cast.[14] Despite the declaration of the Republic of Kosova as an independent State in September 1992, recognized internationally only by Albania, the region was incorporated into what was to be the new State of Serbia and Montenegro, unlike the other four Republics which succeeded in breaking away from Yugoslavia.[15]

Whilst the next few years saw the setting-up of a parallel State structure with its own Government, Parliament, taxes and elections, most authors concur that the Kosovo problem came to a head with the signing of the Dayton Peace Agreement reached in 1995.[16] This brought to an end the conflict in Bosnia and Herzegovina but simultaneously consolidated the frontiers of the FRY within which Kosovo was included.[17] The fact that Kosovo remained outside the Dayton Peace Agreement was a major setback for Ibrahim Rugova's strategy,[18] leaving the matter as no more than an internal problem for Serbia.[19]

From early in 1996, the new course of events led the main intellectuals to commit themselves to the more radicalized protest movements and abandon the policy of pacific resistance followed up till that point.[20] The repressive policies of Belgrade

---

Mazowiecki, Special Rapporteur of the Commission on Human Rights, pursuant to Commission resolution 1992/S-1/1 of 14 August 1992', UN Doc. E/CN.4/1993/50, of 10 February 1993, 78, p. 33. Rrecaj (2011), p. 116.

[13]Cfr. Clark (2000), p. 266. Daskalovski (2003), pp. 11–28. Ghebali (1999), p. 65. Lauwers and Smis (2000), p. 53. Troebst (1999a), p. 50. Strazzari (1998), p. 6.

[14]Cfr. Schmidt (1993), p. 23.

[15]Cfr. Malcolm (1998), p. 346. Williams (2003), p. 396.

[16]Cfr. Dietrich (2010), p. 125. Hilpold (2009a), p. 264.

The 'General Framework Agreement for Peace in Bosnia and Herzegovina' was concluded on 21 November and formally signed in Paris on 14 December 1995. United Nations Documents A/50/790 and S/1995/999, of 30 November 1995, http://peacemaker.un.org/sites/peacemaker.un.org/files/BA_951121_DaytonAgreement.pdf, 35:1 *ILM* (1996), 89–169. *SIPRI Yearbook 1996: Armaments, Disarmament, and International Security*, 232–250.

The signing was preceded by a Peace Implementation Conference held in London on 8 and 9 December, which adopted the Conclusions of the Peace Implementation Conference held at Lancaster House, London, Annex of UN Doc. S/1995/1029, of 12 December 1995, http://peacemaker.un.org/sites/peacemaker.un.org/files/BA_951209_LondonConferenceConclusions.pdf.

On the 'General Framework Agreement for Peace', see: Cox (1998), Ramcharan (1996), Ramón Chornet (1997).

[17]Cfr. Baggett (1999), p. 45. Phillips (1996), p. 827. Suhrke et al. (2000), p. 159, UN Doc. EPAU/2000/001, p. 5, para. 26, http://www.unhcr.org/3ba0bbeb4.html.

[18]Cfr. Strazzari (1998), p. 8. Hehir (2009), p. 90.

[19]Cfr. Hughes (2013), p. 998.

[20]Cfr. Rrecaj (2011), p. 120. Schmidt (1996), pp. 37–39. Lauwers and Smis (2000), p. 54.

induced the Albano-Kosovars into armed struggle and carrying out the first actions of the UÇK.[21]

4.1.2 The Outbreak of Internal Armed Conflict

The chaotic situation affecting the neighbouring State of Albania in Spring 1997, with many police and troops deserting, the resignation of the Alekxandër Meksi Government, and the later defeat of President Sali Berisha, made it easier for Albanian weapons and forces to cross into the central region of Drenica.[22] This situation facilitated the supply of arms to the UÇK, which burst onto the scene by considerably ramping up armed actions in the early months of 1998.[23]

Thereafter, in February 1998 the United Democratic Movement (*Lëvizja e Bashkuar Demokratike*, LBD) was formed, bringing together a number of parties and frustrated members of Ibrahim Rugova's LDK, under the leadership of the writer Rexhep Qosja. Its principal aims were to support the armed struggles carried out by the UÇK against the Serbian regime, and to establish a 'Greater Albania'.[24]

At the same time the FYR Government concentrated numerous troops of the Yugoslav Forces (*Vojska Jugoslavije*, VJ) and other special units in Kosovo.[25] Many skirmishes occurred between Serbian units and the UÇK, culminating in the so-called 'Drenica massacres' the result of an offensive against the populations of Prekaz and Lausa in March 1998 in which more than 80 Albano-Kosovars perished.[26]

The UÇK reacted with its first major offensive and over the course of 5 months succeeded in liberating 30% of the territory of Kosovo.[27] The VJ undertook a counteroffensive that in the next few months gradually recovered the land lost. Simultaneously, the Armed Forces of the Republic of Kosovo (*Forcat e Armatosura të Republikës së Kosovës*, FARK), formed in 1991 on Albanian soil under the guidance of President Rugova, became a competitor to the UÇK.[28]

---

[21]Cfr. Troebst (1999b), p. 782. Williams (2003), p. 397.

[22]Cfr. Hughes (2013), p. 999. Ker-Lindsay (2013), p. 843. A. Suhrke, M. Barutciski, P. Sandison, and R. Garlock, *The Kosovo Refugee Crisis: An Independent Evaluation of the UNHCR's Emergency Preparedness and Response*, UN Doc. EPAU/2000/001, supra, this chapter, note 17, p. 5, para. 26.

[23]Cfr. Sollemberg et al. (1999), p. 16.

[24]Cfr. Kola (2003), p. 350. Weller (1999b), pp. 221-251.

[25]Cfr. Troebst (1999a), p. 51. 'Report of the Secretary-General Prepared Pursuant to Resolution 1160 (1998) of the Security Council', UN Doc. S/1998/470, of 4 June 1998, 13, p. 4, para. 14.

[26]Cfr. 44:3 *Keesing's Record of World Events* (1998), p. 42156. Troebst (1999a), p. 51. Lauwers and Smis (2000), p. 54. OSCE (1999), p. 30, http://www.osce.org/odihr/17772?download=true.

[27]Cfr. Lauwers and Smis (2000), p. 54.

[28]Cfr. Janssen (2015), p. 60.

A balance-sheet of the confrontations up to October 1998 showed deaths of around 100 Serbian police, 40 VJ soldiers, an unknown number of Serbian and Montenegrin civilians, and more than 1500 Albano-Kosovars,[29] in what looked like a campaign of ethnic cleansing in Kosovo.[30] The extent of what was the sole active conflict in Europe in 1998 put it into the category of 'major armed conflict' and led to fears that it could cause a new humanitarian crisis, with consequent destabilization of the whole region.[31]

The international community began to involve itself more seriously in the situation. At this point, the Security Council determined that the state of affairs constituted a threat to international peace and security, and called on the parties to resolve their differences peacefully.[32] This highlighted the fact that the situation in Kosovo was now perceived as a problem that was no longer merely internal.[33]

4.1.3 Regional Action Seeking Peaceful Resolution of the Conflict

From the last few months of 1997 onwards, the Contact Group on Bosnia-Herzegovina began to look at the problem of the Kosovo crisis.[34] By taking upon itself the handling of this without a specific mandate from the Security Council it could be seen as converting itself, *de facto*, into a sort of 'Security Council for the Balkans'.[35] However, from the start there was no unanimous stance on the steps to be taken to confront the crisis.

---

[29]Cfr. Troebst (1999a), pp. 47 and 48.

[30]Cfr. Williams (2003), p. 397.

[31]Cfr. 'Report of the Secretary-General Prepared Pursuant to Resolution 1160 (1998) of the Security Council', UN Doc. S/1998/608, of 2 July 1998, 14, p. 4, para. 13. Sollemberg et al. (1999), p. 19. Independent International Commission on Kosovo, *The Kosovo Report: Conflict, International Response, Lessons Learned*, supra, note 288, pp. 33–83.

According to Birger Heldt's criteria, followed by these authors, 'a 'major armed conflict' is defined as prolonged use of armed force between the military forces of two or more governments, or of one government and at least one organized armed group, incurring the battle-related deaths of at least 1000 people during the entire conflict and in which the incompatibility concerns government and/or territory' (Cfr. Heldt (1992), Chap. 3).

[32]Cfr. UN Doc. S/RES/1199 (1998) , of 23 September, para. 15. UN Doc. S/RES/1203 (1998), of 24 October, para. 15.

Cfr. Wilson (2009), p. 458.

[33]Cfr. Rrecaj (2011), p. 122.

[34]Cfr. Schwegmann (2000), p. 12, http://www.iss.europa.eu/uploads/media/occ016.pdf.

[35]The Contact Group on Bosnia-Herzegovina was set up on 25 April 1994 by the Ministries of Foreign Affairs of France, Germany, the Russian Federation, the United Kingdom, the United States of America, the Commissioner of the European Union for Foreign Affairs, and the two Permanent Co-Chairmen of the Steering Committee of the International Conference of the Former Yugoslavia (ICFY). From May 1996 onwards, Italy also joined. Representatives of the Presidency

Until the Contact Group's meeting in London on 9 March 1998, the actions of the international community were 'a pattern of neglect' relative to the Kosovo problem.[36] The Conference on Security and Co-operation in Europe (CSCE) was the first multilateral forum to take an interest in the situation,[37] as against the main international organizations in the European regional sphere, which had not put in place policies on what was happening in Kosovo.[38] Most were wrapped up in the on-going conflict in Bosnia-Herzegovina. However, the CSCE limited itself to sending an exploratory mission to Kosovo, Vojvodina and Sandjak in August 1992, and to establishing several permanent missions in these territories that ended their work in June 1993.[39]

Even when the matter was discussed within the Contact Group, a major division manifested itself as to the way the crisis should be handled. Where the United States and the United Kingdom proposed rapid, energetic action, France, Italy and the Russian Federation were opposed to this sort of measures, and Germany advocated mediation.[40]

The meeting ended by adopting a declaration that condemned both 'the use of excessive force by Serbian police against civilians' and 'terrorist actions by the Kosovo Liberation Army or any other group or individual'.[41] Although not supporting the independence of Kosovo, it equally did not accept the *status quo* at that point,[42] and denounced the arising of events in which human rights were infringed:

> Our commitment to human rights values means that we cannot ignore such disproportionate methods of control. Government authorities have a special responsibility to protect the

---

of the Council of the EU, of the Chairperson-in-Office of the OSCE, and of the Office of the High Representative established by the Dayton Peace Agreement also attended. Cfr. Leight-Phippard (1998), p. 308.

[36] Caplan (1998), p. 747.

[37] In the session of the First Ministerial Council of the CSCE held in Berlin on 19 and 20 June 1991, the Yugoslav crisis was discussed at the request of the Federal Secretary for Foreign Affairs of Yugoslavia, Budimir Lončar. At the meeting's end, a 'Statement on the situation in Yugoslavia' was adopted in which the Ministers stated their support for democratic evolution, territorial unity and integrity, full application of human rights throughout Yugoslavia, including those of minorities, and a peaceful solution to the crisis http://www.osce.org/mc/40234?download=true.

[38] Cfr. Troebst (1999a), pp. 51 and 52. Troebst (1998), pp. 21–71, http://www.ecmi.de/uploads/tx_lfpubdb/working_paper_1.pdf.

[39] Cfr. OSCE (2007), pp. 46–47, http://www.osce.org/files/documents/b/3/22624.pdf.

The FRY had been suspended from participation in the CSCE, and Slobodan Milošević, elected President of the FRY in 1992, demanded full participation in order to become involved with the CSCE once again. Cfr. Ghebali (1999), p. 68.

[40] Cfr. Troebst (1999a), p. 52.

[41] 'Statement on Kosovo Adopted by the Members of the Contact Group, Meeting in London on 9 March 1998', Annex of the UN Doc. S/1998/223, of 12 March 1998, at para. 2 and 3.

[42] Cfr. Id. at para. 9.

human and civil rights of all citizens and to ensure that public security forces act judiciously and with restraint.[43]

The same declaration adopted a broad range of measures intended to oblige President Slobodan Milošević to stop the violence and make a commitment to seeking a political solution through dialogue.[44]

Over the course of that month of March, the activity of both the Organization for Security and Co-operation in Europe (OSCE) and the Contact Group intensified. The Permanent Council of the OSCE held that the Kosovo crisis no longer constituted a purely internal matter, because of the violations of the principles and human rights envisaged within the framework of the Organization and their major consequences for security in the region.[45] Among the measures adopted was the sending of a new mission headed by Felipe González Márquez. Nonetheless, the mission was denied access by the Belgrade Government as a reaction to the suspension of the FRY as a member of the OSCE.[46]

For its part, the Contact Group set a new limit of 4 weeks for the Belgrade Government to comply with all the requirements of the statement adopted in London.[47] Unfortunately, far from these being met, there was a fresh upsurge of violence. Consequently, when the time-limit expired, the Contact Group took the step of freezing all funds held externally by the Governments of the FRY and Republic of Serbia, in a meeting held in Rome, by now in April.[48] However, in doing so it no longer had the support of the Russian Federation.

[43]Id. at para. 5.

[44]Among other steps, a time-limit of ten days was set for the withdrawal of special police units, ending operations by security forces against the civilian population and making a public commitment to initiating dialogue. Cfr. 'Statement on Kosovo Adopted by the Members of the Contact Group, Meeting in London on 9 March 1998', Annex of the UN Doc. S/1998/223, of 12 March 1998, at paragraph 7. See also Troebst (1999b), p. 785.

[45]Cfr. Decision 'OSCE Action in Relation to Kosovo Crisis', OSCE Doc. PC.DEC/218, of 11 March 1998, at Preamble, para. 5, http://www.osce.org/pc/20518?download=true. Also in UN Doc. S/1998/246, of 17 March 1998, Annex.

[46]Cfr. Ghebali (1999), p. 71.

[47]Cfr. 'Statement on Kosovo issued by members of the Contact Group in Bonn on 25 March 1998', Annex of the UN Doc. S/1998/272, of 27 March 1998, at para. 8 https://documents-dds-ny.un.org/doc/UNDOC/GEN/N98/082/72/pdf/N9808272.pdf?OpenElement.

[48]Cfr. 'Statement on Kosovo adopted by the members of the Contact Group in Rome on 29 April 1998', Annex of the UN Doc. S/1998/355, of 30 April 1998, para. 9 https://documents-dds-ny.un.org/doc/UNDOC/GEN/N98/118/03/pdf/N9811803.pdf?OpenElement.

4.2 The Humanitarian Crisis and the Use of Force by NATO in 1999

4.2.1 The Humanitarian Crisis and the Recrudescence of Armed Conflict

Despite all the warnings from the West, Slobodan Milošević undertook a new offensive in the Decani region, intended to destroy the operational base of the UÇK.[49] A large number of places suffered bombardment by artillery and tanks, leading to a mass exodus of population to Montenegro and Albania.[50] In this situation the VJ set up a barrier of minefields along the frontier with Albania and launched attacks against villages west of Dakovica where hundreds of refugees had gathered.

Faced with the developing events and obstruction from the Russian Federation in the Contact Group, the United States and United Kingdom decided to take steps within NATO and the European Union (EU) In this new context, the decision was taken to carry out the 'Determined Falcon' exercise along the frontiers between the FRY and Albania and Macedonia.[51] The action was taken on 15 June 1998 by NATO aircraft 'with the aim of demonstrating NATO's capability to project power rapidly into the region'.[52] In contrast, France, Italy, Denmark and Germany stated that they would not support the use of force in the Security Council in view of the threat of vetoes from the Russian Federation and China.[53] The Russian Federation declared its opposition to any UN resolution that would affect the territorial integrity of the FRY and urged a diplomatic solution.[54]

As an outcome of the advances made by the VJ and the taking of villages, the humanitarian crisis grew to dimensions seen by the international community as a new 'humanitarian disaster', or even genocide.[55] The number of refugees and

---

[49]Cfr. 44:5 *Keesing's Record of World Events* (1998), p. 42301.

[50]During May the first mass flows of refugees to Albania occurred. In June, the UNHCR had recorded 6500. The Montenegrin authorities noted a total of 10,177 internally displaced persons from Kosovo, and the UNHCR stated that there were 45,000 displaced within Kosovo. Cfr. 'Report of the Secretary-General Prepared Pursuant to Resolution 1160 (1998) of the Security Council', UN Doc. S/1998/470, of 4 June 1998, 13, p. 4, paragraph 16; and 5, para. 20. 'Report of the Secretary-General Prepared Pursuant to Resolution 1160 (1998) of the Security Council', UN Doc. S/1998/608, of 2 July 1998, 14, p. 3, para. 10. Troebst (1999b), p. 785.

[51]Cfr. 44:6 *Keesing's Record of World Events* (1998), p. 42356.

[52]'Statement on Kosovo' issued at the meeting of the North Atlantic Council in Defence Ministers Session, 11 June 1998, doc. M-NAC-D-1(98)77, of 11 June http://nato.int/docu/pr/1998/p98-077e.htm.

[53]Cfr. Baggett (1999), p. 465.

[54]Cfr. Schwegmann (2000), p. 12.

[55]Cfr. 44:9 *Keesing's Record of World Events* (1998), p. 42512. 'Report of the Secretary-General Prepared Pursuant to Resolution 1160 (1998) of the Security Council', UN Doc. S/1998/712, of 5 August 1998, 20, p. 3, paras 12 and 13. Hughes (2013), p. 1001.

internal displaced persons was estimated at 230,000, of whom 60,000 had chosen to leave Kosovo.[56] The situation was worsened by massive generalized violations of basic human rights, with murders of civilians, arbitrary arrests and individuals "disappeared" by both sides.[57]

Despite the cease-fire agreed in October 1998, violence persisted, the situation relative to infringements of basic human rights steadily deteriorating.[58] Renewed combat, generalized from mid December 1998 onwards, triggered a fresh mass exodus by the Kosovar population of Albanian origin.[59] By the start of 1999, the figures had grown in a truly alarming manner, as according to the United Nations High Commissioner for Refugees (UNHCR) there were some 180,000 persons displaced within Kosovo, whilst outside the province there were 20,000 in Serbia and 25,000 in Montenegro.[60] Outside the State there were calculated to be 22,000 refugees in Albania, 10,000 in Bosnia-Herzegovina and 3000 in the Republic of Macedonia, besides the some 94,000 people from the FRY who were in other European countries, of whom 90% were Albano-Kosovar.[61] Relative to the population census of 1991, this implied that 17.6% of the inhabitants of Kosovo had fled their homes.

4.2.2 Resort to Force by NATO

On 23 September, the Security Council adopted Resolution 1199 (1998), in which, 'acting under Chapter VII of the UN Charter', among other things it requested the parties involved in the conflict to cease hostilities immediately and establish a cease-

[56]Cfr. 'Report of the Secretary-General Prepared Pursuant to Resolution 1160 (1998) of the Security Council', Addendum Annex 'Information on the situation in Kosovo and measures taken by the Organization for Security and Cooperation in Europe, submitted pursuant to paragraphs 13 and 16 of Security Council resolution 1160 (1998)', UN Doc. S/1998/834/Add.1, of 21 September 1998, 6, p. 2, para. 6.

[57]Cfr. 'Report of the Secretary-General Prepared Pursuant to Resolution 1160 (1998) of the Security Council', UN Doc. S/1998/834, of 4 September 1998, 9, p. 2, para. 7; 4, para. 16; and 5, para. 17. Bellamy (2001), pp. 105–126.

[58]Cfr. 'Report of the Secretary-General Prepared Pursuant to Resolutions 1160 (1998), 1199 (1998) and 1203 (1998) of the Security Council', UN Doc. S/1999/99, of 30 January 1999, 22, p. 3, para. 11.

[59]Cfr. Id., at Annex I 'Information on the Situation in Kosovo and measures taken by the Organization for Security and Cooperation in Europe, submitted pursuant to para. 13 of the Security Council resolution 1160 (1998), para. 2.

[60]Cfr. Cfr. Id., p. 8, para. 29 and 30.

[61]Cfr. Id., p. 8, para. 30. *Refugees and Others of Concern to UNHCR – 1998 Statistical Overview* (UNHCR, 1998), 120, at Table I.2. 'Refugee population by country of asylum and origin, 1997-1998' http://www.unhcr.org/cgi-bin/texis/vtx/home/opendocPDFViewer.html?docid=3bfa31ac1&query=refugees%20and%20others.

fire, withdrawing security units used for repression.[62] For its part, China abstained from voting, as it held that the Kosovo question was an internal matter of the FRY and so that the principle 'of respect for and maintenance of the sovereignty and territorial integrity of the FRY' should be respected.[63] However, the resolution received a favourable vote from the Russian Federation, whose Permanent Representative, Sergey Lavrov, stated that the basic provisions of the draft resolution:

> [...] correspond to the fundamental stance taken by the Russian Federation which favours settlement of the conflict in Kosovo exclusively through peaceful and political means on the basis of granting broad autonomy to Kosovo, with strict respect for the territorial integrity of the Federal Republic of Yugoslavia. [...] In particular, the use of unilateral measures of force in order to settle this conflict is fraught with the risk of destabilizing the Balkan region and of all of Europe and would have long-term adverse consequences for the international system [...].[64]

The following day, the North Atlantic Council approved an activation warning (ACTWARN) decision on the possibility of carrying out 'a limited air option and a phased air campaign in Kosovo', which gave decided backing for the resolution approved by the Security Council.[65]

The resolution was also backed by the Contact Group, which decided to commission the Special Envoy of the United States to the Balkans, Richard Holbrooke, to go to Belgrade in order to achieve compliance with the requirements of Resolution 1199 (1998).[66] The result was an informal agreement between the Special Envoy and Slobodan Milošević on 13 October.[67] The terms included a cease-fire and the setting up of a verification mission of the OSCE, together with progress towards attaining a political solution that would concede an increasing degree of self-determination to Kosovo.[68]

When these commitments were not kept, NATO hardened its stance, changing from 'activation warnings' to 'activation orders' (ACTORDs) for both 'limited air strikes and a phased air campaign in Yugoslavia'.[69] The Belgrade Government was called on to fulfil its commitments within 96 h.[70] At the point when the 96 h were about to expire, NATO ceded a fresh time-limit of 10 days, as recognition of the signing of an agreement between the Supreme Allied Commander in Europe

---

[62] Cfr. UN Doc. S/RES/1199 (1998) , of 23 September, at para. 1, 4.a) and 4.c).

[63] Intervention of Mr. Qin Huasun (China), UN Doc. S/PV.3930, of 23 September 1998, 5, p. 3.

[64] Intervention of Mr. Lavrov (Russian Federation), UN Doc. S/PV.3930, of 23 September 1998, 5, p. 3.

[65] 'Statement by the Secretary General following the ACT WARM Decision', Vilamoura, 24 September 1998 http://nato.int/docu/pr/1998/p980924e.htm.

[66] Cfr. Troebst (1999b), p. 787.

[67] Cfr. Ghebali (1999), p. 71. 44:10 *Keesing's Record of World Events* (1998), p. 42580.

[68] Cfr. 'Serbian Government Endorses Accord Reached by President Milosevic', Belgrade, 13 October 1998. The document may be seen in: Weller (1999a), Vol. I, p. 279.

[69] 'Statement to the press by the Secretary General following decision on the ACTORD', NATO Headquarters, 13 October 1998 http://nato.int/docu/speech/1998/s981013a.htm.

[70] Id.

(SACEUR), General Wesley Clark, and the Chief of the General Staff of the VJ, Momčilo Perišić, relating to the establishment of a NATO Verification Mission in Kosovo.[71]

At the same time, the Chairman-in-Office of the OSCE, Bronislaw Geremek, signed another accord with the Minister of Foreign Affairs of the FRY, Živadin Jovanović, on the deployment of the KVM.[72]

The Security Council took on board the agreements reached in Belgrade and backed the creation and establishment of the KVM, as well as the carrying out of Operation 'Eagle Eye' by NATO in its Resolution 1203 (1998).[73] In this same resolution it demanded full compliance with Resolutions 1160 (1998) and 1199 (1998), and co-operation with the KVM both by the FRY and by the leaders and members of the Albano-Kosovar community.[74]

Against general wishes, the cease-fire was observed for barely 2 months. Confrontations worsened as December went by, and the conflict became general.[75] Faced with this situation, the Contact Group members announced that they would attempt to find a political solution for the crisis. With this aim, they joined with the EU in inviting the Belgrade Government and the representatives of the Albano-Kosovar community to meet with the aim of negotiating a settlement.

In order to avoid rejection of the negotiations, NATO issued an ultimatum to the FRY Government stating that it would undertake necessary measures as a function of fulfilment by the two parties of international commitments and their responses to the demands of the Contact Group.[76] In the text, permission was granted to the Secretary General to 'authorise air strikes against targets on FRY territory'.[77] The response of the Belgrade Government came in the shape of a declaration calling NATO's decision an open threat of aggression against the sovereignty and territorial integrity of the FRY. It also claimed that NATO had no authorization from the

[71]Cfr. 'Kosovo Verification Mission Agreement between the North Atlantic Treaty Organization and the Federal Republic of Yugoslavia' done at Belgrade on 15 October 1998, UN Doc. S/1998/991, of 23 October 1998, 7, at Annex.

[72]Cfr. 'Agreement on the Kosovo Verification Mission of the Organization for Security and Cooperation in Europe' done at Belgrade on 16 October 1998, UN Doc. S/1998/978, of 20 October 1998, 9, at Annex.

[73]Cfr. UN Doc. S/RES/1203 (1998), of 24 October, at para. 1.

[74]Cfr. Id., at para. 3.

The KVM was set up in accordance with the decision of the Permanent Council of the OSCE, PC.DEC/263, of 25 October 1998. It constituted the widest, most complex and varied action undertaken by the OSCE up to that point. Among its functions was verifying compliance with the Security Council resolutions, maintaining the cease-fire, controlling movements of forces, aiding refugees and displaced persons, supervising elections, promoting human rights, and building up democracy. Cfr. OSCE (2007), p. 47, http://www.osce.org/files/documents/b/3/22624.pdf.

[75]Cfr. Troebst (1999b), p. 790. Posen (2000), p. 43.

[76]Cfr. 'Statement by the North Atlantic Council on Kosovo', Press Release (99) 12, of 30 January 1999, at para. 5 http://nato.int/docu/pr/1999/p99-012e.htm. Also in UN Doc. S/1999/107, of 3 February 1999, 5, at Appendix.

[77]Cfr. Id., at Appendix.

Security Council or right to take coercive action against an independent State that was a member of the UN.[78]

Negotiations went on in Rambouillet in France from 6 to 23 February and in Paris from 15 to 19 March 1999.[79] The outcome was two documents with considerable divergences. On the one hand, the Albano-Kosovar delegation finally on 23 March accepted the so-called 'Interim Agreement for Peace and Self-Government in Kosovo' proposed by the mediators.[80] However, on the other, the Serbian representatives rejected the 'Interim Agreement' and put forward a counterproposal consisting of an 'Agreement for Self-Government in Kosmet' dated 18 March and drawn up by Belgrade with the collaboration of representatives of Albanian political parties in tune with it and of the six non-Albanian communities in Kosovo.[81] The failure of negotiations was perceived as the outcome of influence from the Russians who acted as the Serbs' advocates.[82]

Faced with this refusal, on 24 March NATO announced the start of air raids against targets in the FRY, an operation that was to be called 'Allied Force'.[83] These military actions, as stated by the NATO Secretary General, Javier Solana Madariaga, were supporting the political wishes of the international community and were not a war against Yugoslavia, but rather intended to prevent human suffering, repression and violence against the civilian population of Kosovo.[84] A last measure before the beginning of the attacks, aimed at avoiding the need for them, was the sending of a NATO and EU mission to Belgrade. Sadly, the Special Envoy, Richard Holbrooke, was obliged to inform the North Atlantic Council that this last chance had failed.

Finally, on 24 March bombing commenced against FRY targets in Pristina. The aim was clear, the Secretary General once again repeated, 'to halt the violence and to stop further humanitarian catastrophe'.[85] This intervention involved a change in the practice of International law which is still unresolved. What is true is that majority opinion saw the intervention of NATO as contrary to international law,[86] although it

---

[78]Cfr. 'Statement of the Federal Government Concerning NATO Decisions', Belgrade, 1st February 1999. See Krieger (2001), p. 300.

[79]Cfr. Troebst (1999b), p. 791. Weller (1999b). Herring (2000), p. 225, Vidmar (2011), p. 147.

[80]UN Doc. S/1999/648, of 7 June 1999, 86, at Annex. Krieger (2001), p. 261.

[81]Reprinted in Krieger (2001), p. 280.

Cfr. Ghebali (1999), p. 73. Judah (2002), p. 220. Posen (2000), p. 44.

[82]Cfr. Talbott (2002), p. 303.

[83]Cfr. Ronzitti (1999), p. 478.

[84]Cfr. 'Press Statement by Dr. Javier Solana, Secretary General of NATO', Press Release (1999) 040, of 23 March 1999, http://nato.int/docu/pr/1999/p99-040e.htm.

[85]Id.

[86]Cfr. Cassese (1999), p. 23. Chinkin (2000), p. 916. Falk (1999), p. 854. Gutiérrez Espada (2000), p. 108. Kohen (1999), p. 132. Kritsiotis (2000), pp. 330–359. Lowe (2000), p. 936. Picone (2000), p. 343. Simma (1999), pp. 11 and 22. Sur (1999), pp. 280–291. Zappalà (1999), p. 996.

might be considered legitimate as a collective responses to very serious crimes, in the light of the doctrine of 'humanitarian intervention'.[87]

4.2.3 Russian Opposition and the Consequences of Intervention

The Government of the Russian Federation opposed Operation 'Allied Force' from the very first. The Kosovo conflict had given rise to the most critical moment in relations between Russia and the United States since the end of the Cold War. The new NATO 'Strategic Concept' of April 1999 was interpreted by the Russian Federation as a form of multilateralism excluding her from the new post-Cold War security architecture of Europe and a change from the idea of collective defence to one of 'collective interference' outside the NATO area.[88] Its attempt to universalize the international response to the Kosovo crisis also ran counter to Russian policies relating to internal and regional 'frozen conflicts'.[89]

The same day the raids began, the Permanent Representative of the Russian Federation, Sergey Lavrov, requested an emergency meeting of the Security Council in which he declared his strong opposition to military intervention and it became clear that China, Belarus, and India backed this view.[90] Among the arguments put forward was that unilateral action by NATO infringed fundamental precepts of the UN Charter:

> Those who are involved in this unilateral use of force against the sovereign Federal Republic of Yugoslavia —carried out in violation of the UN Charter and without the authorization of the Security Council— must realize the heavy responsibility they bear for subverting the Charter and other norms of international law and for attempting to establish in the world, de facto, the primacy of force and unilateral diktat.[91]

After 2 days, Belarus, India and the Russian Federation presented a draft resolution condemning NATO's actions and calling for 'an immediate cessation of the use of force against the FRY and urgent resumption of negotiations'.[92] However, during the Security Council meeting held that same 26 March, the draft resolution was

[87]Cfr. Charney (1999), p. 841. Greenwood (1999), p. 161. Henkin (1999), p. 826. Mertus (2001), p. 133. Wippman (2001), pp. 129–150.

[88]Cfr. Hughes (2013), p. 993.

[89]Cfr. Id., p. 994.

[90]Cfr. Intervention of Mr. Qin Huasun (China); intervention of Mr. Martynov (Belarus); and intervention of Mr. Sharma (India), UN Doc. S/PV.3988, of 24 March 1999, 20, p. 13, 15 and 16.

[91]Intervention of Mr. Lavrov (Russian Federation), UN Doc. S/PV.3988, of 24 March 1999, 20, p. 2.

[92]UN Doc. S/1999/328, of 26 March, at para. 1.

rejected by 12 votes against to 3 votes in favour.[93] The declaration by the Permanent Representative of Slovenia, Danilo Türk, summed up to the justification accepted by the majority of the members of the Security Council: 'The use of force by the Belgrade Government against the civilian population created a situation that made the current military action inevitable'.[94]

Among the States considering NATO's actions illegal was the FRY which pulled out all the stops in trying to get official recognition of NATO's responsibility.[95] Among the claims it made were the suits brought before the ICJ on 29 April 1999 against 10 NATO member States, based on violation of obligations such as those 'not to use force against another State' and 'not to intervene in the affairs of another State', basic human rights, the freedom of navigation on international rivers, together with the 'Convention on the Prevention and Punishment of the Crime of Genocide'.[96] The ICJ avoided pronouncing on the merits of these claims.[97] Finally, the FRY was held not to be the successor to the SFRY and the new State of Serbia and Montenegro, not being part of the UN and thus of the ICJ Statute, did not 'have access to the Court under either paragraph 1 or paragraph 2 of Art. 35 of the Statute'.[98]

[93]The votes in favour were from China, Namibia and Russian Federation. Those against were from Argentina, Bahrain, Brazil, Canada, France, Gabon, Gambia, Malaysia, Netherlands, Slovenia, the United Kingdom of Great Britain and Northern Ireland, and the United States of America. Cfr. UN Doc. S/PV.3989, of 26 March, 16, p. 6.

[94]Intervention of Mr. Türk (Slovenia), UN Doc. S/PV.3989, of 26 March, 16, p. 3.

[95]Hilpold (2009a), p. 266.

[96]See Legality of Use of Force, Yugoslavia v. ten NATO States (Belgium, Canada, France, Germany, Italy, the Netherlands, Portugal, Spain and the United States of America). See http://www.icj-cij.org/en/list-of-all-cases.

[97]The same day that the applications were lodged, Serbia and Montenegro presented a request for an indication of provisional measures relating to each of the matters. The Court pronounced on this petition in the shape of ten orders issued on 2 June 1999. In the *prima facie* examination of its jurisdiction, the ICJ decided that it manifestly lacked jurisdiction in the case of Spain and the United States (*Legality of Use of Force (Yugoslavia* v. *Spain), Provisional Measures, Order of 2 June 1999, I.C.J. Reports 1999*, 761–774, p. 773, para. 35; *Legality of Use of Force (Yugoslavia* v. *United States of America), Provisional Measures, Order of 2 June 1999, I.C.J. Reports 1999*, 916–926, p. 925, para. 29). In the remaining eight cases, it declared that *prima facie* it lacked jurisdiction, without this prejudging the question of the jurisdiction to deal with the merits of the cases. Consequently, the matters of Spain and the United States were removed from the List, while for the others the provisional measures requested were not adopted and judgements were delayed until 15 December 2004.

See: Boisson de Chazournes (1999), Heselhaus (2000), Shen (2001), Shifman (1999), pp. 117–120.

[98]*Legality of Use of Force (Serbia and Montenegro* v. *Belgium), Preliminary Objections, Judgment, I.C.J. Reports 2004*, 279–329, p. 327, para. 127 http://www.icj-cij.org/files/case-related/105/105-20041215-JUD-01-00-BI.pdf. Similarly, in judgements relating to Canada (para. 114), France (para. 114), Germany (para. 113), Italy (para. 114), the Netherlands (para. 126), Portugal (para. 117), and the United Kingdom (para. 113).

See Gray (2005), pp. 787–794. Olleson (2005), pp. 237–255. Vitucci (2006), pp. 105–127.

The numbers of refugees grew greater even than the worst predictions. According to an OSCE report, violence inflicted on the Albano-Kosovar population from 20 March onwards led to 69,500 people leaving the province of Kosovo by 23 March personas and by June the total number of refugees had reached 863,000.[99] The root of this was the Serbian strategy of trying to represent the NATO raids as the true cause of the humanitarian disaster.[100] In the light of these figures, it could be stated that more than 90% of the population of Kosovo province, that is almost all those of Albanian origin, had been forced to abandon their homes.[101] The humanitarian catastrophe has reached dimensions comparable to that suffered by the Kurds in northern Iraq in 1991, or the Rwandan genocide of 1994. In the eleven-week period that the conflict lasted it is estimated that 10,000 Albano-Kosovars died.[102]

After 78 days of raids, Slobodan Milošević, together with the National Assembly of the Republic of Serbia and the Government of the FRY, decided to accept the principles of the peace plan drawn up by the new mediating group, made up of the Group of Seven plus Russia (Group of Eight, G-8).[103] The project was presented by the President of Finland, Martti Ahtisaari, representing the EU, and the Special Representative of the President of the Russian Federation, Viktor Chernomyrdin.[104]

The G-8, after a number of meetings in Bonn, on 6 May gained acceptance of the principles on which peace should be founded.[105] Once agreement was reached the Contact Group was completely side-lined from the political handling of the conflict and the G-8 commenced preparation of a project for a Security Council resolution that would provide the basis for a reasonable and viable political solution.[106]

---

[99] OSCE (1999), p. 167, http://www.osce.org/odihr/17772?download=true. Hodge (2000), p. 47.

The figures provided by the UNHCR reached 860,000, of whom 444,000 were in Albania, 344,500 in the Former Yugoslav Republic of Macedonia, and 69,900 in Montenegro. Cfr. A. Suhrke, M. Barutciski, P. Sandison, and R. Garlock, *The Kosovo Refugee Crisis: An Independent Evaluation of the UNHCR's Emergency Preparedness and Response,* Doc. EPAU/2000/001, supra, this chapter, note 4, p. 6, para. 31.

On the same lines, the United States Department of State's Bureau of Population, Refugees, and Migration, 'Kosovo Humanitarian Situation Update, April 2, 1999', http://www.state.gov/www/global/prm/rpt_990402_humsitrep.html. O'Connell (1999), p. 80.

[100] Cfr. Posen (2000), p. 53. Dietrich (2010), p. 125.

[101] Cfr. Westendorp (1999), p. 45.

[102] Cfr. Posen (2000), p. 62.

[103] On the NATO campaign, see Independent International Commission on Kosovo, *The Kosovo Report: Conflict, International Response, Lessons Learned*, supra, this chapter, note 4, pp. 85–97.

[104] The agreement on the principles to move towards a resolution of the Kosovo crisis is to be found in UN Doc. S/1999/649, of 7 June 1999, 3, at Annex. Independent International Commission on Kosovo, *The Kosovo Report: Conflict, International Response, Lessons Learned*, supra, this chapter, note 4, p. 95.

[105] 'Statement by the Chairman on the Conclusion of the Meeting of the G-8 Foreign Ministers held at the Petersberg Centre on 6 May 1999', UN Doc. S/1999/516, of 6 May 1999, 2, at Annex.

[106] Cfr. Ghebali (1999), p. 78. 'Conclusions of the Meeting of the G8 Foreign Ministers, Cologne, 10 June 1999', p. 6 Regional Issues, http://www.g8.utoronto.ca/foreign/fm9906010.htm.

The end of hostilities was attained on 9 June 1999 with the signing of the 'Military Technical Agreement between the International Security Force (KFOR) and the Government of the Federal

Without delay, the Security Council adopted Resolution 1244 (1999) on 10 June, backed by the Russian Federation and with only China abstaining.[107] The text of the draft resolution was supported by the G-8 along with Bahrain, Gabon, Slovenia, the Netherlands and the Ukraine, and returned the main role in resolving the conflict to the UN.[108] Although the majority of the members of the Security Council expressed satisfaction at the solution of the conflict and the adoption of a resolution laying the foundations for construction, the representative de la Russian Federation stated:

> [...] Russia has strongly condemned the NATO aggression against a sovereign State. This action on the part of the Alliance, which was undertaken in violation of the United Nations Charter and in circumvention of the Security Council, has severely destabilized the entire system of international relations based on the primacy of international law. The humanitarian crisis in Kosovo was transformed by the NATO bombing into the most serious humanitarian catastrophe, [...].[109]

The new Resolution 1244 (1999) authorized Member States to deploy an international civilian presence and security arrangements in Kosovo.[110] The international civilian presence had as its aim the setting up of a provisional administration that would let the people of Kosovo enjoy substantial autonomy with provisional democratic government institutions for a peaceful life.[111] As for the international security presence, a Kosovo International Security Force (KFOR) would be deployed that would attempt to verify the withdrawal of Serbian troops and to disarm the UÇK.[112]

4.2.4 Administration of Kosovo as a Premise for the Unilateral Declaration of Independence

The Security Council maintained an essentially pragmatic attitude when faced with a situation that was complex both from a political and legal viewpoint and from that of deep internal divisions.[113] Resolution 1244 (1999) implied the start of a new period that would last from March 1999 to July 2010, marked by tensions between recollections and forgetting, the desire being to get over events so as to re-establish peace.[114]

Republic of Yugoslavia and the Republic of Serbia', at Kumanovo, Republic of Macedonia, http://nato.int/kosovo/docu/a990609a.htm. Cfr. Milano (2003), p. 1004.

[107] Cfr. UN S/PV.4011, of 10 June 1999, 21, p. 9.

[108] Cfr. UN Doc. S/1999/661, of 10 June 1999, 8. Balmond and Weckel (1999), p. 739.

[109] Cfr. Intervention of Mr. Lavrov (Russian Federation), UN Doc. S/PV.4011, of 10 June 1999, 21, p. 7.

[110] Cfr. UN Doc. S/RES/1244 (1999), of 10 June 1999, at para. 5.

[111] Cfr. Id., at para. 10.

[112] Cfr. Id., at para. 9.

[113] Cfr. Hilpold (2009a), p. 267.

[114] Cfr. Ibid.

Under the aegis of the UN, the Kosovo question now once again was formally set in a multilateral context. However, NATO stuck to its position of not ceding any military sector to the Russian Federation, and the United States of America (US) put pressure on Rumania and Bulgaria so that they would not allow passage through their airspace by Russian forces.[115] Faced with this foot-dragging, the Russian Federation undertook one of the riskiest manoeuvres in the whole Kosovo crisis, sending elements of its contingent in the Bosnia-Herzegovina peacekeeping force in the direction of Serbia with the aim of taking control of the strategic airport at Pristina.[116] This episode could have been one of the most dangerous in the recent history of Europa, as the NATO Supreme Commander, General Wesley Clark, ordered the British troops stationed in Pristina to expel the Russian forces from the airport.[117] Fortunately, the British Commander, General Michael Jackson, rejected this order, saying that he was not ready to 'start World War Three'.[118]

The UNIMIK was responsible for the civil administration of Kosovo.[119] The task set for UNIMIK was delimited as 'performing basic civilian administrative functions where and as long as required'.[120] However, the actions of both UNIMIK and KFOR were the grounds for repeated protests from the FRY Government, which saw them as running counter to Resolution 1244 (1999) in that they infringed its sovereignty and territorial integrity, declared in that resolution.[121] Thus, UNIMIK carried out *de facto* government in Kosovo completely independently of the FRY, in a way that some authors consider contrary to international law.[122]

Resolution 1244 (1999) entrusted UNIMIK with the task of 'facilitating a political process designed to determine Kosovo's future status'.[123] Although Regulation No. 2001/9 was adopted on 15 May 2001 regarding a 'Constitutional Framework for Provisional Self-Government' for the establishment of Provisional Institutions of Self-Government of Kosovo,[124] the question of determining their final status

[115]Cfr. Hughes (2013), p. 1005.

[116]Cfr. Gordon (1999), http://www.nytimes.com/1999/06/12/world/crisis-in-the-balkans-news-analysis-kremlin-vs-its-army.html.

[117]Cfr. Erlanger (1999) , http://www.nytimes.com/1999/06/12/world/crisis-balkans-overview-russians-enter-kosovo-early-but-moscow-calls-it-mistake.html.

[118]Cfr. Myers (1999), http://www.nytimes.com/1999/06/13/world/crisis-balkans-troops-british-forces-reaching-kosovo-capital-find-russians.html.

[119]On UNMIK, see: Ardault et al. (2006), Bothe and Marauhn (2001), Von Carlowitz (2003), Daase (2009), Fox (2008), Friedrich (2005), Garcia (2000), Irmscher (2001), Lagrange (1999), Serra (2008).

[120]UN Doc. S/RES/1244 (1999), of 10 June 1999, at para. 11.b).

[121]Cfr. Id., at Preamble, para. 10.

[122]Cfr. Ingravallo (2012), p. 223. Santori (2004), Vol. III, pp. 1689–1721.

[123]UN Doc. S/RES/1244 (1999), of 10 June 1999, at para. 11.e).

[124]See http://www.unmikonline.org/regulations/2001/reg09-01.htm.

remained unresolved.[125] In November 2005, the Secretary-General, Kofi Atta Annan, named Martti Ahtisaari as Special Envoy for the process of determining the future status of Kosovo.[126]

After a year and a half of negotiations with the parties aimed at reaching a compromise, the Special Envoy reached the conclusion that no agreed solution could be attained and on 10 March 2007 presented his plan for solving the problem.[127] His proposal focused on granting independence at a future date, initially under international supervision.[128] This rested on the premise that over times ethnic tensions could only worsen, so that independence was the remedy for Kosovo as a *sui generis* case, the solution to which should not be taken to set a precedent for similar situations: 'Kosovo is a unique case that demands a unique solution. It does not create a precedent for other unresolved conflicts'.[129]

---

[125]The Independent International Commission on Kosovo (IICK) proposed a status termed 'conditional independence', which would emerge from a consultation process. *The Kosovo Report: Conflict, International Response, Lessons Learned*, supra, this chapter, note 4, p. 273.

The IICK was set up in August 1999 by the Swedish Government on the initiative of Prime Minister Göran Persson, and composed of 11 members. Richard Goldstone of South Africa and Carl Tham of Sweden were appointed as the first co-chairmen. Its report was presented to the Secretary-General on 23 October 2000. Cfr. Williams (2003), p. 411, note 116.

[126]'Secretary-General Appoints Former President Martti Ahtisaari of Finland as Special Envoy for Future Status Process for Kosovo', 15 November 2005, http://www.un.org/press/en/2005/sga955.doc.htm.

[127]Cfr. Hilpold (2009a), p. 270. Ker-Lindsay (2009), 272 pp. Perritt (2009), p. 157.

[128]Cfr. 'Report of the Special Envoy of the Secretary-General on Kosovo's future status', UN Doc. S/2007/168, of 26 March 2007, 9, p. 2, para. 5. 'Comprehensive Proposal for the Kosovo Status Settlement', UN Doc. S/2007/168/Add.1, of 26 March 2007, 61.

[129]'Report of the Special Envoy of the Secretary-General on Kosovo's future status', UN Doc. S/2007/168, of 26 March 2007, 9, p. 4, para. 15.

Cfr. Christakis (2011), p. 80.

The Council of the EU, in its Council Meeting No. 2851 on General Affairs and External Relations, Brussels, February 18, 2008, discussed developments in Kosovo and adopted the following conclusion:

> The Council reiterates the EU's adherence to the principles of the UN Charter and the Helsinki Final Act, inter alia the principles of sovereignty and territorial integrity and all UN Security Council resolutions. It underlines its conviction that in view of the conflict of the 1990s and the extended period of international administration under SCR 1244, Kosovo constitutes a sui generis case which does not call into question these principles and resolutions.

Council of the European Union, General Affairs and External Relations, Brussels, 18 February 2008, Press Release, doc. 6496/08 (Presse 41), 18, p. 7.

The arguments for claiming that this was a 'unique case' were the internal conflict in Kosovo with its grave violations of human rights and the subsequent period of administration by the United Nations. Cfr. Jia (2009), p. 30. Ker-Lindsay (2013), p. 847. Marxsen (2014), p. 386.

The plan proposed by Martti Ahtisaari, though backed by the Secretary-General, was not adopted by the Security Council because of differences of opinion among the Permanent Members and the opposition of Serbia.[130] There was a further round of negotiations in which the Belgrade Government proposed the so-called 'Åland Islands Model' for Kosovo with a duration of 20 years.[131] However, all that became clear was the main defect of the Security Council: its inability to act on matters where there was disagreement between East and West.[132]

Thanks to the Ahtisaari Plan, the will of the Albanian Kosovar representatives was strengthened. The Assembly of Kosovo's Provisional Institutions of Self-Government finally declared independence on 17 February 2008.[133]

This declaration of independence was not unanimously accepted by the international community and caused friction both within the Security Council and in the EU At the present day, the independence of Kosovo has been recognized by the majority of Western countries, but remains opposed by the Russian Federation, China, Spain and India.[134] The Permanent Representative of the Russian Federation, Vitaly

---

[130]The matter was discussed behind closed doors by the Security Council in its session of 3 April 2007, UN Doc. S/PV.5654, of 3 April 2007. 'Ahtisaari's proposal unacceptable and illegitimate for Serbia', 7 February 2007, http://www.srbija.gov.rs/vesti/vest.php?id=31550. Muharremi (2008), p. 412.

During a visit to Moscow by President Boris Tadić and Prime-Minister Vojislav Koštunica, Vladimir Putin re-iterated that Russia was:

> categorically against any unilateral declaration of independence by Kosovo. This would risk doing serious damage to the whole system of international law and have negative consequences for the Balkans and for stability in other regions of the world'. 'Press Statement following Russian-Serbian Talks,

Press Service of the President of Russia, 34:1 *European Neighbourhood Watch* (2008), p. 4, https://www.ceps.eu/sites/default/files/old/NW/NWatch34.pdf.

Cfr. 'President Vladimir Putin met at the Kremlin with Serbian President Boris Tadic and Serbian Prime Minister Vojislav Kostunica', January 25, 2008, http://en.kremlin.ru/events/president/news/43702.

[131]Basically, under the proposed model the Belgrade Government would exercise control of foreign policy, control of borders, protection of Serb religious and cultural heritage, and defence. Remaining competencies were to be exercised by Kosovo exclusively. Cfr. 'Belgrade's Proposal Freezes Kosovo Status for 20 Years', *Tanjug*, November 20, 2007, http://www.mfa.gov.rs/Bilteni/Engleski/b211107_e.html#N1.

On the case of the Åland Islands see *infra*, p. 156.

[132]Cfr. Hilpold (2009a), p. 274.

[133]'Kosova Declaration of Independence' 17 February 2008, supra, Chap. 1, note 13. Statement by Secretary Condolezza Rice 'United States Recognizes Kosovo as Independent State', US Department of State Press Statement No. 2008/117 (18 February 2008), 102:2 *AJIL* (2008), p. 640. Warbrick (2008), p. 675.

Among many, intervention of Mr. Ban Ki-moon (Secretary-General), UN Doc. S/PV.5839, of 17 February 2008, 23, p. 2.

[134]It currently has diplomatic recognition from 113 of the 193 UN Member States, 23 of the 28 EU States and 24 of the 28 members of NATO. Cfr. 'International Recognitions of the Republic of Kosovo', http://www.mfa-ks.net/?page=2,224. For its part, the Serbian Government has not recognized Kosovo as a sovereign State, although it does maintain relations with the Kosovo

Churkin, following the Russian foreign policy of preserving the territorial integrity of the FRY,[135] stressed that it broke norms and principles of international law:

> We fully understand the reaction of President Tadić and the Serbian leadership to the Kosovo developments, and we support Belgrade's legitimate demands to restore the territorial integrity of the country.
>
> [. . .] The 17 February declaration by the local assembly of the Serbian province of Kosovo is a blatant breach of the norms and principles of international law — above all of the UN Charter — which undermines the foundations of the system of international relations.
>
> [. . .] The illegal acts of the Kosovo Albanian leadership and of those who support them set a dangerous precedent'.[136]

In view of the inability of the Security Council to adopt a resolution relating to the situation in Kosovo and the desire of the Provisional Institutions to take on the functions performed by UNMIK, the Secretary General declared that he would not continue with the Ahtisaari Plan and that the UN would maintain 'strict neutrality' with regard to the final status of Kosovo.[137] As an alternative he proposed a review of the functions and budget for UNMIK, which ended with the setting up of a new independent mission called EULEX Kosovo.[138]

Box 4.1 The Declaration of Independence of Kosovo
Kosova Declaration of Independence

1. We, the democratically-elected leaders of our people, hereby declare Kosovo to be an independent and sovereign state. This declaration reflects the will of our people and it is in full accordance with the recommendations of UN Special Envoy Martti Ahtisaari and his Comprehensive Proposal for the Kosovo Status Settlement.
2. We declare Kosovo to be a democratic, secular and multi-ethnic republic, guided by the principles of non-discrimination and equal protection under the law. We shall protect and promote the rights of all communities in Kosovo and create the conditions necessary for their effective participation in political and decision-making processes.

(continued)

Government in accordance with the 'First Agreement of Principles Governing the Normalization of Relations' concluded, although not signed by either party, on 19 April 2013 in Brussels under the auspices of the EU Cfr. 'Serbia and Kosovo Reach Landmark Deal', European Union External Action 19 April 2013 http://eeas.europa.eu/top_stories/2013/190413__eu-facilitated_dialogue_en.htm.

135Cfr. 'The Foreign Policy Concept of the Russian Federation. Approved by the President of the Russian Federation V. Putin on June 28, 2000', http://www.bits.de/EURA/russia052800.pdf.

136Intervention of Mr. Churkin (Russian Federation), UN Doc. S/PV.5839, of 17 February 2008, 23, pp. 6 and 7.

137Cfr. 'Report of the Secretary-General on the United Nations Interim Administration Mission in Kosovo', UN Doc. S/2008/458, of 15 July 2008, 21, p. 9, para. 29.

138Cfr. Id., p. 9, para. 30.

Box 4.1 (continued)

3. We accept fully the obligations for Kosovo contained in the Ahtisaari Plan, and welcome the framework it proposes to guide Kosovo in the years ahead. We shall implement in full those obligations including through priority adoption of the legislation included in its Annex XII, particularly those that protect and promote the rights of communities and their members.
4. We shall adopt as soon as possible a Constitution that enshrines our commitment to respect the human rights and fundamental freedoms of all our citizens, particularly as defined by the European Convention on Human Rights. The Constitution shall incorporate all relevant principles of the Ahtisaari Plan and be adopted through a democratic and deliberative process.
5. We welcome the international community's continued support of our democratic development through international presences established in Kosovo on the basis of UN Security Council resolution 1244 (1999). We invite and welcome an international civilian presence to supervise our implementation of the Ahtisaari Plan, and a European Union-led rule of law mission. We also invite and welcome the North Atlantic Treaty Organization to retain the leadership role of the international military presence in Kosovo and to implement responsibilities assigned to it under UN Security Council resolution 1244 (1999) and the Ahtisaari Plan, until such time as Kosovo institutions are capable of assuming these responsibilities. We shall cooperate fully with these presences to ensure Kosovo's future peace, prosperity and stability.
6. For reasons of culture, geography and history, we believe our future lies with the European family. We therefore declare our intention to take all steps necessary to facilitate full membership in the European Union as soon as feasible and implement the reforms required for European and Euro-Atlantic integration.
7. We express our deep gratitude to the United Nations for the work it has done to help us recover and rebuild from war and build institutions of democracy. We are committed to working constructively with the United Nations as it continues its work in the period ahead.
8. With independence comes the duty of responsible membership in the international community. We accept fully this duty and shall abide by the principles of the United Nations Charter, the Helsinki Final Act, other acts of the Organization on Security and Cooperation in Europe, and the international legal obligations and principles of international comity that mark the relations among states. Kosovo shall have its international borders as set forth in Annex VIII of the Ahtisaari Plan, and shall fully respect the sovereignty and territorial integrity of all our neighbors. Kosovo shall also refrain from the threat or use of force in any manner inconsistent with the purposes of the United Nations.
9. We hereby undertake the international obligations of Kosovo, including those concluded on our behalf by the United Nations Interim Administration Mission in Kosovo (UNMIK) and treaty and other obligations of the former Socialist Federal Republic of Yugoslavia to which we are bound as a former constituent part, including the Vienna Conventions on diplomatic and consular relations. We shall cooperate fully with the International Criminal Tribunal for the Former Yugoslavia. We intend to seek membership in international organizations, in which Kosovo shall seek to contribute to the pursuit of international peace and stability.
10. Kosovo declares its commitment to peace and stability in our region of southeast Europe. Our independence brings to an end the process of Yugoslavia's violent dissolution. While this process has been a painful one, we shall work tirelessly to

(continued)

Box 4.1 (continued)

contribute to a reconciliation that would allow southeast Europe to move beyond the conflicts of our past and forge new links of regional cooperation. We shall therefore work together with our neighbors to advance a common European future.

11. We express, in particular, our desire to establish good relations with all our neighbors, including the Republic of Serbia with whom we have deep historical, commercial and social ties that we seek to develop further in the near future. We shall continue our efforts to contribute to relations of friendship and cooperation with the Republic of Serbia, while promoting reconciliation among our people.
12. We hereby affirm, clearly, specifically, and irrevocably, that Kosovo shall be legally bound to comply with the provisions contained in this Declaration, including, especially, the obligations for it under the Ahtisaari Plan. In all of these matters, we shall act consistent with principles of international law and resolutions of the Security Council of the United Nations, including resolution 1244 (1999). We declare publicly that all states are entitled to rely upon this declaration, and appeal to them to extend to us their support and friendship.

D- 001
Pristina, 17 February 2008
President of the Assembly of Kosova
Jakup KRASNIQI

For their part, the Serbian authorities at all times deemed the unilateral declaration illegal because it infringed their sovereignty and territorial integrity.[139] As a reaction to the declaration of independence they brought in a draft resolution in the UN General Assembly requesting the ICJ 'to render an advisory opinion on the following question'[140]:

> Is the unilateral declaration of independence by the Provisional Institutions of Self-Government of Kosovo in accordance with international law?.[141]

[139]Intervention of Mr. Tadić (President of the Republic of Serbia), UN Doc. S/PV.5839, of 17 February 2008, 23, p. 4. Intervention of Mr. Jeremić (Minister for Foreign Affairs of Serbia), UN Doc. S/PV.5850, of 11 March 2008, 5, p. 2. Intervention of Mr. Jeremić (Minister for Foreign Affairs of Serbia), UN Doc. A/63/PV.22, of 8 October 2008, 15, p. 1.

[140]See 'Request for an advisory opinion of the International Court of Justice on whether the unilateral declaration of independence of Kosovo is in accordance with international law', UN Doc. A/63/L.2, of 23 September 2008, 1, at para. 5.

[141]'Draft resolution submitted by Serbia: Request for an advisory opinion of the International Court of Justice on whether the unilateral declaration of independence of Kosovo is in accordance with international law', UN Doc. A/63/L.2, of 23 September 2008, 1, at para. 5.

This resolution was adopted by the General Assembly as Resolution 63/3 by a vote of seventy-seven in favour to six against and seventy-four states abstaining from voting.[142]

When the ICJ received the request for an advisory opinion, it issued an order requesting member states to draw up reports on the legality of the declaration.[143] The deadline for these written reports was 17 April 2009. The ICJ delivered its Opinion on the case on 22 July 2010, concluding that the declaration of Independence by Kosovo:

> [. . .] did not violate general international law, Security Council resolution 1244 (1999) or the Constitutional Framework. Consequently the adoption of that declaration did not violate any applicable rule of international law.[144]

References

Ardault, K., C.-M. Arion, D. Gnamou-Petauton, and M. Yetongnon. 2006. L'administration internationale du territoire à l'épreuve du Kosovo et du Timor Oriental: la pratique à la recherche d'une théorie. *RBDI* 39: 300–383.

Baggett, T. 1999. Human Rights Abuses in Yugoslavia: To Bring an End to Political Oppression, the International Community Should Assist in Establishing and Independent Kosovo. *Ga.J. Int'l & Comp L.* 27: 45–59.

Balmond, L., and Ph. Weckel. 1999. Chronique des faits internationaux – OTAN/Yougoslavie. *RGDIP* 103: 733–741.

Bellamy, A.J. 2001. Human Wrongs in Kosovo: 1974–1999. In *The Kosovo Tragedy. The Human Rights Dimension*, ed. K. Booth, 105–126. London: Frank Cass.

Boisson de Chazournes, L. 1999. La Cour internationale de justice aux prises avec la crise du Kosovo: à propos de la demande en mesures conservatoires de la République fédérale de Yougoslavie. *AFDI* 45: 452–471.

Bothe, M., and T. Marauhn. 2001. UN Administration of Kosovo and East Timor: Concept, Legality and Limitations of Security Council-Mandated Trusteeship Administration. In *Kosovo and the International Community. A Legal Assessment*, ed. C. Tomuschat, 217–242. The Hague: Kluwer.

---

[142]The six countries voting against adoption of the resolution were Albania, the Marshall Islands, the Federated States of Micronesia, Nauru, Palau and the United States of America. UN Doc. A/63/PV.22, of 8 October 2008, 15, p. 10.

'Request for an advisory opinion of the International Court of Justice on whether the unilateral declaration of independence of Kosovo is in accordance with international law', UN Doc. A/RES/63/3, of 8 October 2008.

[143]See *Accordance with International Law of the Unilateral Declaration of Independence by the Provisional Institutions of Self-Government of Kosovo, Order of 17 October 2008, I.C.J. Reports 2008*, 409–410, p. 410, para. 2. http://www.icj-cij.org/docket/files/141/14813.pdf.

[144]*Accordance with International Law of the Unilateral Declaration of Independence in Respect of Kosovo, Advisory Opinion,* supra, Chap. 1, note 3.

The voting in the case was ten to four in support of the Opinion it delivered, Id. p. 452. In favour: President Owada, Judges Al-Khasawneh, Buergenthal, Simma, Abraham, Keith, Sepúlveda-Amor, Cançado Trindade, Yusuf, Greenwood. Against: Vice-President Tomka, Judges Koroma, Bennouna, Skotnikov.

Caplan, R. 1998. International Diplomacy and the Crisis in Kosovo. *International Affairs* 74: 745–761.

Cassese, A. 1999. *Ex iniuria jus oritur*. Are We Moving Towards International Legitimation of Forcible Humanitarian Countermeasures in the World Community? *EJIL* 10: 23–30.

Charney, J. 1999. Anticipatory Humanitarian Intervention in Kosovo. *AJIL* 93: 834–841.

Chinkin, C. 2000. The Legality of NATOs Action in the Former Republic of Yugoslavia (FRY) Under International Law. *ICLQ* 49: 910–925.

Christakis, T. 2011. The ICJ Advisory Opinion on Kosovo: Has International Law Something to Say About Secession? *LJIL* 24: 73–86.

Clark, H. 2000. *Civil Resistance in Kosovo*. London: Pluto Press.

Cox, M. 1998. The Dayton Agreement in Bosnia and Herzegovina: A Study of Implementation Strategies. *BYIL* 69: 201–243.

Daase, C. 2009. Die UN-Mission im Kosovo 1999-2008: zur Umsetzung völkerrechtlicher Standards für state-building durch eine internationale Übergangsverwaltung. *Friedens-Warte* 84: 83–124.

Daskalovski, Z. 2003. Claims to Kosovo: Nationalism and Self-Determination. In *Understanding the War in Kosovo*, ed. F. Bieber and Z. Daskalovski, 11–28. London: Frank Cass.

Dietrich, F. 2010. The Status of Kosovo - Reflections on the Legitimacy of Secession. *Ethics & Global Politics* 3: 123–142.

Dogo, M. 1992. Kosovo: Albanesi e Serbi: le radici del conflitto. In *Lungo di Cosenza*. Italia: Marco.

Duijzings, G., D. Janjić, and S. Maliqi, eds. 1996. *Kosovo – Kosova: Confrontation or Coexistence*. Nijmegen: Peace Research Centre, University of Nijmegen.

Erlanger, S. 1999. Crisis in the Balkans: The Overview; Russians Enter Kosovo Early but Moscow Calls It a Mistake; British Lead NATO'S Vanguard. *The New York Times*, June 12. http://www.nytimes.com/1999/06/12/world/crisis-balkans-overview-russians-enter-kosovo-early-but-moscow-calls-it-mistake.html.

Falk, A. 1999. Kosovo, World Order, and the Future of International Law. *AJIL* 93: 847–857.

Fox, G.H. 2008. *Humanitarian Occupation*. Cambridge: Cambridge University Press.

Friedrich, J. 2005. UNMIK in Kosovo: Struggling with Uncertainty. *Max Planck YUNL* 9: 225–293.

Garcia, T. 2000. La Mission d'administration intérimaire des Nations Unies au Kosovo (MINUK). *RGDIP* 104: 61–71.

Ghebali, V.-Y. 1999. Le Kosovo entre la guerre et la paix. *Déf. Nat.* 55: 62–79.

Gordon, M.R. 1999. Crisis in the Balkans: News Analysis; Kremlin vs. Its Army. *The New York Times*, June 12. http://www.nytimes.com/1999/06/12/world/crisis-in-the-balkans-news-analysis-kremlin-vs-its-army.html.

Gray, C. 2005. Legality of Use of Force (Serbia and Montenegro v. Belgium) (Serbia and Montenegro v. Canada) (Serbia and Montenegro v. France) (Serbia and Montenegro v. Germany) (Serbia and Montenegro v. Italy) (Serbia and Montenegro v. Netherlands) (Serbia and Montenegro v. Portugal) (Serbia and Montenegro v. United Kingdom): Preliminary Objections. Judgment of 15 December 2004. *ICLQ* 54: 787–794.

Greenwood, C. 1999. Humanitarian Intervention: The Case of Kosovo. *Finnish YIL* 10: 141–175.

Gutiérrez Espada, C. 2000. Uso de la fuerza, intervención humanitaria y libre determinación (La Guerra de Kosovo). *ADI* 16: 93–132.

Hehir, A. 2009. Independence, Intervention and Great Power Patronage: Kosovo, Georgia and the Contemporary Self-Determination Penumbra. *Amsterdam Law Forum* 1: 88–99.

Heldt, B., ed. 1992. *States in Armed Conflict 1990–1991*. Uppsala: Department of Peace and Conflict Research, Uppsala University.

Henkin, L. 1999. Kosovo and the Law of Humanitarian Intervention. *AJIL* 93: 824–828.

Herring, E. 2000. From Rambouillet to the Kosovo Accords: NATO's War Against Serbia and its Aftermath. *IJHR* 4: 224–245.

Heselhaus, S. 2000. Die Entscheidungen des IGH über den Erlass vorsorglicher Massnahmen in den Fällen Legality of Use of Force vom 2.Juni 1999. *AVR* 38: 328–375.

Hilpold, P. 2008. Das Kosovo-Problem – ein Testfall für das Völkerrecht. *ZaöRV/HJIL* 68: 779–801.

———. 2009a. The International Court of Justices Advisory Opinion on Kosovo: Perspectives of a Delicate Question. *ARIEL* 14: 259–310.

———. 2009b. The Kosovo Case and International Law: Looking for Applicable Theories. *Chinese JIL* 8: 47–61.

Hodge, C.C. 2000. Casual War: NATO's Intervention in Kosovo. *Ethics & International Affairs* 14: 39–54.

Hughes, J. 2013. Russia and the Secession of Kosovo: Power, Norms and the Failure of Multilateralism. *Europe-Asia Studies* 65: 992–1016.

Ingravallo, I. 2012. Kosovo after the ICJ Advisory Opinion: Towards a European Perspective? *ICLR* 14: 219–241.

Irmscher, T.H. 2001. The Legal Framework for the Activities of the United Nations Interim Administration Mission in Kosovo: The Charter, Human Rights, and the Law of Occupation. *German YIL* 44: 353–395.

Jaber, T. 2011. A Case for Kosovo? Self-determination and Secession in the 21st Century. *IJHR* 15: 926–947.

Janssen, J. 2015. *State-building in Kosovo. A Plural Policing Perspective*. Antwerp, Belgium: Maklu.

Jia, B.B. 2009. The Independence of Kosovo: A Unique Case of Secession? *Chinese JIL* 8: 27–46.

Judah, T. 2002. *Kosovo: War and Revenge*. 2nd ed. New Haven, CT: Yale University Press.

Ker-Lindsay, J. 2009. *Kosovo: The Path to Contested Statehood in the Balkans*. London: I.B. Tauris.

———. 2013. Preventing the Emergence of Self-determination as a Norm of Secession: An Assessment of Kosovo Unique Case Argument. *Europe-Asia Studies* 65: 837–856.

Kohen, M.G. 1999. L'emploi de la force et la crise du Kosovo: vers un nouveau désordre juridique international. *RBDI* 32: 122–148.

Kola, P. 2003. *The Search for Greater Albania*. London: C. Hurst & Co.

Krieger, H. 2001. *The Kosovo Conflict and International Law: An Analytical Documentation 1974–1999*. Cambridge: Cambridge University Press.

Kritsiotis, D. 2000. The Kosovo Crisis and NATOs Application of Armed Force Against the Federal Republic of Yugoslavia. *ICLQ* 49: 330–359.

Lagrange, E. 1999. La Mission intérimaire des Nations Unies au Kosovo, nouvel essai d'administration directe d'un territoire. *AFDI* 45: 335–370.

Lauwers, G., and S. Smis. 2000. New Dimensions of the Right to Self-determination: A Study of the International Response to the Kosovo Crisis. *N & EP* 6: 43–70.

Leight-Phippard, H. 1998. The Contact Group on (and in) Bosnia: An Exercise in Conflict Mediation? *International Journal* 53: 306–324.

Lowe, V. 2000. International Legal Issues Arising in the Kosovo Crisis. *ICLQ* 49: 934–943.

Lukic, R., A. Lynch, and SIPRI. 1996. *Europe from the Balkan to the Urals. The Disintegration of Yugoslavia and the Soviet Union*. Oxford: Oxford University Press.

Malcolm, N. 1998. *Kosovo: A Short History*. London: Macmillan.

Marxsen, C. 2014. The Crimea Crisis – An International Law Perspective. *ZaöRV/HJIL* 74: 367–391.

Mertus, J. 2001. Legitimizing the Use of Force in Kosovo. *Ethics & Intl A.* 15: 133–150.

Milano, E. 2003. Security Council Action in the Balkans: Reviewing the Legality of Kosovo's Territorial Status. *EJIL* 14: 999–1022.

Montaz, D. 2000. 'L'intervention d'humanité' de l'OTAN au Kosovo et la règle du non-recours à la force. *RICR/IRRC* 82: 89–101.

Muharremi, R. 2008. Kosovo's Declaration of Independence: Self-Determination and Sovereignty Revisited. *RCEEL* 33: 401–435.

Myers, S.L. 1999. Crisis in the Balkans: The Troops; British Forces Reaching Kosovo Capital Find Russians, and Confusion. *The New York Times*, June 13. http://www.nytimes.com/1999/06/13/world/crisis-balkans-troops-british-forces-reaching-kosovo-capital-find-russians.html.

Navarro Nijssen, H. 1999. *Kosovo: Causas y consecuencias de la sinrazón*. Barcelona: Asociación para las Naciones Unidas en España.
O'Connell, M.E. 2000. The UN, NATO and International Law after Kosovo. *HRQ* 22: 57–89.
Olleson, S. 2005. Killing Three Birds with One Stone? The Preliminary Objections Judgments of the International Court of Justice in the Legality of Use of Force Cases. *LJIL* 18: 237–255.
OSCE. 1999. *Kosovo/Kosova, As Seen, As Told: An Analysis of the Human Rightss Findings of the OSCE Kosovo Verification Mission, October 1998 to June 1999*. Warsaw: OSCE, Office for Democratic Institutions and Human Rights. http://www.osce.org/odihr/17772?download=true.
———. 2007. *OSCE Handbook*. Vienna: OSCE Press and Public Information Section. http://www.osce.org/files/documents/b/3/22624.pdf.
Perritt, H.H. 2008. *Kosovo Liberation Army: Inside Story of an Insurgency*. Baltimore, MD: University of Illinois Press.
———. 2009. *The Road to Independence for Kosovo: A Chronicle of the Ahtisaari Plan*. Cambridge: Cambridge University Press.
Pettifer, J. 2012. *The Kosova Liberation Army: Underground War to Balkan Insurgency, 1948–2001*. London: Hurst.
Phillips, D.L. 1996. Comprehensive Peace in the Balkans: The Kosovo Question. *HRQ* 18: 821–832.
Picone, P. 2000. La guerra del Kosovo e il diritto internazionale generale. *RDI* 83: 309–360.
Posen, B.R. 2000. The War for Kosovo. Serbia's Political-Military Strategy. *International Security* 24: 39–84.
Ramcharan, B. 1996. The Bosnian Peace Accords. *LJIL* 9: 131–140.
Ramón Chornet, C. 1997. Balance provisional de la aplicación de los Acuerdos de Dayton. *ADI* 13: 547–560.
Ronzitti, N. 1999. Raids aerei contro la Repubblica federale di Iugoslavia e Carta delle Nazioni Unite. *RDI* 82: 476–482.
Roux, M. 1992. *Les Albanais en Yougoslavie: minorité nationale, territoire et développement*. Paris: Éditions de la Maison des sciences de l'Homme.
———. 1999. *La guerre du Kosovo: dix clés pour comprendre*. Paris: La Découverte.
Rrecaj, B. 2011. A Contemporary Interpretation of the Principles of Sovereignty, Territorial Integrity and Self-Determination, and the Kosovo Conundrum. In *Kosovo: A Precedent?: The Declaration of Independence, the Advisory Opinion and Implications for Statehood, Self-Determination and Minority Rights*, ed. J. Summers, 109–141. Leiden, Boston: Martinus Nijhoff Publishers.
Santori, V. 2004. The United Nations Interim Mission in Kosovo and the Sovereignty and Territorial Integrity of the Federal Republic of Yugoslavia. In *Studi di diritto internazionale in onore di Gaetano Arangio-Ruiz*, vol. III, 1689–1721. Naples: Editoriale Scientifica.
Schmidt, F. 1993. Kosovo: The Time Bomb that has not Gone Off. *Radio Free Europe/Radio Liberty Research Report* 39: 21–29.
———. 1996. Teaching the Wrong Lesson in Kosovo. *Transition* 2: 37–39.
Schubert, P. 1997. *Zündstoff im Konfliktfeld des Balkan: Die albanische Frage*. Baden-Baden: Nomos Verlag.
Schwegmann, C. 2000. *The Contact Group and Its Impact on the European Institutional Structure*. Paris: Institute for Security Studies, Western European Union. http://www.iss.europa.eu/uploads/media/occ016.pdf.
Serra, G. 2008. The International Civil Administration in Kosovo: A Commentary on Some Major Legal Issues. *Italian YIL* 18: 63–87.
Shen, J. 2001. The ICJ's Jurisdiction in the 'Legality of Use of Force' Cases. In *International Law in the Post-Cold War World: Essays in Memory of Li Haopei*, 480–495. London, New York: Routledge.
Shifman, B. 1999. International Court of Justice: Cases Concerning Legality of Use of Force: No Provisional Measures against NATO Member States. *International Law FORUM du droit international* 1: 117–120.

Simma, B. 1999. NATO, the UN and the Use of Force: Legal Aspects. *EJIL* 10: 1–22.

Sollemberg, M., P. Wallensteen, and A. Jato. 1999. 1. Major armed conflicts. *SIPRI Yearbook 1999: Armaments, Disarmament, and International Security*: 15–25.

Strazzari, F. 1998. De Kosovo a Kosova, y vuelta a empezar. *Meridiano Ceri* 23: 4–11.

Šturanović, R., and J. Jelinčić, eds. 1989. *The Constitution of the Socialist Federal Republic of Yugoslavia*. Beograd: Jugoslovenski Pregled.

Suhrke, A., M. Barutciski, P. Sandison, and R. Garlock. 2000. *The Kosovo Refugee Crisis: An Independent Evaluation of the UNHCR's Emergency Preparedness and Response*, 159. Geneva: UNHCR, Evaluation and Policy Analysis Unit.

Sundhaussen, H. 1999. Kosovo: 'Himmlisches Reich' und irdischer Kriegsschauplatz: Kontroversen über Recht, Unrecht und Gerechtigkeit. *Südosteuropa* 48: 237–257.

Sur, S. 1999. L'affaire du Kosovo et le droit international points et contrepoints. *AFDI* 45: 280–291.

Talbott, S. 2002. *The Russia Hand. A Memoir of Presidential Diplomacy*. New York: Random House.

Troebst, S. 1997. Still Looking for an Answer to the 'Albanian Question. *Transition* 3: 24–27.

———. 1998. *Conflict in Kosovo: Failure of Prevention? An Analytical Documentation, 1992–1998*. Flensburg: European Centre for Minority Issues.

———. 1999a. Appendix 1C. The Kosovo Conflict. *SIPRI Yearbook 1999: Armaments, Disarmament, and International Security*: 47–62.

———. 1999b. Chronologie einer gescheiterten Prävention: vom Konflikt zum Krieg im Kosovo, 1989–1999. *Östeuropa* 49: 777–795.

———. 1999c. Conflict in Kosovo: Causes and Cures. An Analytical Documentation. In *The Southeast European Challenge. Ethnic Conflict and the International Response*, ed. H.-G. Ehrhart and A. Schnabel, 85–116. Baden-Baden: Nomos Verlag.

Velebit, V. 1999. Kosovo: A Case of Ethnic Change of Population. *East European Quarterly* 33: 177–194.

Vickers, M. 1998. *Between Serb and Albanian: A History of Kosovo*, 1998. London: Hurst.

Vidmar, J. 2011. Kosovo: Unilateral Secession and Multilateral State-Making. In *Kosovo: A Precedent?: The Declaration of Independence, the Advisory Opinion and Implications for Statehood, Self-Determination and Minority Rights*, ed. J. Summers, 143–177. Leiden, Boston: Martinus Nijhoff Publishers.

Vitucci, M. 2006. Has Pandora's Box Been Closed? The Decisions on the Legality of Use of Force Cases in Relation to the Status of the Federal Republic of Yugoslavia (Serbia and Montenegro) within the United Nations. *LJIL* 19: 105–127.

Von Carlowitz, L. 2003. UNMIK Lawmaking between Effective Peace Support and Internal Self-Determination. *AVR* 41: 336–393.

Warbrick, C. 2008. Kosovo: The Declaration of Independence. *ICLQ* 57: 675–690.

Weller, M. 1999a. *The Crisis in Kosovo 1989-1999, International Documents and Analysis*. Cambridge: Documents and Analysis Publishing.

———. 1999b. The Rambouillet Conference on Kosovo. *International Affairs* 75: 221–251.

———. 2009. *Contested Statehood: Kosovo's Struggle for Independence*. Oxford: Oxford University Press.

Westendorp, C. 1999. Kosovo: las lecciones de Bosnia. *Política Exterior* 70: 45–58.

Williams, P.R. 2003. Earned Sovereignty: The Road to Resolving the Conflict over Kosovo's Final Status. *DJILP* 31: 387–425.

Wilson, G. 2009. Self-Determination, Recognition and the Problem of Kosovo. *NILR* 56: 455–481.

Wippman, D. 2001. Kosovo and the Limits of International Law (NATOs Bombing of Kosovo Under International Law). *Fordham Intl L.J* 25: 129–150.

Yee, S. 2010. Notes on the International Court of Justice (Part 4): The Kosovo Advisory Opinion. *Chinese JIL* 9: 763–782.

Zappalà, S. 1999. Nuovi sviluppi in tema di uso della forza armata in relazione alle vicende del Kosovo. *RDI* 82: 975–1004.

Chapter 5
The Crimea's Declaration of Independence and Annexation to Russia in 2014

5.1 Calls for Independence and the Crisis of the Ukrainian State

Historically, Crimea is one of the cradles of Russian origin and identity, the site of Russian military glories and tragedies, a centre of cultural renewal, occupying a special place in the Russian heart.[1] Within the turbulent history of the region, the ceding at the behest of the Ukrainian Nikita Khrushchev of the Crimean Oblast to the Ukrainian Soviet Socialist Republic on 19 February 1954 may be seen as one of the roots of the present crisis in the Ukraine with regard to Crimea.[2]

As more than 200,000 Crimean Tartars, along with a large number of Greeks and Armenians, had been deported and Crimea was a truly Russian region, it was unusual for Nikita Khrushchev to make this 'symbolic gesture' in commemoration of the three hundredth anniversary of the Pereyaslav Agreement. According to the official interpretation of the Communist Party of the Soviet Union, this summed up the desire of Ukrainians and Russians to remain united.[3] In the Decree, the measure

---

[1]Cfr. Saluschev (2014), p. 37.

On the Siege of Sebastopol as a key event in the conclusion of the Crimean War and instance of 'Russian valour', *infra*, this chapter, note 14.

[2]Cfr. Decree (указ, *ukase*) of the Presidium of the Supreme Soviet 'On the Transfer of the Crimean Oblast'. The text of the Decree is in: 'Meeting of the Presidium of the Supreme Soviet of the Union of Soviet Socialist Republics', February 19, 1954, History and Public Policy Program Digital Archive, GARF. F.7523. Op.57. D.963, L1-10. Published in "Istoricheskii arkhiv," issue 1, Vol. 1 (1992). Translated for CWIHP by Gary Goldberg. digitalarchive.wilsoncenter.org/document/119638. It is possible to consult in the original Russian under the heading *zakony* the collection of texts adopted during the Soviet period and down to 1991 that relate to Crimea and Sebastopol en http://kro-krim.narod.ru/ZAKON/zakoni.htm.

[3]Cfr. Subtelny (2000), p. 135. Hilpold (2015), p. 241. As seen by Orest Subtelny, the Agreement has been subject to five major interpretations, as apart from that noted above it has been taken to be a 'personal union' between Muscovy and the Ukraine (Vasilii Sergeevich, 1910), 'personal

J. F. Escudero Espinosa, *Self-Determination and Humanitarian Secession in International Law of a Globalized World*,
https://doi.org/10.1007/978-3-319-72622-9_5

was justified 'taking into account the integral character of the economy, the territorial proximity and the close economic ties between Crimea Province and the Ukraine Republic'.[4]

It was an administratively logical measure, as the Ukraine provided much of the water, electricity and raw materials needed by Crimea.[5] Thus, a region that had formed a part of Russia, was gifted to the Ukraine in a way it was hoped 'will promote the further strengthening of the fraternal link between the Ukrainian and Russian peoples'.[6] However, the peninsula remained linked to Moscow and continued to be a centre of military production, of naval bases, and of resources.[7]

5.1.1 The Evolution of the Crimean Oblast into the Autonomous Republic of Crimea

The Crimean Oblast was turned into an Autonomous Soviet Socialist Republic by the Supreme Soviet of the Ukrainian Soviet Socialist Republic on 12 February 1991, after a referendum held the previous 20 January, in which 93% of the population voted "yes".[8] The disintegration of the Soviet Union meant that Crimea formed part of the Ukraine from its Declaration of Independence on 24 August 1991.[9] In the

---

subjugation' to the Tsar (Nikolai Diakonov, 1919), a 'form of vassalage' (Venedik Miakotin and Mykhailo Hrushevsky), or a 'military alliance' between Moscow and the Ukrainians (Viacheslav Lypynsky).

See: Basarab (1982), Ohloblyn (1954), Prokopovych (1955), Ukrainian Canadian Committee (1954).

[4]Decree (указ, *ukase*) of the Presidium of the Supreme Soviet 'On the transfer of the Crimean Oblast', supra, this chapter, note 2, at para. 1.

[5]Cfr. Stewart (1997), p. 15, http://www.dtic.mil/dtic/tr/fulltext/u2/a341002.pdf. Rudnytsky (1954), p. 28. Schwartz (1954), p. 2.

[6]Speech by Mikhail Tarasov, Chairman of the Presidium of the Supreme Soviet of the Russian Soviet Federative Socialist Republic, in the 'Meeting of the Presidium of the Supreme Soviet of the Union of Soviet Socialist Republics', February 19, 1954, History and Public Policy Program Digital Archive, GARF. F.7523. Op.57. D.963, L1-10. Published in "Istoricheskii arkhiv," Issue 1, Vol. 1 (1992). Translated for CWIHP by Gary Goldberg, http://digitalarchive.wilsoncenter.org/document/119638.

Cfr. Calamur (2014), http://www.npr.org/sections/parallels/2014/02/27/283481587/crimea-a-gift-to-ukraine-becomes-a-political-flash-point. Taylor (2014).

[7]Stewart (1997), p. 22.

[8]Cfr. Beissinger (2002), p. 197. Wilson (2014), p. 105.

[9]Cfr. Van den Driest (2015), p. 332.

The text is to be found in: http://static.rada.gov.ua/site/postanova_eng/Rres_Declaration_Independence_rev12.htm.

The Declaration of Independence was based on the results of the referendum on continuation of the Soviet Union held on 17 March in nine of the fifteen component republics of the Union. The opinion of some authors was that the referendum, having been boycotted by six republics could not constitute a legal basis for adopting the instruments liquidating the Soviet Union. This was also

referendum held some months later, 92% of those voting, with 84% participation, expressed clear support for independence throughout the new State, with the significant exception of Crimea and Sebastopol City, where the percentages in favour were 54 and 57% respectively, with turn-out being 60%.[10]

In an accord signed at Minsk on 8 December 1991, known as the Belavezha Agreement, the leaders of three of the four founder states that subscribed to the treaty creating the Union of Soviet Socialist Republics, Russian President Boris Yeltsin, Ukrainian President Leonid Kravchuk, and Belarusian Supreme Soviet Chairman Stanislav Shushkevich, declared the Union dissolved and the Commonwealth of Independent States (CIS) established.[11] On a basis of mutual recognition of respect for State sovereignty, the inalienable right to self-determination, the principles of equality and non-intervention in internal affairs, and of abstention from the use of force,[12] the fifth Article of the pact stated, that the countries involved would: 'acknowledge and respect each other's territorial integrity and the inviolability of existing borders within the Commonwealth'.[13]

On 21 December 1991, Russia, the Ukraine and all the other former Soviet republics except Georgia signed a protocol to the Belavezha Agreement in Alma Ata into which they incorporated as an annex the Alma Ata Declaration.[14] In the

---

stated by the State Duma or Federal Assembly of Russia in its Resolution 'On the Validity for the Russian Federation of the Results of a Referendum of the USSR on 17 March 1991 on the Issue of the Preservation of the USSR', done on 15 March 1996, No. 157-II GD, *Rossiyskaya Gazeta*, 20.3.1996 (Cfr. A. Salenko, 'Legal Aspects of the Dissolution of the Soviet Union in 1991 and Its Implications for the Reunification of Crimea with Russia in 2014', 75:1 *ZaöRV/HJIL* (2015), 141–166, p. 165). However, Art. 72 of the 1977 Constitution of the Soviet Union envisaged the right of Soviet Republic freely to withdraw from the USSR Moreover, Art. 80 laid down the right of Soviet Republics to keep up relations with other States, to conclude international treaties, to maintain diplomatic and consular representatives, and to participate in the activities of international organizations. This meant that not just the USSR, but each Soviet Republic, was a sovereign State and subject to international law enjoyed the same legal status. They formed a federation, but in Soviet literature it was termed a 'soft federation'. Thus, the Ukraine was a sovereign State before the formation of the USSR and throughout its existence, and continued to be an independent State after its dissolution (Cfr. Merezhko (2015), p. 168).

[10]Cfr. Delahunty (2015), p. 127. Nahaylo (1999), p. 419. Subtelny (2000), p. 583. 'Independence – over 90% vote yes in referendum; Kravchuk elected president of Ukraine', *The Ukrainian Weekly*, December 8, 1991, No. 49, Vol. LIX. http://www.ukrweekly.com/old/archive/1991/499101.shtml.

[11]'Armenia-Azarbaijan-Belarus-Kazakhstan-Kyrgyzstan-Moldova-Russia-Tajikistan-Turkmenistan-Uzbekistan-Ukraine: Agreements Establishing the Commonwealth of Independent States', 31:1 *ILM* (1992), 138–154, p. 143. 'Letter dated 12 December 1991 from the Permanent Representative of Belarus to the United Nations addressed to the Secretary-General', UN Doc. A/46/771, of 13 December 1991, 6, p. Annex II 'Agreement Establishing the Commonwealth of Independent States'.

[12]'Agreement establishing the Commonwealth of Independent States' signed at Minsk on 8 December 1991, at Preamble, para. 4.

[13]Id., at Art. 5.

[14]'Armenia-Azarbaijan-Belarus-Kazakhstan-Kyrgyzstan-Moldova-Russia-Tajikistan-Turkmenistan-Uzbekistan-Ukraine: Agreements Establishing the Commonwealth of Independent States', 31:1 *ILM* (1992), 138–154, p. 147. 'Letter dated 27 December 1991 from the Permanent

preamble to that Declaration, the signatory States jointly agreed to 'recognize and respect each other's territorial integrity and the inviolability of existing borders'.[15] So, during December 1991 Russia twice committed herself to respecting the current frontiers of the Ukraine which hence included Crimea.[16]

The years following the break-up of the Soviet Union, under the Presidency of Leonid Kravchuk (1991 to 1994), were marked by catastrophic developments in the economic situation, such that 70% of the population was at or below the poverty threshold.[17] The former Soviet élite set the course of events by failing to undertake necessary reforms and by establishing a sort of 'crony capitalism coupled with political oligarchy'.[18]

Any measures adopted were far from constituting a programme, being rather the outcome of struggles for power and of the use of the same old administrative methods.[19] Among the most controversial decisions, one that stood out was the mass imposition of the Ukrainian language throughout civil administration and education.[20]

The crisis brought with it angry social protests and the assumption of the Presidency in 1994 by Leonid Kuchma (1994 to 2005).[21] Kuchma cleverly blamed the problems of the economy on the march towards Ukrainianization and gained power with a promise to re-establish links with Russia and protect the Russian language.[22] His election slogan was: 'Russia and the Ukraine: Fewer Walls, More Bridges'.[23]

However, in reality he carried on with Ukrainianization and in foreign policy went further than his predecessor by signing an agreement for co-operation with NATO on 8 February 1994, making his country the first in the CIS to join the Partnership for Peace programme.[24] Kuchma declared that NATO was 'the only real

---

Representative of Belarus to the United Nations addressed to the Secretary-General', UN Doc. A/47/60, of 30 December 1991, 11, at Annex II 'Alma Ata Declaration'.

[15]'Alma Ata Declaration', at para. 3.

[16]Cfr. Delahunty (2015), p. 128, note 13.

[17]Cfr. Nahaylo (1999), p. 446. Yekelchyk (2007), pp. 193 and 198.

[18]Cfr. Åslund (2015), p. 4. Yekelchyk (2007), p. 193. According to this author: 'The only social group that found the situation to their liking was the new rich: a mixture of high government officials moonlighting as big-league traders and private businesspeople, who were often former Soviet industrial managers, Komsomol functionaries, or black marketeers', *id.*, p. 197.

[19]Cfr. Åslund (2015), pp. 60 and 61. Harasymiw (2002), p. 164. Harasymiw (2003), p. 323.

[20]Cfr. Armandon (2013), p. 57. Evers (2010), p. 223. Yekelchyk (2007), p. 200.

[21]Cfr. Subtelny (2000), p. 618. Yekelchyk (2007), p. 198.

[22]Cfr. Bowring (2005), p. 82. Yekelchyk (2007), p. 201.

[23]Cfr. Åslund (2015), p. 61.

[24]Cfr. Cfr. Yekelchyk (2007), p. 202. *NATO* (2006), p. 219, http://www.nato.int/docu/handbook/2006/hb-en-2006.pdf. Feldhusen (1999), pp. 119–138, 124.

The Partnership for Peace Framework Document was published by NATO at the 1994 Brussels summit. Text in 42:1 *NATO Review* (1994), p. 28.

guarantor of security on the continent'.[25] After a time the economic situation stabilized in the final years of the decade, thanks to considerable aid from the United States, the European Bank for Reconstruction and Development, the International Monetary Fund and Russia, and recovery began by 2000.[26]

The aspirations of Crimea were summed up in the adoption of the name Republic of Crimea in 1992. The movement for independence was channeled into the proclamation as a sovereign State and the adoption of a Constitution on 5 May 1992 by the Supreme Council.[27] At the same time, a referendum was called for 2 August that was finally not held, since the declaration of independence was deemed unconstitutional by the *Verkhovna Rada* of Ukraine.[28] The Supreme Council of Crimea rectified and modified the Constitution to incorporate a declaration that Crimea was a constituent part of the Ukraine and suspended the holding of the referendum.[29] However, at this same period the Supreme Soviet of Russia declared on 21 May that the 1954 Decree ceding Crimea was null and void, as it was deemed contrary to the Russian Constitution and legislation.[30]

The long-standing roots of many of the Russians living in Crimea, Russians constituting 67% of the population of 1.6 million in 1989,[31] explains why most of them did not wish to leave the peninsula after the break-up of the Soviet Union.[32] More than 50% of the Russians resident in Crimea had been born there and only 3% emigrated in 1989, this being the year with the largest outflow in the period from 1989 to 1995.[33]

The legislative reforms granting more autonomy to Crimea did not stop the Supreme Council from adopting decisions such as the approval of a flag and national anthem in 1992, the consolidation of institutions like the post of President of the Republic, and the holding of elections to this position in 1994.[34] The result was that the candidate of the Russian Bloc, Yuri Meshkov, won 72.9% of the votes in the

---

Later, in Madrid on 9 July 1997, a 'Charter on a Distinctive Partnership between Ukraine and the North Atlantic Treaty Organization' was signed http://www.nato.int/cps/en/natohq/official_texts_25457.htm?selectedLocale=en, and a 'Declaration to Complement the Charter' followed on 21 August 2009, http://www.nato.int/cps/en/natohq/official_texts_57045.htm. See Buffa (2010).

[25]Cfr. Zlenko (1997), p. 53.

[26]D'Anieri et al. (1999), 344 pp. Nahaylo (1999), p. 501. Yekelchyk (2007), pp. 205 and 208. Wilson (2015), p. 262.

[27]Cfr. Subtelny (2000), p. 609. Schmemann (1992a), http://www.nytimes.com/1992/05/06/world/crimea-parliament-votes-to-back-independence-from-ukraine.html.

[28]Cfr. Yekelchyk (2007), p. 195. Wydra (2004), p. 116.

[29]Cfr. Wydra (2004), p. 117.

[30]Cfr. Bowring (2005), p. 82. Solchanyk (1995), p. 7. Wydra (2004), p. 117. Schmemann (1992b), http://www.nytimes.com/1992/05/22/world/russia-votes-to-void-cession-of-crimea-to-ukraine.html.

[31]Cfr. Armandon (2013), p. 36.

[32]Cfr. Id., p. 40.

[33]Cfr. Id., pp. 40 and 41.

[34]*The Crimea: Chronicle of Separatism (1992–1995)* (1996), p. 28. Subtelny (2000), *passim*.

second round and among other measures held the referendum that had been postponed in 1992 and managed to re-establish the Constitution of 1992.[35]

Internal developments towards increasing tension between the President and the Supreme Council led this body to curtail the competencies of the President. As a response the President dissolved the Supreme Council.[36] In this context of institutional crisis, the *Verkhovna Rada* of the Ukraine intervened by passing a 'Law on the Autonomous Republic of Crimea' on 17 March 1995, reducing the autonomy of Crimea, repealing the 1992 Constitution and removing President Yuri Meshkov from office, in an atmosphere of some opposition.[37]

At the end of 1995, the Supreme Council voted a new Constitution, amended after 2 months, and approved by the Ukrainian *Verkhovna Rada* in April 1996 with major modifications arising from its running counter to the laws of the Ukraine in aspects such as Crimean citizenship, State symbols, control over core areas of Ministerial competence, property rights, State languages, and the name, which became the 'Autonomous Republic of Crimea'.[38]

5.1.2 The Intricate Relationship Between Russia and the Ukraine

Relations with Russia saw growing detente after the acceptance of the 'Treaty of Friendship, Co-operation, and Partnership between the Ukraine and the Russian Federation' (Treaty of Friendship), signed in in Kiev on 31 May 1997, which once again recognized the frontiers of the Ukraine and mutual respect for territorial integrity.[39] This was the culmination of nearly 6 years' negotiations and the reaching of other agreements on the division of the Black Sea Fleet and the status of its base in Sebastopol, which was ceded for 20 years, until 2017.[40] At the moment the Treaty of

[35]Cfr. Wydra (2004), p. 118.

[36]Cfr. Ibid.

[37]Cfr. Gartnett (1997), p. 27. Wolczuk (2002), p. 71. Wydra (2004), p. 116. 'Ukraine Moves to Oust Leader of Separatists', *The New York Times*, March 19, 1995. http://www.nytimes.com/1995/03/19/world/ukraine-moves-to-oust-leader-of-separatists.html.

[38]Cfr. Hilpold (2015), p. 244. Wolczuk (2002), p. 71. Wydra (2004), p. 119.

[39]Annex I to the 'Letter dated 6 June 1997 from the Permanent Representatives of the Russian Federation and the Ukraine to the United Nations addressed to the Secretary-General', UN Doc. A/52/174, 9 June 1997, p. 2. Cfr. Specter (1997), http://www.nytimes.com/1997/06/01/world/setting-past-aside-russia-and-ukraine-sign-friendship-treaty.html. Delahunty (2015), p. 128. Hilpold (2015), p. 243. Luchterhandt (2014), p. 137.

[40]In the 'Memorandum on Security Assurances in connection with Ukraine's Accession to the Treaty on the Non-Proliferation of Nuclear Weapons' (Budapest Memorandum), signed in Budapest on 5 December 1994, by the Ukraine, the United States, the United Kingdom, and the Russian Federation, basic guidelines were established to safeguard 'the independence and sovereignty and the existing borders of the Ukraine' (Art. 1 of the Budapest Memorandum). For the text, see Annex to 'Letter dated 7 December 1994 from the Permanent Representatives of the Russian Federation,

Friendship was concluded, some 40,000 Russian soldiers and sailors assigned to the Black Sea Fleet were still stationed in Crimea in the city of Sebastopol, seen as a symbol of 'Russian valour'.[41] Many Russians who had retired from the forces remained in the region, taking an active part in politics.[42] This was a clear indication of the intention of the Russian authorities to retain military bases in the States composing the CIS and to promote their military integration.[43] Likewise, defending the rights of Russians living outside Russia was one of the objectives mentioned in the programmes of the political parties contending elections to the State Duma on 17 December 1995, in which the Communist Party won an ample majority.[44]

The outcome of the bilateral negotiations was that Russia agreed to minimize its demands for the repayment of debt and the Ukraine consented to make minimal claims to Sebastopol.[45] Further, the Ukraine would make concessions in its Constitution relating to a limited presence of foreign forces in its territory and Russia

---

the Ukraine, the United Kingdom of Great Britain and Northern Ireland and the United States of America to the United Nations addressed to the Secretary-General', UN Doc. A/49/765-S/1994/1399, 19 December 1994, https://documents-dds-ny.un.org/doc/UNDOC/GEN/N94/507/64/pdf/N9450764.pdf?OpenElement. Cfr. Tancredi (2014c), p. 6, http://www.qil-qdi.org/wp-content/uploads/2014/05/CRIMEA_Tancredi_FINAL-1.pdf.

The set of Agreements between the Russian Federation and the Ukraine on the Parameters of Division of the Black Sea Fleet, on the Status and Conditions of the Presence of the Russian Black Sea Fleet in the Territory of the Ukraine, and on Payments Associated with the Division of the Black Sea Fleet and Its Presence in the Territory of the Ukraine were signed on 28 May 1997. Cfr. Gordon (1997), http://www.nytimes.com/1997/05/29/world/russia-and-ukraine-finally-reach-accord-on-black-sea-fleet.html.

Cfr. Stewart (1997), p. 8.

[41]Cfr. Id., p. 22. Gordon (1997).

During the Crimean War, in which the British and French Empires, together with the Kingdom of Sardinia, came to the aid of the Ottoman Empire against the Russian Empire, Sebastopol was besieged until 9 September 1855, when it fell into the hands of Franco-British troops after 11 months of siege. The outcome of this defeat was that Russia was obliged to sue for peace, this taking the form of the signing of a 'Peace Treaty Concerning the Termination of the Crimean War' ('Treaty of Paris') on 30 March 1856 (Grewe (1992), Vol. III/1: 1815–1945, 681, pp. 19–37). The siege of Sebastopol has been seen as a symbol of 'Russian valour' and as unequalled in military history (Cfr. Gorizontov (2012), pp. 65–94). See Von Todleben (1863), 2 Vol.

The fleet comprised a total of 400 vessels. Land and sea air forces amounted to some 400 aircraft, 126 of them bombers, and 85 combat helicopters. There were a total of 11 air bases in the peninsula. Land forces were made up of the Sebastopol brigade of marines, equipped with 100 combat vehicles, and the Simferopol motorized rifle division, with some 300 tanks and 600 combat vehicles. Additionally, there were numerous military store depots, arsenals of weapons, and training and manoeuvre grounds (Cfr. Kuzio (1995), p. 93).

[42]Cfr. Armandon (2013), p. 108. Gartnett (1997), p. 27. Kuzio (2012), p. 573.

[43]Cfr. Armandon (2013), p. 264. Jaworsky (1995), p. 137. Evers (2010), p. 237.

In mid campaign, on 14 September, the Russian President, Boris Yeltsin, adopted a ukase on Russia's strategic policies in relation to member States of the CIS in which it was stated that the territory of States emerging from the Soviet Union constituted a vital interest for Russia. Cfr. Armandon (2013), p. 265.

[44]Cfr. Armandon (2013), p. 264.

[45]Cfr. Stewart (1997), p. 50.

recognized the frontiers of the Ukraine and its territorial integrity, and agreed to supply it with natural gas.[46] So, once again in 1998 the Supreme Council adopted a fresh Constitution that was agreed by the Ukrainian *Verkhovna Rada* before the year's end.[47]

On the political stage, Kuchma's second mandate was marked by corruption, the scandal known as 'Kuchmagate', and presidential elections held in 2004, which ostensibly were won by the candidate Viktor Yanukovych, whose campaign was financed by Russia.[48] Nevertheless, the new President had to leave office shortly afterwards as a consequence of peaceful protests in favour of the opposition candidate Viktor Yushchenko, who had been the victim of an attempted poisoning because the results fell under suspicion of electoral fraud, this being termed the Orange Revolution.[49]

Inability to handle internal conflicts and the scandalous lifestyle of his family circle gradually eroded Yushchenko's reputation.[50] Finally, Viktor Yanukovych won the elections of 25 February 2010 and became President of the Ukraine with the support of the Party of Regions, largely composed of Russian speakers.[51] In the following months, the politics of the Ukraine and its national security policies were brought into line with those of Vladimir Putin in Russia.[52] Parliament was marginalized for the first time and policies of the Party of Regions of an authoritarian neo-Soviet nature were adopted, with the aim of preventing a second Orange Revolution.[53] In reality, the Russian leadership was trying to establish a regency in the Ukraine led by somebody under the thumb of Moscow.[54]

On these lines, 21 April 2010 saw the conclusion of an 'Agreement Governing the Presence of the Russian Black Sea Fleet in the Territory of the Ukraine' (Kharkiv

---

[46]Cfr. Article 2 of the *Treaty of Friendship*. Marxsen (2014), p. 371. Subtelny (2000), p. 599. Stewart (1997), p. 50.

[47]Cfr. Wydra (2004), p. 120.

[48]Cfr. Kuzio (2007), p. 42. Yekelchyk (2007), pp. 206 and 215.

[49]Cfr. Herron (2009), pp. 58–77. Kuzio (2005), p. 42. Wilson (2005), 232 pp. Åslund and McFaul (2006). Karatnycky (2005), pp. 35–52.

[50]Cfr. Åslund (2015), p. 81. Yekelchyk (2007), p. 221.

[51]Cfr. Kuzio (2012), p. 561.

[52]Cfr. Id., p. 559.

[53]Cfr. Ibid.

[54]During the NATO-Russia Council in Bucharest, in April 2008, Vladimir Putin said: 'The country obtained from Russia vast territories in what is now eastern and southern Ukraine.' and went on to argue that the 'Ukraine is home to as many as 17 million ethnic Russians. Who will dare to claim that we don't have any interests there? Southern Ukraine is entirely populated with ethnic Russians.' Cfr. Åslund (2015), p. 77. However, the census figures for Russians in the Ukraine in 2001 amounted to 8.3 million or 17.3% of the population and the sole region with a Russian ethnic majority was the Crimea. Cfr. Kuzio (2012), p. 559.

Accord), which renewed commitments until 2042.[55] Its authorization by the *Verkhovna Rada* was questioned as it violated the prohibition on the establishment of foreign bases envisaged by the 1996 Constitution, with the sole temporary exception for the Black Sea Fleet under the Treaty of Friendship, which was to run only until 2017.[56] However, renewal of the agreements brought with it détente in relations in Crimea, where Sebastopol 'ensures the geo-strategic balance in southern Russia',[57] and a reduction of 30% in the price of gas as a sweetener.[58] All the agreements were unilaterally abrogated by Russia on 31 March 2014.[59]

Viktor Yanukovych's continuance in power was a crucial strategic objective, as the opposition had declared its intention to annul the Kharkiv Accord, which some saw as criminal.[60] This was especially relevant for the 2015 presidential elections.[61]

---

[55] Marxsen (2014), p. 371.

[56] The Ukrainian Constitution, adopted under Ukrainian Law No. 254к/96-ВР, on 28 June 1996, lays down in Art. 17(7), within Chap. I (General Principles):

> The location of foreign military bases shall not be permitted in the territory of the Ukraine.

For its part, Chap. XV, on Transitional Provisions, has a Point 14 stating:

> The use of existing military bases in the territory of the Ukraine for the temporary stationing of foreign military formations is possible under the terms of the lease, by the procedure determined by the international treaties of Ukraine ratified by the Verkhovna Rada of Ukraine.

The original text is to be found on http://zakon4.rada.gov.ua/laws/show/en/254%D0%BA/96-%D0%B2%D1%80. The unofficial translation of the text of the Constitution of the Ukraine with amendments by Ukrainian Law No. 2222-IV of 8 December 2004 can be seen on the site of the European Commission for Democracy through Law (Venice Commission), 'Constitution of Ukraine as of 25 May 2006', 56, CDL (2006)070 https://web.archive.org/web/20120427012054/http://www.venice.coe.int/docs/2006/CDL%282006%29070-e.pdf. Amendments came into force on 1 January 2006.

Article 40 of the Treaty of Friendship, supra, note 467, included the following provision:

> This Treaty is concluded for a period of 10 years. It shall subsequently be extended automatically for further 10-year periods unless one of the High Contracting Parties notifies the other High Contracting Party in writing of its desire to terminate it at least six months before the expiry of the current 10-year period.

[57] Press Conference on 22 July in Moscow by Yuri Luzhkov, Mayor of Moscow until September 2010 and founder of the United Russia party, 'Controversial Moscow Mayor Back in Crimea', *KyivPost*, July 27, 2010, https://www.kyivpost.com/content/politics/controversial-moscow-mayor-back-in-crimea-75601.html?flavour=mobile.

[58] Cfr. Åslund (2015), p. 82.

[59] Cfr. 'State Duma approves denunciation of Russian-Ukrainian agreements on Black Sea Fleet', ITAR-TASS (31 March 2014), http://tass.ru/en/russia/725964.

[60] Cfr. Kuzio (2012), p. 574.

[61] Cfr. Ibid.

5.1.3 The Outbreak of Generalized Conflict in the Ukraine

It may be held that the recent crisis suffered by the Ukraine is closely linked to the tension stirred up by the process of attachment to one of two opposing poles, the EU and the Russian Federation.[62] After 3 years of negotiations promoted by Viktor Yushchenko, on 30 March 2012 the EU and the Ukraine had reached an agreement on what was intended to lead to a future association agreement for establishing a free trade zone. The 'Partnership and Co-operation Agreement between the European Communities and their Member States, and the Ukraine' of 14 June 1994 had come into force on 1 March 1998, constituting the framework within which relations between the Ukraine and the EU were developing.[63] However, during the EU-Ukraine annual summit meeting held in Evian in 2008, it was agreed that the partnership and co-operation agreement that had been in place for a decade would be replaced by an association agreement that would 'facilitate the deepening of our relations in all areas, strengthen political association and economic integration'.[64]

Against the backdrop of a catastrophic economic situation triggered by the 'predatory regime' of Viktor Yanukovych,[65] the most crucial events in the current situation go back to November 2013. At that point a crisis arose because of mass protests by young people in the Maidan Square against the decision to suspend the signing of the association agreement with the EU.[66] Protests developed into hostility towards President Yanukovych on the part of extreme right-wing nationalists hostile

---

[62]Cfr. Martucci (2014), p. 766.

[63]See 'Partnership and Cooperation Agreement between the European Communities and their Member States, and Ukraine - Protocol on mutual assistance between authorities in customs matters - Final Act - Joint Declarations - Exchange of Letters in relation to the establishment of companies - Declaration of the French Government', *OJEC* L49, 18.02.1998, 3–46.

Cfr. Martucci (2014), p. 766.

[64]Cfr. Twelfth annual EU-Ukraine Summit in Evian, France, 9 September 2008, at para. 5, http://delukr.sdv.com.ua/press_releases.html?id=48778.

[65]Cfr. Åslund (2015), p. 4.

[66]Cfr. Bismuth (2014), p. 720. Delahunty (2015), p. 129. Kuruneri-Millet (2014), p. 11. Marxsen (2014), p. 369. Ruys and Verlinden (2014), p. 325.

Prior to this a 'Partnership and Cooperation Agreement between the European Communities and their Member States, and Ukraine' had been concluded on 14 June 1994, entering into force in 1998 (*OJEC* L49, 18.02.1998, 3–46), this having a very different perspective (Cfr. Sciso (2014), p. 993). Negotiations for an Association Agreement were started by Viktor Yushchenko's Orange government in March 2007. The EU demanded the Ukraine become a member of the World Trade Organization (WTO) before a free trade agreement could be concluded. The Ukraine joined the WTO on 16 May 2008. The election of Viktor Yanukovych in February 2010 caused problems for the EU, because of his opposition to membership of NATO, although negotiations continued. At the end of 2010, the EU deemed Yanukovych's regime corrupt and authoritarian and insisted on the need to respect human rights and the rule of law. In March 2012 a start was made on drawing up a text and on 19 July 2012 it was put before Yanukovych and the EU leaders, but was not signed. Later, it was again proposed during the EU's Eastern Partnership summit in Vilnius on 28 and 29 November 2013, but in the end the Association Agreement was not signed. Cfr. Åslund (2015), pp. 43 and 44. Mantovani and Rickenbacher (2014), p. 46.

to both Russia and Europe and the generality of opponents of the regime demanding he resign together with the whole group of those in power.[67] As the nationalists confronted those in power, the populations of eastern and western regions mobilized and became more radical about their ethnic identity.[68]

Faced with this situation, Yanukovych met with Putin on 17 December 2013, concluding a series of agreements aimed at changing the situation in the Ukraine.[69] Under their terms, the Ukraine was given a loan sufficient for financing foreign transactions until the elections scheduled for March 2014, the price of gas was reduced for the first four months of 2014, sanctions on Ukrainian exports to Russia were lifted, co-operation in weapons manufacture was agreed, and the construction of a bridge over the disputed Kerch Strait of the Sea of Azov was mooted, this being likely to undermine Ukrainian sovereignty in Crimea.[70]

In an extraordinary session, and in violation of constitutional procedure, taking advantage of a mass absence of the 'Partija regioniv' (Party of Regions) in protest against the massacres, on 22 February the *Verkhovna Rada* removed Viktor Yanukovych from power. He fled to Russia, designated a provisional government, restored the Constitution as amended in 2004 and called elections for 25 May.[71] Although removing Yanukovych technically infringed the Constitution by not fulfilling all the requirements for a motion of no confidence, it cannot be seen as a 'coup d'état' or a violation of popular sovereignty.[72]

5.2 Russia's Intervention in Crimea

After the overthrow of Viktor Yanukovych, the new government met opposition from Vladimir Putin, who held it was illegitimate, the result of a 'coup d'état', and hostile to the ethnic Russian populations.[73] This stance was re-asserted in the

[67]Cfr. Kuruneri-Millet (2014), p. 13.

[68]Cfr. Ibid. Marxsen (2014), p. 367.

[69]Cfr. Åslund (2015), p. 104. Wilson (2014), p. 79. Mantovani and Rickenbacher (2014), p. 47.

[70]Cfr. Åslund (2015), p. 104.

[71]Cfr. Luchterhandt (2014), p. 140. Marxsen (2014), p. 369. Perpetua (2014), http://www.nytimes.com/video/world/europe/100000002728851/parliament-votes-to-dismiss-yanukovych.html. Saluschev (2014), p. 42. 'Yanukovich Tried to Flee Ukraine: Parliamentary Speaker', *The New York Times*, February 22, 2014, http://www.nytimes.com/reuters/2014/02/22/world/europe/22reuters-ukraine-crisis-plane.html. Urquhart (2014), http://www.theguardian.com/world/2014/feb/23/ukraine-crisis-yanukovych-tymoshenko-live-updates.

[72]Viktor Yanukovych's removal from power was voted by a large majority of the *Verkhovna Rada*. However, it did not fulfil the formal requirements laid down by Art. 108 to 111 of the Constitution. Article 111 requires the support of three-quarters of the members, in other words 338 of the total of 450, as well as a prior judgement by the Constitutional Court. Nevertheless, it was unanimously approved by the 328 representatives present. Sciso (2014), p. 994. Hilpold (2015), p. 250.

[73]Cfr. Bismuth (2014), p. 721. Repeated in successive speeches such as the 'Address by President of the Russian Federation on March 18, 2014', supra, Chap. 1, note 1. Among other passages, the

declarations of the Chairman of the State Duma Committee on Commonwealth of Independent States Affairs, Leonid Slutsky, in Simferopol.[74]

The fears of the population of Russian origin were heightened by measures adopted, such as the unwise prohibition of the Russian language and the establishment of Ukrainian as the sole official language, accompanied by the closure of Russian-medium schools.[75] In a territory like Crimea which was less intrinsically linked to the Ukraine, this stoked the fires of historical claims to independence. Moreover, in this case the population, who had had Russian passports for years, looked for protection from its ally against the extension of anti-Russian moves by the authorities in Kiev.[76]

At this time several steps were taken by the Russian authorities indicating there would progressively be integration into Russia. Among others, some of the more striking were the guaranteeing of citizenship, building work on the project for a bridge over the Kerch Strait,[77] and later, in April, the provision of resources for the northern frontier of Crimea, which the Russian Deputy Prime Minister, Dmitry Rogozin, now formed part of the frontier between Russia and the Ukraine.[78]

5.2.1 The Russian Military Presence in Crimea

During the following days, control points were set up by men wearing uniforms without rank or unit badges, whom the media nicknamed 'little green men',[79] similar units also occupying the Crimean Parliament and both international airports.[80] Although Vladimir Putin initially denied that they were Russian troops, claiming

following is striking: '[...] those who stood behind the latest events in Ukraine had a different agenda: they were preparing yet another government takeover; they wanted to seize power and would stop short of nothing. They resorted to terror, murder and riots. Nationalists, neo-Nazis, Russophobes and anti-Semites executed this coup', Intervention of Mr. Churkin (Russian Federation), UN Doc. S/PV.7125, of 3 March 2014, p. 3.

[74]Cfr. 'Top Lawmaker Vows to Protect Russians in Ukraine', *The New York Times*, February 25, 2014, http://www.nytimes.com/aponline/2014/02/25/world/europe/ap-eu-ukraine-russia.html.

[75]Cfr. Ayres (2014), http://www.csmonitor.com/World/Europe/2014/0228/Is-it-too-late-for-Kiev-to-woo-Russian-speaking-Ukraine. Van den Driest (2015), p. 332. Mantovani and Rickenbacher (2014), p. 47. Verkhovna Rada of Ukraine, 'On Principles of the State Language Policy', Law on Jule 3, 2012 No. 5029-VI, http://zakon4.rada.gov.ua/laws/anot/en/5029-17.

[76]Cfr. Kuruneri-Millet (2014), p. 13.

[77]Cfr. Reuters, 'Russia Says It Will Build Bridge to Crimea', *The New York Times*, March 3, 2014, http://www.nytimes.com/reuters/2014/03/03/world/europe/03reuters-ukraine-crisis-crimea-bridge.html.

[78]Cfr. Saluschev (2014), p. 43. 'Russian State Border in North Crimea to Be Fully Equipped in Early May', *ITAR TASS*, April 29, 2014, http://tass.ru/en/russia/729980.

[79]Cfr. Olson (2014), p. 20. Shevchenko (2014), http://www.bbc.com/news/world-europe-26532154.

[80]Cfr. Åslund (2015), p. 18. Reeves and Wallace (2015), p. 367.

they were 'local self-defence units' spontaneously emerging to protect ethnic Russians in Crimea,[81] he later admitted that Russian forces had indeed been se deployed in Crimea.[82]

In fact, on 27 February pro-Russian troops took control and the local government announced it had voted a proposal for a secession motion and for organizing a referendum. Everything points to the likelihood of these steps being taken under duress from the threat of armed force.[83]

In a letter of 28 February, the Ukraine asked for a meeting of the Security Council 'due to the deterioration of the situation in the Autonomous Republic of Crimea, Ukraine, which threatens the territorial integrity of Ukraine'.[84] The Security Council addressed the issue in its 1 March session, in which the Permanent Representative of Ukraine, Yuriy Sergeyev, requested it 'to react immediately in order to prevent intervention'.[85]

That same first day of March Viktor Yanukovych asked Russia to send troops: 'So in this regard I would call on the President of Russia, Mr. Putin, asking him to use the armed forces of the Russian Federation to establish legitimacy, peace, law and order, stability and defending the people of Ukraine'.[86] At the behest of the Russian President, the Russian Federation's Upper House (the Council of the Federation) authorized deployment of troops in the Ukraine with the aim of bringing the situation in the territories of Crimea under control.[87] The authorization was

[81]Cfr. Ruys and Verlinden (2014), p. 325. Sciso (2014), p. 995.

[82]Cfr. 'Putin Admits Russian Soldiers Were in Crimea, Slams West for Role in Ukraine Crisis', *Huffington Post*, 17 April 2014, www.huffingtonpost.com/2014/04/17/putin-ukraine_n_5165913.html.

[83]Cfr. Wilson (2014), p. 110. According to sources quoted by this author, the forces came from 'military units of the Black Sea Fleet; from the 'East' Chechen battalion, the 31st Guards brigade, the 22nd brigade of special GRU [Main Intelligence Directorate] troops, and other military units'. Cfr. Vasiliev (2014), http://www.opendemocracy.net/od-russia/andrei-vasiliev/crimean-%E2%80%98army%E2%80%99.

[84]Cfr. UN Doc. S/2014/136, of 28 February 2014.

Cfr. Douhan (2015), p. 199.

[85]Cfr. Intervention of Mr. Sergeyev, UN Doc. S/PV.7124, of 1 March 2014, p. 3.

The situation in Crimea was discussed in meetings 7123, of 28 February 2014; 7124, of 1 March 2014; 7125, of 3 March 2014; 7134, of 13 March 2014; 7138, of 15 March 2014; and 7144, of 19 March 2014.

[86]UN Doc. S/PV.7125, of 3 March 2014, p. 4. Cfr. Arcari (2014), p. 473. Lagerwall (2014), p. 60, http://www.qil-qdi.org/wp-content/uploads/2014/12/CRIMEA_Lagerwall_FINAL.pdf. 'Russia: Yanukovich Asks Putin for Russian Military in Ukraine', *The New York Times*, February 3, 2014, http://www.nytimes.com/reuters/2014/03/03/world/europe/03reuters-ukraine-crisis-un-russia.html.

[87]Cfr. Dmitriev (2014), p. 24. Marxsen (2014), p. 372. Olson (2014), p. 20. Smale and Erlanger (2014), http://www.nytimes.com/2014/03/02/world/europe/ukraine.html. 'Putin's letter on use of Russian army in Ukraine goes to upper house', 1 March 2014, http://tass.ru/en/russia/721586 (Use of Armed Forces Request).

During the following 2 days, Russian forces besieged or captured a number of Ukrainian military installations, forcing the surrender or defection of numerous land and naval units. Cfr. UN Doc.

revoked by Council of the Federation at the request of President Vladimir Putin on 25 June.[88]

5.2.2 The Holding of a Referendum and the Ensuing Declaration of Independence

The attempts at 'Ukrainianization', the hasty actions of the Ukrainian opposition, and the inability of the US and the EU to cannel protests effectively, seen by some as 'strategic mistakes',[89] triggered the secession of Crimea.[90] On 11 March, the *Verkhovna Rada* of the Autonomous Republic of Crimea and the Sebastopol City Council voted a 'Declaration of Independence of the Autonomous Republic of Crimea and Sebastopol' in which the intention was expressed of declaring Independence if the results of referendum to be held on 16 March were in favour of ado unification with the Russian Federation.[91]

At the urging of a group of 41 member States of the UN, headed by the US and including all 28 members of the EU, a draft resolution in respect of the referendum on the status of Crimea was submitted to the Security Council.[92] Basically, this proposed resolution was to declare that the referendum was not valid and could not constitute the basis for changing the status of Crimea.[93] The session on 15 March

---

S/PV.7125, of 3 March 2014, p. 2. 'Russian state flags raised over most of Ukrainian mil units, ships in Crimea', 22 March 2014, http://tass.ru/en/russia/724901.

[88]Cfr. 'Putin asks Federation Council to cancel resolution on use of Russian forces in Ukraine', 24 June 2014, http://tass.ru/en/russia/737498. 'Upper house speaker warns against statements which may hamper talks on Ukraine', *TASS Russian News Agency*, June 25, 2014, http://tass.ru/en/russia/737705. Sciso (2014), p. 995.

[89]Cfr. Saluschev (2014), p. 41.

[90]Cfr. Id., p. 38.

[91]Cfr. The Declaration, at para. 1, stated:

> 1. If a decision to become part of Russia is made at the referendum of the March 16, 2014, Crimea including the Autonomous Republic of Crimea and the city of Sevastopol will be announced an independent and sovereign state with a republican order.

The original text may be seen on: http://www.rada.crimea.ua/act/11726.

[92]The States sponsoring the draft resolution were Albania, Australia, Austria, Belgium, Bulgaria, Canada, Croatia, Cyprus, the Czech Republic, Denmark, Estonia, Finland, France, Georgia, Germany, Greece, Hungary, Iceland, Ireland, Italy, Japan, Latvia, Liechtenstein, Lithuania, Luxembourg, Malta, Montenegro, New Zealand, Norway, Poland, Portugal, the Republic of Moldova, Rumania, Slovakia, Slovenia, Spain, Sweden, Turkey, Ukraine, the Netherlands, the United Kingdom of Great Britain and Northern Ireland and the United States of America, UN Doc. S/2014/189, of 15 March 2014, https://documents-dds-ny.un.org/doc/UNDOC/GEN/N14/266/57/pdf/N1426657.pdf?OpenElement.

[93]The most crucial paragraphs of the draft resolution were the following:

> 4. Notes that Ukraine has not authorized the referendum on the status of Crimea;

discussed its adoption but the Permanent Representative of the Russian Federation, Vitaly Churkin, stated 'It is a secret to no one that the Russian Federation will vote against the draft resolution'[94] and 'to confirm that we will respect the will of the Crimean people during the referendum of 16 March'.[95] The result was 13 votes in favour, one vote against by Russia, and the abstention of China.[96]

Secession followed on the heles of the referendum, the legitimacy of which was challenged by the Ukrainian Government, the EU[97] and the US.[98] The results showed a turn-out of 83.1%, with 96.77% of those voting favourable to integration into Russia.[99] The two questions asked were controversial, as no provision was made for retaining the *status quo* prior to the referendum, so that Independence was effectively preordained.[100] Similarly, it was held under conditions of strong support and assistance from Russia, as Vladimir Putin declared: 'our goal was to ensure proper conditions for the people of Crimea to be able to freely express their will'.[101]

The next day, Crimea and Sebastopol declared their Independence as the Republic of Crimea,[102] which was recognized by the Russian Federation,[103] and requested

> 5. Declares that this referendum can have no validity, and cannot form the basis for any alteration of the status of Crimea; and calls upon all States, international organizations and specialized agencies not to recognize any alteration of the status of Crimea on the basis of this referendum and to refrain from any action or dealing that might be interpreted as recognizing any such altered status;

[94]Intervention of Mr. Churkin, UN Doc. S/PV.7138, of 15 March 2014, p. 2, para. 2.

[95]Id., p. 3, para. 10.

[96]Cfr. UN Doc. S/PV.7138, of 15 March 2014, p. 3.

[97]The results of the referendum were not recognized by the EU as noted in the Statement of the High Representative of the Union for Foreign Affairs and Security Policy, Catherine Ahston, of 12 May 2014. Cfr. 'Remarks by EU High Representative Catherine Ashton following the Foreign Affairs Council', Brussels, 12 May 2014, http://eeas.europa.eu/statements/docs/2014/140512_02_en.pdf.

Similarly, the EU condemned the accession of Crimea to Russia and consequent deterioration in the human rights situation in Crimea. Cfr. 'Statement of the Heads of State or Government on Ukraine', 27 May 2014, at para. 2, http://www.consilium.europa.eu/workarea/downloadAsset.aspx?id=15303.

[98]Cfr. Cimiotta (2014), p. 491.

[99]Cfr. Dmitriev (2014), p. 22. Van den Driest (2015), p. 333. Wilson (2014), p. 113.

[100]Cfr. Marxsen (2014), p. 382. Tancredi (2014a), p. 480.

[101]Cfr. Sciso (2014), p. 998. 'Direct Line with Vladimir Putin', 17 April 2014, http://en.kremlin.ru/events/president/news/20796.

[102]Cfr. 'Crimea Parliament Declares Independence from Ukraine Ahead of Referendum', 11 March 2014, https://www.rt.com/news/crimea-parliament-independence-ukraine-086/.

[103]Executive Order on Recognising the Republic of Crimea, signed on March 17, 2014, http://en.kremlin.ru/acts/news/20596. The Executive Order reads, in part:

> Given the declaration of will by the Crimean people in a nationwide referendum held on March 16, 2014, the Russian Federation is to recognise the Republic of Crimea as a sovereign and independent state, whose city of Sebastopol has a special status.

to be accepted as subjects of that Federation.[104] Effectively, the Sebastopol City Council requested incorporation into the Russian Federation as a federal city.[105] From this point onwards, Russian troops marched in openly and started driving Ukrainians out of the peninsula.[106]

Box 5.1 The Declaration of Independence of Crimea
Declaration of Independence of the Autonomous Republic of Crimea and Sebastopol

We, the members of the parliament of the Autonomous Republic of Crimea and the Sebastopol City Council, with regard to the charter of the United Nations and a whole range of other international documents and taking into consideration the confirmation of the status of Kosovo by the United Nations International Court of Justice on July 22, 2010, which says that unilateral declaration of independence by a part of the country does not violate any international norms, make this decision jointly:

1. If a decision to become part of Russia is made in the referendum of 16 March 2014, Crimea including the Autonomous Republic of Crimea and the city of Sebastopol will be announced an independent and sovereign state with a republican order.
2. The Republic of Crimea will be a democratic, lay and multinational state, with an obligation to maintain peace, international and intersectarian consent in its territory.
3. If the referendum brings the respective results, the Republic of Crimea as an independent and sovereign state will turn to the Russian Federation with the proposition to accept the Republic of Crimea on the basis of a respective interstate treaty into the Russian Federation as a new constituent entity of the Russian Federation.

Declaration approved by the Resolution of the Supreme Council of the Autonomous Republic of Crimea at the extraordinary plenary session on March 11, 2014 (signed by the Chairman of the Supreme Council of the Autonomous Republic of Crimea Vladimir Konstantinov) and by the Decision of the Sebastopol City Council at the extraordinary plenary session on 11 March 2014 (signed by the Chairman of the Sebastopol City Council Yury Doynikov).

As the crisis developed, reaction by the international community was unanimously expressed. Thus, the Parliamentary Assembly of the Council of Europe passed Resolution 1990 (2014) on 1 March 2014, where the question was minutely examined, the result of the referendum was not recognized, the use of force by Russia in Crimea was condemned and Russia's voting rights in the Assembly were suspended until the end of the session.[107] On similar lines, the North Atlantic

[104]Cfr. Herszenhorn (2014), http://www.nytimes.com/2014/03/17/world/europe/crimea-ukraine-secession-vote-referendum.html, http://kremlin.ru/events/president/news/20605.

[105]Cfr. Herszenhorn and Cowell (2014), http://www.nytimes.com/2014/03/18/world/europe/european-union-ukraine.html?hpw&rref=world&_r=1.

[106]Cfr. Marxsen (2014), p. 369. Herszenhorn et al. (2014), http://www.nytimes.com/2014/03/23/world/europe/ukraine.html?_r=0. Reeves and Wallace (2015), p. 378.

[107]See COE Doc. Resolution 1990 (2014), 'Reconsideration on Substantive Grounds of the Previously Ratified Credentials of the Russian Delegation', at para. 15, was passed by 145 for, 21 against, and 22 abstained http://assembly.coe.int/nw/xml/XRef/X2H-Xref-ViewPDF.asp?FileID=20882&lang=en.

Council issued a statement on the situation in the Ukraine on 2 March, in which it 'condemns the Russian Federation's military escalation in Crimea and expresses its grave concern regarding the authorisation by the Russian Parliament to use the armed forces of the Russian Federation on the territory of Ukraine'.[108] Likewise the G-7 nations condemned the 'Russian Federation's clear violation of the sovereignty and territorial integrity of Ukraine, in contravention of Russia's obligations under the UN Charter and its 1997 basing agreement with Ukraine'.[109]

5.2.3 *The Accession of Crimea to the Russian Federation*

On 18 March, the Republic of Crimea and the federal city of Sebastopol signed an agreement to join the Russian Federation.[110] In a speech President Putin stated that the 'Crimea is our common historical legacy and a very important factor in regional stability. And this strategic territory should be part of a strong and stable sovereignty, which today can only be Russian'.[111] However, Crimea was Russian for 73 years, from the Crimean War in 1853 until 1917, when it became an independent Soviet Republic, and from 1945 until 1954, whilst it was Ukrainian for the 60 years from

---

The condemnation of Russia's actions in relation to Crimea was expressed in the following terms in paragraph 3:

> The Assembly considers that the actions of the Russian Federation leading up to the annexation of Crimea, and in particular the military occupation of the Ukrainian territory and the threat of the use of military force, the recognition of the results of the illegal so-called referendum and subsequent annexation of Crimea into the Russian Federation constitute, beyond any doubt, a grave violation of international law, including of the United Nations Charter and the Organization for Security and Co-operation in Europe (OSCE) Helsinki Final Act.

[108] 'North Atlantic Council Statement on the Situation in Ukraine', Press Release (2014) 033, http://www.nato.int/cps/en/natolive/official_texts_107681.htm?selectedLocale=en. See also the statement by NATO Secretary-General Anders Fogh Rasmussen: 'What Russia is doing now in Ukraine violates the principles of the United Nations Charter. It threatens peace and security in Europe. Russia must stop its military activities and its threats', www.nato.int/cps/en/natolive/opinions_107663.htm.

[109] 'Statement by the G-7 Nations', Ottawa, 2 March 2014, http://news.gc.ca/web/article-en.do?nid=820669.

[110] Cfr. 'Agreement on the Accession of the Republic of Crimea to the Russian Federation submitted to State Duma for ratification', 19 March 2014, http://en.kremlin.ru/acts/news/20616. 'Treaty between the Russian Federation and the Republic of Crimea on the Acceptance of the Republic of Crimea into the Russian Federation and on Creation of New Federative Entities within the Russian Federation', signed on 18 March 2014 in Moscow. The text can be found on the site http://www.kremlin.ru/events/president/news/20605, and as not official translation in the Annex of the Pronin (2015), p. 137, http://www.russianlawjournal.org/index.php/jour/article/view/72/78. Sciso (2014), p. 998.

[111] 'Address by President of the Russian Federation on March 18, 2014', supra, Chap. 1, note 1, at para. 50.

1954 to 2014, 'which isn't so different'.[112] The next day, groups of demonstrators and Russian troops and threw Ukrainian troops out of their bases, the Ukraine stating that it was withdrawing them from Crimean territory.[113]

Accession was completed on 21 March with the signing of two federal laws by President Vladimir Putin.[114] This was the very same day that the association agreement between the Ukraine and the EU was signed, and establishing that a Deep and Comprehensive Free Trade Area was to be a vital element of the association agreement.[115]

For its part, the General Assembly of the UN in its session of 27 March, passed Resolution 68/262 co-sponsored by Canada, Costa Rica, Germany, Lithuania, Poland, the Ukraine and the US on the 'Territorial Integrity of Ukraine'.[116] This stated that 'the referendum held in the Autonomous Republic of Crimea and the city of Sebastopol on 16 March 2014, having no validity, cannot form the basis for any alteration of the status of the Autonomous Republic of Crimea or of the city of Sebastopol'.[117] The text gained one hundred votes in favour, eleven against, and fifty-eight abstentions,[118] at first sight a majority in favour of nearly two-thirds of the States voting, although in fact only 59% of the States represented in the meeting, and 51% of member States actually supported the resolution, so that its impact was somewhat limited.[119] During the debates, various States condemned the Russian intervention as a breach of the Ukraine's sovereignty and territorial integrity, as a 'use of force', or as an act of 'aggression'.[120]

---

[112]Wilson (2014), p. 100.

[113]Cfr. Herszenhorn and Kramer (2014), http://www.nytimes.com/2014/03/20/world/europe/crimea.html. 'Ukraine 'Preparing Withdrawal of Troops from Crimea'', *BBC News*, March 19, 2014, http://www.bbc.com/news/world-europe-26656617. Reeves and Wallace (2015), p. 378.

[114]Vladimir Putin signed a 'Federal Constitutional Law on Admitting to the Russian Federation the Republic of Crimea and Establishing within the Russian Federation the New Constituent Entities of the Republic of Crimea and the City of Federal Importance Sebastopol', and a 'Federal Law on Ratifying the Agreement between the Russian Federation and the Republic of Crimea on Admitting to the Russian Federation the Republic of Crimea and Establishing within the Russian Federation New Constituent Entities'. Cfr. 'Laws on admitting Crimea and Sevastopol to the Russian Federation', March 21, 2014, http://en.kremlin.ru/acts/news/20625. Milano (2014), p. 35.

[115]'European Agreement Between the European Union and its Member States, of the one part, and Ukraine, of the other part', *OJEU* L 161, 29.5.2014, pp. 3-2135. See, 'A Look at the EU-Ukraine Association Agreement', European Union External Action 2012, http://eeas.europa.eu/top_stories/2012/140912_ukraine_en.htm.

[116]Cfr. UN Doc. A/68/L.39 and Add.1, of 24 March 2014.

[117]Resolution on 'Territorial Integrity of Ukraine', UN Doc. A/RES/68/262, of 27 March 2014, at para. 5.

[118]Cfr. UN Doc. A/68/PV.80, of 27 March 2014, p. 17.

The States voting against were: Armenia, Belarus, Bolivia, Cuba, Democratic People's Republic of Korea, Nicaragua, the Russian Federation, the Sudan, the Syrian Arab Republic, Venezuela, and Zimbabwe.

[119]Cfr. Douhan (2015), p. 201.

[120]Cfr. UN Doc. A/68/PV.80, of 27 March 2014, pp. 1–2 (Ukraine: 'act of aggression'), 5 (European Union: 'acts of aggression'), 5–6 (United States: 'occupation'), 7 (Liechtenstein, referring to the

Together with many other internal measures, on 3 April the Moscow government sent a diplomatic note to the Ukraine on the termination of agreements relating to the deployment of the Russian Federation's Black Sea Fleet in Ukrainian territory.[121] The Moscow government deemed the bases no longer to be situated in the Ukraine, so that there was no cause to continue observing agreements that should be seen as ended.[122]

One month after the referendum, the State Council of Crimea approved a new constitution for the Republic of Crimea, with 88% of the votes in favour, in which the inseparable unity of the Russian Federation is asserted.[123] On that same date, 11 April, an amendment was made to the existing 1993 Russian Constitution so as to include the Republic of Crimea and the federal city of Sebastopol in the list of the 'constituent entities of the Russian Federation'.[124]

On 15 April, the *Verkhovna Rada* declared that the Autonomous Republic of Crimea and Sebastopol were under 'provisional occupation by the Russian military' and asserted that the territories were 'inalienable parts of the Ukraine'.[125] All goes to

---

prohibition on the threat or use of force and to the Kampala resolution on the ICC's Definition of aggression), 8 (Costa Rica: 'illegitimate violation by force of Ukraine's territorial integrity'), 9 (Canada: 'illegal military occupation', 'aggression'), 10 (Japan), 12 (Iceland), 14 (Norway, Cyprus), 19 (Singapore).

[121]Cfr. 'A Proposal to Terminate a Number of Russia-Ukrainian Agreements Submitted to the State Duma', March 28, 2014, http://en.kremlin.ru/acts/news/20654. Wilson (2014), p. 116.

See supra, Sect. 5.1.2, note 40.

[122]The termination is based on Art. 61 and 62 of the 1969 Vienna Convention on the Law of Treaties relating to the occurrence of 'supervening impossibility of performance' and 'fundamental change of circumstances'. 1115 *UNTS* (1980), No. 18232, 331-512. Also in UN Doc. A/CONF.39/11/Add.2, 287–301.

This is an interpretation in accordance with Soviet doctrine on international law. During a press conference held on 4 March in Novo-Ogaryovo, Vladimir Putin consistently declared that there had been a revolution in the Ukraine, so there was a new State with which Russia had not made any agreements (Cfr. Marxsen (2014), p. 371).

> Yes, but if this is revolution, what does this mean? In such a case it is hard not to agree with some of our experts who say that a new state is now emerging in this territory. This is just like what happened when the Russian Empire collapsed after the 1917 revolution and a new state emerged. And this would be a new state with which we have signed no binding agreements,

V. Putin, 'Vladimir Putin answered journalists' questions on the situation in Ukraine', March 4, 2014, http://en.kremlin.ru/events/president/transcripts/20366.

[123]Cfr. 'Crimean Constitution comes into legal force', *The Voice of Russia*, April 12, 2014, http://sputniknews.com/voiceofrussia/news/2014_04_12/Crimean-Constitution-comes-into-legal-force-7799/.

[124]Cfr. Constitution of the Russian Federation, adopted on 12 December 1993, at Art. 65(1), http://constitution.kremlin.ru/. 'Russia Amends Constitution to Include Crimea, Sevastopol', *Sputnik International*, April 11, 2014, http://sputniknews.com/russia/20140411/189160173.html.

[125]Cfr. 'Ukraine's Parliament Declares Crimea, Sevastopol 'Occupied Territory'', *Sputnik International*, April 15, 2014, http://sputniknews.com/world/20140415/189236902.html. The *Verkhovna Rada* of Ukraine adopted the Resolution 'On the Statement of the Verkhovna Rada of Ukraine 'On

show that Russian troops played a major part in gaining control over Crimea and in besieging Ukrainian military units, although it is hard to be precise about the exact moment when their deployment began.[126]

In a context of negotiations aimed at bringing to a close the Ukrainian crisis, which in early April had been extended by pro-Russian and anti-government groups to other regions, especially parts of the Oblasts of Donetsk, Luhansk and Kharkiv, the US, the EU, Russia and the Ukraine agreed to meet in Geneva on 17 April.[127] Discussions culminated in the acceptance of a document termed the 'Geneva Statement on Ukraine', in which all agreed as to the steps needed to 'de-escalate tensions and restore security for all citizens'.[128] Sadly, as noted by the Under-Secretary-General for Political Affairs of the UN, Jeffrey Feltman, 'the situation in parts of eastern and southern Ukraine continues to deteriorate'.[129]

The secessionist movement has been seen as not arising from any internal rebellion, but as a real military aggression by Russia in which the participants were not just local military forces, but also Russian regular troops and mercenaries.[130] Vladimir Putin alone knows if he had a master plan to move into the eastern Ukraine after annexing Crimea.[131] However, others say that what happened should be understood as an outcome of the links between the Russian people and the peninsula combined with nationalistic Ukrainian policies that alienated the Russian community.[132] What seems clear is that the operation in Crimea, with its twofold structure as what is known as 'hybrid war', was highly successful.[133]

---

the initiative of international negotiations on de-escalation of situation around Ukraine', April 16, 2014, http://iportal.rada.gov.ua/en/news/News/page/en/news/News/91700.html.

[126]Cfr. Marxsen (2014), p. 370.

[127]Cfr. Christakis (2014), p. 734. Mantovani and Rickenbacher (2014), p. 49.

[128]Cfr. Ruys and Verlinden (2014), p. 328. Christakis (2014), p. 734. 'Text of Joint Diplomatic Statement on Ukraine', *The New York Times*, April 17, 2014, http://www.nytimes.com/2014/04/18/world/europe/text-of-joint-diplomatic-statement-on-ukraine.html?_r=0.

The full text of the Joint Statement is on the websites of External Action of the European Union http://www.eeas.europa.eu/statements/docs/2014/140417_01_en.pdf, and of the US Department of State http://www.state.gov/r/pa/prs/ps/2014/04/224957.htm.

[129]Intervention of Mr. Feltman (Under-Secretary-General for Political Affairs), UN Doc. S/PV.7165, of April 29, 2014, p. 2.

[130]Cfr. Åslund (2015), p. 19.

[131]Cfr. Wilson (2015), p. 117.

[132]Cfr. Saluschev (2014), p. 44.

[133]Cfr. Wilson (2015), p. 117.

Faced with the increasing complexity of contemporary conflicts, some American academics, particularly Frank G. Hoffman, have proposed the expression 'hybrid war', defined as follows: 'Hybrid Wars can be conducted by both states and a variety of non-state actors. *Hybrid Wars incorporate a range of different modes of warfare, including conventional capabilities, irregular tactics and formations, terrorist acts including indiscriminate violence and coercion, and criminal disorder*' (Hoffman (2007), p. 14). On this idea, Michael Swetnam notes 'we are entering a time when multiple types of warfare will be used simultaneously by flexible and sophisticated adversaries. These adversaries understand that successful conflict takes on a variety of forms that are designed to fit one's goals at that particular time [...] Non-state actors may mostly employ irregular

It is definitely the case that in the end the new President Petro Poroshenko and Vladimir Putin on 5 September came to a cease-fire agreement called the 'Minsk Protocol'.[134]

References

Arcari, M. 2014. Violazione del divieto di uso della forza, aggressione o attacco armato in relazione all'intervento militare della Russia in Crimea? *DUDI* 8: 473–479.

Armandon, E. 2013. *La Crimée entre la Russie et Ukraine. Un conflit qui n'a pas eu lieu*. Bruxelles: Bruylant.

Åslund, A. 2015. *Ukraine: What Went Wrong and How to Fix It*. Washington: Peterson Institute for International Economics.

Åslund, A., and M. McFaul, eds. 2006. *Revolution in Orange: The Origins of Ukraine's Democratic Breakthrough*. Washington: Carnegie Endowment for International Peace.

Ayres, S. 2014. Is it too late for Kiev to woo Russian-speaking Ukraine?. *The Christian Science Monitor*, February 28. http://www.csmonitor.com/World/Europe/2014/0228/Is-it-too-late-for-Kiev-to-woo-Russian-speaking-Ukraine.

Basarab, J. 1982. *Pereislav 1654: A Historiographical Study*. Edmonton: Canadian Institute of Ukrainian Studies, University of Alberta.

Beissinger, M.R. 2002. *Nationalist Mobilization and the Collapse of the Soviet State*. Cambridge: Cambridge University Press.

Bismuth, R. 2014. Odysée dans le conundrum des réactions décentralisées à l'illicite. *JDI* 141: 719–731.

---

forms of warfare, but will clearly support, encourage, and participate in conventional conflict if it serves their ends (Swetnam (2007), p. 5, http://www.potomacinstitute.org/images/stories/publications/potomac_hybridwar_0108.pdf.

In an attempt to sharpen definition of the concept, Josef Schroefl and Stuart J. Kaufman suggested a deeper approach looking not just at the means used but also the sorts of participant involved, political, social and financial factors, the varying motives, and failure to observe International humanitarian law. Cfr. Schroefl and Kaufman (2014), p. 867.

[134]The 'Protocol on the Results of Consultations of the Trilateral Contact Group' which met in Minsk on 5 September 2014 were signed by the Swiss diplomat Heidi Tagliavini as representative of the OSCE, the former President of the Ukraine Leonid Kuchma as the Ukrainian representative, the Russian Ambassador to the Ukraine Mikhail Zurabov as the Russian representative, and the leaders of the Donetsk People's Republic (*Donets'ka Narodna Respublika*, DNR) and the Luhansk People's Republic (*Luganskaya Narodnaya Respublika*, LNR), Alexander Zakarchenko and Igor Plotnitski http://mfa.gov.ua/en/news-feeds/foreign-offices-news/27596-protocolon-the-results-of-consultations-of-the-trilateral-contact-group-minsk-05092014. The official text in Russian is on http://www.osce.org/ru/home/123258?download=true. The agreement was expanded by a Memorandum of 19 September 2014 outlining the parameters for the implementation of commitments of the Minsk Protocol of 5 September 2014, clarifying the application of the Protocol, the text of which is available only in Russian on http://www.osce.org/ru/home/123807?download=true.

When the Minsk Protocol collapsed, a summit held on 11 and 12 February 2015 adopted a new Package of Measures for the Implementation of the Minsk Agreements, in order to end the confrontations in the Donbass region. The official text in Russian is on: http://www.osce.org/ru/cio/140221?download=true. The English version is on: http://peacemaker.un.org/sites/peacemaker.un.org/files/UA_150212_MinskAgreement_en.pdf.

Bowring, B. 2005. The Crimean Autonomy: Innovation or Anomaly. In *Autonomy, Self-Governance and Conflict Resolution*, ed. M. Weller and S. Wolff, 75–97. London; New York: Routledge.
Buffa, D.G. 2010. A Proposed Remedy for the Dilemma of Innumerable Futures: Ukraine, Russia, and NATO Membership. *Brook. J. Int'l L.* 35: 593–626.
Calamur, K. 2014. Crimea: A Gift to Ukraine Becomes a Political Flash Point'. *NPR*, February, 27. http://www.npr.org/sections/parallels/2014/02/27/283481587/crimea-a-gift-to-ukraine-becomes-a-political-flash-point.
Christakis, T. 2014. Les conflits de sécession en Crimée et dans l'Est de l'Ukraine et le droit international (The Conflicts of Secession in Crimea and Eastern Ukraine and International Law). *JDI* 141: 733–764.
Cimiotta, E. 2014. Le reazioni alla 'sottrazione' della Crimea all'Ucraina. Quali garanzie del diritto internazionale di fronte a gravi illeciti imputati a grandi potenze? *DUDI* 8: 491–504.
D'Anieri, P., R. Kravchuk, and T. Kuzio, eds. 1999. *Politics and Society in Ukraine*. Boulder: Westview Press.
Delahunty, R. 2015. The Crimean Crisis, Legal Studies Research Paper Series. *University of St. Thomas Journal of Law and Public Policy* 9: 125–168.
Dmitriev, Y.A. 2014. Crimea as a Bone of Contention Between Russia, the European Union and the USA. *ПРАВО И ЖИЗНЬ Независимый научно-правовой журнал* 189: 22–50.
Douhan, A.F. 2015. International Organizations and Settlement of the Conflict in Ukraine. *ZaöRV/HJIL* 75: 195–214.
Evers, F. 2010. Damaged Prospects/Damaged Dialogue in Ukraine and Crimea. The Current Situation in Ukraine and Future Co-operation with the OSCE. *OSCE Yearbook* 16: 221–243.
Feldhusen, A. 1999. 'The 'Russian Factor' in Ukrainian Foreign Policy'. *Fletcher Forum of World Affairs* 23 (2): 119–138.
Gartnett, S.W. 1997. *The Keystone in the Arch: Ukraine in the Emerging Security Environment of Central and Eastern Europe*. Washington, D.C.: The Carnegie Endowment for International Peace.
Gordon, M.R. 1997. Russia and Ukraine Finally Reach Accord on Black Sea Fleet. *The New York Times*, May 29. http://www.nytimes.com/1997/05/29/world/russia-and-ukraine-finally-reach-accord-on-black-sea-fleet.html.
Gorizontov, L.E. 2012. The Crimean War as a Test of Russia's Imperial Durability. *Russian Studies in History* 51: 65–94.
Grewe, W.G., ed. 1992. *Fontes Historiae Iuris Gentium. Quellen zur Geschichte des Völkerrechts/Sources Relating to the History of the Law of Nations*. Berlin; New York: Walter de Gruyter.
Harasymiw, B. 2002. *Post-Communist Ukraine*. Edmonton: Canadian Institute of Ukrainian Studies Press.
———. 2003. Policing, Democratization and Political Leadership in Postcommunist Ukraine. *Canadian Journal of Political Science/Revue canadienne de science politique* 36: 319–340.
Herron, E.S. 2009. State Institutions, Political Context and Parliamentary Election Legislation in Ukraine, 2000–2006. In *Democratic Revolution in Ukraine: From Kuchmagate to Orange Revolution*, ed. T. Kuzio, 58–77. London; New York: Routledge.
Herszenhorn, D.M. 2014. Crimea Votes to Secede From Ukraine as Russian Troops Keep Watch. *The New York Times*, March 16. http://www.nytimes.com/2014/03/17/world/europe/crimea-ukraine-secession-vote-referendum.html.
Herszenhorn, D.M., and A. Cowell. 2014. Lawmakers in Crimea Move Swiftly to Split From Ukraine. *The New York Times*, March 17. http://www.nytimes.com/2014/03/18/world/europe/european-union-ukraine.html?hpw&rref=world&_r=1.
Herszenhorn, D.M., and A.E. Kramer. 2014. Ukraine Plans to Withdraw Troops from Russia-Occupied Crimea. *The New York Times*, March 19. http://www.nytimes.com/2014/03/20/world/europe/crimea.html.

Herszenhorn, D.M., P. Reevell, and N. Sneider. 2014. Russian Forces Take Over One of the Last Ukrainan Bases in Crimea. *The New York Times*, March 22. http://www.nytimes.com/2014/03/23/world/europe/ukraine.html?_r=0.

Hilpold, P. 2015. Ukraine, Crimea and New International Law: Balancing International Law with Arguments Drawn from History. *Chinese JIL* 14: 237–270.

Hoffman, F.G. 2007. *Conflict in the 21st Century: The Rise of Hybrid Wars*. Arlington, VA: Potomac Institute for Policy Studies.

Jaworsky, J. 1995. Crimea's Importance to Ukraine and its Future Security. In *Crimea: Dynamics, Challenges and Prospects*, ed. M. Drohobycky, 135–156. Lanham, Maryland: Rowman & Littlefield.

Karatnycky, A. 2005. Ukraine's Orange Revolution. *Foreign Affairs* 84: 35–52.

Kuruneri-Millet, A. 2014. 2014: l'Ukraine à la croisée des chemins. *Déf. Nat.* 769: 11–16.

Kuzio, T. 1995. *Ukrainian Security Policy*. Westport, CT, London: Praeger.

———. 2005. From Kuchma to Yushchenko. Ukraine's 2004 Presidential Elections and the Orange Revolution. *Problems of Post-Communism* 52: 29–44.

———. 2007. Oligarchs, Tapes and Oranges: 'Kuchmagate' to the Orange Revolution. *Journal of Communist Studies and Transition Politics* 23: 30–56.

———. 2012. Russianization of Ukrainian National Security Policy under Viktor Yanukovych. *The Journal of Slavic Military Studies* 25: 558–581.

Lagerwall, A. 2014. L'agression et l'annexion de la Crimée para la Fédération de Russie: Quels enseignements au sujet du droit international. *Questions of International Law, Zoom Out* I 57–72. www.qil-qdi.org.

Luchterhandt, O. 2014. Der Anschluss der Krim an Russland aus völkerrechtlicher Sicht. *Archiv des Völkerrecht* 52: 137–174.

Mantovani, M., and D. Rickenbacher. 2014. Crimea Going East - A Clash of Great Power Strategies. *ML & LWR* 53: 45–68.

Martucci, F. 2014. La réaction multidimensionnelle de l'Union européenne dans la crise ukrainienne. *JDI* 141: 765–785.

Marxsen, C. 2014. The Crimea Crisis - An International Law Perspective. *ZaöRV/HJIL* 74: 367–391.

Merezhko, O. 2015. Crimea's Annexation by Russia – Contradictions of the New Russian Doctrine of International Law. *ZaöRV/HJIL* 75: 167–194.

Milano, E. 2014. The Non-Recognition of Russia's Annexation of Crimea: Three Different Legal Approaches and One Unanswered Question. *Questions of International Law, Zoom Out* I 35–55. www.qil-qdi.org.

Nahaylo, B. 1999. *The Ukrainian Resurgence*. London: Hurst & Co.

NATO. 2006. *Handbook*. Brussels: Public Diplomacy Division. http://www.nato.int/docu/handbook/2006/hb-en-2006.pdf.

Ohloblyn, O. 1954. *Treaty of Pereyaslav, 1654*. Toronto: Canadian League for Ukraine's Liberation, Organization for Defence of Four Freedoms for Ukraine.

Olson, P.M. 2014. The Lawfulness of Use of Force in Crimea. *ML & LWR* 53: 17–44.

Perpetua, S. 2014. Parliament Votes to Dismiss Yanukovych. *The New York Times*, February 22. http://www.nytimes.com/video/world/europe/100000002728851/parliament-votes-to-dismiss-yanukovych.html.

Prokopovych, V. 1955. The Problem of the Juridical Nature of the Ukraine's Union with Muscovy. *Annals of the Ukrainian Academy of Arts and Sciences in the United States* 4: 926–946.

Pronin, A. 2015. Republic of Crimea A Two-Day State. *Russian LJ* 3: 133–142.

Reeves, S.R., and D.A. Wallace. 2015. The Combatant Status of the Little Green Men and Other Participants in the Ukraine Conflict. *International Law Studies* 91: 361–401.

Rudnytsky, I.L. 1954. Status of the Crimea; Recent Move is Seen as Concession to Ukraine Demand. *The New York Times*, March 16.

Ruys, T., and N. Verlinden. 2014. Digest of State Practice 1 January – 30 June 2014. *JUFIL* 1: 324–340.

Saluschev, S. 2014. Annexation of Crimea: Causes, Analysis & Global Implications. *Global Societies Journal* 2: 37–46.
Schmemann, S. 1992a. Crimea Parliament Votes to Back Independent from Ukraine. *The New York Times*, May 6. http://www.nytimes.com/1992/05/06/world/crimea-parliament-votes-to-back-independence-from-ukraine.html.
———. 1992b. Russia Votes to Void Cession of Crimea to Ukraine. *The New York Times*, May 22. http://www.nytimes.com/1992/05/22/world/russia-votes-to-void-cession-of-crimea-to-ukraine.html.
Schroefl, J., and S.J. Kaufman. 2014. Hybrid Actors, Tactical Variety: Rethinking Asymmetric and Hybrid War. *Studies in Conflict & Terrorism* 37: 862–880.
Schwartz, H. 1954. Concession to the Ukraine. *The New York Times*, February 27.
Sciso, E. 2014. La crisi ucraina e lintervento russo: profile di diritto internazionale. *RDI* 97: 992–1031.
Shevchenko, V. 2014. 'Little green men' or 'Russian invaders'? *BBC News* March 11. http://www.bbc.com/news/world-europe-26532154.
Smale, A., and S. Erlanger. 2014. Ukraine Mobilizes Reserve Troops, Threatening War. *The New York Times*, March 1. http://www.nytimes.com/2014/03/02/world/europe/ukraine.html.
Solchanyk, R. 1995. Crimea: Between Ukraine and Russia. In *Crimea: Dynamics, Challenges and Prospects*, ed. M. Drohobycky, 3–13. Lanham, Maryland: Rowman & Littlefield.
Specter, M. 1997. Setting Past Aside, Russia and Ukraine Sign Friendship Treaty. *The New York Times*, June 1. http://www.nytimes.com/1997/06/01/world/setting-past-aside-russia-and-ukraine-sign-friendship-treaty.html.
Stewart, D.B. 1997. *The Russian-Ukrainian Friendship Treaty and the Search for Regional Stability in Eastern Europe*. Monterey, CA: Naval Postgraduate School. Thesis.
Subtelny, O. 2000. *Ukraine: A History*. Toronto: Toronto University Press.
Swetnam, M. 2007. Foreword. In *Conflict in the 21st Century: The Rise of Hybrid Wars*, ed. F.G. Hoffman, 5–6. Arlington, VA: Potomac Institute for Policy Studies. http://www.potomacinstitute.org/images/stories/publications/potomac_hybridwar_0108.pdf.
Tancredi, A. 2014a. Crisi in Crimea, referéndum ed autodeterminazione dei popoli. *DUDI* 8: 480–490.
———. 2014c. The Russian Annexation of the Crimea: Questions Relating to the Use of Force. *Questions of International Law, Zoom Out* I 5–34. www.qil-qdi.org.
Taylor, A. 2014. To understand Crimea, take a look back at its complicated history. *The Washington Post*, February, 27. http://www.washington.com.
The Crimea: Chronicle of Separatism (1992–1995). 1996. Kiev: Ukrainian Centre for Independent Political Research.
Ukrainian Canadian Committee. 1954. *Bastion of Resistance: Comments on the Treaty of Pereyaslav between Ukraine and Russia*. Winnipeg: Ukrainian Canadian Committee.
Urquhart, C. 2014. Ukraine MPs appoint interim president as Yanukovych allies dismissed – 23 Februray as it happened. *The Guardian*, February 23. http://www.theguardian.com/world/2014/feb/23/ukraine-crisis-yanukovych-tymoshenko-live-updates.
Van den Driest, S.F. 2015. Crimea's Separation from Ukraine: An Analysis of the Right to Self-Determination and (Remedial) Secession in International Law. *NILR* 62: 329–363.
Vasiliev, A. 2014. The Crimean 'Army'. Open Democracy website. March, 14. http://www.opendemocracy.net/od-russia/andrei-vasiliev/crimean-%E2%80%98army%E2%80%99.
Von Todleben, F.E. 1863. *Défense de Sébastopol*. Saint-Petersburg: N. Thieblin.
Wilson, A. 2005. *Ukraine's Orange Revolution*. New Haven: Yale University Press.
———. 2014. *Ukraine Crisis: What It Means for the West*. New Haven: Yale University Press.
———. 2015. *The Ukrainians: Unexpected Nation* ([S.l.]: Yale University Press.
Wolczuk, K. 2002. Catching up with Europe? Constitutional Debates on the Territorial-Administrative Model in Independent Ukraine. *Regional & Federal Studies* 12: 65–88.
Wydra, D. 2004. The Crimea Conundrum: The Tug of War Between Russia and Ukraine on the Questions of Autonomy and Self-Determination. *IJGR* 10: 111–130.

Yekelchyk, S. 2007. *Ukraine: Birth of a Modern Nation*. New York; Oxford: Oxford University Press.

Zlenko, A.M. 1997. Foreign Policy Interests of Ukraine and Problems of European Security. *Fordham Int'l L.J.* 21: 45–64.

Chapter 6
The Legality of the Secessions of Kosovo and Crimea

Contemporary international law does not prohibit secessions. However, in certain circumstances, an attempt at secession may be illicit because it infringes some norm of general international law, or a *lex specialis*, as explained in Chap. 3.[1] Thus, effectiveness is not the only requirement for the appearance of a new entity; it is necessary for the creation to be licit through observing the peremptory norms forming international *jus cogens*, or the requirements in respect of the legal status of the territory set out in a *lex specialis*.[2] Conformity with international law must be seen as a criterion for statehood alongside the needed effectiveness, so that the latter is a necessary, but not a sufficient requirement.[3]

6.1 Interventions by NATO in Kosovo and Russia in Crimea

Necessary effectiveness must at all times comply with observance of the peremptory norm prohibiting the threat or actual use of international relations.[4] The ICJ had occasion to highlight various precedents where the declaration of independence was condemned by the Security Council because of being the outcome of illicit use of force or other serious violations of peremptory norms of international law.[5]

---

[1]See supra, Sect. 3.3.

[2]This was the stance taken by Serbia in its 'Written Statement'. See supra, Sect. 3.1.2.

[3]Cfr. Tancredi (2012), p. 83.

[4]Cfr. Christakis (2014), p. 749.

[5]Cfr. *Accordance with the International Law of the Unilateral Declaration of Independence in Respect of Kosovo, Advisory Opinion,* supra, Chap. 1, note 3, p. 437, para. 81.
Cfr. Arcari (2014), p. 478. Sciso (2014), p. 1009.

J. F. Escudero Espinosa, *Self-Determination and Humanitarian Secession in International Law of a Globalized World*,
https://doi.org/10.1007/978-3-319-72622-9_6

These precedents, particularly the Turkish Republic of Northern Cyprus, whose proclamation of independence on 15 November 1983 was deemed 'legally invalid' by the Security Council,[6] raise the question of a legal assessment of the events in the cases of Kosovo and Crimea. To sum up, in all these instance it became clear that there was tension between the principles of self-determination and protection of human rights, on one hand, and preservation of territorial integrity of States, the foundation of the world order established by the UN Charter, on the other.[7]

6.1.1 The Illegality of NATO's Intervention in Kosovo

The legality of NATO's intervention in Kosovo has been the subject of wide-ranging debate among international academic lawyers, experts in the law of nations.[8] The question could have been the object of a pronouncement by the ICJ when judging the suit brought by the then FRY, but it never went into the depths of the matter.[9] The international community, in contrast, has overwhelmingly evinced disapproval of this action, seeing it as entailing a clear infringement of the prohibition of the use of force and thus a breach of *jus cogens*.[10]

However, NATO attacks on the FRY, whilst constituting a violation of the prohibition on the use of force, were not aimed to infringe its territorial integrity or aimed at ensuring the secession of Kosovo.[11] The unilateral declaration of independence by Kosovo was not one of the objectives of the assault on the FRY.[12] Hence, as most authors have done, it may be stated that the unilateral

[6]UN Doc. S/RES/541 (1983), of 18 November, at para. 2.

The international community never saw this supposed Republic as a State and it was recognized only by Turkey. See supra, Sect. 3.3.

[7]Cfr. Burke-White (2014), p. 71. Wilson (2009), p. 65.

[8]See supra, Sect. 4.2.2, notes 86 and 87.

Apart from the authors previously quoted, see also: Cvijić (2007), Francioni (2000), Gray (2001), Greenwood (1999), Hilpold (2009b), Jennings (1999), Kälin (2000), Kessedjian (1999), Krisch (1999), Murase (2002), Nolte (1999), O'Connell (2000), Sofaer (2000), Thürer (2000), Wall (2002), Wippman (2001).

[9]Cfr. Brown (2005), pp. 267–271. Gray (2005), pp. 787–794.

[10]Cfr. "Final Document of the XIII Conference of Heads of State Government of the Non-Aligned Movement, Kuala Lumpur, 24–25 February 2003", para. 5 http://www.nam.gov.za/media/030227e.htm. Brownlie (1990), p. 744. 'Letter dated 26 March 1999 from the Permanent Representative of Mexico to the United Nations addressed to the Secretary-General' Annex: Communiqué issued on 25 March 1999 by the Rio Group, UN Doc. A/53/884, S/1999/347, of 26 March 1999. Krieger (2001), p. 493.

[11]Cfr. Orakhelashvili (2011), p. 83.

[12]Cfr. Ibid.

declaration of independence of Kosovo in 2008 was not a consequence arising from armed attacks by NATO in 1999.[13] Even Serbia agreed that there was no causal link between the attacks and the unilateral declaration of independence by Kosovo during proceedings before the ICJ.

6.1.2 *The Flagrant Breach of International Law in the Russian Intervention*

More depth is needed when considering the events in Crimea, described in some detail in Chap. 5. In the view of a large number of States, the authorization to deploy Russian Federation forces in the territory of the Ukraine granted by the Council of the Federation of the Russian Parliament on 1 March 2014 at the request of President Vladimir Putin on the basis of Art. 102(1)(d) of the Russian Constitution[14] may be seen as 'a clear and unambiguous violation of the sovereignty, independence and territorial integrity of Ukraine, and is a flagrant breach of international law'.[15]

Russia initially denied involvement, hence considering no justification necessary.[16] However, Russia's actions were soon defended by President Vladimir Putin

---

[13]Cfr. Christakis (2011), p. 83. Corten (2008), p. 748. Orakhelashvili (2011), p. 83. Tancredi (2012), p. 105.

[14]See supra, Sect. 5.2.1.

Article 102(1)(d) grants the Council of the Federation powers for:

> d) deciding on the possibility of using the Armed Forces of the Russian Federation outside the territory of the Russian Federation;

Constitution of the Russian Federation, adopted on 12 December 1993, supra, Chap. 5, note 124.

[15]Intervention of Sir Mark Lyall Grant (United Kingdom), UN Doc. S/PV.7125, of 3 March 2014, p. 6. Cfr. Intervention of Sir Mark Lyall Grant (United Kingdom), UN Doc. S/PV.7124, of 1 March 2014, p. 6; and intervention of Mr. Araud (France), UN Doc. S/PV.7124, of 1 March 2014, p. 7.

Within the Council of Europe (COE), the Parliamentary Assembly adopted Resolution 1990 (2014) on 10 April, 'Reconsideration on Substantive Grounds of the Previously Ratified Credentials of the Russian Delegation', paragraph 3 stating:

> considers that the actions of the Russian Federation leading up to the annexation of Crimea, and in particular the military occupation of the Ukrainian territory and the threat of the use of military force, the recognition of the results of the illegal so-called referendum and subsequent annexation of Crimea into the Russian Federation constitute, beyond any doubt, a grave violation of international law, including of the United Nations Charter and the Organization of Security and Co-operation in Europe (OSCE) Helsinki Final Act.

For its part, the NATO view was manifested in the 'North Atlantic Council statement on the situation in Ukraine' on 2 March 2014, que la 'Military Action against Ukraine by Forces of the Russian Federation is a Breach of International Law' http://www.nato.int/cps/en/natohq/official_texts_107681.htm.

[16]See supra, Sect. 5.2.1.

Lagerwall (2014), p. 59.

and the Russian authorities, it being alleged that they fell outside the scope of Art. 2 (4) of the UN Charter and that the use of force was justified.[17]

6.1.2.1 Threat to the Life of Russian Citizens

In its first statements, Russia claimed there was a threat to the life and well-being of Russian citizens in Crimea, including the Russian forces stationed in the peninsula under the bilateral agreements with the Ukraine.[18] The argument was 'one of defending our citizens and compatriots' against the *coup d'état* by extremists in Kiev who took measures to cut the rights of Russian-speaking minorities.[19] Likewise, Russia cited the call for help from the Chairman of the Council of Ministers of Crimea, Sergey Aksyonov, supported by the President of the Ukraine, Viktor Yanukovych.[20] Both had appealed to President Vladimir Putin to provide assistance 'in ensuring peace and tranquillity on the territory of the Autonomous Republic of Crimea'.[21]

The combination of the two justifications put forward by the Russian Federation involves mutual exclusion at some points. In fact the simultaneous allegations that resort was had to force in order to rescue nationals abroad and because of an invitation to intervene are contradictory.[22]

The doctrine relating to protecting nationals in foreign parts has been extensively debated.[23] It has been understood to mean that there is a right to offer protection to citizens abroad through the use of force as an exercise of the right to self-defence.[24] Similarly, the practice of some States, including the Russian Federation, pointed to

---

[17]Cfr. Olson (2014), p. 24.

[18]See supra, Sect. 5.2.1.

Cfr. Bismuth (2014), p. 722. Lagerwall (2014), p. 58. Ruys and Verlinden (2014), p. 329.

[19]Cfr. Intervention of Mr. Churkin (Russian Federation), UN Doc. S/PV.7125, of 3 March 2014, p. 3. In this same speech, Vitaly Churkin noted the request from President Yanukovych:

> As the legitimately elected President of Ukraine, I wish to inform you that events in my country and capital have placed Ukraine on the brink of civil war. Chaos and anarchy reign throughout the country. The lives, security and rights of the people, particularly in the south-east and in Crimea, are under threat. Open acts of terror and violence are being committed under the influence of Western countries. People are being persecuted on the basis of their language and political beliefs. I therefore call on President Vladimir Vladimirovich Putin of Russia to use the armed forces of the Russian Federation to establish legitimacy, peace, law and order and stability in defence of the people of Ukraine.

[20]Cfr. Bismuth (2014), p. 722. Lagerwall (2014), p. 58. Intervention of Mr. Churkin (Russian Federation), UN Doc. S/PV.7124, of 1 March 2014, p. 5.

[21]Intervention of Mr. Eliasson (Deputy Secretary-General), UN Doc. S/PV.7124, of 1 March 2014, p. 2.

[22]Cfr. Hilpold (2015), p. 251.

[23]See Akehurst (1977), Bowett (1986), and Gordon (1977).

[24]Cfr. Bowett (1986), p. 49. Ruys (2008), p. 234.

acceptance of the view that an attack against nationals of a State in a foreign country equated to an attack against the State itself, thus giving rise to a right to self-defence in accordance with Art. 51 of the UN Charter.[25] However, practice is not conclusive with this line of reasoning and it was also possible to see it as an exception to the prohibition in Art. 2(4) based on customary law.[26] It is true that in practice there was a relative acceptance of this sort of intervention, but only as long as the intervening power did not at the same time attempt to achieve any other aims.[27]

The criterion of nationality is a distinguishing feature relative to other concepts, such as humanitarian intervention, in which there would also be a use of force for the protection of human rights beyond the frontiers of the State employing it, which have varying legal bases. In any of these cases there is implicit a greater or lesser degree of interposition between the people whose human rights are being infringed and the State in which these people are present.[28]

Natalino Ronzitti even contemplated the possibility of interventions to protect one's own nationals in another country with the consent of the territorial State, which would rule out the act being illegitimate.[29] However, it is clear that this action on the basis of international customary law is far from definitively established.[30] This author pointed out that the consent of the local State could not serve as an *erga omnes* defence, but rather that the intervening State would be liable for any possible illicit actions against other members of the international community.[31] Moreover, consent from the local State could not infringe a peremptory norm of international law in the event that the actions of the intervening State ran counter to the local State and remaining members of the international community.[32]

As Sir Humphrey Waldock stated, the right was subject to fulfilment of three conditions: '(1) an imminent threat of injury to nationals, (2) a failure or inability on the part of the territorial sovereign to protect them and (3) measures of protection strictly confined to the object of protecting them against injury'.[33]

Examination of how events developed makes plain how dubious the justification for intervention by the Russian Federation was in the light of doctrine on the

[25]Cfr. Burke-White (2014), p. 69, note 16.

[26]Cfr. Ronzitti (1985), p. 68.

[27]Cfr. Hilpold (2015), p. 252.

[28]Cfr. Bowett (1986), p. 49.

[29]Cfr. Ronzitti (1985), p. 84.

[30]Cfr. Hilpold (2015), p. 252. Ruys (2008), pp. 233–271.

[31]Cfr. Ronzitti (1985), p. 85. 'Eighth Report on State Responsibility, by Mr. Roberto Ago, Special Rapporteur. The Internationally Wrongful Act of the State, Source of International Responsibility (continued)', UN Doc. A/CN.4/318 and Add.1-4, of 24 January, 5 February and 15 June 1979, p. 37, para. 74.

[32]Cfr. Ronzitti (1985), p. 86. 'Eighth Report on State Responsibility, by Mr. Roberto Ago, Special Rapporteur. The Internationally Wrongful Act of the State, Source of International Responsibility (continued)', UN Doc. A/CN.4/318 and Add.1-4, of 24 January, 5 February and 15 June 1979, p. 38, para. 75.

[33]Waldock (1952), p. 467.

protection of nationals abroad.[34] Indeed, the conclusion that may be reached hangs on the difficulty of discerning 'an imminent threat of injury to nationals', whether objectively or subjectively.[35] Firstly, it is highly doubtful whether the situation in the Ukraine had immediate repercussions for Crimea such as to imply an imminent danger for the life and safety of the Russian-speaking Crimean population.[36] From a subjective viewpoint, it is also not possible to say that the actions of the Russian Federation were aimed at protecting Russian nationals.[37] Although Vladimir Putin alleged that millions of Russians were threatened, the number in Crimea was in fact lower than that.[38] As a number of authors have pointed out, even the census figure is a consequence of the policy of mass issue of Russian passports that began in Crimea in 2008 as a preparation for annexation.[39] This policy of "passportization" undermines the requirements of international law for according international projection to citizens, as it should be a case of 'real and effective' nationality.[40]

Following the line of argument put forward by the Russian Federation, allusion was also made to the concept of humanitarian intervention (which, however, had never been accepted by Russia[41]), an example being the statements by Vitaly Churkin before the Security Council.[42] This argument lacks validity, since the

[34]Cfr. Arcari (2014), p. 473. Lagerwall (2014), p. 62.

[35]Cfr. Hilpold (2015), p. 253.

[36]Cfr. Green (2014), p. 8. Olson (2014), p. 34.

[37]Cfr. Hilpold (2015), p. 253.

[38]Cfr. 'Address by President of the Russian Federation on March 18, 2014', supra, Chap. 1, note 1. Intervention of Mr. Churkin (Russian Federation), UN Doc. S/PV.7125, of 3 March 2014, p. 3.

[39]Cfr. Gray (2009), pp. 133–151. Green (2014), p. 8. Green (2010), pp. 54–79. Hilpold (2015), pp. 253 and 255. Natoli (2010), pp. 389–417.

The Honorary Professor of the European University Yuri Albertovich Dmitriev commented on President Putin's arguments that Order No.340-R of the Government of Russia, dated 10 March 2014, submitted to the Duma a draft law 'On Amendments to the Federal Law 'On Citizenship of the Russian Federation' and Particular Legislative Acts of the Russian Federation' http://asozd2c.duma.gov.ru. This law was passed in 2002 and among its amendments granting of citizenship was made conditional upon the applicant's knowledge of the Russian language, while authorization of residence was excluded and the deadline for deciding to accept citizenship was cut to three months. Cfr. Dmitriev (2014), p. 26.

[40]Cfr. Green (2014), p. 4.

According to the ICJ in its Judgement on the Nottebohm Case, nationality:

> is a legal bond having as its basis a social fact of attachment, a genuine connection of existence, interests and sentiments, together with the existence of reciprocal rights and duties. It may be said to constitute the juridical expression of the fact that the individual upon whom it is conferred, either directly by the law or as the result of an act of the authorities, is in fact more closely connected with the population of the State conferring nationality than with that of any other State. *Nottebohm Case (second phase) (Liechtenstein v. Guatemala), Judgment of April 6th, 1955, I.C.J. Reports 1955*, 27, p. 23.

[41]Cfr. Merezhko (2015), p. 190. Olson (2014), p. 38, note 53.

[42]Cfr. Intervention of Mr. Churkin (Russian Federation), UN Doc. S/PV.7125, of 3 March 2014, p. 17.

absence of any widespread serious violation of human rights by the Ukrainian Government rules out legitimization as an intervention of a humanitarian nature.[43] Moreover, the Russian Federation never made any accusations to this effect before the various international tribunals of which it is a member.[44] On the contrary, reports on the situation in Crimea submitted to these International Organizations make it plain that there was no record of violations of human rights by the Ukrainian authorities.[45]

6.1.2.2 Intervention by Invitation

The Russian Federation simultaneously argued that there had been a request for aid from the Ukrainian authorities, specifically from the overthrown President Viktor Yanukovych.[46] Consent expressed by this invitation was claimed to rule out any wrongfulness of the Russian military intervention, which otherwise would have been an infringement of the prohibition on the use of force in international relations.[47]

The International Law Commission's (ILC) comments on Art. 29 of the 'Draft Articles on State Responsibility' laid down the general requirements needed for a

---

[43]Cfr. Christakis (2014), p. 751.

[44]Cfr. Delahunty (2015), p. 129. Merezhko (2015), p. 192.

On these lines, the Foreign Secretary of the United Kingdom, William Hague, stated that 'international diplomatic mechanisms exist to provide assurance on the situations of national minorities, including within the Organisation for Security and Cooperation in Europe and the Council of Europe'. 'The Foreign Secretary William Hague has updated Parliament on the situation in Ukraine and the UK government's response', 4 March 2014, https://www.gov.uk/government/speeches/uks-response-to-the-situation-in-ukraine.

[45]Cfr. Merezhko (2015), p. 192.

In contrast, Anatoly Kapustin referred to the UNHCHR, *Report on Human Rights Situation in Ukraine*, of 15 May 2014, at para. 103 and 104, http://www.ohchr.org, and United Nations Human Rights Council (UNHRC), *Report on the Situation of Human Rights in Ukraine*, of September 2014, UN Doc. A/HCR/27/75, at para. 23. Cfr. Kapustin (2015), p. 116, note 44. It must be objected that the violations of human rights related were a long way from constituting serious, massive human rights infringements, as the author recognizes 117, such as to justify an action. Moreover, the cases did not even fall within Sect. 'VI Particular Human Rights Challenges in Crimea', paragraphs 117–154, which does look at violations occurring after annexation.

[46]See supra, Sect. 5.2.1. Cfr. V. Putin, 'Vladimir Putin answered journalists' questions on the situation in Ukraine', March 4, 2014, http://en.kremlin.ru/events/president/transcripts/20366. Intervention of Mr. Churkin (Russian Federation), UN Doc. S/PV.7125, of 3 March 2014, pp. 3 and 4. Marxsen (2014), p. 374.

[47]The ILC's comments on Art. 29 on Consent, within Chap. V relating to 'Circumstances Precluding Wrongfulness' of the 'Draft Articles on State Responsibility', referring expressly to the entry of foreign troops into a State, says that it 'is normally considered a serious violation of State sovereignty and often, an act of aggression [. . .] is clear that such action ceases to be so characterized and becomes perfectly lawful if it occurred at the request or with the agreement of the State'. 'Report of the International Law Commission on the Work of its Thirty-first Session, 14 May–3 August 1979', UN Doc. A/34/10, of 14 August 1979, 528, p. 294, para. (5).

valid expression of consent.[48] The present case raises the question of whether the consent declared by Viktor Yanukovych could be attributed to the State.[49] The classic view, confirmed by the ICJ in the *Nicaragua* case, is that the prerogative of requesting an intervention lies with the legitimate government and cannot be exercised by the opposition.[50]

This was the starting point for various objections to the justification of the Russian intervention.[51] The first of these is rooted in Ukrainian law, as Art. 85 (23) of the Constitution lays down the condition that authorization from the *Verkhovna Rada* is needed for request for assistance from a foreign army.[52] Secondly, although it is dubious whether the change of government was carried out within the constitutional framework envisaged by Art. 108 relating to 'removal from office by the procedure of impeachment', and following the procedure foreseen in Art. 111 'in the event that he or she commits state treason or other crime',[53] it also

---

[48]In order to be considered as a circumstance precluding wrongfulness, the consent must be (1) valid under the rules of international law, (2) clearly established, (3) really expressed, (4) internationally attributable to the State, (5) must also have been given prior to the commission of the act, and (6) precludes the wrongfulness of a particular act only within the limits which the State expressing the consent intends with respect to its scope and duration. Finally, 'the conduct of a State which is not in conformity with an obligation imposed by one of the rules of jus cogens must remain an internationally wrongful act, even if the injured State has given its consent to the conduct in question'. 'Report of the International Law Commission on the Work of its Thirty-first Session, 14 May–3 August 1979', UN Doc. A/34/10, of 14 August 1979, 528, pp. 300–305, and 307, paragraphs 12–17, and 21.

[49]Cfr. Commentary on Art. 20 del 'Draft Articles on Responsibility of States for Internationally Wrongful Acts', 'Report of the International Law Commission on the Work of its Fifty-third Session, 23 April–1 June and 2 July–10 August 2001', UN Doc. A/56/10, 536, p. 175, para. 5.

[50]According to the ICJ, if intervention could be requested both by the government and by the opposition this would allow any State to intervene at any time in the internal affairs of any other State:

> [...] Indeed, it is difficult to see what would remain of the principle of non-intervention in international law if intervention, which is already allowable at the request of the government of a State, were also to be allowed at the request of the opposition. This would permit any State to intervene at any moment in the internal affairs of another State, whether at the request of the government or at the request of its opposition. *Military and Paramilitary Activities in and Against Nicaragua (Nicaragua v. United States of America), Merits, Judgment, I.C.J. Reports 1986*, 12–150, p. 126, para. 246.

On the same lines, *Armed Activities on the Territory of the Congo (Democratic Republic of the Congo v. Uganda), Judgment, I.C.J. Reports 2005*, 165–283, p. 196, para. 45.

[51]Cfr. Mansour (2010), p. 443. Commentary on Art. 20 del 'Draft Articles on Responsibility of States for Internationally Wrongful Acts', supra, Chap. 6, note 49, p. 174, para. 4.

[52]The text of Art. 85(23) of the Ukrainian Constitution, supra, Chap. 5, note 56, runs as follows:

> The authority of the Verkhovna Rada of Ukraine comprises: [...]
>
> (23) approving decisions on providing military assistance to other states, on sending units of the Armed Forces of Ukraine to a foreign state, or on admitting units of armed forces of foreign states onto the territory of Ukraine;

[53]Cfr. Marxsen (2014), p. 375.

must be stated that when he made his request to Russia, Yanukovych no longer had 'effective control' of the Ukraine as President.[54]

It is certainly true, on the one hand, that his removal was voted without required majority of three quarters of the parliament, in violation of the Constitution,[55] and on the other that his abandonment of power and loss of majority support among the people make it hard to determine whether he was entitled to make such an invitation.[56] Moreover, Viktor Yanukovych's legitimacy has been questioned in view of the 'serious violations of human rights' like the excessive use of force, killings, disappearances, torture and ill-treatment committed during his mandate, these having been denounced by the Office of the United Nations High Commissioner for Human Rights (UNHCHR) in 2014.[57]

A response would seem to be found, regardless of questions of 'effective control' or of the legality of an intervention requested by a President who had been deposed, although not by constitutional means, in the application of the 'negative equality principle'. This lays down that no assistance should be given to either of the two parties involved in a situation of internal conflict.[58] Even if there had been a *coup d'état,* as Russian academics have claimed,[59] it would still be a matter of domestic jurisdiction in which resort to the use of force by another State would not be justified.[60]

Examination of the Crimean crisis leads to the conclusion that the actions of the la Russian Federation in Crimea is hard to justify either as protecting Russian nationals or as responding to an invitation to intervene from Viktor Yanukovych. The views expressed both by States and International Organizations and by legal doctrine have

[54]Cfr. Ibid. Merezhko (2015), p. 187. Wilson (2015), p. 221.

In contexts of internal conflict, civil war and revolutionary change account has been taken of the criterion of 'effective control' over specific parts of the territory. Under this principle, the authority entitled to invite in foreign troops would be the one exercising some effectiveness of a government. The criterion of 'effective control' was the exclusive or the main requisite. However, in more recent times this has been questioned, with governments seen as needing not just control but also legitimacy. Cfr. Nolte (2010), para. 17, http://opil.ouplaw.com/view/10.1093/law:epil/9780199231690/law-9780199231690-e1702?prd=EPIL.

[55]Cfr. Hilpold (2015), p. 250.

[56]Cfr. Marxsen (2014), p. 377.

In Resolution 1988 (2014), adopted on 9 April 2015, the Parliamentary Assembly of the COE declared by 154 votes to 26, with 14 abstentions, that it 'therefore fully recognises the legitimacy of the new authorities in Kyiv and the legality of their decisions. It regrets attempts to question the legitimacy of the new authorities, which can only serve to destabilise the country', COE Doc. Resolution 1988 (2014), at para. 3.

[57]Cfr. Office of the UNHCHR, *Report on the Human Rights Situation in Ukraine*', 15 April 2014, 28. http://www.ohchr.org/Documents/Countries/UA/Ukraine_Report_15April2014.doc.

[58]Cfr. Fox (2015), p. 829.

[59]See Voronin et al. (2015), pp. 11–28. Russian with English summary. According to these authors, the situation of civil war in the Ukraine was a consequence of a *coup d'état* and the attempts by the new authorities to subject those regions no supporting the new government.

[60]Cfr. Merezhko (2015), p. 187. Wilson (2015), p. 221.

unanimously held that presence of Russian troops was a use of force as prohibited by Art. 2(4) of the UN Charter in violation of the principle of non-intervention and the territorial integrity of the Ukraine that can be described as flagrant.[61] Many commentators have also claimed that the Russian Federation had committed an act of aggression as defined in Resolution 3314 (XXIX),[62] in particular Art. 3(e),[63] and even Art. 3(a) (invasion or attack by the armed forces of a State), 3(c) (military naval blockade), and 3(g) ('indirect aggression').[64] According to the eloquent speech to the Security Council by the representative of the US, Samantha Power, 'What is happening today is not a human rights protection mission or a consensual intervention. What is happening today is a dangerous military intervention in Ukraine. It is an act of aggression'.[65]

To go further into the arguments, there is a clear authorization for using force given by the Russian Federation's Upper House on 1 March 2014, at the request of President Vladimir Putin. Under its terms, a campaign was undertaken by Russian troops who seized control of Crimea, captured Ukrainian military material, and forced Ukrainian troops to surrender by violating the territorial integrity of the

[61]Among States, the declarations by the representatives of the United Kingdom, Sir Mark Lyall Grant, UN Doc. S/PV.7125, of 3 March 2014, 20, p. 7; of Lithuania, Raimonda Murmokaitè, UN Doc S/PV.7134, of 13 March 2014, 19, p. 16; and of France, Gérard Araud, UN Doc. S/PV.7138, of 15 March 2014, 12, p. 5, are of particular note. Also noteworthy were the statements by the representatives of Liechtenstein, Christian Wenaweser, and of Canada, Guillermo Rishchynski, before the General Assembly, UN Doc. A/68/PV.80, of 27 March 2014, 27, pp. 7 and 9.

Within the United Nations, the Security Council debated a draft resolution sponsored by forty-two States, the first paragraph of the Preamble of which read: '*Recalling* the obligation of all States under Art. 2 of the United Nations Charter to refrain in their international relations from the threat or use of force' (UN Doc. S/2014/189, of 15 March 2014, supra, Chap. 5, note 92). However, this was not adopted, because of the negative vote of the Russian Federation. Thereafter, the General Assembly adopted Resolution A/RES/68/262, of 1 April 2014, see supra, Sect. 5.2.3, note 118, the second paragraph of the Preamble of which had this very same wording. For its part, the Special Meeting of the European Council held in Brussels on 30 August 2014, concluded by saying 'It condemns the increasing inflows of fighters and weapons from the territory of the Russian Federation into Eastern Ukraine as well as the aggression by Russian armed forces on Ukrainian soil', European Council, Brussels, 30 August 2014, Conclusions, EU Doc. EUCO 163/14, 8, p. 3, para. 8.

Cfr. Bílkovà (2015), p. 32. Christakis (2014), p. 750. Hilpold (2015), p. 245. Sciso (2014), p. 1003. Tancredi (2014b), p. 9. Van den Driest (2015), p. 359. Vidmar (2015), p. 376. Wilson (2015), p. 221.

[62]Cfr. Bílkovà (2015), p. 49. Tancredi (2014b), pp. 19–20. Walter (2014), pp. 307–309.

[63]Cfr. Arcari (2014), p. 476. Sciso (2014), p. 1005.

> The use of armed forces of one State which are within the territory of another State with the agreement of the receiving State, in contravention of the conditions provided for in the agreement or any extension of their presence in such territory beyond the termination of the agreement;. Article 3(e) of the 'Definition of Aggression' UN Doc. A/RES/3314 (XXIX), Annex, 14 December 1974.

[64]Cfr. Tancredi (2014b), p. 20.

[65]Intervention of Ms. Power (United States of America), UN Doc. S/PV.7125, of 3 March 2014, 20, p. 5.

Ukraine.[66] This was the first time in the 20 years that the current Russian Constitution had been in force that a measure was voted to authorize 'using the Armed Forces of the Russian Federation outside the territory of the Russian Federation' under the terms of Art. 102(1).[67] This step was far from justified under international law, had not been authorized by the Security Council and infringed Art. 2(4) of the UN Charter.[68]

6.2 Referenda as the Basis for Declarations of Independence

The conclusion has been reached that international law does not envisage any regulation of processes that might culminate in secession. These remain within the scope of the internal jurisdiction of States.[69] Holding a referendum through which the direct expression of the general will is manifested constitutes a matter lying inside domestic jurisdiction, which itself is not regulated by international law.[70] Nonetheless, this does not mean that those processes having material consequences at an international level are of no interest to other States.[71] Some of these referenda, known as 'sovereignty referenda', have an impact on the concept of statehood, acquisitions of territory, territorial changes, the international status of states, the extinction of states, or mergers of territories and states, directly linked to state creation and of particular interest to the international community.[72]

6.2.1 International Standards for Referenda

In its Western Sahara Advisory Opinion the ICJ stated that 'the application of the right of self-determination requires a free and genuine expression of the will of the peoples concerned'.[73] Hence from a formal angle there is a requirement for

[66]Cfr. Marxsen (2014), p. 389.

[67]Cfr. Dmitriev (2014), p. 24.

See supra, Sect. 6.1.2. Constitution of the Russian Federation, adopted on December 12, 1993, supra, Chap. 5, note 124.

[68]Cfr. Marxsen (2014), p. 750.

[69]See supra, Sect. 3.1.2.

[70]Cfr. Şen (2015), 298 pp. Tolstykh (2015), p. 133.

[71]Cfr. Şen (2015), p. 50.

[72]Cfr. Ibid.

[73]*Western Sahara, Advisory Opinion*, supra, Chap. 2, note 70, p. 32, para. 55.

fulfilment by States of certain basic international rules on holding referenda, these constituting what might be termed 'international standards on referenda'.[74] Such general principles for organizing votes are laid down at a universal level in Art. 25 of the 'International Covenant on Civil and Political Rights'.[75] In the European regional sphere, they are covered by Art. 3 of the 'Protocol to the European Convention on Human Rights'.[76] The principles may be summed up as a recognition of citizens' rights to take part in the conduct of public affairs through periodic, free, universal, equal, and secret elections ensuring the freedom of expression.[77]

In pursuit of its aims, the European Commission for Democracy through Law (Venice Commission) drew up a 'Code of Good Practice on Referendums' that provides some practical rules for applying the principles in question to the holding of elections.[78] The document presents the international standards stated in the main norms of international law and observed in practice by States, forming part more specifically of 'Europe's electoral heritage'.[79]

---

[74] Cfr. Tolstykh (2015), p. 133.

[75] On the 'International Covenant on Civil and Political Rights', supra, Chap. 2, note 51.

The text of Art. 25 runs as follows:

> Every citizen shall have the right and the opportunity, without any of the distinctions mentioned in article 2 and without unreasonable restrictions:
>
> (a) To take part in the conduct of public affairs, directly or through freely chosen representatives;
>
> (b) To vote and to be elected at genuine periodic elections which shall be by universal and equal suffrage and shall be held by secret ballot, guaranteeing the free expression of the will of the electors;
>
> (c) To have access, on general terms of equality, to public service in his country.

[76] The 'Protocol to the Convention for the Protection of Human Rights and Fundamental Freedoms', signed in Paris, 20 March 1952, *European Treaty Series* No. 9, entry into force on 18 May 1954, http://www.coe.int/en/web/conventions/search-on-treaties/-/conventions/treaty/005, and was amended by Protocol No. 11, signed in Strasbourg, 11 May 1994, *European Treaty Series* No. 155, and entry into force on 1 November 1998, http://www.coe.int/en/web/conventions/search-on-treaties/-/conventions/treaty/009.

The text of Art. 3 runs as follows:

> The High Contracting Parties undertake to hold free elections at reasonable intervals by secret ballot, under conditions which will ensure the free expression of the opinion of the people in the choice of the legislature.

[77] Cfr. Marxsen (2014), p. 381.

[78] Cfr. Hilpold (2015), p. 260. Marxsen (2014), p. 381. Tolstykh (2015), p. 133.

The Venice Commission was established in May 1990 by eighteen COE Member States. By 2016, it was composed of sixty-one member states, including fourteen non-European members and Kosovo, with five observer countries and one associate member.

The 'Code of good practice on Referendums' was adopted by the Council for Democratic Elections at its nineteenth meeting (Venice, 16 December 2006) and the Venice Commission at its 70th plenary session (Venice, 16–17 March 2007), CDL-AD(2007)008rev http://www.venice.coe.int/webforms/documents/CDL-AD(2007)008rev.aspx.

[79] Cfr. Venice Commission, 'Code of good practice on Referendums', Strasbourg, 20 January 2009, Study No. 371/2006, CDL-AD(2007)008rev, 24, p. 4, para. 3.

Moreover, Russian legal doctrine has also produced a listing of the requirements to be observed by a plebiscite, which differs from a referendum in specifically dealing with territorial questions. Among other points, Professor Larisa Ivanovna Volova notes the need for preparation time, supervision by an international commission, the forming of panels to oversee voting from representatives of all parties, and, most strikingly, the evacuation of all foreign troops from the territory concerned.[80]

Examples of this sort of referendum are numerous in the course of the recent history of international society. Some were held at the end of the First World War under the aegis of the League of Nations and related to the legal status of certain European territories. A considerable number also occurred during the process of decolonization that took place after the Second World War. A third peak came at the end of the Cold War period with the emergence of new States as a consequence of the collapse of the Soviet Bloc and the consequent break-up of the Union of Soviet Socialist Republics (USSR) and the la SFRY, together with further processes involving Eritrea, East Timor, Montenegro and South Sudan.[81]

Jure Vidmar stresses that alongside these instances there were other cases, such Czechoslovakia and Kosovo, in which no prior referendum on independence was held.[82] There were already precedents in the decolonization process in which no referenda were held because it was assumed that the will of the people was sufficiently clear. This was noted by the ICJ in its Western Sahara Advisory Opinion when it held that an authority 'has dispensed with the requirement of consulting the inhabitants of a given territory. [...] on the conviction that a consultation was totally unnecessary'.[83] In the case of Kosovo, the basis for independence was understood not to lie in the holding of a referendum as an expression of the general will in exercising the right to self-determination but rather was the response to 'the call of the people to build a society that honours human dignity'.[84]

To sum up, international practice has made it feasible to state several conclusions relating to independence referenda. Firstly, international law has no clear requirement for territorial changes in States to be legitimized by holding a referendum.[85] Secondly, it is not possible to demand a referendum must be held for any territorial

---

Prior to this, the Parliamentary Assembly of the COE had adopted Recommendation 1704 (2005), on 'Referendums: Towards Good Practices in Europe' on 29 April 2005 http://assembly.coe.int/nw/xml/XRef/Xref-XML2HTML-en.asp?fileid=17329&lang=en.

[80]Cfr. Merezhko (2015), p. 185, cites Volova (1972), pp. 54 and 122.

[81]Cfr. Vidmar (2013), pp. 65–115.

[82]Cfr. Id., p. 190.

[83]*Western Sahara, Advisory Opinion*, supra, Chap. 2, note 70, p. 25, para. 59.

[84]'Kosova Declaration of Independence' 17 February 2008, supra, Chap. 1, note 13, at Preamble, para. 2.

See also supra, p. 77, especially note 417.

Cfr. Jia (2009), pp. 31–32. Wilson (2009), p. 477.

[85]Cfr. Hilpold (2015), p. 258. Radan (2012), pp. 18–21.

change,[86] but neither does the holding of an independence referendum have a direct or self-executing legal effect at the international level, so that the results do not cause the independence of a territory.[87] Consequently, an independence referendum merely provides a certain democratic legitimacy relative to changes in sovereignty over a given territory, but legitimization of such changes must be sought in the rules of international law.[88] Thirdly and finally, the holding of an independence referendum by one State within another State must be deemed to run counter to international law, as it constitutes a violation of the right to self-determination and of the territorial integrity principle.[89]

6.2.2 The Illicit Nature of the Crimean Referendum

In the case of Crimea an attempt was made to legitimize the declaration of independence with the results of the referendum held on 16 March 2014.[90] This justification

[86]Cfr. Crawford (2012), p. 243.

[87]Cfr. Vidmar (2015), p. 379.

[88]Cfr. Hilpold (2015), p. 259.

[89]Cfr. Tancredi (2014a), p. 484.

When the Government of South Africa proposed holding a referendum in Namibia, the ICJ held that once the mandate had run out the presence of South Africa in Namibia was illegal and hence 'its acts on behalf of or concerning Namibia are illegal and invalid', *Legal Consequences for States of the Continued Presence of South Africa in Namibia (South West Africa) notwithstanding Security Council Resolution 276 (1970), Advisory Opinion*, supra, Chap. 2, note 70, p. 58, para. 132.

On the same lines, during debates relating to the situation in the Ukraine in the Security Council, the representative of the Russian Federation, Vitaly Churkin, alluded to the referendum held by France in February 1976 on the island of Mayotte, belonging to the recently independent State of the Comoro Islands, as to whether it was to refrain from joining the Comoros and become part of France. The result was a majority for Independence from the Comoros (Cfr. Intervention of Mr. Churkin (Russian Federation), UN Doc S/PV.7134, of 13 March 2014, 19, p. 16). The matter was brought to the Security Council and the representative of the Comoros called the actuation a 'flagrant aggression' ('Telegram dated 28 January 1976 from the Head of State of the Comoros addressed to the President of the Security Council', UN Doc. S/11953, of 30 January 1976). The draft resolution, sponsored by Benin, Guyana, Libyan Arab Republic, Panama and the United Republic of Tanzania, claimed that holding the referendum constituted 'an interference in the internal affairs', and called for France 'to respect the independence, sovereignty, unity and territorial integrity of the Comorian State' (UN Doc. S/11967, of 5 February 1976, 2, at 1 paragraphs 1 and 3). The resolution in support of the Comorian position was vetoed by France, as the representative of the Russian Federation remarked in his speech on events in Crimea (Cfr. Intervention of Mr. Churkin (Russian Federation), UN Doc S/PV.7134, of 13 March 2014, 19, p. 16).

The argument put forward by Russia, and supported by an appreciable number of international legal scholars, was linked to the traditional view of Soviet international law according to which an expansion of the territory of the Soviet Union would be possible through the holding of plebiscites addressing the question of territorial accession by a region transferred or a State incorporated. The plebiscite could be used as a way of bringing back into the Soviet Union of former Soviet territories that had been seized by force. Cfr. Pronin (2015), p. 134.

[90]See supra, Sect. 5.2.2.

was strongly disputed, because the referendum infringed Ukrainian national law and did not comply with the formal requirements of 'international standards on referenda'.[91]

Article 2 of the Ukrainian Constitution proclaims the indivisibility and inviolability of the Ukraine's territory within its current borders,[92] and Art. 134 declares the Autonomous Republic of Crimea to be 'an inseparable constituent part of Ukraine' exercising its competences within limits established by the Constitution.[93] Among these competences, Art. 138(2) grants the possibility of holding local referenda.[94] The status of Crimea is that of an autonomous region within the unitary Ukrainian State, as stated in the Constitution of the Autonomous Republic of Crimea, voted by the Crimean *Verkhovna Rada* on 21 October 1998, on the basis of an amended draft law of 1995, and approved by the Ukrainian *Verkhovna Rada* on 23 December 1998 in accordance with Art. 135 of the Ukrainian Constitution.[95] Article 1 re-affirms its status: 'The Autonomous Republic of Crimea shall be an integral part of the Ukraine and it shall solve, within the powers conferred upon it by the Constitution of the Ukraine, any and all matters coming within its terms of reference'.[96]

As held by the Venice Commission in the 'Code of Good Practice on Referendums': 'the referendums cannot be held if the Constitution or a statute in conformity with the Constitution has not provided for them'.[97] Contrarily to this rule, the

---

[91]Cfr. Merezhko (2015), pp. 182–185.

[92]The text of Art. 2 runs:

> The sovereignty of Ukraine extends throughout its entire territory.
> Ukraine is a unitary state.
> The territory of Ukraine within its present border is indivisible and inviolable.

On the Ukrainian Constitution, see supra, Chap. 5, note 56.

[93]The text of Art. 134 runs:

> The Autonomous Republic of Crimea is an inseparable constituent part of the Ukraine and decides on the issues ascribed to its competence within the limits of authority determined by the Constitution of the Ukraine.

[94]Article 138(2) de la Ukrainian Constitution lays down that:

> The competence of the Autonomous Republic of Crimea comprises:
> 1) [...]
> 2) organising and conducting local referendums;

[95]According to Art. 135(1) of the Ukrainian Constitution 'The Autonomous Republic of Crimea has the Constitution of the Autonomous Republic of Crimea that is adopted by the Verkhovna Rada of the Autonomous Republic of Crimea and approved by the Verkhovna Rada of Ukraine by no less than one-half of the constitutional composition of the Verkhovna Rada of Ukraine'.

Cfr. Sciso (2014), p. 997.

[96]An unofficial text can be found on http://web.archive.org/web/20150510004739/http://www.rada.crimea.ua/en/bases-of-activity/konstituciya-ARK.

[97]Venice Commission, 'Code of Good Practice on Referendums', Strasbourg, 20 January 2009, Study No. 371/2006, CDL-AD(2007)008rev, 24, p. 12, point III.1.

referendum held in Crimea was organized in contravention of the Ukrainian Constitution, both Art. 134 and Art. 73, which expressly provides that 'Issues of altering the territory of Ukraine are resolved exclusively by an All-Ukrainian referendum'.[98] The Venice Commission also stressed that if the possibility of amending Art. 134 of the Constitution of the Ukraine was mooted, Art. 157(1) excluded such an option if the intention was 'the liquidation of the independence or violation of the territorial indivisibility of Ukraine'.[99] Consequently, it must be stated that the referendum was held in breach of the Ukrainian Constitution.[100] As Barack Obama stated 'The proposed referendum on the future of Crimea would violate the Ukrainian Constitution and violate international law'.[101]

Apart from Ukrainian national law, the referendum was also void because it broke other basic 'international standards on referenda'. Although Vladimir Putin claimed that 'the referendum was fair and transparent, and the people of Crimea clearly and convincingly expressed their will and stated that they want to be with Russia',[102] the questions it asked were seen as obscure, misleading or suggestive, and contrary to the criteria established in the 'Code of Good Practice on Referendums'.[103] In fact, the referendum was unclear and ambiguous in offering the alternatives of independence or a return to the 1992 Constitution.[104] As the Venice Commission highlighted, the possibility of retaining the Constitution currently in force was

[98]Cfr. Venice Commission, 'Opinion on 'Whether the Decision Taken by the Supreme Council of the Autonomous Republic of Crimea in Ukraine to Organize a Referendum on Becoming a Constituent Territory of the Russian Federation or Restoring Crimea's 1992 Constitution is Compatible with Constitutional Principles', 21 March 2014, Opinion 762/2014, CDL-AD(2014) 002, 6, p. 3, para. 13.

[99]Cfr. Id., p. 3, para. 14.

[100]The General Assembly stressed that the referendum was held without the authorization of the Ukraine, Resolution on 'Territorial Integrity of Ukraine', UN Doc. A/RES/68/262, of 1 April 2014, at Preamble, para. 7.

Cfr. Bismuth (2014), p. 723. Hilpold (2015), p. 260.

[101]White House, 'Statement by the President on Ukraine', 6 March 2014, https://obamawhitehouse.archives.gov/the-press-office/2014/03/06/statement-president-ukraine.

[102]'Address by President of the Russian Federation on March 18, 2014', supra, Chap. 1, note 1, at para. 59.

[103]Cfr. Venice Commission, 'Code of Good Practice on Referendums', Strasbourg, 20 January 2009, Study No. 371/2006, CDL-AD(2007)008rev, 24, p. 8, point III.1.c.

[104]Cfr. Hilpold (2015), p. 261. Vidmar (2015), p. 381.

The referendum of 16 March 2014 put the following two questions:

> Are you in favour of unifying Crimea with Russia as a part of the Russian Federation?
> Are you in favour of restoring the 1992 Constitution and the status of Crimea as a part of Ukraine?

For a different wording, see also Dmitriev (2014), p. 22. Marxsen (2014), p. 382.

omitted.[105] Even the reference to the 1992 Constitution was not clear, as the text adopted in May 1992 was extensively amended in September 1992.[106]

The most serious aspect affecting the referendum was the context in which it was held, both its announcement and the actual voting process thereafter.[107] This was doubtless the most blameworthy infringement, the violation of the prohibition of the threat or use of force.[108] In brief, although the results were very clear, they were discredited, as noted by the representative of the United Kingdom, Sir Mark Lyall Grant, by the vote's being illegal 'under the Ukrainian Constitution, arranged at 10 days' notice, met none of the OSCE standards for democratic elections, was held under Russian military occupation and gave the people of Crimea no option to vote for the status quo'.[109]

The referendum was not in itself a violation of international law, but it did not observe the most basic international standards on referenda.[110] The surrounding circumstances described meant the referendum lacked legitimacy and because it had international repercussions, State have not accepted its results as a basis for its intended effects at an international level.

The assessment of the referendum incorporated in the draft resolution finally vetoed by the Russian Federation stated 'that this referendum can have no validity, and cannot form the basis for any alteration of the status of Crimea'.[111] Similar views were expressed throughout the debates arising within the Security Council.[112]

6.3 Kosovan Independence Versus Crimean Secession

6.3.1 The Debatable Legality of Kosovan Independence

The question: 'Is the unilateral declaration of independence by the Provisional Institutions of Self-Government of Kosovo in accordance with international law?'

---

[105]Cfr. Venice Commission, Opinion 762/2014, CDL-AD(2014)002, supra, Chap. 6, note 98, p. 5, para. 23. Marxsen (2014), p. 382. Vidmar (2015), p. 381.

[106]Cfr. Venice Commission, Opinion 762/2014, CDL-AD(2014)002, supra, Chap. 6, note 98, p. 5, para. 23.

[107]On the outcome of the vote, see supra, Sect. 5.2.2.

[108]Cfr. Hilpold (2015), p. 261. Kranz (2014), p. 212. Vidmar (2015), p. 382.

[109]Intervention of Sir Mark Lyall Grant (United Kingdom), UN Doc. S/PV.7144, of 19 March 2014, 20, p. 15.

[110]Cfr. Marxsen (2014), p. 382.

[111]UN Doc. S/2014/189, of 15 March 2014, at para. 5.

Cfr. Burke-White (2014), p. 72.

[112]Cfr. Douhan (2015), p. 200.

The representative of France, Gérard Araud, stated that 'the referendum it had instigated in Crimea was illegal and null and void under international law' (Intervention of Mr. Araud, UN Doc. S/PV.7144, of 19 March 2014, 20, p. 6).

was put to the ICJ by the General Assembly and its response, the Kosovo Advisory Opinion, did not investigate whether the population of Kosovo had the right to create a new State as a manifestation of its right to external self-determination.[113] The declaration of independence likewise did not refer to the right to self-determination.[114] Hence, attempts have been made to base it on various legal concepts that do not really provide an answer, some dubious in international law.[115] Consideration of the Kosovan declaration of independence, which alludes to "democratically elected leaders of our people" who are reflecting "the will of our people", might lead to the view that it is based on the people's will for its democratic legitimacy.[116] It is true that the right to internal self-determination is solidly based in international law, but it is also necessary to keep in mind the order created by Security Council Resolution 1244 (1999).[117]

A large group of authors see the unilateral declaration of independence as breaching 1244 (1999).[118] Among the reasons cited by Judge Abdul Gadire Koroma in his dissenting opinion was the infringement of the mandate to seek a negotiated solution between all the parties with regard to the final status of the territory, the mandate to base any solution on respect for the territorial integrity of the FRY and the autonomy of Kosovo, and finally the fact that the declaration entailed the ending of the international presence in Kosovo established by the Security Council resolution.[119]

As others have noted, the declaration of independence of Kosovo was possibly not in conformity with Resolution 1244 (1999), but the resolution itself already fractured the territorial integrity of Serbia and established mechanisms leading towards independence.[120] The setting up of UNIMIK undermined Serbian sovereignty and constituted a legal basis for the future independence of Kosovo.[121] Effectively, as pointed out by Peter Hilpold, the failure to find a negotiated solution, as required by Resolution 1244 (1999) left a unilateral decision as the only way out.[122] This determination was based on prior measures like the election of the Kosovar Assembly on 17 November 2007 in conformity with Resolution 1244

[113]Cfr. Ryngaert and Griffioen (2009), p. 573. Yee (2010), p. 777.

[114]Cfr. Jia (2009), p. 35.

[115]Cfr. Hilpold (2009a), pp. 272 and 273.

[116]Cfr. Ibid.

[117]See supra, Sect. 4.2.4. UN Doc. S/RES/1244 (1999), of 10 June 1999, at para. 11.

[118]Cfr. Ryngaert (2010), p. 493.

[119]Cfr. 'Dissenting Opinion of Judge Koroma', *Accordance with International Law of the Unilateral Declaration of Independence in Respect of Kosovo, Advisory Opinion, I.C.J. Reports 2010*, 467–477, p. 470, para. 11. http://www.icj-cij.org/files/case-related/141/141-20100722-ADV-01-02-BI.pdf.

[120]Cfr. Ryngaert and Griffioen (2009), p. 586.

[121]Cfr. Id., p. 586.

[122]Cfr. Hilpold (2009a), p. 274. Jia (2009), p. 32.

(1999). As its first measure, the Assembly, exercising its autonomy, adopted the declaration of independence on 17 February 2008.[123]

However, as the ICJ recognized, the authors of the declaration 'did not act, or intend to act, in the capacity of an institution created by and empowered to act within that legal order but, rather, set out to adopt a measure the significance and effects of which lie outside that order'.[124] On these lines, Resolution 1244 (1999) did not envisage a final status for Kosovo and so lacked provisions for institutions of self-government for Kosovo, thus the action fell outside the competences attributed to UNIMIK.[125] The declaration of independence was made outside the agreement between the parties called for by Resolution 1244 (1999) and must thus be considered to lie outside any *lex specialis* of international law.

More clarity is achieved by starting from the premise that unilateral declarations of independence are not regulated in international law.[126] Likewise, a right to secession cannot be said to be recognized in international law.[127] Consequently, Kosovo was able to make a unilateral declaration of independence, but this action did not mean it had any right to secede from Serbia.[128] This was the view of the ICJ in the Kosovo Advisory Opinion: 'it is entirely possible for a particular act—such as a unilateral declaration of independence—not to be in violation of international law without necessarily constituting the exercise of a right conferred by it'.[129] Hence, States are not obliged to recognize the new State and it is not surprising that one sector of the international community considered its recognition inappropriate.[130]

Finally, it is also true that it did not breach any peremptory norm of international law, as had happened with Southern Rhodesia, Northern Cyprus or the Republika Srpska, which were condemned by the Security Council, as the ICJ noted in its Kosovo Advisory Opinion.[131] In conclusion, unless it is considered an immediate

---

[123]See supra, Sect. 4.2.4.
Cfr. Hilpold (2009a), p. 274. Jacobs and Radi (2011), p. 345.

[124]*Accordance with the International Law of the Unilateral Declaration of Independence in Respect of Kosovo, Advisory Opinion,* supra, Chap. 1, note 3, p. 446, para. 105.
Cfr. Arcari (2014), p. 473.

[125]Cfr. *Accordance with the International Law of the Unilateral Declaration of Independence in Respect of Kosovo, Advisory Opinion,* supra, Chap. 1, note 3, pp. 450–451, paragraphs 116–117.
Cfr. Cirkovic (2010), p. 903.

[126]See supra, Sect. 3.2.

[127]See supra, Sect. 3.1.2.

[128]Cfr. Ryngaert (2010), p. 493.

[129]*Accordance with the International Law of the Unilateral Declaration of Independence in Respect of Kosovo, Advisory Opinion,* supra, Chap. 1, note 3, p. 426, para. 56.

[130]Cfr. Borgen (2009), pp. 10–16. Efevwerhan (2012), pp. 120–127. Oeter (2014), p. 59.

[131]See supra, Sect. 3.3. Cfr. *Accordance with the International Law of the Unilateral Declaration of Independence in Respect of Kosovo, Advisory Opinion,* supra, Chap. 1, note 3, p. 437, para. 81.
Cfr. Tancredi (2008), p. 58.

consequence of NATO intervention,[132] it cannot be claimed to be an illicit act and recognition of Kosovo is not illegal under general international law.[133]

6.3.2 *The Illegality of the Crimea's Declaration of Independence*

The Crimean declaration of independence refers to the UN Charter and the ICJ Advisory Opinion, arguing that the ICJ opines that declarations of independence do not violate international law.[134] Similarly, the parliament of the Autonomous Republic of Crimea and the Sebastopol City Council claimed that the referendum of 16 March 2014 constituted a basis for independence as a sovereign State and for accession to the Russian Federation.[135] The Russian Federation held that the referendum had been conducted in conformity with international norms in an exercise of the right to self-determination, as President Vladimir Putin proclaimed:

> As it declared independence and decided to hold a referendum, the Supreme Council of Crimea referred to the United Nations Charter, which speaks of the right of nations to self-determination. Incidentally, I would like to remind you that when Ukraine seceded from the USSR it did exactly the same thing, almost word for word. Ukraine used this right, yet the residents of Crimea are denied it.[136]

According to these statements, it would seem the Russian Federation considers the right to self-determination to imply a right to independence and constitutes a basis for it.[137] The first question that must be answered hinges on the recognition of a right to self-determination for Crimea.

As a starting point, it is somewhat debatable whether the population of Crimea constitutes a people, as it is hard to pick out any homogeneous group representing the identity of Crimea.[138] As Vladimir Putin said, 'Russians and Ukrainians, Crimean Tatars and people of other ethnic groups have lived side by side in Crimea, retaining their own identity, traditions, languages and faith', making Crimea 'a

[132]See supra, Sect. 6.1.1. Cfr. Orakhelashvili (2011), p. 101.

[133]Cfr. Arcari (2014), p. 478. Orakhelashvili (2011), p. 102. Tancredi (2008), p. 58. Vidmar (2009), p. 831. See also, by the same author Vidmar (2011), p. 383.

[134]See supra, Sect. 5.2.2.
Cfr. Van den Driest (2015), p. 330.

[135]Cfr. 'Declaration of Independence of Crimea', of 11 March 2014, para. 1 and 3.

[136]'Address by President of the Russian Federation on March 18, 2014', supra, Chap. 1, note 1, at para. 28. On the same lines, intervention of Mr. Churkin (Russian Federation), UN Doc. S/PV.7144, of 19 March 2014, 20, p. 8.

[137]Cfr. Van den Driest (2015), p. 331.

[138]Cfr. Merezhko (2015), p. 183. Peters (2015), p. 258. Van den Driest (2015), pp. 351 and 360. Wilson (2015), pp. 219–220.

unique blend of different peoples' cultures and traditions'.[139] Russian legal doctrine has even pointed out that if part of the population of a State has the same ethnic origin as the majority population of another State this does not give it a right to self-determination.[140] This makes it difficult to accept that the population concerned constitutes a group with its own identity, sufficiently preponderant and identified with the territory of Crimea for it to be considered a 'people'.[141]

It is only on territorial criteria that there could be any attribution of a right to self-determination to a population living in a given territory.[142] However, such a view is not admissible, as already explained in relation to the idea of a people as entitled to a right to self-determination.[143] Even if a strictly territorial criterion applied, it would not seem that the Autonomous Republic of Crimea could exercise a right to secession in conformity with Ukrainian domestic law.[144]

Despite these arguments, the Russian Federation, traditionally opposed to any right to secession, has still defended the secession of Crimea, putting forward the Kosovo case as a relevant precedent and denying it is a unique instance that should not set precedents, as stated by Special Envoy Martti Ahtisaari and Western states.[145] The first paragraph of the declaration of independence alluded to a status arising from the Kosovo declaration of independence,[146] and President Vladimir Putin also tried to give Crimean secession foundations in the Kosovan precedent 'the Crimean authorities referred to the well-known Kosovo precedent—a precedent our western colleagues created with their own hands in a very similar situation, when they agreed that the unilateral separation of Kosovo from Serbia, exactly what Crimea is doing now, was legitimate and did not require any permission from the country's central authorities'.[147]

---

[139]'Address by President of the Russian Federation on March 18, 2014', supra, Chap. 1, note 1, at para. 6.

[140]Cfr. Merezhko (2015), p. 183, citing Chernichenko (1999), Vol. II., p. 174.

[141]See supra, Sect. 5.1.1.

Cfr. Luchterhandt (2014), p. 150.

Several Russian authors, such as Anatoly Kapustin, took the opposite view, stating that 'there is no doubt the people of Crimea may be considered a people by the standards of international law', 'which in is composition is poly-ethnic'. Cfr. Kapustin (2015), p. 115.

[142]Cfr. Brilmayer (1991), p. 201. Weller (2009), p. 17.

[143]See supra, Sect. 2.2.2.

Cfr. Vidmar (2011), p. 364.

[144]See supra, Sect. 6.2.2.

Cfr. Marxsen (2014), p. 387.

[145]See supra, Sect. 4.2.4.

Cfr. Ibid.

[146]See supra, Sect. 5.2.2.

[147]'Address by President of the Russian Federation on March 18, 2014', supra, Chap. 1, note 1, at para. 29.

The Russian Federation, which opposed the secession of Kosovo and held that the situation could be resolved internally,[148] nevertheless referred to the Kosovo Advisory Opinion to provide a basis for Crimean independence. For their part, Western states, who had justified Kosovan independence as a *sui generis* case, opposed Crimean independence, a stance described by President Vladimir Putin in the following terms 'This is not even double standards; this is amazing, primitive, blunt cynicism. One should not try so crudely to make everything suit their interests, calling the same thing white today and black tomorrow'.[149] As stated by the representative of Saint Vincent and the Grenadines, Inga Rhonda King, during the debates in the General Assembly, all this goes to show 'the sad irony that those most supportive of Kosovo's unilateral declaration of independence now reject such a declaration by Crimea, while those with the strongest arguments against the decision of the International Court of Justice on the legality of the Kosovar unilateral declaration of independence now cite it approvingly. [. . .] the legal defenders and dissenters have switched places this time'.[150]

The situation of Kosovo has been used as a precedent for the secession of Crimea, despite the fact that those justifying Kosovan independence stressed that it was a unique instance. The independence of Kosovo was a unique matter because no precedents existed in which similar circumstances had arisen.[151] However, it could not be ruled out that it might set a precedent for future instances that could overcome the assertion that it was a *sui generis* case.[152] As is well known in legal circles, judges are not and never will be able to predict the consequences of their decisions for later cases.[153] Apart from other reasons, this is because they cannot foresee developments in general norms.[154] Moreover, in politics uniqueness in itself can never legitimize or legalize decisions or actions, nor determine future cases, as it is not even subject to the doctrine of *stare decisis*, not to mention other motives.[155] Precedent has no formal authority in international law.[156]

Apart from any other circumstances occurring in Kosovo, the Crimean case differs essentially in the unlawful military intervention on the peninsula carried out

[148] See supra, Sect. 4.2.4.
Cfr. Jaber (2011), p. 942.

[149] 'Address by President of the Russian Federation on March 18, 2014', supra, Chap. 1, note 1, at para. 31.

[150] Intervention of Ms. King (Saint Vincent and the Grenadines), UN Doc. A/68/PV.80, of 27 March 2014, 27, p. 15. Cfr. Lagerwall (2014), p. 69.

[151] Cfr. Jia (2009), p. 30.
See supra, Sect. 4.2.4.

[152] Cfr. Marxsen (2014), p. 388.

[153] Cfr. Caminker (1994), pp. 1–82.

[154] Cfr. Fleiner (2011), p. 881.

[155] Cfr. Id., p. 882.

[156] Cfr. Pelc (2014), p. 547.

by the Russian Federation bringing with it the unlawfulness of the declaration of independence.[157] As concluded by the ICJ in its Kosovo Advisory Opinion, declarations of independence are illegal when 'connected with the unlawful use of force or other egregious violations of norms of general international law'.[158] The authorization given by the Council of the Federation to deploy troops on Ukrainian territory clearly reveals the use of force by the la Russian Federation.[159] Furthermore, it constituted an intervention aimed at the final annexation of Crimea, which distinguishes it from any other instance of secession.[160] This intention is plainly indicated in the wording of the 'Declaration of Independence', which stated that in the referendum independence was linked to a decision on annexation to the Russian Federation.[161]

6.4 The Infringement of International Law in Russia's Annexation of Crimea

The apparent underlying logic relative to the annexation of Crimea in Russian Federation policy chimes with the traditional doctrines of Soviet international law. This stated that territorial changes, such as expansions of the lands of the Soviet Union, could be achieved by holding plebiscites putting the question of accession, which would be a mechanism for re-incorporating any territories that had been stripped from it by force.[162]

In the Crimean case, independence was aimed at accession to Russia through the signature of the 'Treaty between the Russian Federation and the Republic of Crimea on the Acceptance of the Republic of Crimea into the Russian Federation and on Creation of New Federative Entities within the Russian Federation' on 18 March 2014.[163] In fact, Russian constitutional law required a treaty for accession under the terms of Federal Constitutional Law No. 6 FKZ on the 'Procedure of Admission to the Russian Federation and Creation of a New Subject with the Russian Federation',

---

[157]Cfr. Marxsen (2014), p. 384. Kranz (2014), p. 212. Müllerson (2014), p. 141. Van den Driest (2015), p. 361. Vidmar (2015), p. 383.

[158]*Accordance with the International Law of the Unilateral Declaration of Independence in Respect of Kosovo, Advisory Opinion,* supra, Chap. 1, note 3, p. 437, para. 81.
See supra, Sect. 3.3.

[159]See supra, Sect. 5.2.1.
Cfr. Marxsen (2014), p. 389.

[160]Cfr. Kranz (2014), p. 212. Pronin (2015), p. 134. Walter (2014), p. 297.

[161]See supra, Sect. 5.2.2.
Cfr. Walter (2014), p. 297.

[162]See supra, Chap. 6, note 89.
Cfr. Kozhevnikov (ed.) (1960), 477 pp. Tunkin (1975), p. 25.

[163]See supra, Chap. 5, note 110.

adopted on 17 December 2001 and implementing Art. 65(2) of the Constitution of the Russian Federation.[164]

It is of relevance that Art. 4(2) of Federal Constitutional Law No. 6 FKZ laid down that a foreign State or any part of it may be admitted as a new component of the Russian Federation on the basis of mutual accord between the Russian Federation and the relevant State in the shape of an international treaty concluded between the two countries.[165] The admission process must be initiated by the foreign State concerned and the request directed to the President of the Russian Federation, who is required to report to the chambers of the Parliament and the Government.[166]

Nevertheless, the treaty with the Crimean Republic was in breach of Russian constitutional law and the 'Vienna Convention on the Law of Treaties' of 23 May 1969,[167] and is thus of no effect and void.[168] The treaty was the sole pact signed by the self-determining new State of the Republic of Crimea which under international law would have had to have had recognition as a State and recognition of its incorporation into another State.[169] In reality the Republic of Crimea did not exist as a State for the Russian Federation, yet the Federation claimed it could incorporate it using the mechanism envisaged by Art. 4(2) of Federal Constitutional Law No. 6 FKZ, in fact intended for entities recognized as States or parts of States.[170] Likewise, an international treaty cannot be concluded by an entity that exists only in its own view and which is thus not a subject of international law. The consequence is that Crimea had no power to sign a supposed treaty with the Russian Federation, so that its accession to Russia lacks legal effect within the framework of international law.[171]

The situation had already been considered theoretically by the Venice Commission when formulating the opinion requested by the Secretary General of the Council of Europe, Thorbjørn Jagland, on the compatibility with international law of Draft Federal Constitutional Law No. 462741-6, of 28 February 2014, amending the

---

[164]The text of Art. 65(2) of the Constitution of the Russian Federation, adopted on December 12, 1993, supra, Chap. 5, note 124, is as follows:

> The admission to the Russian Federation and the creation in it of a new subject shall be carried out according to the rules established by the federal constitutional law.

[165]Cfr. 'Opinion on 'Whether Draft Federal Constitutional Law No. 462741-6 on Amending the Federal Constitutional Law of the Russian Federation on the Procedure of Admission to the Russian Federation and Creation of a New Subject within the Russian Federation is Compatible with International Law', adopted by the Venice Commission at its 98th Plenary Session (Venice, 21–22 March 2014), CDL-AD(2014)004, 12, p. 2, para. 7. http://www.venice.coe.int/webforms/documents/default.aspx?pdffile=CDL-AD(2014)004-e. Luchterhandt (2014), p. 171.

[166]Cfr. 'Opinion on 'Whether Draft Federal Constitutional Law No. 462741-6', CDL-AD(2014)004, supra, Chap. 6, note 165, p. 2, para. 8. Luchterhandt (2014), p. 171.

[167]On the 'Vienna Convention on the Law of Treaties', supra, Chap. 5, note 122.

[168]Cfr. Marxsen (2014), p. 367. Luchterhandt (2014), p. 171.

[169]Cfr. Pronin (2015), p. 135.

[170]Cfr. Id., p. 136.

[171]Cfr. Marxsen (2014), p. 390.

procedure for admission to the Russian Federation and the creation of a new entity within the Federation that had been proposed by a group of deputies of the State Duma of the Russian Federation. The amendment did away with the need for mutual accord and an international treaty between the Federation and the foreign State. The Draft Law laid down that if it was impossible to conclude a treaty by reason of the absence of any efficient sovereign state government, admission to the Federation of a part of a foreign State in the capacity of a new subject could be accomplished on the basis of a referendum held in accordance with the legislation of the foreign State, in the territory of that part of the foreign State in which accession was approved or requested by the authorities of the given part of the foreign state.[172] This proposed modification was seen by the Venice Commission as not compatible with international law, as it implied violation of the principles of territorial integrity, national sovereignty, and non-intervention in the internal affairs of another state, and the *pacta sunt servanda* rule.[173] On 20 March the Draft Law was withdrawn from the order paper of the Duma at its proposers' initiative.[174] The text of the Draft Law betrayed the fact that certain actions corresponding exactly to the contents of the proposal were illicit.

The Venice Commission recalled in its opinion a renunciation of rights and ownership of a territory by one State in favour of another is a cession that can take place only through a 'mutual, freely reached accord' between the previous and the new entities and must have the consent of the State owning the territory.[175] This requirement was also enshrined in the provisions of Art. 2 of the Ukrainian Constitution, which proclaimed national indivisibility, and of Art. 1 of the Constitution of the Autonomous Republic of Crimea, which likewise stated that Crimea was 'an integral part of Ukraine', as noted previously.[176] The Russian Federation had made a commitment to preserving this territorial Integrity in the el Treaty of Friendship of 1997, Art. 2 of which envisaged an obligation to 'respect each other's territorial integrity and confirm the inviolability of their common borders'.[177]

The conclusion reached by the Venice Commission was quite forthright and held that 'a transfer of territory from one state to the other without the valid consent of the government of the state whose territory is concerned is no lawful cession of territory, but rather amounts to an annexation of territory which is prohibited under international law'.[178] The annexation of Crimea by the Russian Federation constitutes an

---

[172]On the doctrines of Soviet international law on the accession of new territories, see supra, Chap. 6, note 89.

Cfr. 'Opinion on 'Whether Draft Federal Constitutional Law No. 462741-6', CDL-AD(2014) 004, supra, Chap. 6, note 165, p. 3, para. 9.

[173]Cfr. Id., p. 12, para. 46.

[174]Cfr. Id., p. 12, para. 47.

[175]Cfr. Id., p. 5, para. 17.

[176]See supra, Sect. 6.2.2.

[177]See supra, Sect. 5.1.2.

[178]Cfr. 'Opinion on 'Whether Draft Federal Constitutional Law No. 462741-6', CDL-AD(2014) 004, supra, Chap. 6, note 165, p. 6, para. 22.

infringement of a number of principles and norms of international law comprised in the UN Charter, in other texts of a regional nature, and in the bilateral treaties concluded with the Ukraine.[179]

References

Akehurst, M. 1977. The Use of Force to Protect Nationals Abroad. *International Relations* 5: 3–23.

Arcari, M. 2014. Violazione del divieto di uso della forza, aggressione o attacco armato in relazione all'intervento militare della Russia in Crimea? *DUDI* 8: 473–479.

Bílkovà, V. 2015. The Use of Force by the Russian Federation in Crimea. *ZaöRV/HJIL* 75: 27–50.

Bismuth, R. 2014. Odysée dans le conundrum des réactions décentralisées à l'illicite. *JDI* 141: 719–731.

Borgen, C.J. 2009. The Language of Law and the Practice of Politics: Great Powers and the Rhetoric of Self-Determination in the Cases of Kosovo and South Ossetia. *Chicago JIL* 10: 1–33.

Bowett, D.W. 1986. The Use of Force for the Protection of Nationals Abroad. In *The Current Legal Regulation for the Use of Force*, ed. A. Cassese, 39–55. Dordrecht: Martinus Nijhoff Publishers.

Brilmayer, L. 1991. Secession and Self-Determination: A Territorial Interpretation. *YJIL* 16: 177–202.

Brown, C. 2005. Access to International Justice in the Legality of Use of Force Cases. (Yugoslavia v. The 10 NATO Countries which Militarily Intervened in Kosovo, in which the International Court of Justice Ruled it did not have Jurisdiction). *Cambridge LJ* 64: 267–271.

Brownlie, I. 1990. *Principles of Public International Law*. 4th ed. Oxford: Oxford University Press.

Burke-White, W.W. 2014. Crimea and the International Legal Order. *Survival* 56: 65–80.

Caminker, E.H. 1994. Precedent and Prediction: The Forward-Looking Aspects of Inferior Court Decisionmaking. *Texas Law Review* 73: 1–82.

Chernichenko, S.V. 1999. *Teoria mezhdunarodnogo prava*. Moscow: NIMP.

Christakis, T. 2011. The ICJ Advisory Opinion on Kosovo: Has International Law Something to Say about Secession? *LJIL* 24: 73–86.

———. 2014. Les conflits de sécession en Crimée et dans l'Est de l'Ukraine et le droit international (The Conflicts of Secession in Crimea and Eastern Ukraine and International Law). *JDI* 141: 733–764.

Cirkovic, E. 2010. An Analysis of the ICJ Advisory Opinion on Kosovo's Unilateral Declaration of Independence. *German LJ* 11: 895–912.

Corten, O. 2008. Déclarations unilatérales d'indépendance et reconnaissance prématurées: du Kosovo à l'Ossétie du sud et à l'Abkhazie. *RGDIP* 112: 721–759.

Crawford, J. 2012. *Brownlie's Principles of Public International Law*. 8th ed. Oxford: Oxford University Press.

Cvijić, S. 2007. Self-Determination as a Challenge to the Legitimacy of Humanitarian Intervention: The Case of Kosovo. *German LJ* 8: 57–80.

Delahunty, R. 2015. The Crimean Crisis, Legal Studies Research Paper Series. *U.St.Thomas J.L. & Pub. Poly* 9: 125–168.

Dmitriev, Y.A. 2014. Crimea as a Bone of Contention Between Russia, the European Union and the USA. *ПРАВО И ЖИЗНЬ Независимый научно-правовой журнал* 189: 22–50.

Douhan, A.F. 2015. International Organizations and Settlement of the Conflict in Ukraine. *ZaöRV/HJIL* 75: 195–214.

Efevwerhan, D.I. 2012. Kosovo's Chances of UN Membership: A Prognosis. *GoJIL* 4: 93–130.

[179]Cfr. Merezhko (2015), p. 194.

Fleiner, T. 2011. The Unilateral Secession of Kosovo as a Precedent in International Law. In *From Bilateralism to Community Interests: Essays in Honour of Judge Bruno Simma*, ed. U. Fastenrath, 877–894. Oxford: Oxford University Press.

Fox, G.H. 2015. Intervention by Invitation. In *The Oxford Handbook of the Use of Force in International Law*, ed. M. Weller, 816–840. Oxford: Oxford University Press.

Francioni, F. 2000. Of War, Humanity and Justice in International Law After Kosovo. *Max Planck YUNL* 4: 107–126.

Gordon, D.J. 1977. Use of Force for the Protection of Nationals Abroad: The Entebbe Incident Note. *Case W.Res.J. Int'l L.* 9: 117–134.

Gray, C. 2001. The Legality of NATOs Military Action in Kosovo: Is There a Right of Humanitarian Intervention? In *International Law in the Post-Cold War World: Essays in Memory of Li Haopei*, 240–253. London: Routledge.

———. 2005. Legality of Use of Force. (Serbia & Montenegro v. Belgium, Canada, France, Germany, Italy, Netherlands, Portugal, and the United Kingdom; Cases Stemming from NATO Action in Yugoslavia and Kosovo). *ICLQ* 54: 787–794.

———. 2009. The Protection of Nationals Abroad: Russia's Use of Force in Georgia. In *The Diversity of International Law: Essays in Honour of Professor Kalliopi K. Koufa*, ed. A. Constantinides and N. Zaiker, 133–151. Leiden, Netherlands; Boston, MA: Martinus Nijhoff Publishers.

Green, J.A. 2010. Passportization, Peacekeepers and Proportionality: The Russian Claim on the Protection of Nations Abroad in Self-Defence. In *Conflict in the Caucasus: Implications for International Legal Order*, ed. J.A. Green and C.P.M. Waters, 54–79. Basingstoke, England; New York: Palgrave Macmillan.

———. 2014. The Annexation of Crimea: Russia, Passportisation and the Protection of Nationals Revisited. *JUFIL* 1: 3–10.

Greenwood, C. 1999. Humanitarian Intervention: The Case of Kosovo. *Finnish YIL* 10: 141–175.

Hilpold, P. 2009a. The International Court of Justices Advisory Opinion on Kosovo: Perspectives of a Delicate Question. *ARIEL* 14: 259–310.

———. 2009b. The Kosovo Case and International Law: Looking for Applicable Theories. *Chinese JIL* 8: 47–61.

———. 2015. Ukraine, Crimea and New International Law: Balancing International Law with Arguments Drawn from History. *Chinese JIL* 14: 237–270.

Jaber, T. 2011. A Case for Kosovo? Self-Determination and Secession in the 21st Century. *IJHR* 15: 926–947.

Jacobs, D., and Y. Radi. 2011. Waiting for Godot: An Analysis of the Advisory Opinion on Kosovo. *LJIL* 24: 331–353.

Jennings, R.Y. 1999. Kosovo and International Lawyers. *International Law FORUM du droit international* 1: 166–170.

Jia, B.B. 2009. The Independence of Kosovo: A Unique Case of Secession? *Chinese JIL* 8: 27–46.

Kälin, W. 2000. Humanitäre Intervention: Legitimation durch Verfahren? Zehn Thesen zur Kosovo-Krise. *SZIER/RSDIE* 10: 159–176.

Kapustin, A. 2015. Crimea's Self-Determination in the Light of Contemporary International Law. *ZaöRV/HJIL* 75: 101–118.

Kessedjian, C. 1999. La légalité de l'intervention de l'OTAN au Kosovo. *International Law FORUM du droit international* 1: 147–148.

Kozhevnikov, F.I., ed. 1960. *International Law. A Textbook for Use in Law Schools*. Moscow: Foreign Languages Publishing House.

Kranz, J. 2014. Imperialism, the Highest Stage of Sovereign Democracy: Some Remarks on the Annexation of Crimea by Russia. *AVR* 52: 205–221.

Krieger, H. 2001. *The Kosovo Conflict and International Law: An Analytical Documentation 1974–1999*. Cambridge: Cambridge University Press.

Krisch, N. 1999. Unilateral Enforcement of the Collective Will: Kosovo, Iraq, and the Security Council. *Max Planck YUNL* 3: 59–103.

Lagerwall, A. 2014. L'agression et l'annexion de la Crimée para la Fédération de Russie: Quels enseignements au sujet du droit international. *Questions of International Law, Zoom Out* I: 57–72. www.qil-qdi.org.
Luchterhandt, O. 2014. Der Anschluss der Krim an Russland aus völkerrechtlicher Sicht. *AVR* 52: 137–174.
Mansour, A.B. 2010. Circumstances Precluding Wrongfulness in the ILC Articles on State Responsibility. Consent. In *The Law of International Responsibility*, ed. J. Crawford, A. Pellet, and S. Olleson, 439–449. Oxford: Oxford University Press.
Marxsen, C. 2014. The Crimea Crisis – An International Law Perspective. *ZaöRV/HJIL* 74: 367–391.
Merezhko, O. 2015. Crimea's Annexation by Russia – Contradictions of the New Russian Doctrine of International Law. *ZaöRV/HJIL* 75: 167–194.
Müllerson, R.A. 2014. Ukraine: Victim of Geopolitics. *Chinese JIL* 13: 133–146.
Murase, S. 2002. The Relationship Between the UN Charter and General International Law Regarding Non-Use of Force: The Case of NATOs Air Campaign in Kosovo Crisis of 1999. In *Liber amicorum Judge Shigeru Oda*, vol. 2, 1543–1554. The Hague; New York: Kluwer Law International.
Natoli, K. 2010. Weaponizing Nationality: An Analysis of Russia's Passport Policy in Georgia. *B. U. Int'l L.J.* 28: 389–417.
Nolte, G. 1999. Kosovo und Konstitutionalisierung: Zur humanitären Intervention der NATO-Staaten. *ZaöRV/HJIL* 59: 941–960.
———. 2010. Intervention by Invitation. In *Max Planck Encyclopedia of Public International Law*. Oxford Public International Law, Online edition. http://opil.ouplaw.com/view/10.1093/law:epil/9780199231690/law-9780199231690-e1702?prd=EPIL.
O'Connell, M.E. 2000. The UN, NATO and International Law After Kosovo. *HRQ* 22: 57–89.
Oeter, S. 2014. The Role of Recognition and Non-Recognition with Regard to Secession. In *Self-Determination and Secession in International Law*, ed. C. Walter et al., 45–67. Oxford: Oxford University Press.
Olson, P.M. 2014. The Lawfulness of Use of Force in Crimea. *ML & LWR* 53: 17–44.
Orakhelashvili, A. 2011. The International Courts Advisory Opinion on the UDI in Respect of Kosovo: Washing Away the Foam on the Tide of Time. *Max Planck YUNL* 15: 65–104.
Pelc, K.J. 2014. The Politics of Precedent in International Law: A Social Network Application. *APSR* 108: 547–564.
Peters, A. 2015. The Crimean Vote of March 2014 as an Abuse of the Institution of the Territorial Referendum. In *Staat und Mensch im Kontext des Völker- und Europarechts. Liber Amicorum für Torsten Stein*, ed. C. Calliess, 255–280. Baden-Baden: Nomos Verlag.
Pronin, A. 2015. Republic of Crimea A Two-Day State. *Russian LJ* 3: 133–142.
Radan, P. 2012. Secessionist Referenda in International and Domestic Law. *Nationalism and Ethic Politics* 18: 8–21.
Ronzitti, N. 1985. *Rescuing Nationals Abroad Through Military Coercion and Intervention on Grounds of Humanity*. Dordrecth: Martinus Nijhoff Publishers.
Ruys, T. 2008. The 'Protection of Nationals' Doctrine Revisited. *Journal of Conflict and Security Law* 13: 233–271.
Ruys, T., and N. Verlinden. 2014. Digest of State Practice 1 January–30 June 2014. *JUFIL* 1: 324–340.
Ryngaert, C. 2010. The ICJs Advisory Opinion on Kosovo's Declaration of Independence: A Mixed Opportunity?: International Court of Justice, Accordance with International Law of the Unilateral Declaration of Independence in Respect of Kosovo, Advisory Opinion of 22 July 2010. *NILR* 57: 481–494.
Ryngaert, C., and C. Griffioen. 2009. The Relevance of the Right to Self-Determination in the Kosovo Matter: In Partial Response to the Agora Papers. *Chinese JIL* 8: 573–587.
Sciso, E. 2014. La crisi ucraina e lintervento russo: profile di diritto internazionale. *RDI* 97: 992–1031.

Şen, İ.G. 2015. *Sovereignty Referendums in International and Constitutional Law*. Dordrecht, Boston, New York: Springer.
Sofaer, A.D. 2000. International Law and Kosovo. *SJIL* 36: 1–21.
Tancredi, A. 2008. Neither Authorized nor Prohibited? Secession and International Law After Kosovo, South Ossetia and Abkhazia. *Italian YIL* 18: 37–62.
———. 2012. Some Remarks on the Relationship Between Secession and General International Law in the Light of the ICJs Kosovo Advisory Opinion. In *Kosovo and International Law: The ICJ Advisory Opinion of 22 July 2010*, ed. P. Hilpold, 79–108. Leiden; Boston: M. Nijhoff Publishers.
———. 2014a. Crisi in Crimea, referéndum ed autodeterminazione dei popoli. *DUDI* 8: 480–490.
———. 2014b. The Russian Annexation of the Crimea: Questions Relating to the Use of Force. *Questions of International Law, Zoom Out* I: 5–34. www.qil-qdi.org.
Thürer, D. 2000. Der Kosovo-Konflikt im Lichte des Völkerrechts: Von drei-echten und scheinbaren – Dilemmata. *AVR* 38: 1–22.
Tolstykh, V. 2015. Three Ideas of Self-Determination in International Law and the Reunification of Crimea with Russia. *ZaöRV/HJIL* 75: 119–139.
Tunkin, G.I. 1975. International Law in the International System. *Recueil des cours* 147: 1–218.
Van den Driest, S.F. 2015. Crimea's Separation from Ukraine: An Analysis of the Right to Self-Determination and (Remedial) Secession in International Law. *NILR* 62: 329–363.
Vidmar, J. 2009. International Legal Responses to Kosovo's Declaration of Independence. *Vand. J. Transnatl L.* 42: 779–851.
———. 2011. The Kosovo Advisory Opinion Scrutinized. *LJIL* 24: 355–383.
———. 2013. *Democratic Statehood in International Law: The Emergence of New States in Post-Cold War Practice*. Oxford: Hart Publishing.
———. 2015. The Annexation of Crimea and the Boundaries of the Will of the People. *German LJ* 16: 365–383.
Volova, L.I. 1972. *Plebistsit v mezhdunarodnom prave*. Moscow: Mezhdunar. otnosheniia.
Voronin, E.R., V.N. Kulebyakin, and A.V. Nikolaev. 2015. Государственный переворот в Киеве в феврале 2014 г.: международно–правовые оценки и последствия [The coup d'état in Kiev in February 2014: International Law Context and Consequences]. *Московский журнал международного права/Moscow Journal of International Law* 97: 11–28.
Waldock, H. 1952. The Regulation of the Use of Force by Individual States in International Law. *Recueil des cours* 81: 455–515.
Wall, A.E. 2002. Legal and Ethical Lessons of NATOs Kosovo Campaign. *International Law Studies* 78: 571.
Walter, C. 2014. Postscript: Self-Determination, Secession and the Crimean Crisis 2014. In *Self-Determination and Secession in International Law*, ed. C. Walter, A. Von Ungern-Sternberg, and K. Abushov, 293–311. Oxford: Oxford University Press.
Weller, M. 2009. *Contested Statehood: Kosovo's Struggle for Independence*. Oxford: Oxford University Press.
Wilson, G. 2009. Self-Determination, Recognition and the Problem of Kosovo. *NILR* 56: 455–481.
———. 2015. Crimea: Some Observations on Secession and Intervention in Partial Response to Müllerson and Tolstykh. *Chinese JIL* 14: 217–223.
Wippman, D. 2001. Kosovo and the Limits of International Law (NATOs Bombing of Kosovo Under International Law). *Fordham Intl L.J.* 25: 129–150.
Yee, S. 2010. Notes on the International Court of Justice (Part 4): The Kosovo Advisory Opinion. *Chinese JIL* 9: 763–782.

Part III
The Emergence of Humanitarian Secession as a Response to Humanitarian Crises

Chapter 7
The International Community Faced with Illegal Secessions by Sub-State Units

In the pages above an attempt has been made to show how events developed, and to analyse the fundamentals asserted, with regard to the unilateral declarations of independence by Kosovo and Crimea from the viewpoint of international law. This chapter will endeavour to study the scope of these declarations within the international community and the consequences they may have on the impact of secession in international law.

There is a contrast between the stances adopted in respect of the Kosovo precedent and the statements of recognition made by a large group of States, on the one hand, and the attitudes towards the annexation of Crimea and limited number of declarations of recognition of it, on the other. This raises a fundamental question with regard to the scope of the Kosovan and Crimean episodes.

Indeed, a major group of States recognized Kosovo as an independent State very shortly after its unilateral declaration of independence.[1] In contrast, with regard to the events in Crimea only the Russian Federation and ten other States recognized the new status of the Republic.[2] It may be said that States departed from the traditional practice of not stating their recognition for a territory attempting to secede while territorial sovereignty was still in dispute with the State from which it was trying to break away.[3]

---

[1]See supra, Chap. 4, note 134.

The day after the unilateral declaration of independence, on 18 February 2008, it was recognized by Afghanistan, Albania, Costa Rica, France, Senegal, Turkey, the United Kingdom, and the United States. Three of these are permanent members of the Security Council. In the following 2 days, recognition was also granted by Australia (19 February), and Latvia and Germany (20 February), until 21 recognitions had been made during the month of February. By the end of 2010, this figure had reached 53 recognitions.

[2]The States recognizing the new situation were Afghanistan, Bolivia, Cuba, Kyrgyzstan, Nicaragua, North Korea, Sudan, Syria, Venezuela and Zimbabwe.

[3]Cfr. Frowein (2010), at para. 6, http://opil.ouplaw.com/view/10.1093/law:epil/9780199231690/law-9780199231690-e1086?rskey=0y3Wx1&result=1&prd=EPIL.

J. F. Escudero Espinosa, *Self-Determination and Humanitarian Secession in International Law of a Globalized World*,
https://doi.org/10.1007/978-3-319-72622-9_7

As an aftermath of the Kosovan and Crimean events, a strong disinclination to grant recognition has emerged, giving rise to substantial differences in views on its impact on the international community.[4] The question posed turns on the response that the international community should give to secession and its reaction to situations running counter to international law. Hasty statements of recognition in the matter of Kosovo and non-recognition in the Crimean affair, respectively, have sharpened debate on the part these can play with regard to a possible secession.[5] In these discussions, the case of Kosovo had become a key element in developments in changing laws on statehood and related norms on recognition.[6]

7.1 The Difficulty of Reacting to the Illicit and the Obligation to Deny Recognition

The problem that has always arisen with regard to recognition lies in its legal nature and consequences.[7] The extent of the debate in legal doctrine on this matter can be summed up as the traditionally termed declaratory and constitutive theories.[8] The most widespread stance in practice by States, according to the main authorities in the field, has been declarative theory.[9] As Jochen Abraham Frowein stressed, in contrast to the views of Sir Hersch Lauterpacht, Dionisio Anzilotti and Hans Kelsen, who saw recognition as having a constitutive scope in a system of law based on understandings between States,[10] it would seem that recognition does not create a State.[11] Following this line, the Arbitration Commission of the Peace Conference on Yugoslavia declared in its Opinion No. 1 that 'the existence or disappearance of the State

[4]Cfr. Oeter (2014), p. 45.

[5]Cfr. Tomuschat (2012), p. 31.

[6]Cfr. Jia (2009), p. 42.

[7]Cfr. Dugard (2011), p. 13.

[8]Cfr. Roth (2010), pp. 396–398. Talmon (2005a), p. 180. For an explanation of the debate between the two views see: Grant (1999).

[9]Cfr. Brownlie (1982), p. 206. Frowein (2010), at para. 10. Vidmar (2015), p. 372. Wilson (2009), p. 459.

[10]In the words of Hans Kelsen: 'By the legal act of recognition the recognized community is brought into legal existence in relation to the recognizing state, and thereby international law becomes applicable to the relations between these states. Hence the legal act of recognition has a specifically constitutive character'. Kelsen (1941), p. 609. Lauterpacht (1947). Anzilotti (1999), pp. 159–177.

Cfr. Briggs (1949), p. 114. Pronin (2015), p. 135.

[11]Cfr. Frowein (2010), at para. 10. Jia (2009), p. 43.

On these lines, James Crawford maintains that 'an entity is not a State because it is recognized; it is recognized because it is a State'. Crawford (2007), pp. 22–26.

is a question of fact; the effects of recognition by other States are purely declaratory'.[12]

Some authors have stated that recognition may have a declaratory or constitutive effect, depending on circumstances, as shown by the Kosovo case.[13] Thus, for instance, in the 'Letter from President George W. Bush to the President of Kosovo' of 18 February 2008, the United States recognized the fact of the existence of Kosovo as a sovereign State and simultaneously expressed a desire to establish diplomatic relations.[14] This was a manifestation of the classic double legal function of recognition. On the one hand, statehood was asserted, on the other, the establishment of bilateral relations.[15] This distinction implies a recognition of the legal status and the exercise of rights by a State, the first having a declarative nature, the second a constitutive.[16]

However, it must be noted that legal doctrine has developed the view that recognition should be based on proof of the effective existence of a State, rather than upon a mere declaration of independence.[17] The new entity should meet the classic criteria for statehood envisaged by Art. 1 of the Montevideo Convention,[18] termed recognition requirements.[19] Nevertheless, as has been seen in international practice, acceptance by the international community is also of importance in deploying all the legal effects inherent in statehood.[20] For this reason, it may be stated that recognition has a function of securing, rather than creating, the emergence of a new State in the international community. This function has been seen as a consolidating effect by some authors.[21]

---

[12]Opinion No. 1, of 29 November 1991, at para. 1(a). 31:6 *ILM* (1992), 1494; 3:1 *EJIL* (1992), 182–183, http://ejil.org/pdfs/3/1/1175.pdf.

The Arbitration Commission of the Peace Conference on Yugoslavia of the EEC, known as the Badinter Arbitration Committee, issued Opinion No. 1 in which it confirmed the process of dissolution of the SFRY. Cfr. Opinion No. 1, of 29 November 1991, supra, Chap. 3, note 70, at para. 2 and 3. See Craven (1995).

[13]Cfr. Jia (2009), p. 43. Vidmar (2015), p. 372.

[14]Cfr. 'Letter from the President to the President of Kosovo' of 18 February 2008, at para. 1 and 3. https://georgewbush-whitehouse.archives.gov/news/releases/2008/02/20080218-3.html. United States Recognizes Kosovo as an Independent State, 2008, *AJIL* 102:638–640, p. 640.

[15]Cfr. Brownlie (1990), p. 93. Jia (2009), p. 44.

[16]Cfr. Brownlie (1990), p. 93, note 3.

[17]Cfr. Vidmar (2012), p. 153.

[18]See supra, Chap. 3, note 68.

[19]Cfr. Talmon (2005a), p. 126. Ryngaert and Sobrie (2011), p. 489.

[20]Cfr. Supreme Court of Canada, *Reference re Secession of Quebec*, supra, Chap. 2, note 71, p. 274, para. 106.

[21]Cfr. Dugard and Raič (2006), p. 135. Hilpold (2009), p. 59.

7.1.1 The Effectiveness of Non-Recognition

The question arising from the declarations of independence by Kosovo and Crimea centres on whether reaction by the international community in respect of recognition is in conformity with international law.

In the first instance it is possible to hold that the effective fulfilment of the criteria for statehood was not reached. Statements of recognition in this sort of affair have been seen as premature recognition and such acts should be deemed null and void.[22] Some authors have even affirmed that such an untimely recognition would constitute a form of illicit intervention.[23]

In the case of Crimea, the majority of the international community has opted not to recognize the claimed new entity. In its Kosovo Advisory Opinion the ICJ had confirmed that there are certain declarations of independence that are illegal 'from the fact that they were, or would have been, connected with the unlawful use of force or other egregious violations of norms of general international law, in particular those of a peremptory character',[24] as was already explained in detail in Sect. 3.3 of Chap. 3.[25] These illegal situations, the outcome of a serious violation of a norm of peremptory nature, give rise to consequences in the area of international responsibility, among which may be an obligation not to recognize them.[26]

7.1.1.1 The Emergence of an Obligation Not to Recognize in International Law

The obligation not to recognize under certain circumstances had as one of its first instances what was called the Stimson Doctrine, which was put forward in relation to situations running counter to the 'General Treaty for Renunciation of War as an Instrument of National Policy' (Kellogg-Briand Pact) of 1928.[27] Faced with Japan's policy of unilateral acquisition of Manchuria, the United States Secretary of State, Henry Lewys Stimson, stated his non-recognition of international territorial changes achieved by means of the use of force:

---

[22] Cfr. Crawford (2007), p. 21.

[23] Cfr. Oppenheim et al. (1992), Vol. I, p. 143.

[24] *Accordance with the International Law of the Unilateral Declaration of Independence in Respect of Kosovo, Advisory Opinion,* supra, Chap. 1, note 3, p. 437, para. 81.

[25] See supra, Sect. 3.3.

[26] Cfr. Bismuth (2014), p. 724. Lagerwall (2014), p. 66. Christakis (2011), p. 82. Wilson (2015), p. 220.

[27] On the Stimson Doctrine, see: Current (1954), Turns (2003).

The 'General Treaty for Renunciation of War as an Instrument of National Policy', signed at Paris, on 27 August 1928, which was to come into effect on 24 July 1929. 94:1–4 *LNTS* (1929), No. 2137, 57–64 https://treaties.un.org/doc/Publication/UNTS/LON/Volume%2094/v94.pdf.

> [...] that it does not intend to recognize any situation, treaty or agreement which may be brought about by means contrary to the covenants and obligations of the Pact of Paris of August 27, 1928, to which Treaty both China and Japan, as well as the United States, are parties.[28]

Later practice and *opinio iuris* by States confirmed the existence of an obligation of a deep-rooted customary law nature arising from the Stimson Doctrine.[29] This doctrine was rapidly fleshed out in a number of American instruments such as the 'Anti-War Treaty of Non-Aggression and Conciliation' (Saavedra Lamas Treaty) of 1933[30] and the Montevideo Convention' of 1933.[31] It was also backed up by international practice that served to confirm the existence of an obligation to non-recognition in general international law.[32]

In the period starting with the UN Charter, practice has had to react to events such as the claim to secede made by Southern Rhodesia in 1965, which led both the General Assembly and the Security Council of the UN to request it should not be recognized because it infringed the right of self-determination.[33] Similar lines were

---

[28]'The Secretary of State to the Consul General at Nanking (Peck), Washington, January 7, 1932', *Foreign Relations of the United States Diplomatic Papers, 1932, The Far East*, Vol. III, 782, pp. 7–8. https://history.state.gov/historicaldocuments/frus1932v03/pg_7.

[29]Cfr. Christakis (2005), p. 135. Grant (2014), at para. 14, http://opil.ouplaw.com/view/10.1093/law:epil/9780199231690/law-9780199231690-e697?prd=EPIL. Himmer (1992), p. 272. Lagerwall (2014), p. 64. Milano (2014), p. 36.

[30]'Anti-war Treaty of Non-aggression and Conciliation', signed in Rio de Janeiro on 10 October 1933, at Art. 2. 163 *LNTS* (1935), No. 3781, 394–413.

[31]'Convention on Rights and Duties of States' adopted by the Seventh International Conference of American States, signed at Montevideo on 26 December 1933, supra, Chap. 3, note 68, at Art. 11.

[32]Théodore Christakis highlights among others the resolution adopted by the General Assembly of the League of Nations on 11 March 1932 after the occupation of Manchukuo by Japan in 1931, which requested members 'not to recognize any situation, treaty, or agreement which may be brought about by means contrary to the Covenant of the League of Nations or to the Pact of Paris' (*League of Nations Official Journal* 87) (Cfr. Turns (2003), p. 123). This same obligation was restated in the context of the Gran Chaco Conflict (1928–1935) between Bolivia and Paraguay in the shape of the 'Declaration of Nineteen American Republics' of 3 August 1932, and of the Leticia Conflict between Colombia and Peru in the resolution of the Council of the League of Nations of 18 March 1933. The hiatus arising from the annexation of Ethiopia by Italy in 1935 in practices prior to the Second World War was no hindrance to non-recognition of this by some States and support for the continuity of the Ethiopian State at the end of World War II. See Christakis (2005), pp. 137–138.

One particularly relevant event was the annexation of the Baltic States by the USSR in June 1940. This seizure was given no recognition by a large number of states, but triggered a movement opposing non-recognition on the grounds of the negative consequences it had for the population. With the break-up of the Soviet Union in 1990, the Baltic States argued that their independence had been restored and that they had no need to make any declaration of independence. This reasoning was supported by various States that had refused recognition of the original annexation. See Christakis (1999), pp. 200–201. Himmer (1992), pp. 253–291. Rich (1993), p. 37. Vidmar (2010), p. 44.

[33]Cfr. UN Doc. A/RES/2022 (XX), of 5 November 1965, at para. 9. UN Doc. S/RES/216 (1965), of 12 November, para. 1. Gowlland-Debbas (1990), p. 282.

See supra, Sect. 3.3.

taken at the end of the South African mandate in Namibia in 1966,[34] on the creation of Homelands by South Africa from 1976 onwards, these being seen as a form of 'forced secession',[35] on the break-away of Northern Cyprus in 1983, which was considered 'legally invalid' by the Security Council,[36] on the annexation of certain territories occupied by Israel in 1967 and 1973,[37] and on the invasion of Kuwait by Iraq in 1990.[38]

Throughout this period a large number of texts enshrining the obligation not to recognize were also issued, among them resolutions taken by the General Assembly. Of particular note would be 2625 (XXV) 'Declaration on Principles of International Law Concerning Friendly Relations and Co-operation among States in Accordance with the Charter of the United Nations', especially its First Principle,[39] 3314 (XXIX) 'Definition of Aggression', in particular Art. 5(3),[40] 36/103 'Declaration on the Inadmissibility of Intervention and Interference in the Internal Affairs of States',[41] and 42/22 'Declaration on the Enhancement of the Effectiveness of the Principle of Refraining from the Threat or Use of Force in International Relations'.[42]

This doctrine has also been included in further texts drawn up by the ILC. Of these, attention should be drawn to Art. 41(2) of the 'Draft Articles on the Responsibility of States for Internationally Wrongful Acts' de 2001[43] and to Art. 42(2) of

---

[34]Cfr. UN Doc. S/RES/269 (1969), of 12 August, para. 7.

Text of the 'Draft Articles on Responsibility of States for Internationally Wrongful Acts - Article 41 Commentary', supra, Chap. 6, note 49, p. 289, para. 8.

See supra, Sect. 3.3.

[35]Cfr. UN Doc. A/RES/31/6A, of 26 October 1976; A/RES/3411D (XXX), of 28 November 1975; A/RES/32/105N, of 14 December 1977; and A/RES/37/69A, of 9 December 1982. UN Doc. S/RES/402 (1976), of 22 December, and S/RES/407 (1977), of 25 May.

Text of the 'Draft Articles on Responsibility of States for Internationally Wrongful Acts - Article 41 Commentary', supra, Chap. 6, note 49, p. 289, para. 8.

See supra, Sect. 3.3.

[36]Cfr. UN Doc. S/RES/541 (1983), of 18 November, at para. 2 and 7.

See supra, Sects. 3.3 and 6.1, note 6.

[37]An account of the resolutions may be found in: Dugard (1987), p. 112.

[38]Cfr. UN Doc. S/RES/662 (1990), of 9 August.

[39]UN Doc. A/RES/2625 (XXV), of 24 October 1970, at Annex, 'The Principle that States shall refrain in their international relations from the threat or use of force against the territorial integrity or political independence of any State, or in any other manner inconsistent with the purposes of the United Nations', para. 10.

[40]UN Doc. A/RES/3314 (XXIX), of 14 December 1974, at Annex.

[41]UN Doc. A/RES/36/103, of 9 December 1981, at Annex, para. 2(III) (e).

[42]UN Doc. A/RES/42/22, of 18 November 1987, at Annex, para. 10.

[43]The text of Art. 41(2) of the 'Draft Articles on Responsibility of States for Internationally Wrongful Acts,' supra, Chap. 6, note 49, pp. 43–59), runs as follows:

> No State shall recognize as lawful a situation created by a serious breach within the meaning of article 40, nor render aid or assistance in maintaining that situation.

the 'Draft Articles on the Responsibility of International Organizations' de 2011.[44] These envisage a prohibition on the recognition as valid of any situation caused by infringement of a peremptory norm.[45]

At a regional level, the principle was incorporated in Art. 17 of the 'Charter of the Organization of American States' of 1948,[46] confirmed by Art. 20 of the 'Protocol of Buenos Aires' of 1967.[47] In a European context, there was also the 'Declaration of Principles Guiding Relations between Participating States' forming a part of the Helsinki Final Act of 1975, issued by the CSCE.[48] At a later stage, there was the 'Declaration of the European Council on the Guidelines on the Recognition of the New States in Eastern Europe and in the Soviet Union' of 1991,[49] together with the opinions stated by the Arbitration Commission of the Peace Conference on Yugoslavia, likewise from 1991.[50]

As Judge *ad hoc* Krysztof Skubiszewski stated with regard to his dissenting opinion in the East Timor Case:

---

[44]The text of Art. 44(2) of the 'Draft Articles on the Responsibility of International Organizations' adopted by the ILC in its sixty-third session ('Report of the International Law Commission, Sixty-third Session (26 April–3 June and 4 July–12 August 2011)', UN Doc. A/66/10, 384, pp. 54–69), is the following:

> No State or international organization shall recognize as lawful a situation created by a serious breach within the meaning of article 41, nor render aid or assistance in maintaining that situation.

[45]Cfr. Vidmar (2012), p. 166.

[46]Article 17 of the 'Charter of the Organization of American States', signed in Bogotá, on 30 April 1948, 119 *UNTS* (1952), No. 1609, 3-97, declares:

> The territory of a State is inviolable; it may not be the object, even temporarily, of military occupation or of other measures of force taken by another State, directly or indirectly, on any grounds whatever. No territorial acquisitions or special advantages obtained either by force or by other means of coercion shall be recognized.

[47]'Protocol of amendment to the Charter of the Organization of American States', signed in Buenos Aires, on 27 February 1967, 721 UNTS (1970), No. 1609, 322–389.

[48]'Conference on Security and Co-operation in Europe Final Act', Helsinki, 1 August 1975, supra, Chap. 2, note 61, at 'Declaration of Principles Guiding Relations between Participating States' (IV) 'Territorial Integrity of States', in which the States declare:

> The participating States will likewise refrain from making each other's territory the object of military occupation or other direct or indirect measures of force in contravention of international law, or the object of acquisition by means of such measures or the threat of them. No such occupation or acquisition will be recognized as legal.

[49]'Declaration of the European Council on the Guidelines on the Recognition of the New States in Eastern Europe and in the Soviet Union', of 16 December 1991, 31:6 *ILM* (1992), 1485–1487, UN Doc. A/46/804, of 18 December 1991, at Annex, the last paragraph of which reads:

> The Community and its member States will not recognize entities which are the result of aggression. They would take account of the effects of recognition on neighbouring States.

[50]See supra, this chapter, note 12.

For a more detailed study of its content, see: Türk (1993), pp. 66–71.

> The *policy* of non-recognition, which goes back to before the First World War, started to be transformed into an *obligation* of non-recognition in the thirties. Through the Stimson doctrine, the United States of America played a pioneering, and beneficial, role in this development. The rule or, as Sir Hersch Lauterpacht says, the principle of non-recognition now constitutes part of general international law. The rule may be said to be at present in the course of possibly reaching a stage when it would share in the nature of the principle of which it is corollary, i.e., the principle of the non-use of force. In that hypothesis non-recognition would acquire the rank of a peremptory norm of that law (*jus cogens*).[51]

This reasoning was supported in an Advisory Opinion of the ICJ in the *Palestinian Wall* matter, which declared: 'Given the character and the importance of the rights and obligations involved, the Court is of the view that all States are under an obligation not to recognize the illegal situation resulting from the construction of the wall in the Occupied Palestinian Territory'.[52] In consequence, it may be stated that in current general international law there is an obligation to withhold recognition of illicit situations arising from infringements of certain peremptory norms (*jus cogens*).

7.1.1.2 Scope and Effectiveness of the Obligation for Non-Recognition

The extent of the obligation not to recognize is limited to situations arising directly or indirectly in relation to a territory affected by the infringement of a peremptory norm of international law.[53] This is an obligation applying to all States, as an outcome of the *erga omnes* nature of the illegality and invalidity involved.[54] Its content has been defined as a *minimum* reaction to an illicit action: 'a prerequisite for any concerted community response against such breaches and [it] marks the minimum necessary response by States to the serious breaches referred to in article 40'.[55]

---

[51] 'Dissenting Opinion of Judge Skubiszewski', *East Timor (Portugal v. Australia), Judgment*, supra, Chap. 2, note 70, p. 262, para. 125.

[52] *Legal Consequences of the Construction of a Wall in the Occupied Palestinian Territory, Advisory Opinion, I.C.J. Reports 2004*, 136–271, p. 200, para. 159.

Cfr. Christakis (2005), p. 142. Vidmar (2011), p. 371, note 93.

[53] Cfr. Bismuth (2014), p. 725.

[54] Cfr. Cimiotta (2014), p. 493. Milano (2014), p. 39.

During its Cracow meeting of 2005, the Institut de Droit International passed a resolution on 'Obligations *Erga Omnes* in International Law', Art. 1(a) of which defines obligations *erga omnes*:

> an obligation under general international law that a State owes in any given case to the international community, in view of its common values and its concern for compliance, so that a breach of that obligation enables all States to take action; or.

71:2 *Annuaire de l'Institut de droit international* (2005), p. 287.

[55] 'Text of the 'Draft Articles on Responsibility of States for Internationally Wrongful Acts - Article 41 Commentary', supra, Chap. 6, note 49, p. 289, para. 8.

Its content comprises various abstention measures intended to isolate the illicit regime or authority. These may include refusal to establish conventional relations,[56] not setting up diplomatic links in the form of accrediting or receiving diplomatic missions, rejecting admission to international organizations, or avoiding connections of an economic or commercial nature.[57] There is no requirement for the active imposition of sanctions, just abstention from all acts that imply recognition.[58]

This obligation for non-recognition is certainly a duty, but it is hard to demand performance from States, so that its reach is limited.[59] When it comes down to it, it is a matter of choice for a State or group of States rather than a mandate derived from a rule of international law establishing reactive measures against the violation of primary obligations.[60] This is the reason that it may be seen more as a 'social sanction' in the context of the international community rather than a true international sanction. Nevertheless, the effects of the isolation arising from non-recognition may be similar to those caused by the latter.[61]

The effectiveness of non-recognition has often been questioned in view of its impotence in the face of increasingly numerous illegal actions.[62] Despite this, the obligation not to recognize constitutes 'the minimum necessary response by States to serious breaches',[63] and fulfils an important function of reasserting the legal basis of the international order as against illicit *de facto* situations.[64]

As indicated, international practice in relation to non-recognition demonstrates that it cannot be disregarded as if it were a totally inefficacious obligation. On the contrary, almost all the affairs noted above in which non-recognition of an illegal situation was called for ended in a failure to consolidate this illicit circumstance. Whilst it is not possible to ascribe the outcome achieved exclusively to application of the obligation for non-recognition, it must be accepted that a substantial role was played in isolating the illicit action in the majority of cases. The independence of Southern Rhodesia failed, the presence of South Africa in Namibia was not prolonged, as the country became independent in 1990, the Homelands never came to constitute independent States, the Turkish Republic of Northern Cyprus is

---

[56]Cfr. *Legal Consequences for States of the Continued Presence of South Africa in Namibia (South West Africa) notwithstanding Security Council Resolution 276 (1970), Advisory Opinion*, supra, Chap. 2, note 70, p. 55, para. 122.

[57]Cfr. Id., p. 55, para. 124.

On this set of measures, see Christakis (2005), p. 144. See also, by the same author Christakis (2014), p. 759. Milano (2014), p. 51.

[58]Cfr. Christakis (2014), p. 758.

[59]Cfr. Talmon (2005b), p. 125.

[60]Cfr. Milano (2014), p. 49.

[61]Cfr. Ibid.

[62]Cfr. Verhoeven (1975), p. 288.

[63]Text of the 'Draft Articles on Responsibility of States for Internationally Wrongful Acts - Article 41 Commentary', supra, Chap. 6, note 49, p. 289, para. 8.

[64]Cfr. Christakis (2005), p. 133.

not an independent entity, and Kuwait ultimately did not lose its freedom after the occupation and annexation by Iraq in 1990.[65]

7.1.2 Non-Recognition of Crimea

In respect of the situation arising in Crimea, practice in application of the obligation not to recognize was significant and among Western countries, unanimous.[66] In contrast, just eight States have formally recognized the new status of Crimea.[67] Within the UN, the initiative occurred in the context of the Security Council, but in the end the draft resolution presented by 41 States was vetoed by the Russian Federation during the meeting held on 15 March.[68] In its 24 March session, the General Assembly later approved Resolution 68/262,[69] Paragraph 6 of which contained identical wording to Paragraph 5 of the draft resolution rejected in the Security Council, requesting non-recognition of any altered status:

> Calls upon all States, international organizations and specialized agencies not to recognize any alteration of the status of the Autonomous Republic of Crimea and the city of Sevastopol on the basis of the above-mentioned referendum and to refrain from any action or dealing that might be interpreted as recognizing any such altered status.[70]

During the debates, numerous States requested non-recognition both of the results of the referendum and of the subsequent annexation by Russia. Among others, the interventions of France, the United Kingdom, Lithuania, Australia and Luxemburg in the Security Council meetings,[71] and of the delegation of the EU, Norway, Georgia, Turkey and Liechtenstein in the General Assembly should be highlighted.[72]

This same requirement was expressed in the joint statement of the President of European Council, Herman Van Rompuy, and the President of the European

---

[65]Cfr. Ibid.

With regard to instances of claimed unilateral declarations of independence based on violation of norms of international law, see supra, Sect. 3.3.

[66]Cfr. Christakis (2014), p. 756. Lagerwall (2014), p. 64. Cimiotta (2014), p. 503. Milano (2014), p. 37.

[67]See supra, this chapter, note 2.

[68]See supra, Sect. 5.2.2.

[69]See supra, Sect. 5.2.3.

[70]Resolution on 'Territorial Integrity of Ukraine', UN Doc. A/RES/68/262, of 27 March 2014, at para. 6.

[71]Cfr. Intervention of Mr. Araud (France); intervention of Sir Mark Lyall Grant (United Kingdom); intervention of Ms. Murmokaitė (Lithuania); intervention of Mr. Quinlan (Australia); and intervention of Ms. Lucas (Luxemburg), UN Doc. S/PV.7138, of 15 March 2014, 12, pp. 5, 5, 6, 9, and 11.

[72]Cfr. Intervention of Mr. Mayr-Harting (European Union); intervention of Ms. Power (United States of America); intervention of Mr. Wenaweser (Liechtenstein); intervention of Mr. Imnadze (Georgia); intervention of Mr. Çevik (Turkey); and Intervention of Mr. Pedersen (Norway), UN Doc. A/68/PV.80, of 27 March 2014, 27, pp. 4, 6, 7, 11, 11, and 14.

Commission, José Manuel Durão Barroso, on 18 March.[73] Thereafter, it was included once more in a joint declaration of the leaders of G-7 when they met in The Hague on 24 March.[74]

The statement made by NATO's General Secretary, Anders Rasmussen, also on 18 March, insisted on the same stance: 'Russia continues to violate Ukraine's sovereignty and territorial integrity, and remains in blatant breach of its international commitments. [. . .] Crimea's annexation is illegal and illegitimate and NATO Allies will not recognise it'.[75]

When diplomatic steps failed to achieve resolution of the controversy, non-recognition was followed by proposals by the US, the EU and other Western States to adopt measures of a sanctioning nature of various sorts and intensities against individuals and entities involved in the changes of government that occurred in the Autonomous Republic of Crimea.[76] Among these were the freezing of funds and economic resources, together with a prohibition on entry into their respective territories by a number of individuals of Russian and Ukrainian nationality.[77]

These reactions appeared to be aimed at dissuading the Russian Federation from undertaking expansionist manoeuvres in the region, but from the viewpoint of a

---

[73]Cfr. 'Joint statement on Crimea by the President of the European Council, Herman Van Rompuy, and the President of the European Commission, José Manuel Barroso', Brussels, 18 March 2014, http://europa.eu/rapid/press-release_STATEMENT-14-74_en.htm.

[74]Cfr. 'Declaration of The Hague', of 24 March 2014 http://www.international.gc.ca/g7/2014_hague_declaration.aspx?lang=eng.

[75]'NATO Secretary General condemns moves to incorporate Crimea into Russian Federation', NATO Doc. Press Release (2014) 050, Issued on 18 March 2014, http://www.nato.int/cps/en/natohq/news_108100.htm?selectedLocale=en.

[76]Within the EU, Council Decision 2014/145/CFSP was adopted on 17 March, concerning restrictive measures in respect of actions undermining or threatening the territorial integrity, sovereignty and independence of the Ukraine, *OJEU* L 78, 17.3.2014, 16–21; and the Council Regulation (EU) No. 269/2014, of 17 March, concerning restrictive measures in respect of actions undermining or threatening the territorial integrity, sovereignty and independence of Ukraine, *OJEU* L 78, 17.3.2014, 6–15. Thereafter further measures were adopted: Council Implementing Regulation (EU) No. 284/2014, of 21 March, *OJEU* L 86, 21.3.2014, 27–29; Council Implementing Regulation (EU) No. 433/2014, of 28 April, *OJEU* L 126, 29.4.2014, 48–50; and Council Implementing Regulation (EU) No. 477/2014, of 12 May, *OJEU* L 137, 12.5.2014, 3–4; Council Implementing Regulation (EU) No. 577/2014, of 28 May, *OJEU* L 160, 29.5.2014, 7–10, followed by updates down to the present.

In the United States, the President approved Executive Order 13660 of 6 March 2014, Blocking Property of Certain Persons Contributing to the Situation in Ukraine, *Federal Register* 79, No. 46, Monday, March 10, 2014, 13493–13495; Executive Order 13661 of 16 March 2014, Blocking Property of Additional Persons Contributing to the Situation in Ukraine, *Federal Register* 79, No. 53, Wednesday, March 19, 2014, 15535–15538; Executive Order 13662 of 20 March 2014, Blocking Property of Additional Persons Contributing to the Situation in Ukraine, *Federal Register* 79, No. 56, Monday, March 24, 2014, 16169–16171; and Executive Order 13668, of 19 December 2014, Blocking Property of Certain Persons and Prohibiting Certain Transactions With Respect to the Crimea Region of Ukraine, *Federal Register* 79, No. 247, Wednesday, December 24, 2014, 77357–77359.

[77]Cfr. Cimiotta (2014), p. 492.

return to the *status quo ante* they proved ineffective. In the face of the steadfast reaffirmation of its proposals by the Russian Federation and the impossibility of restoring Crimea to the Ukraine, non-recognition constituted an international legal mechanism for standing up to the illicit, but its effectiveness can only be attained through its generalization and continuance over time. Through this measure, there will be avoidance of the outcome that Henry L. Stimson attributed to recognition:

> The recognition of a new state has been described as the assurance given to it that it will be permitted to hold its place and rank in the character of an independent political organism in the society of nations.[78]

Non-recognition cannot change the situation overnight, but it may prevent its legal consolidation.[79] If this result were to be achieved, it would be the first case in international practice with these characteristics in which such a success occurred.

7.2 Effectiveness in the Consolidation of Illicit Situations Against the International Legal Order

The claimed secession of Crimea ran counter to international law, but it is difficult to envisage a reversal of the situation as a solution.[80] The same might be said with regard to the secession of Kosovo.[81] Inaction and silence on the part of the Ukraine, apparently tacitly accepting the new status, is probably the most realistic choice.[82] However, it is also possible that it will meander on as a frozen conflict until some future date at which non-recognition of the new situation might conceivably play an important role.

To sum up, everything points to acceptance of the *fait accompli* on the lines of the maxim *interest rei publicae ut sit finis litium*, seen by Charles De Visscher as the most 'honourable' option.[83] His reasoning is that non-recognition of a given situation arising from illicit actions cannot retain its legal significance indefinitely. Conflict between reality and law if prolonged over time in the end is resolved in favour of effectiveness.[84] The most likely outcome is that a state of affairs contrary to international law will eventually become consolidated as an effective reality. The conclusion would be that mere effectiveness would ultimately win out, gaining a

---

[78]Henry L. Stimson, Secretary of State, 'Address before the Council on Foreign Relations, 6 February 1931', *Department of State, Latin American Series*, No. 4, p. 6.

[79]Cfr. Hilpold (2015), p. 269.

[80]Cfr. Cimiotta (2014), p. 496.

[81]Cfr. Ryngaert and Griffioen (2009), p. 586.

[82]Cfr. Tolstykh (2015), p. 139.

[83]Cfr. De Visscher (1967), p. 25.

[84]Cfr. Id., pp. 37–38.

legal status from international law, despite this being contrary to the principle *ex injuria jus non oritur.*[85]

These observations lead to the question of determining a theoretical construction that would establish some legal status for such situations. The starting point might be that some consider all States to be *de facto* entities, arising from historical events, in which effectiveness is a manifestation of this that law cannot prevent.[86] At most, law might have some impact on the consequences of the emergence of a State. If this stance is taken, the coming together of the criteria for statehood would determine the creation of a State.[87] Those adopting it hold that arguments striving to require lawfulness as a corollary of statehood are inadmissible, since this in fact is to be characterized merely as a 'capacity to enter into relations with the other States'.[88] A State born from unlawfulness is not inexistent either factually or legally, so that non-recognition of the unlawful State would be no more than a situation of social isolation, a cause of factual limitation of its legal sphere.[89]

Other authors take the line that the emergence of a State is a legal matter, so that certain requirements for legality established in international law should also be fulfilled.[90] At the very least, those adopting this posture hold that the process of converting a *de facto* entity into a new State should not take place in violation of peremptory norms of international law such as the ban on the use of force against the territorial integrity of a State or against the principle of self-determination.[91]

Finally, there is an intermediate stance founded on the idea that the setting up of a State is indeed a *de facto* matter, but at the same time the international community demands observance of certain norms in the process of creation.[92] Breach of these causes a situation of social isolation which would bring with it *de facto* limitation of its sphere.[93] This limitation would imply a certain precariousness in the effectiveness and independence of the new body which could stretch out over time because of collective non-recognition.[94]

It would appear that the process of setting up a new State is complex in nature, because it involves the coming together of multiple aspects making up the idea of statehood. A large number of these *de facto* aspects, which may be seen as matters of

---

[85] See supra, Sect. 3.3.
Cfr. Christakis (2011), p. 82.
[86] Cfr. Tancredi (2008), p. 53.
[87] Cfr. Ibid.
See supra, Chap. 3, note 68, and Sect. 7.1.
[88] Montevideo Convention, at Art. 1.
[89] Cfr. Tancredi (2006), p. 206.
[90] Cfr. Kohen (2006), p. 13. Christakis (2006), p. 165.
[91] Cfr. Tancredi (2006), p. 181.
[92] Cfr. Id., p. 205.
[93] Cfr. Id., p. 206.
[94] Cfr. Tancredi (2008), p. 54.

substance in the terminology used by some academics, are of particular interest for the international community and for this reason are regulated by international law.

When determining the extent of violations of international law during the process of setting up new States, the starting point must be a distinction between infringements of the peremptory norms of international law and those of general norms of particular international law. The consequences of a situation where a peremptory norm of international law was breached would be an impact on the presence of the elements necessary for statehood and rule out the existence of any real new State. The infringement would imply the absence of *de facto* requisites for the emergence of a new State, rather than any judgement on the licit or illicit nature of the creation of this new State. This sort of violation cannot lead to consolidation of statehood by means of effectiveness, since the requirements for statehood would never have been present. These situations would involve the threat or use of force against political independence or territorial integrity, or breach of the principle of self-determination. In such circumstances there is an obligation *erga omnes* for non-recognition.

On the other hand, the birth of a State is certainly a question of fact. However, it cannot be seen as instantaneous and the consolidation of elements of statehood may require the passage of some time before a situation can be seen as effective.

In the light of this, the Kosovo case shows the elements termed substantial acting as decisive in the emergence of statehood. On the lines explained, the secession itself would be illegal, and it cannot be claimed that they were clearly present at the time that it took place.[95] Nonetheless, the international community has expressed itself as in support of the party it saw as the more vulnerable in the controversy. This was aimed at giving decisive backing for the consolidation of the statehood of Kosovo.[96] Thus, recognition burdens the State, which is the stronger party, with the arduous task of refuting the claims that it has behaved inappropriately, constituting a basis for justifying the declaration of independence.[97] In any case, it is not enough to gain the backing of consensus; there must also be continuing effectiveness.[98]

It is harder to find an answer for the state of affairs in Crimea, where independence is also illegal. Its status has not been backed and it can be said that it is in suspense. However, it may be asked what solution might be hoped for in the future for Crimea. A return to its previous situation seems extremely difficult, yet the consolidation of circumstances contrary to peremptory norms of international law is not admissible and does not have the support of the international community. A negotiated solution, in which non-recognition would play an important part,[99] seems to be the sole alternative for achieving resolution of this conflict between illicit effectiveness and law. To this end, it will be necessary to overcome the violations of international law preventing the emergence and consolidation of the *de facto* elements constituting statehood.

[95]Cfr. Ryngaert and Griffioen (2009), p. 586. Tancredi (2012), p. 106.

[96]Cfr. Berlin (2009), p. 590. Ryngaert and Griffioen (2009), p. 586.

[97]Cfr. Müllerson (2009), p. 21. Ryngaert and Griffioen (2009), p. 587.

[98]Cfr. Pegg (1998), p. 122.

[99]Cfr. Christakis (2014), p. 764.

References

Anzilotti, D. 1999. *Cours de droit international*. Paris: Librairie Générale de Droit et Jurisprudence.

Berlin, A.H. 2009. Recognition as Sanction: Using International Recognition of New States to Deter, Punish, and Contain Bad Actors. *University of Pennsylvania Journal of International Law* 31: 531–591.

Bismuth, R. 2014. Odysée dans le conundrum des réactions décentralisées à l'illicite. *JDI* 141: 719–731.

Briggs, H.W. 1949. Recognition of States: Some Reflections on Doctrine and Practice. *AJIL* 43: 113–121.

Brownlie, I. 1982. Recognition in Theory and Practice. *BYIL* 53: 197–211.

———. 1990. *Principles of Public International Law*. 4th ed. Oxford: Oxford University Press.

Christakis, T. 1999. *Le droit à l'autodétermination en dehors des situations de décolonisation*. Paris: La Documentation française.

———. 2005. L'obligation de non-reconnaissance des situations créées par le recours illicite à la force ou d'autres actes enfreignant des règles fondamentales. In *The Fundamental Rules of the International Legal Order: Jus Cogens and Obligations Erga Omnes*, ed. C. Tomuschat and J.M. Thouvenin, 127–166. Leiden, Boston: Martinus Nijhoff.

———. 2006. The State as 'Primary Fact'. Some Thoughts on the Principle of Effectiveness. In *Secession. International Law Perspectives*, ed. M.G. Kohen, 138–170. Cambridge and New York: Cambridge University Press.

———. 2011. The ICJ Advisory Opinion on Kosovo: Has International Law Something to Say about Secession? *LJIL* 24: 73–86.

———. 2014. Les conflits de sécession en Crimée et dans l'Est de l'Ukraine et le droit international (The Conflicts of Secession in Crimea and Eastern Ukraine and International Law). *JDI* 141: 733–764.

Cimiotta, E. 2014. Le reazioni alla 'sottrazione' della Crimea all'Ucraina. Quali garanzie del diritto internazionale di fronte a gravi illeciti imputati a grandi potenze? *DUDI* 8: 491–504.

Craven, M. 1995. The European Community Arbitration Commission on Yugoslavia. *BYIL* 66: 333–413.

Crawford, J. 2007. *The Creation of States in International Law*. 2nd ed. Oxford: Clarendon Press.

Current, R.N. 1954. The Stimson Doctrine and the Hoover Doctrine. *American Historical Review* 59: 513–542.

De Visscher, C. 1967. *Les effectivités du droit international public*. Paris: Pedone.

Dugard, J. 1987. *Recognition and the United Nations*. Cambridge: Cambridge University Press.

———. 2011. The Secession of States and their Recognition in the Wake of Kosovo. *Recueil des cours* 357: 9–222.

Dugard, J., and D. Raič. 2006. The Role of Recognition in the Law and Practice of Secession. In *Secession: International Law Perspectives*, ed. M.G. Kohen, 94–137. Cambridge: Cambridge University Press.

Frowein, J.A. 2010. Recognition. *Max Planck Encyclopedia of Public International Law* (Oxford Public International Law, Online edition. http://opil.ouplaw.com/view/10.1093/law:epil/9780199231690/law-9780199231690-e1086?rskey=0y3Wx1&result=1&prd=EPIL.

Gowlland-Debbas, V. 1990. *Collective Responses to Illegal Acts in International Law: United Nations Action in the Question of Southern Rhodesia*. Dordrecht, Boston: Martinus Nijhoff.

Grant, T. 1999. *The Recognition of States: Law and Practice in Debate and Evolution*. Westport, Conn.: Praeger.

Grant, T.D. 2014. Doctrines (Monroe, Hallstein, Brezhnev, Stimson). *Max Planck Encyclopedia of Public International Law*. Oxford Public International Law, Online edition. http://opil.ouplaw.com/view/10.1093/law:epil/9780199231690/law-9780199231690-e697?prd=EPIL.

Hilpold, P. 2009. The Kosovo Case and International Law: Looking for Applicable Theories. *Chinese JIL* 8: 47–61.

———. 2015. Ukraine, Crimea and New International Law: Balancing International Law with Arguments Drawn from History. *Chinese JIL* 14: 237–270.

Himmer, S.E. 1992. The Achievement of Independence in the Baltic States and Its Justification. *EILR* 6: 253–291.

Jia, B.B. 2009. The Independence of Kosovo: A Unique Case of Secession? *Chinese JIL* 8: 27–46.

Kelsen, H. 1941. Recognition in International Law: Theoretical Observations. *AJIL* 35: 605–617.

Kohen, M.G. 2006. Introduction. In *Secession. International Law Perspectives*, ed. M. Kohen, 1–20. Cambridge and New York: Cambridge University Press.

Lagerwall, A. 2014. L'agression et l'annexion de la Crimée para la Fédération de Russie: Quels enseignements au sujet du droit international. *Questions of International Law, Zoom Out* I 57–72. www.qil-qdi.org.

Lauterpacht, H. 1947. *Recognition in International Law*. Cambridge: Cambridge University Press.

Milano, E. 2014. The Non-Recognition of Russia's Annexation of Crimea: Three Different Legal Approaches and One Unanswered Question. *Questions of International Law, Zoom Out* I 35–55. www.qil-qdi.org.

Müllerson, R.A. 2009. Precedents in the Mountains: On the Parallels and Uniqueness of the Cases of Kosovo, South Ossetia and Abkhazia. *Chinese JIL* 8: 2–25.

Oeter, S. 2014. The Role of Recognition and Non-Recognition with Regard to Secession. In *Self-Determination and Secession in International Law*, ed. C. Walter et al., 45–67. Oxford: Oxford University Press.

Oppenheim, L., R.Y. Jennings, and A.D. Watts. 1992. *Oppenheim's International Law*. 9th ed. Harlow, England: Longman.

Pegg, S. 1998. *International Society and the De Facto State*. Aldershot: Ashgate.

Pronin, A. 2015. Republic of Crimea A Two-Day State. *Russian LJ* 3: 133–142.

Rich, R. 1993. Recognition of States: The Collapse of Yugoslavia and the Soviet Union. *EJIL* 4: 36–65.

Roth, B.R. 2010. Secessions, Coups and the International Rule of Law: Assessing the Decline of the Effective Control Doctrine. *Melbourne Journal of International Law* 11: 393–440.

Ryngaert, C., and C. Griffioen. 2009. The Relevance of the Right to Self-determination in the Kosovo Matter: In Partial Response to the Agora Papers. *Chinese JIL* 8: 573–587.

Ryngaert, C., and S. Sobrie. 2011. Recognition of States: International Law or Realpolitik? The practice of recognition in the wake of Kosovo, South Ossetia and Abkhazia. *LJIL* 24: 467–490.

Talmon, S. 2005a. The Constitutive versus the Declaratory Theory of Recognition: Tertium non Datur? *BYIL* 76: 101–181.

———. 2005b. The Duty Not to 'Recognize as Lawful' a Situation Created by the Illegal Use of Force or Other Serious Breaches of a Jus Cogens Obligation: An Obligation without Real Substance? In *The Fundamental Rules of the International Legal Order: Jus Cogens and Obligations Erga Omnes*, ed. Ch. Tomuschat and J.M. Thouvenin, 99–126. Leiden, Boston: Martinus Nijhoff.

Tancredi, A. 2006. A Normative Due Process in the Creation of States Through Secession. In *Secession. International Law Perspectives*, ed. M. Kohen, 171–207. Cambridge and New York: Cambridge University Press.

———. 2008. Neither Authorized nor Prohibited? Secession and International Law after Kosovo, South Ossetia and Abkhazia. *Italian YIL* 18: 37–62.

———. 2012. Some Remarks on the Relationship Between Secession and General International Law in the Light of the ICJs Kosovo Advisory Opinion. In *Kosovo and International Law: The ICJ Advisory Opinion of 22 July 2010*, ed. P. Hilpold, 79–108. Leiden; Boston: Martinus Nijhoff.

Tolstykh, V. 2015. Three Ideas of Self-Determination in International Law and the Reunification of Crimea with Russia. *ZaöRV/HJIL* 75: 119–139.

Tomuschat, C. 2012. Recognition of New States – The Case of Premature Recognition. In *Kosovo and International Law: The ICJ Advisory Opinion of 22 July 2010*, ed. P. Hilpold, 31–46. Leiden; Boston: Martinus Nijhoff.

Türk, D. 1993. Recognition of States: A Comment. *EJIL* 4: 66–71.

Turns, D. 2003. The Stimson Doctrine of Non-Recognition: Its Historical Genesis and Influence on Contemporary International Law. *Chinese JIL* 2: 105–143.

Verhoeven, J. 1975. *La reconnaissance internationale dans la pratique contemporaine: les relations publiques internationales*. Paris: A. Pedone.

Vidmar, J. 2010. Remedial Secession in International Law: Theory and (Lack of) Practice. *St Antony's International Review* 6: 37–56.

———. 2011. The Kosovo Advisory Opinion Scrutinized. *LJIL* 24: 355–383.

———. 2012. Conceptualizing Declarations of Independence in International Law. *Oxford JLS* 32: 153–177.

———. 2015. The Annexation of Crimea and the Boundaries of the Will of the People. *German LJ* 16: 365–383.

Wilson, G. 2009. Self-Determination, Recognition and the Problem of Kosovo. *NILR* 56: 455–481.

———. 2015. Crimea: Some Observations on Secession and Intervention in Partial Response to Müllerson and Tolstykh. *Chinese JIL* 14: 217–223.

Chapter 8
The Emergence of Humanitarian Secession as an International Response to Serious Violations of Human Rights

The concept of secession is far from having a precise content in current international law. Moreover, this question is particularly controversial when it comes to recognition of a right to secede, which many deem incompatible with the principles upheld by the UN Charter. In view of this, as noted above, it must be concluded that international law takes a neutral position and neither recognizes nor prohibits secession. In contrast, it is unanimously accepted that undertaking secession is illicit when it is linked to infringements of any peremptory norms of international law.

It can be stated that this is a matter of some conflict. Those who hold that it is possible to recognize a right to secession face clear opposition from those who feel it necessary to preserve current international law from a dangerous change.[1]

Among the various arguments upon which recognition of a general right to secession is founded, as is highlighted by Gary Wilson, an academic at Liverpool John Moore's University, is the righting of a 'past injustice' in situations where a geographic unit was created that unjustly incorporated the entity claiming the right to secede.[2] More debatable is the satisfying of the desire of a large majority of the population within an entity,[3] or its existence in itself rather than a reasoned argument.[4] Finally, another argument would be the recognition of the right for the members of a group in those situations in which they are subject to serious violations of human rights on the part of state authorities.[5]

Contrary opinions are also numerous. Among them, reference must be made to those stressing the difficulty of determining groups, or defining the notion of a

[1] Cfr. Wilson (2009), p. 472.

[2] Cfr. Buchanan (1991), pp. 29–32.

[3] Cfr. Ibid.

[4] Cfr. Wilson (2009), p. 474.

[5] Cfr. Ibid.

J. F. Escudero Espinosa, *Self-Determination and Humanitarian Secession in International Law of a Globalized World*,
https://doi.org/10.1007/978-3-319-72622-9_8

people, as supposed holders of a right to secession.[6] According to these authors, recognition of any broad right to secede would constitute a dangerous precedent applicable to any State in which there happened to be a minority, whether racial, religious, linguistic or political.[7] However, the argument most widely put forward by the majority of these analysts lies in the risk of excessive fragmentation of the international community and the emergence of numerous unviable micro-States as the outcome of a recognition of a right to secession.[8] It is even possible to say that the process of disintegration would be never-ending, as there would always be some minority in each newly created State that would also look to secede.[9]

To adopt any of these views is not a simple decision within the framework of current international law. Despite this, it has been feasible to offer a more solid legitimization for secession in certain given circumstances of particular gravity.[10] This legitimization is seen as a 'remedy' for a particular group, aimed at ending a situation in which it is subject to serious persecution by state authorities with genocidal characteristics.[11] This would be a 'qualified' right to 'remedial secession' accepted by international law, in the view of many academics.[12]

According to one grouping, developments in events in Kosovo, even after the decade of administration by UNMIK, would fully correspond to the prerequisites for so-called 'remedial secession'.[13] However, if this conclusion is accepted it must be asked how far back in time it is justifiable to go in relation to abuses in order to be able to invoke a remedial right to secede.[14] Is it really possible to generalize the factors considered in Kosovo, or on the contrary should it remain a unique case?[15]

8.1 The Unclear Theory of the Right to 'Remedial Secession'

The doctrine of 'remedial secession' has been put forward in a large segment of legal teaching, mostly coming from German and American academics, for those special circumstances in which the exercise of an internal right to self-determination within

[6]On the difficulty of determining what constitutes a people, see supra, Sect. 2.2.2.

[7]Cfr. Buchheit (1978), p. 14.

[8]Cfr. Ibid.

[9]Cfr. Higgins (1993), p. 35.

[10]Cfr. Oeter (1992), pp. 741–775.

[11]Cfr. Dinstein (1996), pp. 299–302. Oeter (2012), p. 119.

[12]Cfr. Raič (2002), p. 324.

[13]Before this and during the life of UNMIK, the following are of note: Baggett (1999), p. 472. Charney (2001). Grant (2000), p. 53. Seidel (2001), pp. 203–215.

At the time of the independence declaration by Kosovo, see: Parameswaran (2008), p. 178. Watson (2008), p. 281.

[14]Cfr. Tancredi (2008), p. 43.

[15]Cfr. Tomuschat (2006), p. 38.

a given State might become a right to independent statehood.[16] According to these scholars, remedial secession might be invoked when all attempts to achieve internal self-determination had been frustrated by the State administration, this being clear from the lack of representation and infringements of human rights.[17] These would be exceptional circumstances in which self-determination would also constitute an exceptional remedy going beyond legitimate humanitarian intervention, which in many case may be an undertaking hard to perform.[18]

8.1.1 Towards an **opinio** *on the Lawfulness of Remedial Secession*

Among the precedents for what was later termed the doctrine of remedial secession, some legal bodies have referred to the matter of the Åland Islands from 1921.[19] The question and its solution was seen as unique and special during the 1920s, but it continues to be a benchmark to the present day.[20] The Committee of Rapporteurs designated by the League of Nations to examine the case held that there was no absolute right to unilateral secession and that consequently the archipelago in the Baltic Sea did not have authority to secede from Finland and join Sweden.[21] While recognizing the possibility of secession as a 'last resort',[22] they excluded this option for the inhabitants of the Åland Islands in their conclusions, since no proofs of oppression had been found.[23]

---

[16]Prominent among the fore-runners of the doctrine of remedial secession is Allen E. Buchanan who referred to a remedial right in his works: 1991, *Secession: The Morality of Political Divorce from Fort Sumter to Lithuania and Quebec*; 1997, Theories of Secession, pp. 31–61; and 2004, *Justice, Legitimacy and Self-Determination. Moral Foundations for International Law*, p. 335.

A selection from the most relevant literature on the doctrine of 'remedial secession' would include the following: Buchheit (1978), p. 220. Corten (2008), p. 724. Crawford (2007), p. 120. Grant (2009), p. 29. Hannum (1990), p. 471. Hilpold (2009), p. 55. Kemoklidze (2009), p. 119. Murswiek (1993), pp. 25–27. Raič (2002), at Ch. 7. Ryngaert and Griffioen (2009), p. 575. Schaller (2008), p. 138. Tancredi (2006), p. 175. Tomuschat (2006), p. 33. Thürer (1984), p. 127. Umozurike (1972), p. 196. Vidmar (2009), p. 814.

[17]Cfr. Buchanan (2004), p. 335. Jaber (2011), p. 935. Raič (2002), pp. 368–372.

[18]Cfr. Burke-White (2014), p. 77.

[19]Cfr. Van den Driest (2015), p. 342.

[20]Cfr. Fleiner (2011), p. 882.

[21]Cfr. Cassese (1995), p. 27. Fleiner (2011), p. 884.

On the case of the Åland Islands, see: Barros (1968), 362 pp. Brown (1921), pp. 268–272. Padelford (1939), pp. 465–487. Seyersted (1982), pp. 23–28. De Visscher (1921), pp. 35–56 and 243–284.

[22]Cfr. 'Report Presented to the Council of the League of Nations by the Commission of Rapporteurs', 16 April 1921, League of Nations Council Doc. B7/21/68/106 (1921), pp. 27–28.

[23]Cfr. Id., p. 128. Nanda (1981), p. 266.

One decisive landmark was the adoption of the 'Declaration on Principles of International Law' which envisaged a so-called 'safeguard clause' under which the territorial integrity principle was tied to the representative nature of government.[24] With this text, the international community consolidated a clear *opinio* in recognizing the exception.[25] A more controversial matter was the determination of subjects to which the territorial integrity principle applied and consequently the delimitation of the scope of the exception.

Once the 'Declaration on Principles of International Law' had provided a basis for the theory of remedial secession, attempts were made to lay a foundation for interpretation *a sensu contrario* of the territorial integrity principle for States.[26] In accordance with this interpretation, a State not having a government that represented the entirety of the people belonging to its territory, without distinction of race, creed or colour, could not invoke the principle of the territorial integrity of States to limit to the internal sphere alone the exercise of the people's right to self-determination.[27]

Nevertheless, this interpretation raised various questions, as the territorial integrity principle was considered a core tenet of international law, for which there could be no exceptions, not even the situation cited as a basis for remedial secession.[28] Notwithstanding, this sort of interpretation *a contrario* was not welcomed by the drafters, who expressly warned of such views in their *travaux préparatoires*.[29]

In later decades the theory came to be incorporated in the decisions of a number of national and international bodies, giving limited support for its existence.[30] Among prime instances, it is possible to cite the views of Judge Luzius Wildhaber and Chairman Rolv Ryssdal in 1996 in the case of *Loizidou v. Turkey* before the European Court of Human Rights (ECHR), in the form of a Concurring Opinion stating:

---

[24] Cfr. Kapustin (2015), p. 107. Cfr. 'Declaration on Principles of International Law Concerning Friendly Relations and Co-operation among States in Accordance with the Charter of the United Nations' UN Doc. A/RES/2625 (XXV) , of 24 October 1970, at Annex, 'The Principle of Equal Rights and Self-Determination of Peoples', para. 7. See supra, Sect. 2.1.3.

[25] Cfr. Tancredi (2008), p. 39.

[26] See supra, Sect. 2.1.3. Cfr. 'Declaration on Principles of International Law Concerning Friendly Relations and Co-operation among States in Accordance with the Charter of the United Nations' UN Doc. A/RES/2625 (XXV) , of 24 October 1970, at Annex, 'The Principle of Equal Rights and Self-Determination of Peoples', para. 7. Christakis (2014), p. 742.

[27] Cfr. Ryngaert and Griffioen (2009), p. 581. Tancredi (2006), p. 176; and, by the same author Tancredi (2008), p. 39.

[28] Cfr. Shaw (1997), p. 483.

[29] Cfr. Intervention of Mr. Riphagen (The Netherlands), UN Doc. A/AC.125/SR.114, p. 52. Cited in Tancredi (2008), p. 40, note 11.

[30] Cfr. Jaber (2011), p. 935.

> In recent years a consensus has seemed to emerge that peoples may also exercise a right to self-determination if their human rights are consistently and flagrantly violated or if they are without representation at all or are massively under-represented in an undemocratic and discriminatory way.[31]

The African Commission on Human and Peoples' Rights also reflected the 'safeguard clause' in two cases relating to Katanga examined in 1996 and later in relation to Southern Cameroon in 2009. However, it did not set clear limits for the scope of the exception.[32]

The Supreme Court of Canada has also exercised great influence over the recognition of a claimed right to secession through its decision in the *Reference re Secession of Quebec* case in 1998. According to the Supreme Court there were two instances in which external self-determination was permitted in international law. Alongside these, it stated a third, more controversial, context in which it might be legitimized:

> [...] a right to secession only arises under the principle of self-determination of peoples at international law where 'a people' is governed as part of a colonial empire; where 'a people' is subject to alien subjugation, domination or exploitation; and possibly where 'a people' is denied any meaningful exercise of its right to self-determination within the state of which it forms a part.[33]

The Canadian Court ended by accepting the existence of a right to external self-determination only in those cases in which 'a definable group is denied meaningful access to government to pursue their political, economic, social and cultural development'.[34]

---

[31]Cfr. 'Concurring Opinion of Judge Wildhaber, Joined by Judge Ryssdal', ECHR (Chamber), *Loizidou v. Turkey*, Application No. 15318/89, Judgment (Merits), 28 July 1998, 42, p. 24, para. 1–2. http://hudoc.echr.coe.int/eng?i=001-58007.

See Jaber (2011), p. 936. Van den Driest (2013), pp. 129–131.

[32]Cfr. *Kevin Mgwanga Gunme et al./Cameroon*, Communication No. 266/2003, of 13–27 May 2009, p. 36, para. 190–194.

In the matter *Katangese Peoples' Congress v. Zaire*, Merits, Communication No. 75/92, 8th Annual Activity Report, at para. 6, the African Commission accepted the safeguard clause in the following terms:

> In the absence of concrete evidence of violations of human rights to the point that the territorial integrity of Zaire should be called to question and in the absence of evidence that the people of Katanga are denied the right to participate in Government as guaranteed by Article 13(1) of the African Charter, the Commission holds the view that Katanga is obliged to exercise a variant of self-determination that is compatible with the sovereignty and territorial integrity of Zaire.

A detailed examination of these matters may be found in: Van den Driest (2013), pp. 128–129 and 138–140. Also: Jaber (2011), p. 936. Vashakmadze and Lippold (2010), p. 635.

[33]Supreme Court of Canada, *Reference re Secession of Quebec*, supra, Chap. 2, note 71, p. 295, para. 154.

[34]Id., p. 287, para. 138.

For an examination of this aspect in the case of Quebec, see: Jaber (2011), p. 936. Van den Driest (2013), pp. 131–137.

Finally, the ICJ has highlighted the divisions in the international community concerning the theory of remedial secession on the occasion of the Kosovo case. There were States that accepted the theory during their statements before the ICJ, among them the Russian Federation. A group of at least as many opposed it.[35] The opinion expressed by the ICJ tried to avoid the question by providing an answer exclusively to what was put to it by the General Assembly.[36] This attitude has been criticized both by commentators and by Judges Abdulqawi Ahmed Yusuf and Bruno Simma.[37] The ICJ argued on the same lines taken by the judicial and quasi-judicial, internal or international bodies mentioned above, using very measured language when making pronouncements about the existence and scope of a right to secession as a remedy.

8.1.2 Remedial Secession in State Practice

In parallel with the development of an *opinio*, authors have also mentioned the existence of certain cases supporting the appearance of lawful secession when there is oppression or gross violations of human rights.[38] The clearest instance is that of Bangladesh which was widely recognized as an example of secession under this sort of circumstance.[39] Together with this, authors mention cases in which similar situations arose, such as Eritrea, Croatia and Slovenia, the Baltic Republics, South Sudan and Kosovo.[40]

---

[35]Cfr. Christakis (2014), p. 742. Van den Driest (2015), p. 343.

Among the States supporting remedial secession Théodore Christakis quotes: Albania, Estonia, Germany, Finland, Ireland, Jordan, Lithuania, Maldives, the Netherlands, Poland, the Russian Federation, Slovenia, Switzerland, and Kosovo. Opposed to the theory were: Argentina, Azerbaijan, Belarus, Bolivia, Brazil, Burundi, China, Cyprus, Iran, Romania, Serbia, Slovakia, Spain, Venezuela, and Vietnam. See also Vashakmadze and Lippold (2010), p. 636, note 86, which distinguishes between those accepting remedial secession and those deeming it inapplicable to Kosovo.

[36]Cfr. *Accordance with the International Law of the Unilateral Declaration of Independence in Respect of Kosovo, Advisory Opinion,* supra, Chap. 1, note 3, p. 438, para. 82 and 83.

Cfr. Kapustin (2015), p. 107.

[37]Cfr. Arp (2010), p. 853. Burri (2010), pp. 881–890. Hannum (2011), p. 156. Orakhelashvili (2011), p. 86. Ryngaert (2010), p. 492.

Cfr. 'Separate Opinion of Judge Yusuf', and 'Declaration of Judge Simma', *Accordance with the International Law of the Unilateral Declaration of Independence in Respect of Kosovo, Advisory Opinion,* supra, Chap. 1, note 3, p. 620, para. 5–6; and p. 480, para. 7.

[38]Cfr. Vidmar (2010), pp. 42–50.

[39]Cfr. Dugard and Raič (2006), pp. 120–130. Ryngaert and Griffioen (2009), p. 583. Tancredi (2008), p. 40. Van den Driest (2013), p. 276. Vidmar (2010), p. 43.

On the case of Bangladesh, see supra, Sect. 2.2.2 and Chap. 3.

[40]Cfr. Kapustin (2015), p. 107, note 21. Tancredi (2008), p. 41. Van den Driest (2013), pp. 279–289. Vidmar (2010), pp. 42–48.

Among instances of attempts at secession, many other cases have been examined by academics, including Southern Rhodesia, Katanga, Chechnya, South Ossetia, and Abkhazia.[41] However, these were seen as invalid because in the end secession failed and the international community for the most part refused recognition.[42]

In the end, only Bangladesh and Kosovo have been considered as acceptable cases resulting from a process of unilateral secession, as mentioned above.[43] Hence, they may be said to constitute the sole instances pointing to relevant practice in relation to remedial secession.[44]

Even the case of Kosovo is not unanimously accepted as an instance completely fulfilling the requirements for remedial secession.[45] As certain critics stress, Kosovo's claims for secession were based on a series of abuses that were distant in time and no longer proper grounds for remedial secession.[46] The situation in 1998 might have justified remedial secession, but changes subsequent to NATO bombings made it questionable in 2008 whether such a secession could be seen as legitimate.[47]

The conclusion would appear to be that it must be seen as impossible to claim that there is any widespread and uniform international practice supporting remedial

---

[41]With regard to claims to secede outside a decolonization process, see supra, Sect. 3.1.

[42]Cfr. Ryngaert and Griffioen (2009), p. 578.

In respect of South Ossetia and Abkhazia in relation to Georgia, Antonello Tancredi holds that despite the Russian Federation's claims that they should be seen as instances of remedial secession, in reality they failed in their aims. See supra, Sect. 3.1. Cfr. Tancredi (2008), p. 53.

[43]See supra, Chap. 3.

[44]Cfr. Van den Driest (2013), p. 289. Van den Driest (2015), p. 345.

[45]Cfr. Cismas (2010), p. 582.

[46]Cfr. Goodwin (2007), p. 6. Wilson (2009), p. 477. Vashakmadze and Lippold (2010), p. 636, and note 86.

At the end of the arguments put forward by the Russian Federation during oral statements before ICJ the conclusion was:

> For Kosovo to be able to rely on "remedial secession" in 2008, it has to demonstrate that the situation had aggravated as compared to 1999 [. . .] By 2008, there was clearly no threat to the population of Kosovo coming from the Serbian authorities [. . .] Therefore, the notion of "remedial secession" is obviously inapplicable in the case at hand.

Intervention of Mr. Gevorgian (Russian Federation), 'Public sitting held on Tuesday 8 December 2009, at 10 a.m., at the Peace Palace, President Owada, presiding, on the Accordance with International Law of the Unilateral Declaration of Independence by the Provisional Institutions of Self-Government of Kosovo (*Request for advisory opinion submitted by the General Assembly of the United Nations*)', ICJ Doc. CR 2009/30, 64, p. 44, para. 21–22. http://www.icj-cij.org/files/case-related/141/141-20091208-ORA-01-00-BI.pdf.

On these same lines, see Romania, at para. 24–26. The Russian Federation had previously raised the question: '[C]ould the circumstances, as they were in 2008, be qualified as extreme?'. 'Written Statement by the Russian Federation', *Accordance with the International Law of the Unilateral Declaration of Independence in Respect of Kosovo, (Request for an Advisory Opinion),* of 16 April 2009, 43, p. 37, para. 98. http://www.icj-cij.org/files/case-related/141/15628.pdf.

[47]Cfr. Jaber (2011), pp. 941–942. Ryngaert and Griffioen (2009), p. 585. Van den Driest (2013), p. 273. Vidmar (2010), p. 49. Yee (2010), p. 780.

secession.[48] Indeed, as Stefan Oeter states, practice is 'extremely reluctant' to accept justifications for entitlement to secession.[49] This conclusion is borne out by the arguments advanced by a large group of jurists who held that: 'the post-decolonization practice of State creation does not reflect obvious support for a right to remedial secession being rooted in State practice'.[50]

8.1.3 Remedial Secession as a Unclear Norm of International Customary Law

In view of the conclusion that there is no clear international practice backing remedial secession, it is appropriate to consider whether there are the necessary elements to deem that a norm exists in international customary law. Study of the two cases of Bangladesh and Kosovo has made it evident that it is hard to confirm the presence of any general practice recognizing a right to remedial secession. Nonetheless, despite there being just these two instances, they might suffice if there were in respect of them any *opinion juris* giving grounds for the obligatory nature of remedial secession as a customary international norm.[51]

In the first place, an *opinio juris* might be drawn from the two cases mentioned on the basis of a particular coherence allowing the affirmation that they are consistent with the invocation of remedial secession.[52] This is the opinion supported by authors like Antony D'Amatto, who sees as the clearest expression of such an *opinio juris* acquiescence by the international community when claims opposed to it are raised.[53] Hence, the *opinio juris* may be inferred from the fact that States apparently accepted remedial secession when confirming their recognition.[54] This would be the case for Bangladesh, in relation to which States referred to infringements of human rights, denial of internal self-determination, and the impossibility of resolving an irreversible situation as reasons for granting recognition.

The ICJ had occasion to state in the *Nicaragua* case that it might be feasible to crystalize customary international law in the light of a strong *opinio juris* shown in

---

[48]Cfr. Ryngaert and Griffioen (2009), p. 584. Van den Driest (2015), p. 349.

[49]Cfr. Oeter (2014), p. 58. See also, by the same author Oeter (2012), p. 118.

[50]Van den Driest (2013), p. 290.

[51]Cfr. Tomuschat (2006), p. 42. Cfr. *North Sea Continental Shelf, Judgment, I.C.J. Reports 1969*, 3-57, p. 44, para. 77.

[52]Cfr. *Delimitation of the Maritime Boundary in the Gulf of Maine Area, Judgment, I.C.J. Reports 1984*, 244–352, p. 299, para 111.

[53]See D'Amato (1971), 286 pp.

[54]Cfr. Jaber (2011), p. 941.

international resolutions, even in the absence of uniform State practice.[55] The presence of such a strong *opinio juris* would make up for the relative absence of practice.[56] In such cases there is a need to confirm the existence of a deep-rooted *opinio juris*, over and above mere embodiment in the practice of certain States, tied to the emergence of a new right.[57] In other words, the behaviour of States should be such as to constitute 'evidence of a belief that this practice is rendered obligatory by the existence of a rule of law requiring it'.[58]

Secondly, it must also be pointed out that it should not just be a question of practice corresponding to what might, or ought to, be an explanation of what States have done, seen as in conformity with an emerging new right. More than this, the justifications for their actions actually declared by States should be taken into account. Specifically, in the instances of practice noted, States did not make reference to any right to remedial secession, but rather spoke of other kinds of justification outside the bounds of international law. It has thus been claimed that these were cases that seem to confirm negative practice by States in the sense of their rejection of pretensions to secede.[59]

This is the reason that it is not possible to understand States as having asserted the emergence of any right to secede under the circumstances appropriate for remedial secession.[60] Rather, as some commentators have put it, there is an *opinio non juris*, in other words, a conviction that there is no such right.[61]

The instance of Kosovo similarly does not contribute to demonstrating the existence of the needful strong *opinion juris* leading to acceptance of the presence of international custom.[62] On this point, the ICJ dodged the question and also did not eventually admit any right to remedial secession in relation to the exercise of self-determination.[63]

---

[55]Cfr. *Military and Paramilitary Activities in and Against Nicaragua (Nicaragua v. United States of America), Merits, Judgment*, supra, Chap. 6, note 50, pp. 98–100, para. 186–188.

Cfr. Ryngaert and Griffioen (2009), p. 579.

On the role of *opinio juris* as an autonomous source for contemporary international law, as a sort of collective conscience of the international community as a whole, manifesting itself in the shape of generalized recognition of which special account must be taken by international legal bodies, see: Piza Escalante (1987), p. 171, para. 36.

[56]Cfr. Ryngaert and Griffioen (2009), p. 584.

[57]Cfr. *Military and Paramilitary Activities in and Against Nicaragua (Nicaragua v. United States of America), Merits, Judgment* supra, Chap. 6, note 50, p. 109, para. 207.

Cfr. Ryngaert and Griffioen (2009), p. 584.

[58]*North Sea Continental Shelf, Judgment*, supra, Chap. 8, note 51, p. 44, para. 77.

[59]Cfr. Ryngaert and Griffioen (2009), p. 584.

[60]Cfr. Hilpold (2009), p. 56, para. 15. Jaber (2011), p. 941. Müllerson (2009), p. 19. Yee (2010), p. 780.

[61]Cfr. Tancredi (2008), p. 48.

Some authors have seen this more as an 'extreme version of a collective right to self-defence'. Cfr. Oeter (2012), p. 118. Oeter (1992), p. 758.

[62]Cfr. Van den Driest (2013), p. 360. Yee (2010), p. 780.

[63]Cfr. Van den Driest (2013), p. 344. Orakhelashvili (2011), p. 86. Röben (2010), p. 1075. Tancredi (2014), p. 81.

See supra, Sect. 8.1.1.

The conclusion, backed by a broad sector of legal doctrine, may be summed up as the impossibility of admitting the existence of any right to remedial secession as a part of customary international law.[64] Even if the recognition of Kosovo as a new State by a considerable number of States might be interpreted as a manifestation of a new norm, there are also other States that have unequivocally opposed acceptance of the right of Kosovo to secession. As concluded by the Independent International Fact-Finding Mission on the Conflict in Georgia in its 2009 Report: 'The law does not permit arguing that other states have violated international law and then taking the rule created by the alleged violation as a new rule and to apply it (selectively) to other cases'.[65]

8.1.4 Proposed Requirements for Remedial Secession

Throughout the post-colonial period, opinions matured in the context of legal doctrine that favour recognition of remedial secession have led to the drawing up of an account of the requisites that must come together in order for exercise of it to be deemed legitimate. Along with these, there has been an enumeration of certain decisions by legal bodies. Among these, one of the most impactful was the decision by the Supreme Court of Canada in the case of the *Reference re Secession of Quebec*, which has already been cited a number of times, and in which reference was made to three sets of extraordinary circumstances that might give rise to a right to secession.[66]

On the basis of this description of circumstances, authors such as Cedric Ryngaert and Simone Franciska van den Driest have put forward guidelines summing up four features on which the views of legal doctrine seemed to be in agreement.[67]

In accordance with a broad current of academic thinking, the principles that must be met for there to be a legitimate exercise of a claimed right to remedial secession may be summed up, it would seem, in the following four requirements:

(1) The claim must come from a people representing the majority in the given territory[68];
(2) There must be circumstances involving serious, massive, systematic violation of fundamental human rights[69];

[64]Cfr. Van den Driest (2013), p. 351. Tancredi (2008), p. 49.

[65]*Report of the Independent International Fact-Finding Mission on the Conflict in Georgia*, supra, Chap. 3, note 14, p. 141.

[66]See supra, Sect. 8.1.1.

[67]See Ryngaert and Griffioen (2009), pp. 351, 575–576.

[68]Cfr. Arp (2010), p. 853, note 15. Ioannidis (2015), p. 178. Musgrave (2000), p. 154. Oeter (2012), p. 115. Ryngaert and Griffioen (2009), p. 575.

[69]Cfr. Ioannidis (2015), p. 178. Jaber (2011), p. 935. Ryngaert and Griffioen (2009), p. 576. Van den Driest (2015), p. 351.

(3) Political participation in government must be persistently denied to the group, creating circumstances of domination, subjugation or exploitation verging on a colonial situation[70];
(4) There is a need to carry out a process of external self-determination as the last resort in view of the exhaustion of all forms of negotiation.[71]

Secession is a *de facto* matter which international law neither prohibits nor recognizes as a right.[72] Those entitled to a right to self-determination do not also possess a right to secession, even in the context of the circumstances described as giving rise to remedial secession. However, international law likewise does not prohibit the attaining of Independence without the consent of the State from which there is a break-away.[73] In view of this statement of legal neutrality, it is hard to accept remedial secession construed as a right to secession for peoples oppressed or subjected to grave infringements of their human rights.[74] For the same reason, remedial secession similarly cannot be accepted if it is asserted to be an exception or authorization, a remedy, against a supposed prohibition of secession in international law.[75]

Rather, international practice shows that secession has enjoyed more support from the international community when it has been the outcome of serious violations of human rights, this being shown in terms of recognition.[76] Situations that might trigger remedial secession may be handled by States through the consequences arising from actions such as recognition, rather than constituting any right or entitlement in international law.[77] If they see a claim as legitimate, States can support, promote and grant recognition to the new entity that is calling for independence.

---

[70]Cfr. Ioannidis (2015), p. 178. Jaber (2011), p. 935. Raič (2002), pp. 368–372. Ryngaert and Griffioen (2009), p. 576. Tomuschat (2006), p. 41. Urrutia Libarona (2012), p. 124. Van den Driest (2015), p. 351.

[71]Cfr. Buchanan (2004), p. 335. Ioannidis (2015), p. 178. Jaber (2011), pp. 935 and 942. Lauwers and Smis (2000), p. 64. Oeter (2012), p. 119. Ryngaert and Griffioen (2009), p. 576. Tomuschat (2006), p. 41. Urrutia Libarona (2012), p. 124.

[72]See supra, Sect. 3.1.

[73]Cfr. Corten (2011), p. 93. Vidmar (2012), p. 168.

[74]Cfr. Corten (2011), p. 93.

[75]This view is what underlies the reasoning put forward by the Russian Federation in its 'Written Statement by the Russian Federation', *Accordance with the International Law of the Unilateral Declaration of Independence in Respect of Kosovo, (Request for an Advisory Opinion),* of 16 April 2009, 43, p. 32, para. 88. http://www.icj-cij.org/files/case-related/141/15628.pdf.

[76]Cfr. Shaw (1997), p. 483.

[77]Cfr. Vidmar (2012), p. 168.

8.2 The Legitimacy of 'Humanitarian Secession'

The precedents of Bangladesh and Kosovo cannot be seen as a manifestation in international practice of any supposed right to remedial secession for the reasons given. All the same, the Kosovo case in particular did show that a large part of the international community is prepared to accept the legitimacy of striving for secession in extraordinary situations of grave violations of human rights relating to a specific group.[78] The Foreign Minister of Austria, Ursula Plassnik, when declaring the recognition of the Republic of Kosovo by Austria, stressed the tension between the ideal solution and the way of realism:

> It is not a hasty recognition. We have carefully considered this decision. Unilateral independence is not an ideal solution, but the only realistic and possible path. We must not forget the history of the conflict. Nor can we close our eyes to reality. The status quo could no longer be maintained and was a constant source of instability.[79]

It also seems clear that some States view secession as a consistent option when all other means have failed. This stance was adopted in various written statements introduced in the Kosovo case. Among them, the statement by Switzerland may be highlighted, running:

> A right to secession based on the right of peoples to self-determination can exist, but may only be exercised in exceptional circumstances, when all other means of exercising the right to self-determination have failed or have to be regarded as futile due to grave and systematic violations of human rights.[80]

This new option for secession appears tightly linked to situations described as 'humanitarian catastrophe', 'grave humanitarian crisis' or 'humanitarian tragedy', as was stressed by Judge Antonio Augusto Cançado Trindade in his Separate

---

[78] Cfr. Shany (2014), p. 238.
See supra, Sect. 8.1.1, note 35.

[79] 'Plassnik: 'Letter on Kosovo's Recognition Signed', Vienna, 28 February 2008, at para. 2. https://www.bmeia.gv.at/en/the-ministry/press/announcements/2008/plassnik-letter-on-kosovos-recognition-signed/.

[80] 'Written Statement by the Swiss Confederation', *Accordance with the International Law of the Unilateral Declaration of Independence in Respect of Kosovo, (Request for an Advisory Opinion),* of 17 October 2008, 27, p. 17, para. 67. http://www.icj-cij.org/files/case-related/141/15614.pdf. 'Written Statement by the Federal Republic of Germany', *Accordance with the International Law of the Unilateral Declaration of Independence in Respect of Kosovo, (Request for an Advisory Opinion),* of April 2009, 43, p. 35. http://www.icj-cij.org/files/case-related/141/15624.pdf. 'Written Statement by the Kingdom of the Netherlands', *Accordance with the International Law of the Unilateral Declaration of Independence in Respect of Kosovo, (Request for an Advisory Opinion),* of 17 April 2009, 14, p. 13, para. 3.20. http://www.icj-cij.org/files/case-related/141/15652.pdf.
Legal doctrine also recognizing this right to secession under circumstances of serious infringements of human rights is also abundant. Among many, representative examples would be Crawford (2007), p. 119. Doehring (2002), p. 58. Thürer (2000), p. 371.

Opinion.[81] In brief, the possibility of secession is accepted in extreme situations, as the Venice Commission summed it up when considering the views expressed by the Canadian Supreme Court and the ICJ.[82]

8.2.1 The Safeguarding of Human Rights by the International Community and a Review of the Idea of Secession

The commitment of the international community to defending human rights provides a new viewpoint in the fuzzy context of secession in international law. This new panorama was referred to by Judge Cançado Trindade in his Separate Opinion when he noted that the actions of institutions revealed a new-found consciousness of a 'duty of care for the humankind'.[83] This involvement of States with obligations arising from international law on human rights and international humanitarian law, the so-called 'humanitarian umbrella', especially from the 1990s onwards, and the limitations of the theory of remedial secession makes it appropriate to review this concept within the current international legal order.

The view of secession put forward in the previous period seems to have been transformed in view of the emergence of a widespread *opinio* legitimizing its exercise in situations in which humanitarian action backed by the international community has proved necessary. This *opinio*, as noted above, has emerged through the adoption of a number of texts and resolutions by international institutions and more recently in relation to the matter of Kosovo. In the meeting of the Security Council which passed Resolution 1244 (1999) various representatives stressed the historic nature of the measure, since it provided 'the platform for the future engagement of the entire international community in the effort to resolve the Kosovo crisis',[84] and was 'capable of ensuring the essential humanity of the people concerned as well as the preservation of international order and stability'.[85] Together with this achievement, the most striking and novel feature of the resolution, according to the United States representative US, Peter Burleigh, was that it:

[81]'Separate Opinion of Judge Cançado Trindade', *Accordance with the International Law of the Unilateral Declaration of Independence in Respect of Kosovo, Advisory Opinion,* supra, Chap. 1, note 3, pp. 541 and 560, para. 41, 42, 97 and ss.
Cfr. Cirkovic (2010), p. 907. Hannum (2011), p. 157.

[82]Cfr. Cfr. 'Opinion on 'Whether Draft Federal Constitutional Law No. 462741-6', CDL-AD(2014) 004, supra, Chap. 6, note 165, p. 9, para. 29.

[83]'Separate Opinion of Judge Cançado Trindade', *Accordance with the International Law of the Unilateral Declaration of Independence in Respect of Kosovo, Advisory Opinion,* supra, Chap. 1, note 3, p. 560, para. 96.

[84]Intervention of Mr. Türk (Slovenia), UN Doc. S/PV.4011, of 10 June 1999, 21, p. 10. Cfr. 'Intervention of Mr. Fowler (Canada)', UN Doc. S/PV.4011, of 10 June 1999, 21, p. 13.

[85]Intervention of Mr. Türk (Slovenia), UN Doc. S/PV.4011, of 10 June 1999, 21, p. 11.

> [...] must provide credible assurance of its willingness to engage in a political process aimed at the establishment of an interim political framework agreement providing for substantial self-government for Kosovo.[86]

The recognition granted by a large number of States in this affair was precisely what confirmed this international conviction.[87] If the Kosovo matter was considered a 'unique case', this was, among other reasons, because of the majority response within the UN:

> [...] That Declaration was the product of not one, but three overlapping historical processes, which did not preordain Kosovo's Declaration, but do help to explain it –the disintegration of Yugoslavia; the human rights crisis within Kosovo; the United Nations response.[88]

Taking these views as a starting point, a concept may be built up that integrates the idea of secession and the emerging *opinio* into the new international reality. This new horizon is one of acceptance of the priority of protecting human rights with precedence over the idea of State sovereignty, manifested in the "human rights over sovereignty thesis".[89] Safeguarding human rights is seen as setting limits to the sovereignty of States for reasons of humanity.

The Kosovo case revealed an *opinio* which stated that denial of any part in government together with grave infringements of human rights may legitimize *actions aimed at achieving secession.*[90] These would be situations in which secession is sought as the last resort with the purpose of protecting the most basic human rights for a given group. Gaining self-determination would have to constitute a 'prerequisite for the enjoyment of all other human rights'.[91] It is proposed that this sort of secession, promoted by the actions of the international community, be termed 'humanitarian secession'.

This idea of 'humanitarian secession' is grounded in the nature of a *jus cogens* of the norms regulating human rights, infringement of which in relation to an identifiable group in the population of a State would justify the setting of limits on the exercise of sovereignty by that State. Sovereignty, whether internal or external, and the principles guaranteeing its exercise (the principle of non-intervention and the principle of territorial integrity) would be limited in favour of the protection of the

---

[86]Intervention of Mr. Burleigh (United States of America), UN Doc. S/PV.4011, of 10 June 1999, 21, p. 14.

[87]Cfr. Jacobs and Radi (2011), p. 348.

[88]Intervention of Mr. Hongju Koh (United States of America), (I.C.J. CR 2009/30, of 8 December 2009, *Accordance with the International Law of the Unilateral Declaration of Independence in Respect of Kosovo, (Request for an Advisory Opinion),* of 15 April 2009, 63, p. 25, para. 6. http://www.icj-cij.org/files/case-related/141/141-20091208-ORA-01-00-BI.pdf.

[89]International Commission on Intervention and State Sovereignty, *The Responsibility to Protect. Report of the ICISS* (Ottawa: International Development Research Centre, 2001), 108, p. 8, para. 1.35. http://responsibilitytoprotect.org/ICISS%20Report.pdf.

Cfr. Tancredi (2008), p. 42.

[90]Cfr. Hannum (1993), p. 44. Lauwers and Smis (2000), p. 64. Stromseth (1992), p. 371.

[91]Intervention of Mr. Demchenko (Ukrainian Soviet Socialist Republic), UN Doc. A/C.3/SR.310, of 10 November 1950, 4, p. 4, para. 47. Cfr. Cassese (1981), p. 101.

most fundamental human rights of a group that were being gravely and systematically violated.[92] In many such instances it would be a case of behaviour with genocidal characteristics, like 'massive ethnic cleansing', such that they might threaten the complete destruction of the group involved.[93]

In extreme cases, when a State, one of whose functions is to satisfy the collective interests both of its citizens and of the wider international community,[94] infringes the basic human rights of its population, it is possible to set limits to the principles guaranteeing the exercise of its functions.[95] The concept of sovereignty is not just a prerogative of a State giving rise to rights, but also, and primarily, requires it to fulfil responsibilities and duties.[96] In his Separate Opinion, Judge Cançado Trindade reiterated this idea in the following terms:

> No State can invoke territorial integrity in order to commit atrocities (such as the practices of torture, and ethnic cleansing, and massive forced displacement of the population), nor perpetrate them on the assumption of State sovereignty, nor commit atrocities and then rely on a claim of territorial integrity notwithstanding the sentiments and ineluctable resentments of the 'people' or 'population' victimized. [...] The basic lesson is clear: no State can use territory to destroy the population.[97]

Analogous to humanitarian intervention, humanitarian secession constitutes a limitation of sovereignty in those circumscribed contexts in which grave violations are directed against a group that can be characterized as a people. In humanitarian intervention the use of force is legitimate as an exception to the principle of non-intervention and of the prohibition on threats and use of force. For its part, in humanitarian secession, action in favour of secession is an exception to the principles of non-intervention and of territorial integrity. In both cases, the basis is constituted by the need to safeguard and protect the most fundamental human rights, violations of which perpetrated within a State constitute the most serious crimes of concern to the international community as a whole.[98] However, the two situations do differ. In the first it is a question of serious infringements of human rights inflicted on a whole population, whilst in the second they are directed against a given group that has the characteristics of a 'people'.

In conclusion, in accordance with the most recent practice a definition may be given for humanitarian secession as that form of secession achieved through actions undertaken by the international community, preferably by a major international

---

[92]Cfr. Burke-White (2014), p. 65.

[93]Cfr. Oeter (2014), p. 57.

[94]Cfr. 'Separate Opinion of Judge Cançado Trindade', *Accordance with the International Law of the Unilateral Declaration of Independence in Respect of Kosovo, Advisory Opinion,* supra, Chap. 1, note 3, p. 597, para. 185, 239 and 240.

[95]Cfr. Tancredi (2014), p. 94.

[96]Cfr. Schrijver (1999), p. 98.

[97]'Separate Opinion of Judge Cançado Trindade', *Accordance with the International Law of the Unilateral Declaration of Independence in Respect of Kosovo, Advisory Opinion,* supra, Chap. 1, note 3, p. 593, para. 176.

[98]Cfr. Escudero Espinosa (2002), p. 310.

organization, in favour of a people against its State. It consists of the adoption of all measures aimed at restitution of the exercise of self-determination and safeguarding the most basic human rights, infringement of which is the gravest crime concerning the international community in its entirety.

8.2.2 Principles That Should Govern Humanitarian Secession

In the analysis given above of remedial secession the difficulty of accepting a right to remedial secession as an exception to a non-existent prohibition on secession in international law was emphasized. In contrast, it was shown that on the basis of the preconditions for remedial secession an authentic *opinio* has grown up legitimizing positive action by the international community leading to the secession of a people so as to guarantee its self-determination and the protection of basic human rights infringed by its State, which has here been termed humanitarian secession.

Indeed, one of the prime elements characterizing the Kosovo case were the actions of the international community throughout the process. After many negotiations in various forums, adoption of Resolution 1244 (1999), sponsored by the G-8 plus Bahrain, Gabon, Slovenia, the Netherlands, and the Ukraine, implied committing the Security Council to finding a solution for the crisis. Its provisions also authorized Member States to establish a provisional administration allowing the people of Kosovo to regain their autonomy through democratic self-governing institutions.[99] It marked the start of a ten-year period during which attempts were made under the auspices of the UN to find a solution in a multilateral framework.

The difficulty of reaching consensus on a final status led the Special Envoy to propose as a solution the granting of independence under international supervision. Independence was proposed as the ultimate solution in view of Kosovo's unique situation:

> [...] only in an independent Kosovo will its democratic institutions be fully responsible and accountable for their actions. This will be crucial to ensure respect for the rule of law and the effective protection of minorities. With continued political ambiguity, the peace and stability of Kosovo and the region remains at risk. Independence is the best safeguard against this risk.[100]

The subsequent declaration of independence made by Kosovar institutions was adopted outside the sphere of the competences assigned to UNMIK and the ambit of Resolution 1244 (1999), as pointed out by the ICJ.[101] Nonetheless, the measures

[99]Cfr. UN Doc. S/RES/1244 (1999), of 10 June 1999, at para. 10.

[100]'Report of the Special Envoy of the Secretary-General on Kosovo's Future Status', UN Doc. S/2007/168, of 26 March 2007, 9, p. 4, para. 10. 'Comprehensive Proposal for the Kosovo Status Settlement', UN Doc. S/2007/168/Add.1, of 26 March 2007, 61.

[101]Cfr. *Accordance with the International Law of the Unilateral Declaration of Independence in Respect of Kosovo, Advisory Opinion,* supra, Chap. 1, note 3, pp. 450–451, para. 116–117.

envisaged in the resolution allowed establishment of the institutions that used their autonomy to declare an independence not actually forbidden by international law.[102] As some Security Council members stressed, they were the channel through which the will of the Kosovar people could be expressed in deciding about its own future.[103]

In conclusion, the Special Envoy highlighted the impossibility of reaching any other solution. A look at the progress of negotiations over a whole decade and in particular in the last year had exhausted "every possible avenue to achieve a negotiated settlement". The parties' irreconcilable stances rendered reaching an agreed solution impossible.[104]

The majority of the international community eventually sanctioned independence by recognizing the new entity in the international arena. However, whilst it was accepted that Kosovo was 'a unique case that demands a unique solution', it was not so clear that it did 'not create a precedent for other unresolved conflicts'.[105] The Kosovo case was unique and needed a unique solution because there was great reluctance to extend this solution to cover other analogous contemporary situations: 'The solutions which are being tried to be imposed on the Federal Republic of Yugoslavia set a dangerous precedent for the international community and a great encouragement to separatist and terrorist groups all over the world'.[106]

The solution proposed for Kosovo was unique at the time, but nothing prevents analogous responses from being made to similar situations. It would be desirable to establish a legal framework within which guiding principles for such processes occurring in the post-colonial era could be laid down, just as guidelines were in place to govern decolonization.

Progress made in specifying orientation guidelines for actions of remedial secession provides a useful starting point in formulating the principles that should govern humanitarian secession. Several such guidelines summed up what situations were felt to permit the invocation of a claimed right to remedial secession, and these are equally valid from the angle of humanitarian secession. Among them must be numbered the principles enunciated during the development of the cases of Bangladesh and particularly of Kosovo.

---

[102]See supra, Sect. 6.3.1.

Cfr Intervention of Ms. DiCarlo (United States of America), UN Doc. A/63/PV.22, of 8 October 2008, 15, p. 5.

[103]Intervention of Mr. Nesho (Albania), UN Doc. S/PV.4011 (Reasumption 1), of 10 June, 1999, 20, p. 14.

[104]'Report of the Special Envoy of the Secretary-General on Kosovo's Future Status', UN Doc. S/2007/168, of 26 March 2007, 9, p. 5, para. 16.

[105]Id., p. 4, para. 15.

[106]Intervention of Mr. Jovanović (Federal Republic of Yugoslavia), UN Doc. S/PV.4011, of 10 June 1999, 21, p. 6. Cfr. Intervention of President Tadić (Serbia); and intervention of Mr. Lê Luong Minh (Viet Nam), UN Doc. S/PV.5839, of 18 February 2008, 23, pp. 5 and 14.

It would appear that the criteria that must be fulfilled for the legitimate undertaking of all actions directed towards humanitarian secession may be summed up in the following four features:

(1) The situation must affect a part of the population of a State that constitutes a majority in a given territory and is identifiable as a people;
(2) There must be serious, massive systematic violation of basic human rights tightly linked to denial of political participation in government;
(3) There must be a need to undertake a process of external self-determination as a last resort after exhaustion of all other means of putting an end to the situation;
(4) The secession must have a humanitarian purpose;

In his 2008 report the Secretary-General stressed that the new situation arising from the Declaration of Independence of Kosovo in no wise implied violation of Resolution 1244 (1999), but did involve re-organization of the international presence in Kosovo.[107] This process has continued to this day and highlights the fact that the international community's actions have gradually adopted unique measures for a unique case, but which do correspond to the moves to be made as seen in the 2005 UN World Summit. By the end of this World Summit, Member States had committed themselves to a statement that 'the international community, through the UN, also has the responsibility to use appropriate diplomatic, humanitarian and other peaceful means, in accordance with Chap. VII and VIII of the Charter, to help protect populations from genocide, war crimes, ethnic cleansing and crimes against humanity'.[108]

References

Arp, B. 2010. The ICJ Advisory Opinion on the *Accordance with International Law of the Unilateral Declaration of Independence in Respect of Kosovo* and the International Protection of Minorities. *German LJ* 11: 847–866.

Baggett, T. 1999. Human Rights Abuses in Yugoslavia: To Bring an End to Political Oppression, the International Community Should Assist in Establishing and Independent Kosovo. *Ga.J. Int'l & Comp. L.* 27: 45–59.

Barros, J. 1968. *The Åland Islands Question; Its Settlement by the League of Nations*. New Haven: Yale University Press.

Brown, P.M. 1921. The Aaland Islands Question. *AJIL* 15: 268–272.

Buchanan, A.E. 1991. *Secession: The Morality of Political Divorce from Fort Sumter to Lithuania and Quebec*. Boulder: Westview Press.

———. 1997. Theories of Secession. *Philosophy & Public Affairs* 26: 31–61.

———. 2004. *Justice, Legitimacy and Self-Determination. Moral Foundations for International Law*. Oxford; New York: Oxford University Press.

[107]Cfr. 'Report of the Secretary-General on the United Nations Interim Administration Mission in Kosovo', UN Doc. S/2008/692, of 24 November 2008, 23, pp. 6–7, para. 21–22.

[108]'2005 World Summit Outcome', UN Doc. A/RES/60/1, of 24 October 2005, 38, p. 30, para. 139.

Buchheit, L.C. 1978. *Secession: The Legitimacy of Self-Determination*. New Haven: Yale University Press.

Burke-White, W.W. 2014. Crimea and the International Legal Order. *Survival* 56: 65–80.

Burri, T. 2010. The Kosovo Opinion and Secession: The Sounds of Silence and Missing Links. *German LJ* 11: 881–890.

Cassese, A. 1981. The Self-Determination of Peoples. In *The International Bill of Rights: The Covenant on Civil and Political Rights*, ed. L. Henkin, 95–113. New York: Columbia University Press.

———. 1995. *Self-Determination of Peoples: A Legal Reappraisal*. Cambridge: Cambridge University Press.

Charney, J.I. 2001. Self-Determination: Chechnya, Kosovo, and East Timor. *Vand. J. Transnat'l L.* 34: 455–446.

Christakis, T. 2014. Les conflits de sécession en Crimée et dans l'Est de l'Ukraine et le droit international (The Conflicts of Secession in Crimea and Eastern Ukraine and International Law). *JDI* 141: 733–764.

Cirkovic, E. 2010. An Analysis of the ICJ Advisory Opinion on Kosovo's Unilateral Declaration of Independence. *German LJ* 11: 895–912.

Cismas, I. 2010. Secession in Theory and Practice: The Case of Kosovo and Beyond. *GoJIL* 2: 531–587.

Corten, O. 2008. Déclarations unilatérales d'indépendance et reconnaissance prématurées: du Kosovo à l'Ossétie du sud et à l'Abkhazie. *RGDIP* 112: 721–759.

———. 2011. Territorial Integrity Narrowly Interpreted: Reasserting the Classical Inter-State Paradigm of International Law. *LJIL* 24: 87–94.

Crawford, J. 2007. *The Creation of States in International Law*. 2nd ed. Oxford: Clarendon Press.

D'Amato, A.A. 1971. *The Concept of Custom in International Law*. Ithaca, NY: Cornell University Press.

De Visscher, F. 1921. La question des Iles d'Aaland. *Revue de droit international et de législation comparée* 2: 35–56, and 2: 243–284.

Dinstein, Y. 1996. Is There a Right to Secede? *ASIL Proceedings* 90: 299–302.

Doehring, K. 2002. Self-Determination. In *The Charter of the United Nations: A Commentary*, ed. B. Simma, 2nd ed., 58. Oxford: Oxford University Press.

Dugard, J., and D. Raič. 2006. The Role of Recognition in the Law and Practice of Secession. In *Secession: International Law Perspectives*, ed. M.G. Kohen, 94–137. Cambridge: Cambridge University Press.

Escudero Espinosa, J.F. 2002. *Cuestiones en torno a la intervención humanitaria y el Derecho internacional actual*. León: Universidad, Secretariado de Publicaciones y Medios Audiovisuales.

Fleiner, T. 2011. The Unilateral Secession of Kosovo as a Precedent in International Law. In *From Bilateralism to Community Interests: Essays in Honour of Judge Bruno Simma*, ed. U. Fastenrath, 877–894. Oxford: Oxford University Press.

Goodwin, M. 2007. From Province to Protectorate to State? Speculation on the Impact of Kosovo's Genesis Upon the Doctrines of International Law. *German LJ* 8: 1–20.

Grant, T. 2000. Extending Decolonization: How the United Nations Might Have Addressed Kosovo. *Ga.J. Int'l & Comp. L.* 28: 9–54.

———. 2009. Regulating the Creation of States. From Decolonization to Secession. *JILIR* 5: 11–57.

Hannum, H. 1990. *Autonomy, Sovereignty, and Self-Determination: The Accommodation of Conflicting Rights*, 503. Philadelphia: University of Pennsylvania Press.

———. 1993. Rethinking Self-Determination. *VJIL* 34: 1–69.

———. 2011. The Advisory Opinion on Kosovo: An Opportunity Lost, or a Poisoned Chalice Refused? *LJIL* 24: 155–161.

Higgins, R. 1993. Postmodern Tribalism and the Right to Secession. In *Peoples and Minorities in International Law*, ed. C. Brolmann, R. Lefeber, and M. Zieck, 29–35. Dordrecht: Martinus Nijhoff.
Hilpold, P. 2009. The Kosovo Case and International Law: Looking for Applicable Theories. *Chinese JIL* 8: 47–61.
Ioannidis, N.A. 2015. Constitutional Prohibition of Secession under the Prism of International Law: The Cases of Kosovo, Crimea and Cyprus. *Edimburgh Student Law Review* 2: 169–180.
Jaber, T. 2011. A Case for Kosovo? Self-Determination and Secession in the 21st Century. *IJHR* 15: 926–947.
Jacobs, D., and Y. Radi. 2011. Waiting for Godot: An Analysis of the Advisory Opinion on Kosovo. *LJIL* 24: 331–353.
Kapustin, A. 2015. Crimea's Self-Determination in the Light of Contemporary International Law. *ZaöRV/HJIL* 75: 101–118.
Kemoklidze, N. 2009. The Kosovo Precedent and the Moral Hazard of Secession. *JILIR* 5: 117–140.
Lauwers, G., and S. Smis. 2000. New Dimensions of the Right to Self-Determination: A Study of the International Response to the Kosovo Crisis. *N & EP* 6: 43–70.
Müllerson, R.A. 2009. Precedents in the Mountains: On the Parallels and Uniqueness of the Cases of Kosovo, South Ossetia and Abkhazia. *Chinese JIL* 8: 2–25.
Murswiek, D. 1993. The Issue of a Right to Secession – Reconsidered. In *Modern Law of Self-Determination*, ed. C. Tomuschat, 21–40. The Hague: Martinus Nijhoff Publishers.
Musgrave, T.D. 2000. *Self-Determination and National Minorities*. Oxford: Oxford University Press.
Nanda, V.P. 1981. Self-Determination under International Law: Validity of Claims to Secede. *Case W.Res.J. Int'l L.* 13: 257–280.
Oeter, S. 1992. Selbstbestimmungsrecht im Wandel. Überlegungen zur Debatte um Selbstbestimmung, Sezessionsrecht und 'vorzeitige' Anerkennung. *ZaöRV* 52: 741–775.
———. 2012. Secession, Territorial Integrity and the Role of the Security Council. In *Kosovo and International Law: The ICJ Advisory Opinion of 22 July 2010*, ed. P. Hilpold, 109–138. Leiden; Boston: M. Nijhoff Publishers.
———. 2014. The Role of Recognition and Non-Recognition with Regard to Secession. In *Self-Determination and Secession in International Law*, ed. C. Walter et al., 45–67. Oxford: Oxford University Press.
Orakhelashvili, A. 2011. The International Courts Advisory Opinion on the UDI in Respect of Kosovo: Washing Away the Foam on the Tide of Time. *Max Planck YUNL* 15: 65–104.
Padelford, N.J. 1939. The Aland Islands Question. *AJIL* 33: 465–487.
Parameswaran, K. 2008. Der Rechtsstatus des Kosovo im Lichte der aktuellen Entwicklungen. *AVR* 46: 172–204.
Piza Escalante, R.E. 1987. La '*opinio juris*' como fuente autónoma del Derecho internacional ('*opinio juris*' y '*jus cogens*'). *AHLADI* 8: 131–194.
Raič, D. 2002. *Statehood and the Law of Self-Determination*. The Hague: Martinus Nijhoff Publishers.
Röben, V. 2010. The ICJ Advisory Opinion on the Unilateral Declaration of Independence in Respect of Kosovo: Rules or Principles? *GoJIL* 2: 1063–1086.
Ryngaert, C. 2010. The ICJs Advisory Opinion on Kosovo's Declaration of Independence: A Mixed Opportunity?: International Court of Justice, Accordance with International Law of the Unilateral Declaration of Independence in Respect of Kosovo, Advisory Opinion of 22 July 2010. *NILR* 57: 481–494.
Ryngaert, C., and C. Griffioen. 2009. The Relevance of the Right to Self-Determination in the Kosovo Matter: In Partial Response to the Agora Papers. *Chinese JIL* 8: 573–587.
Schaller, C. 2008. Die Sezession des Kosovo und der völkerrechtliche Status der internationalen Präsenz. *AVR* 46: 131–171.
Schrijver, N. 1999. The Changing Nature of State Sovereignty. *BYIL* 70: 65–98.

Seidel, G. 2001. A New Dimension of the Right of Self-Determination in Kosovo? In *Kosovo and the International Community. A Legal Assessment*, ed. C. Tomuschat, 203–215. The Hague: Kluwer.

Seyersted, F. 1982. The Aaland Autonomy and International Law. *Nordisk Tidsskrift for International Ret* 51: 23–28.

Shany, Y. 2014. Does International Law Grant the People of Crimea and Donetsk a Right to Secede? Revisiting Self-Determination in Light of the 2014 Events in Ukraine. *Brown JWA* 21: 233–244.

Shaw, M.N. 1997. Peoples, Territorialism and Boundaries. *EJIL* 8: 478–507.

Stromseth, J.E. 1992. Self-Determination, Secession and Humanitarian Intervention by the United Nations. *ASIL Proceedings* 86: 370–374.

Tancredi, A. 2006. A Normative 'Due Process' in the Creation of States Through Secession. In *Secession. International Law Perspectives*, ed. M. Kohen, 171–207. Cambridge and New York: Cambridge University Press.

———. 2008. Neither Authorized nor Prohibited? Secession and International Law after Kosovo, South Ossetia and Abkhazia. *Italian YIL* 18: 37–62.

———. 2014. Secession and the Use of Force. In *Self-Determination and Secession in International Law*, ed. C. Walter et al., 68–94. Oxford: Oxford University Press.

Thürer, D. 1984. Das Selbstbestimmungsrecht der Völker. *AVR* 22: 113–137.

———. 2000. Self-Determination. In *Encyclopedia of Public International Law*, ed. R. Bernhardt, vol. Vol. IV, 364–374. Amsterdam: North Holland Publishing.

Tomuschat, C. 2006. Secession and Self-Determination. In *Secession: International Law Perspectives*, ed. M. Kohen, 23–45. Cambridge: Cambridge University Press.

Umozurike, U.O. 1972. *Self-Determination in International Law*. Hamden, Connecticut: Archon Books.

Urrutia Libarona, I. 2012. Territorial Integrity and Self-Determination: The Approach of International Court of Justice in the Advisory Opinion on Kosovo. *Revista destudis autonòmics i federals* 16: 107–140.

Van den Driest, S.F. 2013. *Remedial Secession. A Right to External Self-Determination as a Remedy to Serious Injustices?* Cambridge: Intersentia.

———. 2015. Crimea's Separation from Ukraine: An Analysis of the Right to Self-Determination and (Remedial) Secession in International Law. *NILR* 62: 329–363.

Vashakmadze, M., and M. Lippold. 2010. Nothing But a Road Towards Secession'? The International Court of Justice's Advisory Opinion on Accordance with International Law of the Unilateral Declaration of Independence in Respect of Kosovo. *GoJIL* 2: 619–647.

Vidmar, J. 2009. International Legal Responses to Kosovo's Declaration of Independence. *Vand. J. Transnatl L.* 42: 779–851.

———. 2010. Remedial Secession in International Law: Theory and (Lack of) Practice. *St. Antony's International Review* 6: 37–56.

———. 2012. Conceptualizing Declarations of Independence in International Law. *Oxford JLS* 32: 153–177.

Watson, K.W. 2008. When in the Course of Human Events: Kosovo's Independence and the Law of Secession. *Tul. J. Int'l & Comp. L.* 17: 267–293.

Wilson, G. 2009. Self-Determination, Recognition and the Problem of Kosovo. *NILR* 56: 455–481.

Yee, S. 2010. Notes on the International Court of Justice (Part 4): The Kosovo Advisory Opinion. *Chinese JIL* 9: 763–782.

Chapter 9
Conclusion

Twenty-five years after the historic adoption of Resolution 678 (1990) by the Security Council with the co-operation of all the permanent Member States so as to confront the invasion of Kuwait by Iraq, it would appear that dissent has raised its head once more among Members. That was the first time that authority was given to Member States 'to use all necessary means [. . .] to restore international peace and security'.[1] Among many others, it was followed by Resolution 688 (1991), which attempted 'to address urgently the critical needs of the refugees and displaced Iraqi populations'.[2] The Yalta Conference of February 1945 laid down the broad lines for today's Europe, recognizing an international status for the Ukraine, but also bringing the start of the Cold War. Within this same framework antagonism seems to be emerging in the shape of indignant Russian actions triggered by an aggressive Western stance, so characteristic of what some authors interpret as a return to *realpolitik*.[3]

This aggressive posture had been shown by the NATO intervention in Kosovo in March 1999. Faced with it, the representative of the Russian Federation had declared the need to construct a multipolar world order based on the UN Charter during the debate on Resolution 1244 (1999):

> The draft resolution has even greater significance, going beyond the framework of the Kosovo problem and the Balkan region. It highlights the urgent need to form a truly multi-polar world order based on the UN Charter, a world order in which there will be no room for unilateral diktat or attempts at domination by force. Only on such a collective basis can we achieve lasting solutions to the complex problems of today's world.[4]

---

[1]UN Doc. S/RES/678 (1990), of 28 November 1990, at para. 2.

[2]UN Doc. S/RES/688 (1991), of 5 April 1991, at para. 5.

[3]Cfr. Cimiotta (2014), p. 498. Guillemoles (2014), http://www.politiqueinternationale.com/revue/article.php?id_revue=143&id=1255&content=synopsis.

[4]Intervention of Mr. Lavrov (Russian Federation), UN Doc. S/PV.4011, of 10 June 1999, 21, p. 8.

J. F. Escudero Espinosa, *Self-Determination and Humanitarian Secession in International Law of a Globalized World*,
https://doi.org/10.1007/978-3-319-72622-9_9

However, since the Kosovo conflict the international legal system appeared to have altered and advantage was taken of the Ukraine crisis by Vladimir Putin to take a new role in the world order for the first time since the collapse of the USSR.[5] His new policy seemed to aim at setting the Russian Federation up as a new axis in a multipolar world, going beyond the unilateralism headed by the US, in which other States might spearhead processes that would establish precedents.[6] The Ukrainian crisis was thus the context in which the tension between Russia and western countries became plain. Within it, the Crimea was not just a matter of relations and interference in the Ukraine's internal affairs by Russia.[7]

This was the background against which Vladimir Putin proclaimed that the action in Crimea 'was legitimate and did not require any permission from the country's central authorities'. He alleged that it was a situation similar to that of Kosovo, 'a precedent our western colleagues created with their own hands'.[8] However, it is hard to accept that these are similar situations for which Kosovo might be considered a precedent legitimizing secession by Crimea. Rather, relations between the Ukraine and the Russian Federation are the outcome of a policy of illegal Russian interference in internal matters of 'their Slavonic brothers' culminating in the annexation, against all international law, of part of the territory of these "brother".[9]

International law recognizes a right to self-determination as one of the most basic of all human rights.[10] Guaranteeing this concerns all members of the la international community as an obligation derived from its status as an international *jus cogens*.[11] Ownership of the right to self-determination gains recognition in the post-decolonization era for peoples defined as a social entity possessing a clear identity and its own characteristics, and related to a territory.[12] Although the territorial integrity principle has been seen as a limitation on the exercise of the right to self-determination, in accordance with the reasoning of the ICJ in its Kosovo Advisory Opinion invocation of this cannot be at the level of an internal matter for States, but exclusively in relations among territorial sovereign powers.[13]

---

[5]Cfr. Burke-White (2014), p. 73.

[6]Cfr. Ibid.

[7]Cfr. Wilson (2015), p. 223.

[8]'Address by President of the Russian Federation on March 18, 2014', supra, Chap. 1, note 1, at para. 29.

[9]Cfr. Müllerson (2014), p. 138.

[10]'International Covenant on Civil and Political Rights' and 'International Covenant on Economic, Social and Cultural Rights', of 16 December 1966, supra, Chap. 2, note 51, at Art. 1(1).

[11]Cfr. *East Timor (Portugal v. Australia), Judgment*, supra, Chap. 2, note 70, p. 102, para. 29. *Legal Consequences of the Construction of a Wall in the Occupied Palestinian Territory, Advisory Opinion, I.C.J. Reports 2004*, 136–271, p. 172, para. 88.

[12]Cfr. *The Right of Self-Determination: Historic and Current Development on the Basis of United Nations Instruments.* Study prepared by Aureliu Cristescu, UN Doc. E/CN.4/Sub.2/404/Rev.1, supra, Chap. 2, note 47, p. 41.

[13]Cfr. *Accordance with the International Law of the Unilateral Declaration of Independence in Respect of Kosovo, Advisory Opinion,* supra, Chap. 1, note 3, p. 437, para. 80.

International practice highlights the fact that States have opposed recognition of a right to secession as a realization of the right to self-determination. The cases of Bangladesh and Kosovo alone saw secession recognized, as against some twenty failed attempts at unilateral secession.[14] This absence of any right to secession does not imply that it is prohibited by international law. Rather, secession must be seen as neither recognized nor forbidden by international law, this being a 'deliberate silence'.[15] It is necessary to look at the internal context of each State to assess whether the process directed towards the creation of a new State is licit or illicit in the light of its own inner organization, its national or domestic law.

The making of a unilateral declaration of independence is not regulated by international law and must be considered as an action within the process intended to create a new State. In itself it does not create any new State, so that the presence of elements of statehood and effective exercise of this alone can prove the existence of a State, the status of which 'is a question of fact'.[16] Thus, effective statehood would be the legal title for attributing sovereignty over a given territory.

If doubt is cast on this legal title or legality in relation to a secession process because effectiveness is questioned, the matter of recognition gains particular importance.[17] The condition of effectiveness applies exclusively in the framework of international law and must engage with other principles of international law. Hence, acts contrary to international law can only give rise to *de facto* situations that which may in the end be considered legal because of other circumstances such as the passage of time.[18]

Moreover, any attempt to attain independence must be made in accordance with general or special international law, following the principle *ex injuria jus non oritur*. Secession is not prohibited by international law. However, according to international practice manifested in matters like the attempts to create Northern Cyprus, Southern Rhodesia, the South African Homelands, South Africa's illegal presence in Namibia and the Republika Srpska, it cannot be achieved by violating peremptory norms of international law.[19] International law has no provisions relative to proposals to secede, but it does condemn certain processes undertaken by infringing norms of *jus cogens*, such as the use of force in international relations or violations of human rights.[20] The preservation of international peace and security, and the protection of human rights constitute higher values that must always be observed.

[14]Cfr. Crawford (2007), pp. 388–402.

[15]Cfr. 'Declaration of Judge Simma', *Accordance with the International Law of the Unilateral Declaration of Independence in Respect of Kosovo, Advisory Opinion, I.C.J. Reports 2010*, 478–481, p. 480, para. 9.

[16]Arbitration Commission of the Conference on Yugoslavia, 'Opinion No. 1', of 29 November 1992, supra, Chap. 3, note 70, at para. 1).a).

[17]Cfr. Lauterpacht (1947), pp. 411–412.

[18]Cfr. Salvioli (1933), pp. 51–54.

[19]Cfr. *Accordance with the International Law of the Unilateral Declaration of Independence in Respect of Kosovo, Advisory Opinion,* supra, Chap. 1, note 3, p. 437, para. 81.

[20]Cfr. Vidmar (2012), p. 177.

NATO intervention in Kosovo was the subject of deep and extensive scrutiny by experts in the doctrines of international law, and met with wide disapproval from the international community because it breached the prohibition on the use of force in international relations. However, this assessment of the legality of NATO actions was decoupled from the Kosovo secession process, since the intervention was not aimed against the territorial integrity of the FRY and secession at the end of 2010 was understood as not being a consequence of the attacks.

In contrast, authorization to deploy Russian Federation forces on the territory of the Ukraine, granted by the Council of the Federation of the Russian Parliament on 1 March 2014 at the request of President Vladimir Putin, has been regarded as a flagrant breach of international law. Although attempts have been made to justify it with arguments such as the situation threatening the life of Russian citizens or the authorization received from the overthrown President Viktor Yanukovych, its legality is highly dubious on the basis of the real facts. Even references to the concept of humanitarian intervention by the Russian Federation lack foundation, since this is ruled out by the absence of any massive and serious violation of human rights by the Ukrainian Government. The Russian Federation never brought any charge regarding the human rights situation in Crimea, and the main international organizations made it plain there was no record of violations of human rights by the Ukrainian authorities.[21] The military campaign, far from having any humanitarian character, was directed towards bringing Crimea under the control of the Russian Federation, capturing Ukrainian military material and obliging Ukrainian troops to surrender.

The referendum of 16 March 2014 was held under these conditions, and failed to comply with international standards on referenda guaranteeing 'free and genuine expression of the will of the peoples concerned'.[22] International law requires compliance with certain basic rules laid down in Art. 25 of the 'International Covenant on Civil and Political Rights' or in Art. 3 of the 'Protocol to the European Convention on Human Rights', further elaborated by the 'Code of Good Practice on Referendums' drawn up by the Venice Commission.[23] Even Russian legal doctrine accepts these requirements, among which figures a demand for the evacuation of all foreign troops from the territory involved.

Additionally, international practice regarding referenda has given rise to various further criteria, among them: the lack of sufficient legitimization for territorial changes that arises merely from the holding of a referendum,[24] the absence of any essential need for a referendum to be held in order for territorial changes to be made

[21]UNHCHR, 'Report on Human Rights Situation in Ukraine', supra, Chap. 6, note 45, at para. 103 and 104; y al UNHRC, 'Report of the United Nations High Commissioner for Human Rights on the Situation of Human Rights in Ukraine', of September 2014, UN Doc. A/HCR/27/75, at para. 23.

[22]*Western Sahara, Advisory Opinion*, supra, Chap. 2, note 70, p. 32, para. 55.

[23]See Venice Commission, 'Code of Good Practice on Referendums', Strasbourg, 20 January 2009, Study No. 371/2006, CDL-AD(2007)008rev, 24.

[24]Cfr. Hilpold (2015), p. 258.

or of any binding nature of the results,[25] the fact that referenda held by one State in the territory of another are contrary to international law because they infringe right to self-determination the territorial integrity principle.[26]

Moreover, the referendum must also be seen as breaching the Ukrainian national law, especially Art. 2 and 134, which proclaim the indivisibility and inviolability of the Ukraine's territory and define Crimea as 'an inseparable constituent part of Ukraine', as re-affirmed by Art. 1 of the Constitution of the Autonomous Republic of Crimea in 1998.[27]

The referendum question was far from clear, in that it offered a choice between Independence or a return to the 1992 Constitution, omitting any option of continuing with the current Constitution. However, the most serious aspect was the context in which both the call for a referendum and the actual voting took place, under the threat and actual use of force. This led many States to take no account of the results and to assess them as lacking legitimacy for any change in the status of Crimea. This was reflected in the text of the draft resolution proposed by forty-one States to the Security Council, but finally vetoed by the Russian Federation.[28]

The subsequent annexation of Crimea implied the culmination of a policy of the Russian Federation involving the idea of extending its territory by holding plebiscites putting forward the accession to it of regions previously transferred from it. The instrument intended to incorporate the Crimea into the Russian Federation lacks legal effect, since it was formulated as a supposed international treaty entered into by a body that was seen as a State only by itself, without any international recognition, and by the Russian Federation.[29] This act ran counter to Russian national law, which requires an international treaty to be between two States, whilst Crimea was not yet in existence as a State for the Russian Federation, which was attempting to achieve recognition and incorporation simultaneously.[30]

The Venice Commission had occasion to pronounce its views on a proposal for a Draft Federal Constitutional Law for the Russian Federation of 28 February 2014, in which an attempt was made to avoid the need for mutual accord for admitting and creating a new element within the Russian Federation. At sight of the text, the Venice Commission deemed it incompatible with international law, as it violated the principles of territorial integrity, national sovereignty, non-intervention in the

---

[25]Cfr. Crawford (2012), p. 243. Vidmar (2015), p. 379.

[26]Cfr. *Legal Consequences for States of the Continued Presence of South Africa in Namibia (South West Africa) notwithstanding Security Council Resolution 276 (1970), Advisory Opinion*, supra, Chap. 2, note 70, p. 58, para. 132.

[27]See supra, Sect. 6.2.2.

[28]UN Doc. S/2014/189, of 15 March 2014, at para. 5.

[29]See 'Agreement on the Accession of the Republic of Crimea to the Russian Federation submitted to State Duma for ratification', March 19, 2014, supra, Chap. 5, note 110. 'Treaty between the Russian Federation and the Republic of Crimea on the Acceptance of the Republic of Crimea into the Russian Federation and on Creation of New Federative Entities within the Russian Federation', signed on March 18, 2014 in Moscow, supra, Chap. 5, note 110.

[30]Cfr. Pronin (2015), p. 136.

internal affairs of another state and *pacta sunt servanda*.[31] In concluding its Opinion, it roundly affirmed that the transfer of territory from on State to another without the valid consent of the State owning the territory to be transferred is not a lawful cession, but rather involves an 'annexation of territory which is prohibited under international law'.[32]

In view of the situation arising from the annexation of Crimea, the question arises of what instruments the international community has to hand in order to try to re-establish the status of Crimea. The response of the international community has been to practise wide non-recognition, both by individual States and within international organizations like the UN, the EU and NATO. The failure to resolve the controversy by diplomatic means was followed by the adoption of sanctions applied to individuals and entities involved in the changes of government occurring in the Autonomous Republic of Crimea. Nevertheless, non-recognition continues to be the international legal mechanism for confronting illegal moves, its efficacy depending on its generalization and affirmation over time. The situation will not change immediately, but its legal consolidation can be impeded.[33]

Although international law has been broken, it would appear difficult for the integration of Crimea into the Russian Federation to be reversed. Inaction and silence on the part of the Ukraine, which seems to show tacit admission of the new status, may well be the most realistic option and presage broad tolerance by the international community of acts of secession. Finally, effectiveness will determine new status, contrary to the principle *ex injuria jus non oritur*. What is clear is that the emergence of a new entity has to be seen as a *de facto* matter and that effectiveness is a manifestation of this that law cannot prevent. It is hard to accept that an entity born of unlawfulness has no existence at all, but non-recognition does give rise to a situation of social isolation. When infringements of peremptory norms of international law have taken place, the factual requirements for establishing a new State have not been met, so consolidation of statehood through effectiveness does not occur. This is the reason that in practice there is no case similar to that of Crimea which has had a positive outcome.

When the General Assembly asked the question in relation to the Kosovan declaration of independence, the ICJ took the opinion 'that the declaration of independence of Kosovo adopted on 17 February 2008 did not violate international law'.[34] Throughout the content of the Advisory Opinion, the ICJ left untouched any examination of all the details relating to the possibility of the Kosovan people creating a new State. According to the text of the declaration of independence, it

[31]Cfr. 'Opinion on 'Whether Draft Federal Constitutional Law No. 462741-6', CDL-AD(2014)004, supra, Chap. 6, note 165, p. 3, para. 9.

[32]Id., p. 6, para. 22.

[33]Cfr. Hilpold (2015), p. 269.

[34]*Accordance with the International Law of the Unilateral Declaration of Independence in Respect of Kosovo, Advisory Opinion,* supra, Chap. 1, note 3, pp. 450–451, para. 116–117.

could be assumed that it was made by democratically-elected leaders reflecting the people's will, this constituting its democratic legitimacy.

According to a major argument in legal doctrine, the unilateral declaration of independence breached Resolution 1244 (1999), as it thwarted the mandate to seek a negotiated settlement between the parties for final status and the territorial integrity of the FRY, and because it implied the end of the international presence established by the Security Council.[35] Nevertheless, others noted that Resolution 1244 (1999) already implied breaking up the territorial integrity of Serbia and established mechanisms for self-government, the exercise of which included the possibility of claiming independence. Repeated failures to find the negotiated solution required by the resolution meant that the only way out was a unilateral decision. As pointed out by the ICJ, Resolution 1244 (1999) envisaged no specific final status for Kosovo, and institutions of self-government acted beyond the sphere of competence of UNIMIK.[36]

Despite everything, it is generally accepted that the unilateral declaration of independence did not occur within a context of the infringement of a peremptory norm of international law, as happened in the cases of Southern Rhodesia, Northern Cyprus and the Republika Srpska. Seeing the declaration of independence as an immediate consequence of NATO intervention has to be ruled out, not just because of the time elapsed between them, but also because the intervention did not seek Kosovan secession.

The secession of Kosovo finds its basis not so much in the existence of some unclear right to remedial secession,[37] available to certain populations for whom the exercise of external self-determination would be a 'remedy' against situations of a lack of representation and grave and systematic violations of human rights.[38] Rather, it relies on the legitimacy of secession in situations of grave humanitarian crisis or humanitarian tragedy.

It must be recognized that an *opinio* is emerging in the shape of various international texts and resolutions of international institutions making clear the legitimacy of secession at the behest of the international community when humanitarian action in favour of a population linked to a specific territory becomes needed. The Kosovan case was 'unique' in this way, and Resolution 1244 (1999) provided a platform for the future engagement of the entire international community in the effort to resolve the Kosovo crisis. This triggered a commitment to bring into play a political process driven by the aim of reaching an agreement on a provisional political framework that would give Kosovo substantial self-government. Hence, it was accepted that if there

[35]Cfr. 'Dissenting Opinion of Judge Koroma', *Accordance with International Law of the Unilateral Declaration of Independence in Respect of Kosovo, Advisory Opinion, I.C.J. Reports 2010*, 467–477, p. 470, para. 11. http://www.icj-cij.org/docket/files/141/15991.pdf.

[36]Cfr. *Accordance with the International Law of the Unilateral Declaration of Independence in Respect of Kosovo, Advisory Opinion,* supra, Chap. 1, note 3, p. 453, para. 123.

[37]Id., p. 438, para. 82–83.

[38]Cfr. Buchanan (2004), p. 335.

were to be deprival of participation in government paralleled by grave violations of human rights, this would legitimize the action of the international community in pressing for secession as a last resort.

Exhaustion of all means of reaching a consensual final status for Kosovo led the Special Envoy to propose as the solution the granting of independence under international supervision.[39] The declaration of independence made by the institutions of Kosovo went further than the scope of competence of UNIMIK, and of Resolution 1244 (1999), but the measures envisaged by the Resolution permitted the establishment of institutions that made use of their autonomy to declare an independence not prohibited by international law.[40]

The international community confirmed the new entity through recognition. The case of Kosovo was unique and needed a clearly unique solution for fear of a spread to other similar contemporary situations. However, it was not so clear that it did not constitute a precedent for the future that would legitimize adopting all diplomatic and humanitarian measures of a pacific nature to protect populations against the commission of the most serious crimes. If the secession process of Crimea is disputed under the maxim *ex injuria non oritur jus*, in the case of Kosovo, as argued by Judge Cançado Trindade, the response to serious violations of law gave rise to new rules, *ex factis jus oritur*.[41]

References

Buchanan, A.E. 2004. *Justice, Legitimacy and Self-Determination. Moral Foundations for International Law*. Oxford; New York: Oxford University Press.

Burke-White, W.W. 2014. Crimea and the International Legal Order. *Survival* 56: 65–80.

Cimiotta, E. 2014. Le reazioni alla 'sottrazione' della Crimea all'Ucraina. Quali garanzie del diritto internazionale di fronte a gravi illeciti imputati a grandi potenze? *DUDI* 8: 491–504.

Crawford, J. 2007. *The Creation of States in International Law*. 2nd ed. Oxford: Clarendon Press.

———. 2012. *Brownlie's Principles of Public International Law*. 8th ed. Oxford: Oxford University Press.

Guillemoles, A. 2014. Les cents jours qui ont changé l'Ukraine. *Politique internationale* 143: 45–63.

Hilpold, P. 2015. Ukraine, Crimea and New International Law: Balancing International Law with Arguments Drawn from History. *Chinese JIL* 14: 237–270.

Lauterpacht, H. 1947. *Recognition in International Law*. Cambridge: Cambridge University Press.

Müllerson, R.A. 2014. Ukraine: Victim of Geopolitics. *Chinese JIL* 13: 133–146.

Pronin, A. 2015. Republic of Crimea A Two-Day State. *Russian LJ* 3: 133–142.

[39]Cfr. 'Report of the Special Envoy of the Secretary-General on Kosovo's future status', UN Doc. S/2007/168, of 26 March 2007, 9, p. 4, para. 10.

[40]Cfr. *Accordance with the International Law of the Unilateral Declaration of Independence in Respect of Kosovo, Advisory Opinion,* supra, Chap. 1, note 3, p. 426, para. 56.

[41]Cfr. 'Separate Opinion of Judge Cançado Trindade', *Accordance with the International Law of the Unilateral Declaration of Independence in Respect of Kosovo, Advisory Opinion,* supra, Chap. 1, note 3, p. 577, para. 136.

Salvioli, G. 1933. Les régles générales de la paix. *Recueil des cours* 46: 5–163.
Vidmar, J. 2012. Conceptualizing Declarations of Independence in International Law. *Oxford JLS* 32: 153–177.
———. 2015. The Annexation of Crimea and the Boundaries of the Will of the People. *German LJ* 16: 365–383.
Wilson, G. 2015. Crimea: Some Observations on Secession and Intervention in Partial Response to Müllerson and Tolstykh. *Chinese JIL* 14: 217–223.

Bibliography

Works and Courses

Arcari, M., et al. (dir.). 2011. *Questions de droit international autour de l'avis consultatif de la Cour internationale de Justice sur le Kosovo* [*International Law Issues Arising from the International Court of Justice Advisory Opinion on Kosovo*]. Milano: Giuffrè.

Armandon, E. 2013. *La Crimée entre la Russie et Ukraine. Un conflit qui n'a pas eu lieu*. Bruxelles: Bruylant.

Åslund, A. 2015. *Ukraine: What Went Wrong and How to Fix It*. Washington: Peterson Institute for International Economics.

Åslund, A., and M. McFaul, eds. 2006. *Revolution in Orange: The Origins of Ukraine's Democratic Breakthrough*. Washington: Carnegie Endowment for International Peace.

Bachmann, K., and I. Lyubashenko, eds. 2014. *The Maidan Uprising, Separatism and Foreign Intervention: Ukraine's Complex Transition*. Frankfurt am Main; New York: Peter Lang GmbH; Internationaler Verlag der Wissenschaften.

Bayefsky, A.F., ed. 2000. *Self-Determination in International Law: Quebec and Lessons Learned*. The Hague: Kluwer Law International.

Bokor-Szegö, H. 1970. *New States and International Law*. Budapest: Akadémiai kiadó.

Brolmann, C., R. Lefeber, and M. Zieck, eds. 1993. *Peoples and Minorities in International Law*. Dordrecht: Martinus Nijhoff.

Brown, P.M. 1921. The Aaland Islands Question. *AJIL* 15: 268–272.

Buchanan, A.E. 1991. *Secession: The Morality of Political Divorce from Fort Sumter to Lithuania and Quebec*. Boulder: Westview Press.

———. 2004. *Justice, Legitimacy and Self-Determination. Moral Foundations for International Law*. Oxford; New York: Oxford University Press.

Buchheit, L.C. 1978. *Secession: The Legitimacy of Self-Determination*. New Haven: Yale University Press.

Burke-White, W.W. 2014a. *Crimea and the International Leal Order. Public Law and Legal Theory Research Paper*.

Burri, T. 2010. The Kosovo Opinion and Secession: The Sounds of Silence and Missing Links. *German LJ* 11: 881–890.

Calogeropoulos-Stratis, S. 1973. *Le droit des peuples à disposer d'eux-mêmes*. Bruxelles: E. Bruylant.

J. F. Escudero Espinosa, *Self-Determination and Humanitarian Secession in International Law of a Globalized World*,
https://doi.org/10.1007/978-3-319-72622-9

Cassese, A., ed. 1979. *UN Law Fundamental Rights – Two Topics in International Law*. Alphen aan den Rijn: Sijthoff & Noordhoff.

———. 1995. *Self-Determination of Peoples: A Legal Reappraisal*. Cambridge: Cambridge University Press.

Christakis, T. 1999. *Le droit à l'autodétermination en dehors des situations de décolonisation*. Paris: La Documentation française.

Christakis, T. 2014. Les conflits de sécession en Crimée et dans l'Est de l'Ukraine et le droit international (The Conflicts of Secession in Crimea and Eastern Ukraine and International Law). *JDI* 141: 733–764.

Crawford, J. 2007. *The Creation of States in International Law*. 2nd ed. Oxford: Clarendon Press.

The Crimea: Chronicle of Separatism (1992–1995). 1996. Kiev: Ukrainian Center for Independent Political Research.

Fox, G.H. 2008. *Humanitarian Occupation*. Cambridge: Cambridge University Press.

Fleiner, T. 2011b. The Unilateral Secession of Kosovo as a Precedent in International Law. In *From Bilateralism to Community Interests: Essays in Honour of Judge Bruno Simma*, ed. U. Fastenrath, 877–894. Oxford: Oxford University Press.

Gartnett, S.W. 1997. *The Keystone in the Arch: Ukraine in the Emerging Security Environment of Central and Eastern Europe*. Washington, D.C.: The Carnegie Endowment for International Peace.

Grant, T. 1999. *The Recognition of States: Law and Practice in Debate and Evolution*. Westport, CT: Praeger.

Gros Espiell, H. 1976. *Study on Implementation of United Nations Resolutions Relating to the Right of Peoples under Colonial and Alien Domination to Self-Determination*, UN Doc. E/CN.4/Sub.2/377.

Hannum, H. 1990. *Autonomy, Sovereignty, and Self-Determination: The Accommodation of Conflicting Rights*, 503. Philadelphia: University of Pennsylvania Press.

Hehir, A., ed. 2010. *Kosovo, Intervention and Statebuilding: The International Community and the Transition to Independence*. London; New York: Routledge.

Henkin, L., ed. 1981. *The International Bill of Rights: The Covenant on Civil and Political Rights*. New York: Columbia University Press.

Heraclides, A. 1991. *Self-Determination of Minorities in International Politics*. London: Frank Cass.

Higgins, R. 1963. *The Development of International Law Through the Political Organs of the United Nations*. London; New York: Oxford University Press.

Independent International Commission on Kosovo. 2000. *The Kosovo Report: Conflict, International Response, Lessons Learned*. New York: Oxford University Press.

Köck, H.F., D. Horn, and F. Leidenmuehler. 2009. *From Protectorate to Statehood: Self-Determination v. Territorial Integrity in the Case of Kosovo and the Position of the European Union*. Antwerpen; Berlin; Wien: Intersentia; BWV Berliner Wissenschafts-Verlag; Neuer Wissenschaftlicher Verlag.

Krieger, H. 2001. *The Kosovo Conflict and International Law: An Analytical Documentation 1974–1999*. Cambridge: Cambridge University Press.

Lauterpacht, H. 1947. *Recognition in International Law*. Cambridge: Cambridge University Press.

Macedo, S., and A. Buchanan, eds. 2003. *Secession and Self-Determination*. New York; London: New York University Press.

Malcolm, N. 1998. *Kosovo: A Short History*. London: Macmillan.

Milanovic, M., and M.C. Wood, eds. 2015. *The Law and Politics of the Kosovo Advisory Opinion*. Oxford: Oxford University Press.

Musgrave, T.D. 2000. *Self-Determination and National Minorities*. Oxford: Oxford University Press.

Ofuatey-Kodjoe, W. 1977. *The Principle of Self-Determination in International Law*. New York: Nellen.

Pegg, S. 1998. *International Society and the De Facto State*. Aldershot: Ashgate.

Perritt, H.H. 2009. *The Road to Independence for Kosovo: A Chronicle of the Ahtisaari Plan*. Cambridge: Cambridge University Press.

Pomerance, M. 1982. *Self-Determination in Law and Practice. The New Doctrine in the United Nations*. The Hague: Martinus Nijhoff.

Raič, D. 2002. *Statehood and the Law of Self-Determination*. The Hague: Martinus Nijhoff.

The Right of Self-Determination: Historic and Current Development on the Basis of United Nations Instruments. 1981. Study prepared by Aureliu Cristescu, Special Rapporteur of the Sub-Commission on Prevention of Discrimination and Protection of Minorities. UN Doc. E/CN.4/Sub.2/404/Rev.1, 125.

The Right of Self-Determination: Implementation of the United Nations Resolutions. 1980. Study prepared by Héctor Gros Espiell, Special Rapporteur of the Sub-Commission on Prevention of Discrimination and Protection of Minorities. UN Doc. E/CN.4/Sub.2/405/Rev.1, 86.

Rouet, G., and P. Terem. 2010. *L'Ukaine, entre l'intégration et partenariat [Ukraine, between Integration and Partneship]*. Bruxelles: Bruylant.

Şen, İ.G. 2015. *Sovereignty Referendums in International and Constitutional Law*. Dordrecht; Boston; New York: Springer.

Stewart, D.B. 1997. *The Russian-Ukrainian Friendship Treaty and the Search for Regional Stability in Eastern Europe*. Thesis. Monterey, CA: Naval Postgraduate School.

Subtelny, O. 2000. *Ukraine: A History*. Toronto: Toronto University Press.

Summers, J., ed. 2011. *Kosovo: A Precedent?: The Declaration of Independence, the Advisory Opinion and Implications for Statehood, Self-Determination and Minority Rights*. Leiden; Boston: Martinus Nijhoff.

Tomuschat, C., ed. 1993. *Modern Law of Self-Determination*. The Hague: Martinus Nijhoff.

———., ed. 2001. *Kosovo and the International Community. A Legal Assessment*. The Hague: Kluwer.

———. 2006. Secession and Self-Determination. In *Secession. International Law Perspectives*, ed. M. Kohen, 23–45. Cambridge: Cambridge University Press.

Umozurike, U.O. 1972. *Self-Determination in International Law*. Hamden, CT: Archon Books.

Van den Driest, S.F. 2013. *Remedial Secession. A Right to External Self-Determination as a Remedy to Serious Injustices?* Cambridge: Intersentia.

Vidmar, J. 2013. *Democratic Statehood in International Law: The Emergence of New States in Post-Cold War Practice*. Oxford: Hart Publishing.

———. 2015. The Annexation of Crimea and the Boundaries of the Will of the People. *German LJ* 16: 365–383.

Weller, M., ed. 1999. *The Crisis in Kosovo, 1989–1999: From the Dissolution of Yugoslavia to Rambouillet and the Outbreak of Hostilities*. Cambridge: Documents and Analysis Publications.

———. 2009. *Contested Statehood: Kosovo's Struggle for Independence*. Oxford: Oxford University Press.

Wilson, A. 2005. *Ukraine's Orange Revolution*. New Haven: Yale University Press.

———. 2014. *Ukraine Crisis: What It Means for the West*. New Haven: Yale University Press.

Wilson, S. 2009. *Effectiviness, Legitimacy, and the Use of Force in Modern Wars: The Relentless Battle for Hearts and Minds in NATO's War over Kosovo*. Wiesbaden: VS Verlag für Sozialwissenschaften.

Wittich, S., A. Reinisch, and A. Gattini. 2009. *Kosovo – Staatsschulden – Notstand – EU – Reformvertrag – Humanitätsrecht: Beiträge zum 33. Österr. Völkerrechtstag 2008 in Conegliano*. Frankfurt a.M.: Lang.

Yekelchyk, S. 2007. *Ukraine: Birth of a Modern Nation*. New York; Oxford: Oxford University Press.

Articles and Contributions to Collective Works

Aidan, H. 2009. Independence, Intervention and Great Power Patronage: Kosovo, Georgia and the Contemporary Self-Determination Penumbra. *Amsterdam Law Forum* 1: 88–100.

Anaya, S.J. 1993. A Contemporary Definition of the International Norm of Self-Determination. *TLCP* 3: 131–164.

Andrés Sáenz de Santa María, M.P. 2011. Tu quoque, Corte? La banalización de los poderes del Consejo de Seguridad en la Opinión consultiva sobre la conformidad con el Derecho internacional de la declaración unilateral de independencia relativa a Kosovo. *REDI* 63: 55–78.

Arangio-Ruiz, G. 1983. Autodeterminazione dei popoli e diritto internazionale. Dalla Carta delle Nazioni Unite allAtto di Helsinki (CSCE). *RSPI* 50: 523–552.

Arcari, M. 2014. Violazione del divieto di uso della forza, aggressione o attacco armato in relazione all'intervento militare della Russia in Crimea? *DUDI* 8: 473–479.

Ardault, K., C.-M. Arion, D. Gnamou-Petauton, and M. Yetongnon. 2006. L'administration internationale du territoire à l'épreuve du Kosovo et du Timor Oriental: la pratique à la recherche d'une théorie. *RBDI* 39: 300–383.

Armandon, E. 2015. L'annexion de la Crimée par la Russie: un premier bilan. *Annuaire français de relations internationales* 16: 219–234.

Arp, B. 2010. The ICJ Advisory Opinion on the *Accordance with International Law of the Unilateral Declaration of Independence in Respect of Kosovo* and the International Protection of Minorities. *German LJ* 11: 847–866.

Baggett, T. 1999. Human Rights Abuses in Yugoslavia: To Bring an End to Political Oppression, the International Community Should Assist in Establishing and Independent Kosovo. *Ga.J. Int'l & Comp L* 27: 45–59.

Balci, B. 2014. The Russian Intervention in Crimea: Erdogan's Dilemma. *Eurasia Outlook, Carnegie Endowment for International Peace.*http://carnegieendowment.org/2014/03/14/russian-intervention-in-crimea-erdogan-s-dilemma.

Bebler, A. 2015. Crimea and the Russian-Ukrainian Conflict. *Romanian JEA* 15: 35–54.

Bederman, D.J. 2011. Accordance with International Law of the Unilateral Declaration of Independence in Respect of Kosovo. Advisory Opinion. *AJIL* 105: 301–307.

Bellamy, A.J. 2001. Human Wrongs in Kosovo: 1974–1999. In *The Kosovo Tragedy. The Human Rights Dimension*, ed. K. Booth, 105–126. London: Frank Cass.

———. 2009. Kosovo and the Advent of Sovereignty as Responsibility. In *Kosovo, Intervention and Statebuilding: The International Community and the Transition to Independence*, ed. A. Hehir, 38–59. Florence, KY: Routledge.

Berndtsson, J., and P. Johansson. 2015. Principles on a Collision Course? State Sovereignty Meets Peoples Right of Self-Determination in the Case of Kosovo. *Cambridge RIA* 28: 445–461.

Bílkovà, V. 2015. The Use of Force by the Russian Federation in Crimea. *ZaöRV/HJIL* 75: 27–50.

Binder, G. 1993. The Case for Self-Determination. The Kaplan Lecture on Human Rights. *SJIL* 29: 223–270.

Bismuth, R. 2014. Odysée dans le conundrum des réactions décentralisées à l'illicite. *JDI* 141: 719–731.

Blay, S.K.N. 1986. Self-Determination versus Territorial Integrity in Decolonization. *NYUJILP* 18: 441–472.

Blum, Y.Z. 1975. Reflections on the Changing Concept of Self-Determination. *Israel LR* 10: 509–514.

Borgen, C.J. 2009. The Language of Law and the Practice of Politics: Great Powers and the Rhetoric of Self-Determination in the Cases of Kosovo and South Ossetia. *Chicago JIL* 10: 1–33.

Bothe, M. 2010. Kosovo – So What? The Holding of the International Court of Justice Is Not the Last Word on Kosovo's Independence. *German LJ* 11: 837–840.

———. 2014. The Current Status of Crimea: Russian Territory, Occupied Territory or What? *ML & LWR* 53: 99–116.

Bothe, M., and T. Marauhn. 2001. UN Administration of Kosovo and East Timor: Concept, Legality and Limitations of Security Council-Mandated Trusteeship Administration. In *Kosovo and the International Community. A Legal Assessment*, ed. C. Tomuschat, 217–242. The Hague: Kluwer.

Böttger, K. 2014. Auf dem sicherheitspolitischen Auge blind: Die EU-Außenpolitik augesichts der Ukraine-Krise. *Integration* 37: 95–108.

Bowring, B. 2005. The Crimean Autonomy: Innovation or Anomaly. In *Autonomy, Self-Governance and Conflict Resolution*, ed. M. Weller and S. Wolff, 75–97. London; New York: Routledge.

Brilmayer, L. 1991. Secession and Self-Determination: A Territorial Interpretation. *YJIL* 16: 177–202.

Brown, C. 2005. Access to International Justice in the Legality of Use of Force Cases. (Yugoslavia v. The 10 NATO Countries which Militarily Intervened in Kosovo, in which the International Court of Justice Ruled it did not have Jurisdiction). *Cambridge LJ* 64: 267–271.

Buchanan, A.E. 1997. Theories of Secession. *Philosophy & Public Affairs* 26: 31–61.

Bugajski, J. 2014. Confronting the Putin Doctrine. *Hungarian Review* 5: 10–16.

Burke-White, W.W. 2014b. Crimea and the International Legal Order. *Survival* 56: 65–80.

Burri, T. 2010. The Kosovo Opinion and Secession: The Sounds of Silence and Missing Links. *German LJ* 11: 881–890.

———. 2014. Secession in the CIS: Causes, Consequences, and Emerging Principles. In *Self-Determination and Secession in International Law*, ed. C. Walter et al., 138–154. Oxford: Oxford University Press.

Carrillo Salcedo, J.A. 1976. Libre determinación de los pueblos e integridad territorial de los Estados en el dictamen del Tribunal Internacional de Justicia sobre el Sahara Occidental. *REDI* 29: 33–49.

Cassese, A. 1977. The Helsinki Declaration and Self-Determination. In *Human Rights, International Law & The Helsinki Accord*, T. Buergenthal (ed.) and J.R. Hall, 83–110. Montclair; New York: Allanheld, Osmun & Co.; Universe Books.

———. 1979. Political Self-Determination – Old Concepts and New Development. In *UN Law Fundamental Rights – Two Topics in International Law*, ed. A. Cassese, 137–165. Sijthoff & Noordhoff: Alphen aan den Rijn.

———. 1981. The Self-Determination of Peoples. In *The International Bill of Rights: The Covenant on Civil and Political Rights*, ed. L. Henkin, 95–113. New York: Columbia University Press.

———. 1999. *Ex iniuria jus oritur.* Are We Moving Towards International Legitimation of Forcible Humanitarian Countermeasures in the World Community? *EJIL* 10: 23–30.

Castellino, J. 2014. International Law and Self-Determination. In *Self-Determination and Secession in International Law*, ed. C. Walter et al., 27–45. Oxford: Oxford University Press.

Cerone, J. 2011. The International Court of Justice and the Question of Kosovo's Independence. *ILSA JICL* 17: 335–354.

Charney, J. 1999. Anticipatory Humanitarian Intervention in Kosovo. *AJIL* 93: 834–841.

———. 2001. Self-Determination: Chechnya, Kosovo, and East Timor. *Vand. J. Transnat'l L.* 34: 455–446.

Chase, Ph. 1995. Conflict in the Crimea: An examination of Ethnic Conflict under Contemporary Model of Sovereignty. *Columbia JTL* 34: 219–254.

Chen, L. 1981. Self-Determination: An Important Dimension of the Demand for Freedom. *ASIL Proceedings* 75: 88–94.

Chinkin, C. 2000. The Legality of NATOs Action in the Former Republic of Yugoslavia (FRY) Under International Law. *ICLQ* 49: 910–925.

Chowdhury, S.R. 1977. The Status and Norms of Self-Determination in Contemporary International Law. *NILR* 24: 72–84.

Christakis, T. 2006. The State as 'Primary Fact'. Some Thoughts on the Principle of Effectiveness. In *Secession. International Law Perspectives*, ed. M.G. Kohen, 138–170. Cambridge and New York: Cambridge University Press.

Christakis, T. 2011b. The ICJ Advisory Opinion on Kosovo: Has International Law Something to Say About Secession? *LJIL* 24: 73–86.

———. 2014. Les conflits de sécession en Crimée et dans l'Est de l'Ukraine et le droit international (The Conflicts of Secession in Crimea and Eastern Ukraine and International Law). *JDI* 141: 733–764.

———. 2015. Self-Determination, Territorial Integrity and *Fait Accompli* in the Case of Crimea. *ZaöRV/HJIL* 75: 75–100.

Cimiotta, E. 2014. Le reazioni alla 'sottrazione' della Crimea all'Ucraina. Quali garanzie del diritto internazionale di fronte a gravi illeciti imputati a grandi potenze? *DUDI* 8: 491–504.

Cirkovic, E. 2010. An Analysis of the ICJ Advisory Opinion on Kosovo's Unilateral Declaration of Independence. *German LJ* 11: 895–912.

Cismas, I. 2010. Secession in Theory and Practice: The Case of Kosovo and Beyond. *GoJIL* 2: 531–587.

Corten, O. 2008. Déclarations unilatérales d'indépendance et reconnaissance prématurées: du Kosovo à l'Ossétie du sud et à l'Abkhazie. *RGDIP* 112: 721–759.

———. 2011. Territorial Integrity Narrowly Interpreted: Reasserting the Classical Inter-State Paradigm of International Law. *LJIL* 24: 87–94.

Corten, O., and A. Lagerwall 2013. La doctrine de la sécession-remède à l'épreuve de la pratique récente. In *L'Homme dans la société internationale: mélanges en hommage au Professeur Paul Tavernier*, Coord. J.F. Akandji-Kombé, 187–205. Bruxelles: Bruylant.

Costea, S. 2011. EU-Ukraine Relations and the Eastern Partnership. *EFAR* 16: 259–276.

Crawford, J. 1998. State Practice and International Law in Relation to Secession. *BYIL* 69: 85–117.

———. 2000. State Practice and International Law in Relation to Unilateral Secession. In *Self-Determination in International Law: Quebec and Lessons Learned*, ed. A.F. Bayefsky, 31–62. The Hague: Kluwer Law International.

Cvijić, S. 2007. Self-Determination as a Challenge to the Legitimacy of Humanitarian Intervention: The Case of Kosovo. *German LJ* 8: 57–80.

Cwicinskaja, N. 2017. The Annexation of Crimea and International Law: Review of Thomas D. Grants *Aggression Against Ukraine: Territory, Responsibility and International Law. Israel Law Review* 50: 211–225.

Daase, C. 2009. Die UN-Mission im Kosovo 1999–2008: zur Umsetzung völkerrechtlicher Standards für state-building durch eine internationale Übergangsverwaltung. *Friedens-Warte* 84: 83–124.

Daskalovski, Z. 2003. Claims to Kosovo: Nationalism and Self-Determination. In *Understanding the War in Kosovo*, ed. F. Bieber and Z. Daskalovski, 11–28. London: Frank Cass.

De Deugd, N. 2012. Easier Said than Done: Ukraine as Part of the European Union's Ring of Friends. *Studia Diplomatica* 65: 29–41.

Delahunty, R. 2015. The Crimean Crisis, Legal Studies Research Paper Series. *U.St.Thomas J.L. & Pub Poly* 9: 125–168.

Delcourt, B. 2010. L'indépendance du Kosovo. In *Droit international et relations internationales: Divergences et convergences*, ed. Société Française pour le Droit International, 95–105. Paris: Pedone.

Dietrich, F. 2010. The Status of Kosovo – Reflections on the Legitimacy of Secession. *Ethics & Global Politics* 3: 123–142.

Dinstein, Y. 1976. Collective Human Rights of Peoples and Minorities. *ICLQ* 25: 102–120.

———. 1996. Is There a Right to Secede? *ASIL Proceedings* 90: 299–302.

Dmitriev, Y.A. 2014. Crimea as a Bone of Contention between Russia, the European Union and the USA. *ПРАВО И ЖИЗНЬ Независимый научно-правовой журнал* 189: 22–50.

Douhan, A.F. 2015. International Organizations and Settlement of the Conflict in Ukraine. *ZaöRV/HJIL* 75: 195–214.

Dugard, J. 2011. The Secession of States and their Recognition in the Wake of Kosovo. *Recueil des cours* 357: 9–222.

Dugard, J., and D. Raič. 2006. The Role of Recognition in the Law and Practice of Secession. In *Secession: International Law Perspectives*, ed. M.G. Kohen, 94–137. Cambridge: Cambridge University Press.

Economides, S. 2013. Kosovo, Self-Determination and the International Order. *Europe-Asia Studies* 65: 823–836.

Efevwerhan, D.I. 2012. Kosovo's Chances of UN Membership: A Prognosis. *GoJIL* 4: 93–130.

Eisemann, P.-M. 2010. L'indépendance du Kosovo – le point de vue du juriste. In *Droit international et relations internationales: Divergences et convergences*, ed. Société Française pour le Droit International, 107. Paris: Pedone.

Emerson, R. 1971. Self-Determination. *AJIL* 65: 459–475.

Espósito Massicci, C. 2011. El discreto ejercicio de la función consultiva de la Corte Internacional de Justicia en el asunto Kosovo. *REDI* 63: 125–147.

Evers, F. 2010. Damaged Prospects/Damaged Dialogue in Ukraine and Crimea. The Current Situation in Ukraine and Future Co-operation with the OSCE. *OSCE Yearbook* 16: 221–243.

Evison, J.A. 2014. Mig and Monks in Crimea: Russia Flexes Cultural and Military Muscles, Revealing Dire Need for Balance of *Uti Possidetis* and Internationally Recognized Self-Determination. *MLR* 220: 90–128.

Falk, A. 1999. Kosovo, World Order, and the Future of International Law. *AJIL* 93: 847–857.

Falk, R. 2011. Agora: The ICJs Kosovo Advisory Opinion. The Kosovo Advisory Opinion: Conflict Resolution and Precedent. *AJIL* 105: 50–60.

Falkowski, J.E. 1991. Secessionary Self-Determination: A Jeffersonian Perspective. *B.U. Intl L.J.* 9: 209–242.

Feldbrugge, F.J.M. 2014. Ukraine, Russia and International Law. *RCEEL* 39: 95–97.

Fierstein, D. 2008. Kosovo's Declaration of Independence: An Incident Analysis of Legality, Policy and Future Implications. *B.U. Intl L.J.* 26: 417–442.

Fisher, M.C. 2014. El desafío de Occidente en Ucrania y más allá. *Política exterior* 28: 72–84.

Fleiner, T. 2011. The Unilateral Secession of Kosovo as a Precedent in International Law. In *From Bilateralism to Community Interests: Essays in Honour of Judge Bruno Simma*, ed. U. Fastenrath, 877–894. Oxford: Oxford University Press.

Francioni, F. 2000. Of War, Humanity and Justice in International Law after Kosovo. *Max Planck YUNL* 4: 107–126.

Franck, T.M., R. Higgins, A. Pellet, M.N. Shaw, and C. Tomuschat. 2000. The Territorial Integrity of Québec in the Event of the Attainment of Sovereignty – Experts Report. In *Self-Determination in International Law: Quebec and Lessons Learned*, ed. A.F. Bayefski, 333–342. The Hague: Kluwer Law International.

Friedrich, J. 2005. UNMIK in Kosovo: Struggling with Uncertainty. *Max Planck YUNL* 9: 225–293.

Frowein, J.A. 2011. Kosovo and Lotus. In *From Bilateralism to Community Interests: Essays in Honour of Judge Bruno Simma*, ed. U. Fastenrath, 923–931. Oxford: Oxford University Press.

Garcia, T. 2000. La Mission d'administration intérimaire des Nations Unies au Kosovo (MINUK). *RGDIP* 104: 61–71.

Gdalina, A. 2016. Crimea and the Right to Self-Determination: Questioning the Legality of Crimea's Secession from Ukraine. *Cardozo Journal of International & Comparative Law* 24: 531–563.

Gedmin, J. 2014. Beyond Crimea: What Vladimir Putin Wants. *World Affairs* 177: 8–16.

Geistlinger, M. 2014. Der Beitritt der Republik Krim zur Russ-ländischen Föderation aus der Warte des Selbstbestimmungsrechts der Völker. *AVR* 52: 175–204.

Giuliani, J.-D. 2014. L'Europe après la Crimée. *Déf. Nat.* 771: 122–127.

Grant, T. 2009. Regulating the Creation of States. From Decolonization to Secession. *JILIR* 5: 11–57.

———. 2015. Annexation of Crimea. *AJIL* 109: 68–95.

Gray, C. 2001. The Legality of NATOs Military Action in Kosovo: Is There a Right of Humanitarian Intervention? In *International Law in the Post-Cold War World: Essays in Memory of Li Haopei*, 240–253. London: Routledge.

Green, J.A. 2010. Passportization, Peacekeepers and Proportionality: The Russian Claim on the Protection of Nations Abroad in Self-Defence. In *Conflict in the Caucasus: Implications for*

International Legal Order, ed. J.A. Green and C.P.M. Waters, 54–79. Basingstoke, England; New York: Palgrave Macmillan.
———. 2014. The Annexation of Crimea: Russia, Passportisation and the Protection of Nationals Revisited. *JUFIL* 1: 3–10.
Greenwood, C. 1999. Humanitarian Intervention: The Case of Kosovo. *Finnish YIL* 10: 141–175.
———. 2000. International Law and the NATO Intervention in Kosovo. *ICLQ* 49: 926–934.
Gros Espiell, H. 1979a. En torno al derecho de la libre determinación de los pueblos. *ADI* 3: 49–74.
———. 1979. Self-Determination and Ius Cogens. In *UN Law Fundamental Rights – Two Topics in International Law*, ed. A. Cassese, 167–173. Sijthoff & Noordhoff: Alphen aan den Rijn.
Guillemoles, A. 2014. Les cents jours qui ont changé l'Ukraine. *Politique internationale* 143: 45–63.
Gutiérrez Espada, C. 2000. Uso de la fuerza, intervención humanitaria y libre determinación (La Guerra de Kosovo). *ADI* 16: 93–132.
Hannum, H. 1993. Rethinking Self-Determination. *VJIL* 34: 1–69.
———. 2011. The Advisory Opinion on Kosovo: An Opportunity Lost, or a Poisoned Chalice Refused? *LJIL* 24: 155–161.
Harsch, M.F. 2015. Kosovo: From Intervention to Independence, 1998–2008. In *The Power of Dependence: NATO-UN Cooperation in Crisis Management*, ed. M.F. Harsch, 57–102. Oxford: Oxford University Press.
Haverland, C. 2000. Secession. In *Encyclopedia of Public International Law*, ed. R. Bernhardt, vol. IV, 354–359. Amsterdam: North Holland Publishing.
Heintze, H. 2014. Völkerrecht und Sezession – Ist die Annexion der Krim eine zulässige Wiedergutmachung sowjetischen Unrechts? *Humanitäres Völkerrecht – Informationsschriften [Journal of International Law of Peace and Armed Conflict]* 27: 129–138.
Henkin, L. 1999. Kosovo and the Law of Humanitarian Intervention. *AJIL* 93: 824–828.
Higgins, R. 1993. Postmodern Tribalism and the Right to Secession. In *Peoples and Minorities in International Law*, ed. C. Brolmann, R. Lefeber, and M. Zieck, 29–35. Dordrecht: Martinus Nijhoff.
Hilpold, P. 2006. Self-Determination in the 21st Century – Modern Perspectives for an Old Concept. *IYHR* 36: 247–288.
———. 2008a. Das Kosovo-Problem – ein Testfall für das Völkerrecht. *ZaöRV/HJIL* 68: 779–801.
———. 2008b. Die Sezession – zum Versuch der Verrechtlichung eines faktischen Phänomens. *ZaöRV/HJIL* 63: 117–141.
———. 2009a. The Kosovo Case and International Law: Looking for Applicable Theories. *Chinese JIL* 8: 47–61.
———. 2009b. The International Court of Justices Advisory Opinion on Kosovo: Perspectives of a Delicate Question. *ARIEL* 14: 259–310.
———. 2012b. Secession in International Law: Does the Kosovo Opinion Require a Re-Assesment of this Concept? In *Kosovo and International Law: The ICJ Advisory Opinion of 22 July 2010*, ed. P. Hilpold, 47–78. Leiden; Boston: Martinus Nijhoff.
———. 2015. Ukraine, Crimea and New International Law: Balancing International Law with Arguments Drawn from History. *Chinese JIL* 14: 237–270.
Himmer, S.E. 1992. The Achievement of Independence in the Baltic States and Its Justification. *EILR* 6: 253–291.
Howse, R., and R. Teitel. 2010. Delphic Dictum: How Has the ICJ Contributed to the Global Rule of Law by Its Ruling on Kosovo. *German LJ* 11: 841–846.
Hughes, J. 2013. Russia and the Secession of Kosovo: Power, Norms and the Failure of Multilateralism. *Europe-Asia Studies* 65: 992–1016.
Ingravallo, I. 2012. Kosovo after the ICJ Advisory Opinion: Towards a European Perspective? *ICLR* 14: 219–241.
Instytut Nauk Prawnych Pan. 2009. Polish Advisory Opinion of Kosovo. *Polish YIL* 29: 215–238.
Ioannidis, N.A. 2015. Constitutional Prohibition of Secession under the Prism of International Law: The Cases of Kosovo, Crimea and Cyprus. *Edimburgh Student Law Review* 2: 169–180.

Irmscher, T.H. 2001. The Legal Framework for the Activities of the United Nations Interim Administration Mission in Kosovo: The Charter, Human Rights, and the Law of Occupation. *German YIL* 44: 353–395.

Jaber, T. 2011. A Case for Kosovo? Self-Determination and Secession in the 21st Century. *IJHR* 15: 926–947.

Jacobs, D. 2011. International Court of Justice. Accordance with International Law of the Unilateral Declaration of Independence in Respect of Kosovo, Advisory Opinion of 22 July 2010. *ICLQ* 60: 799–810.

Jacobs, D., and Y. Radi. 2011. Waiting for Godot: An Analysis of the Advisory Opinion on Kosovo. *LJIL* 24: 331–353.

Jaworsky, J. 1995. Crimea's Importance to Ukraine and Its Future Security. In *Crimea: Dynamics, Challenges and Prospects*, ed. M. Drohobycky, 135–156. Lanham, MD: Rowman & Littlefield.

Jennings, R.Y. 1999. Kosovo and International Lawyers. *International Law FORUM du droit international* 1: 166–170.

Jia, B.B. 2009. The Independence of Kosovo: A Unique Case of Secession? *Chinese JIL* 8: 27–46.

Johnson, C.D. 1973. Toward Self-Determination – A Reappraisal as Reflected in the Declaration on Friendly Relations. *Ga.J. Intl & Comp L.* 3: 145–163.

Jovanović, M.A. 2009. Can Constitutions Be of Use in the Resolution of Secessionist Conflicts? *JILIR* 5: 59–87.

Jusufaj, E. 2015. The Kosovo Precedent in the Secession and Recognition of Crimea. *ILIRIA International Review* 5: 267–286.

Kaikobad, K.H. 2011. Another Frozen Conflict: Kosovo's Unilateral Declaration of Independence and International Law. In *Kosovo: A Precedent?: The Declaration of Independence, the Advisory Opinion and Implications for Statehood, Self-Determination and Minority Rights*, ed. J. Summers, 55–85. Leiden; Boston: Martinus Nijhoff.

Kälin, W. 2000. Humanitäre Intervention: Legitimation durch Verfahren? Zehn Thesen zur Kosovo-Krise. *SZIER/RSDIE* 10: 159–176.

Kapustin, A. 2015. Crimea's Self-Determination in the Light of Contemporary International Law. *ZaöRV/HJIL* 75: 101–118.

Kemoklidze, N. 2009. The Kosovo Precedent and the Moral Hazard of Secession. *JILIR* 5: 117–140.

Keohane, R. 2001. Secession Without Independence? Comments on the Report of the Independent Commission on Kosovo. *International Peacekeeping* 7: 360–366.

Ker-Lindsay, J. 2013. Preventing the Emergence of Self-Determination as a Norm of Secession: An Assessment of Kosovo Unique Case Argument. *Europe-Asia Studies* 65: 837–856.

Kessedjian, C. 1999. La légalité de l'intervention de l'OTAN au Kosovo. *International Law FORUM du droit international* 1: 147–148.

Kirgis, F.L., Jr. 1994. The Degrees of Self-Determination in the United Nations Era. *AJIL* 88: 304–310.

Kiss, A. 1986. The Peoples' Right to Self-Determination. *HRLJ* 7: 165–175.

Kohen, M.G. 1999. L'emploi de la force et la crise du Kosovo: vers un nouveau désordre juridique international. *RBDI* 32: 122–148.

———. 2006. Introduction. In *Secession. International Law Perspectives*, ed. M. Kohen, 1–20. Cambridge and New York: Cambridge University Press.

———. 2013. Le Kosovo entre le droit et la puissance: (les questions négligées para l'avis consultatif de la Cour). In *L'Afrique et le droit international: Variations sur l'organisation internationale [Africa and International Law: Reflections on the International Organization. Liber Amicorum Raymond Ranjeva]*, 533–547. Paris: Pedone.

Kohen, M.G., and K. Del Mar. 2011. The Kosovo Advisory Opinion and UNSCR 1244 (1999): A Declaration of Independence from International Law? *LJIL* 24: 109–126.

Kranz, J. 2014. Imperialism, the Highest Stage of Sovereign Democracy: Some Remarks on the Annexation of Crimea by Russia. *AVR* 52: 205–221.

Krisch, N. 1999. Unilateral Enforcement of the Collective Will: Kosovo, Iraq, and the Security Council. *Max Planck YUNL* 3: 59–103.

Kritsiotis, D. 2000. The Kosovo Crisis and NATOs Application of Armed Force Against the Federal Republic of Yugoslavia. *ICLQ* 49: 330–359.

Kuruneri-Millet, A. 2014. 2014: l'Ukraine à la croisée des chemins. *Déf. Nat.* 769: 11–16.

Kuzio, T. 2012. Russianization of Ukrainian National Security Policy under Viktor Yanukovych. *The Journal of Slavic Military Studies* 25: 558–581.

Lagerwall, A. 2014. L'agression et l'annexion de la Crimée para la Fédération de Russie: Quels enseignements au sujet du droit international. *Questions of International Law, Zoom Out* I: 57–72. www.qil-qdi.org.

Lagrange, E. 1999. La Mission intérimaire des Nations Unies au Kosovo, nouvel essai d'administration directe d'un territoire. *AFDI* 45: 335–370.

Laing, E.A. 1991. The Norm of Self-Determination, 1941–1991. *CWILJ* 22: 209–308.

Lasheras, F. de B. 2014. El debate español sobre la crisis de Crimea. *Política exterior* 28: 14–19.

Lauwers, G., and S. Smis. 2000. New Dimensions of the Right to Self-Determination: A Study of the International Response to the Kosovo Crisis. *N & EP* 6: 43–70.

Leonaite, E., and D. Zalimas. 2016. The Annexation of Crimea and Attempts to Justify It in the Context of International Law. *Lithuanian Annual Strategic Review* 14: 11–63.

Lévesque, J. 2009. Les enjeux et contraintes d'un nouveau départ des relations Russie-États-Unies et les effets de la guerre russo-géorgienne. *Conflits dans le monde [Conflicts around the World]*: 67–109.

Levin, D.B. 1962. The Principle of Self-Determination in International Law. *Soviet YIL* 45–48.

López-Jurado Romero de la Cruz, C. 2011. Kosovo ante la Corte Internacional de Justicia: La opinión consultiva de 22 de julio de 2010. *REEI* 21.

Lowe, V. 2000. International Legal Issues Arising in the Kosovo Crisis. *ICLQ* 49: 934–943.

Lu, Jing. 2015. Letter in Partial Response to Vladislav Tolstykh Reunification of Crimea with Russia: A Russian Perspective. *Chinese JIL* 14: 225–228.

Luchterhandt, O. 2014a. Der Anschluss der Krim an Russland aus völkerrechtlicher Sicht. *AVR* 52: 137–174.

———. 2014b. Die Krim-Krise von 2014. Staats- und völkerrechtliche Aspekte [The Crimean Crisis of 2014. Aspects of Constitutional and International Law]. *Osteuropa* 64: 61–86.

MacFarlane, N., and A. Menon. 2014. The EU and Ukraine. *Survival* 65: 95–101.

Magaraševič, A. 1956. A View on the Right to Self-Determination in International Law. *JRMP* 3.

Mankoff, J. 2014. Russia's Latest Land Grab: How Putin Won Crimea and Lost Ukraine. *Foreign Affairs* 93: 60–68.

Mantovani, M., and D. Rickenbacher. 2014. Crimea Going East – A Clash of Great Power Strategies. *ML & LWR* 53: 45–68.

Margueritte, T. 2010. L'avis consultative de la Cour internationale de Justice sur le Kosovo: Une occasion manquée. *L'Observateur des Nations Unies* 28: 257–276.

Martucci, F. 2014. La réaction multidimensionnelle de l'Union européenne dans la crise ukrainienne. *JDI* 141: 765–785.

Marxsen, C. 2014. The Crimea Crisis – An International Law Perspective. *ZaöRV/HJIL* 74: 367–391.

———. 2014b. La réaction multidimensionnelle de l'Union européenne dans la crisis ukrainienne. *JDI* 141: 765–785.

———. 2015. Territorial Integrity in International Law – Its Concept and Implications for Crimea. *ZaöRV/HJIL* 75: 7–26.

McCorquodale, R. 1992. Self-Determination Beyond the Colonial Context and Its Potential Impact on Africa. *AJICL/RADIC* 4: 592–608.

———. 1994. Self-Determination: A Human Rights Approach. *ICLQ* 43: 857–885.

McFarlane, N., and N. Sabanadze. 2013. Sovereignty and Self-Determination: Where Are We? *International Journal* 68: 609–627.

Menon, P.K. 1990. The Problem of Recognition in International Law: Some Thoughts on Community Interest. *Nordic JIL* 59: 247–273.

Merezhko, O. 2015. Crimea's Annexation by Russia – Contradictions of the New Russian Doctrine of International Law. *ZaöRV/HJIL* 75: 167–194.

Mertus, J. 2001. Legitimizing the Use of Force in Kosovo. *Ethics & Intl A.* 15: 133–150.

Milano, E. 2009. The Independence of Kosovo under International Law. In *Kosovo – Staatsschulden – Notstand – EU – Reformvertrag – Humanitätsrecht: Beiträge zum 33. Österr. Völkerrechtstag 2008 in Conegliano*, ed. S. Wittich, A. Reinisch, and A. Gattini, 21–41. Frankfurt a.M.: Lang.

———. 2010. The Security Council and Territorial Sovereignty: The Case of Kosovo. *ICLR* 12: 171–189.

———. 2014. The Non-Recognition of Russia's Annexation of Crimea: Three Different Legal Approaches and One Unanswered Question. *Questions of International Law, Zoom Out* I: 35–55. www.qil-qdi.org.

———. 2015. Russia's Veto in the Security Council: Whither the Duty to Abstain under Art. 27 (3) of the UN Charter? *ZaöRV/HJIL* 75: 215–231.

Mills, A. 2011. The Kosovo Advisory Opinion: If You Don't Have Anything Constructive to Say? *Cambridge LJ* 70: 1–4.

Montaz, D. 2000. 'L'intervention d'humanité' de l'OTAN au Kosovo et la règle du non-recours à la force. *RICR/IRRC* 82: 89–101.

Muharremi, R. 2008. Kosovo's Declaration of Independence: Self-Determination and Sovereignty Revisited. *RCEEL* 33: 401–435.

———. 2010. A Note on the ICJ Advisory Opinion on Kosovo. *German LJ* 11: 867–880.

Müllerson, R.A. 2009. Precedents in the Mountains: On the Parallels and Uniqueness of the Cases of Kosovo, South Ossetia and Abkhazia. *Chinese JIL* 8: 2–25.

———. 2014. Ukraine: Victim of Geopolitics. *Chinese JIL* 13: 133–146.

Murase, S. 2002. The Relationship between the UN Charter and General International Law Regarding Non-Use of Force: The Case of NATOs Air Campaign in Kosovo Crisis of 1999. In *Liber amicorum Judge Shigeru Oda*, vol. 2, 1543–1554. The Hague; New York: Kluwer Law International.

Murswiek, D. 1993. The Issue of a Right to Secession – Reconsidered. In *Modern Law of Self-Determination*, ed. C. Tomuschat, 21–40. The Hague: Martinus Nijhoff.

Nanda, V.P. 1979. Self-Determination Outside the Colonial Context: The Birth of Bangladesh in Retrospect. *Houston Journal of International Law* 1: 71.

———. 1981. Self-Determination under International Law: Validity of Claims to Secede. *Case W. Res.J Int'l L.* 13: 257–280.

Nawaz, M.K. 1965. The Meaning and Range of the Principle of Self-Determination. *Duke Law Journal* 82: 82–101.

Nikouei, M., and M. Zamani. 2016. The Secession of Crimea: Where Does International Law Stand? *Nordic Journal of International Law* 85: 37–64.

Nolte, G. 1999. Kosovo und Konstitutionalisierung: Zur humanitären Intervention der NATO-Staaten. *ZaöRV/HJIL* 59: 941–960.

Norman, W. 2003. Domesticating Secession. In *Secession and Self-Determination*, ed. S. Macedo and A. Buchanan, 193–237. New York; London: New York University Press.

O'Connell, M.E. 2000. The UN, NATO and International Law after Kosovo. *HRQ* 22: 57–89.

Öberg, M.D. 2011a. The Legal Effects of United Nations Resolutions in the Kosovo Advisory Opinion. *AJIL* 105: 60–81.

———. 2011b. Agora: The ICJs Kosovo Advisory Opinion. The Legal Effects of United Nations Resolutions in the Kosovo Advisory Opinion. *AJIL* 105: 81–90.

Oellers-Frahm, K. 2010. Problematic Question or Problematic Answer? Observations on the International Court of Justices Advisory Opinion Concerning Kosovo's Unilateral Declaration of Independence. *German YIL* 53: 793–830.

Oeter, S. 2012. Secession, Territorial Integrity and the Role of the Security Council. In *Kosovo and International Law: The ICJ Advisory Opinion of 22 July 2010*, ed. P. Hilpold, 109–138. Leiden; Boston: Martinus Nijhoff.

———. 2014. The Role of Recognition and Non-Recognition with Regard to Secession. In *Self-Determination and Secession in International Law*, ed. C. Walter et al., 45–67. Oxford: Oxford University Press.

———. 2015. The *Kosovo Case* – An Unfortunate Precedent. *ZaöRV/HJIL* 75: 51–74.

Olson, P.M. 2014. The Lawfulness of Use of Force in Crimea. *ML & LWR* 53: 17–44.

Onica Jarka, B. 2010. Several Reflections on the Significance of the ICJ Advisory Opinion on Accordance with International Law of the Unilateral Declaration of Independence in Respect of Kosovo. *Lex et Scientia International Journal* 17: 49–58.

Orakhelashvili, A. 2008. Statehood, Recognition and the United Nations System: A Unilateral Declaration of Independence in Kosovo. *Max Planck YUNL* 12: 1–44.

———. 2011. The International Courts Advisory Opinion on the UDI in Respect of Kosovo: Washing Away the Foam on the Tide of Time. *Max Planck YUNL* 15: 65–104.

Paço, S. 2016. Sovereignty, Statehood and Self-Determination in International Law – The Kosovo Case. *Academicus: International Scientific Journal* 13: 184–204.

Parameswaran, K. 2008. Der Rechtsstatus des Kosovo im Lichte der aktuellen Entwicklungen. *AVR* 46: 172–204.

Parzymies, S. 2012. L'Ukraine dans la politique de voisinage de l'Union européenne. *Annuaire français de relations internationales* 13: 119–128.

Peters, A. 2011. Does Kosovo Lie in the Lotus-Land of Freedom? *LJIL* 24: 95–108.

———. 2014. Das Völkerrecht der Gebietsreferenden. Das Beispiel der Ukraine 1991–2014 [The International Law of Territorial Referendums. The Example of Ukraine 1991–2014]. *Osteuropa* 64: 101–133.

———. 2015. The Crimean Vote of March 2014 as an Abuse of the Institution of the Territorial Referendum. In *Staat und Mensch im Kontext des Völker- und Europarechts. Liber Amicorum für Torsten Stein*, ed. C. Calliess, 255–280. Baden-Baden: Nomos Verlag.

Picone, P. 2000. La guerra del Kosovo e il diritto internazionale generale. *RDI* 83: 309–360.

Pippan, C. 2010. The International Court of Justices Advisory Opinion on Kosovo's Declaration of Independence: An Exercise in the Art of Silence. *Europäisches Journal für Minderheitenfragen* 3: 145–166.

Piran, K. 2012. La Russie et la sécurité énergétique de l'Union européenne. *AFRI* 13: 129–139.

Pomerance, M. 1976. The United States and Self-Determination: Perspectives on the Wilsonian Conception. *AJIL* 70: 1–27.

Preuß, U.K. 2010. Kosovo – A State sui generis? *Südost-Europa* 58: 389–412.

Pronin, A. 2015. Republic of Crimea A Two-Day State. *Russian LJ* 3: 133–142.

Przetacznik, T. 1990. The Basic Collective Human Right to Self-Determination of Peoples and Nations as a Prerequisite for Peace. *N.Y. Law Sch. J. Hum. Rights* 7: 49–109.

Radan, P. 2012. Secessionist Referenda in International and Domestic Law. *Nationalism and Ethic Politics* 18: 8–21.

Reeves, S.R., and D.A. Wallace. 2015. The Combatant Status of the Little Green Men and Other Participants in the Ukraine Conflict. *International Law Studies* 91: 361–401.

Richmond, S. 2016. Why Is Humanitarian Intervention so Divisive? Revisiting the Debate over the 1999 Kosovo Intervention. *Journal on the Use of Force and International Law* 3: 234–259.

Röben, V. 2010. The ICJ Advisory Opinion on the Unilateral Declaration of Independence in Respect of Kosovo: Rules or Principles? *GoJIL* 2: 1063–1086.

Rossi, C.R. 2016. Impaled on Morton's Fork: Kosovo, Crimea, and the *sui generis* Circumstance. *EILR* 30: 353–390.

Roth, B.R. 2010. Secessions, Coups and the International Rule of Law: Assessing the Decline of the Effective Control Doctrine. *Melbourne Journal of International Law* 11: 393–440.

Rrecaj, B. 2011. A Contemporary Interpretation of the Principles of Sovereignty, Territorial Integrity and Self-Determination, and the Kosovo Conundrum. In *Kosovo: A Precedent?: The*

Declaration of Independence, the Advisory Opinion and Implications for Statehood, Self-Determination and Minority Rights, ed. J. Summers, 109–141. Leiden; Boston: Martinus Nijhoff.

Rusniah, A., and D.I. Efevwerhan. 2010. The ICJ Opinion on Kosovo: Symphony or Cacophony? *Indian JIL* 50: 545–559.

Ruys, T., and N. Verlinden. 2014. Digest of State Practice 1 January – 30 June 2014. *JUFIL* 1: 324–340.

Ryngaert, C. 2010. The ICJs Advisory Opinion on Kosovo's Declaration of Independence: A Mixed Opportunity?: International Court of Justice, Accordance with International Law of the Unilateral Declaration of Independence in Respect of Kosovo, Advisory Opinion of 22 July 2010. *NILR* 57: 481–494.

Ryngaert, C., and C. Griffioen. 2009. The Relevance of the Right to Self-Determination in the Kosovo Matter: In Partial Response to the Agora Papers. *Chinese JIL* 8: 573–587.

Ryngaert, C., and S. Sobrie. 2011. Recognition of States: International Law or Realpolitik? The Practice of Recognition in the Wake of Kosovo, South Ossetia and Abkhazia. *LJIL* 24: 467–490.

Salenko, A. 2015. Legal Aspects of the Dissolution of the Soviet Union in 1991 and Its Implications for the Reunification of Crimea with Russia in 2014. *ZaöRV/HJIL* 75: 141–166.

Salmón, E., and P. Rosales. 2014. Rusia y la anexión de Crimea o la crisis de la post Guerra Fría. *Derecho PUCP* 73:185–204. (Revista de la Facultad de Derecho, Pontificia Universidad Católica del Perú).

Salo, J. 1991. Self-Determination: An Overview of History and Present State with Emphasis on the CSCE Process. *Finnish YIL* 2: 307–321.

Saluschev, S. 2014. Annexation of Crimea: Causes, Analysis & Global Implications. *Global Societies Journal* 2: 37–46.

Santori, V. 2004. The United Nations Interim Mission in Kosovo and the Sovereignty and Territorial Integrity of the Federal Republic of Yugoslavia. In *Studi di diritto internazionale in onore di Gaetano Arangio-Ruiz*, vol. III, 1689–1721. Naples: Editoriale Scientifica.

Scelle, G. 1957. Quelques réflexions sur le droit des peuples à disposer deux-mêmes. In *Grundprobleme Des Internationalen Rechts: Festschrift Für Jean Spiropoulos. [Foundamental Problems of International Law] Problèmes fondamentaux du droit international*, ed. J.C.T. Eustathiades, C.N. Fragistas Spiropoulos, and D.S. Constantopoulos. Bonn: Schimmelbusch.

Schaller, C. 2008. Die Sezession des Kosovo und der völkerrechtliche Status der internationalen Präsenz. *AVR* 46: 131–171.

Sciso, E. 2014. La crisi ucraina e lintervento russo: profile di diritto internazionale. *RDI* 97: 992–1031.

Seidel, G. 2001. A New Dimension of the Right of Self-Determination in Kosovo? In *Kosovo and the International Community. A Legal Assessment*, ed. C. Tomuschat, 203–215. The Hague: Kluwer.

Seminatore, I. 2014. La Russie dans la crise ukrainienne: stratégie, tactique et guerre limitée. *Déf. Nat.* 771: 128–130.

Serra, G. 2008. The International Civil Administration in Kosovo: A Commentary on Some Major Legal Issues. *Italian YIL* 18: 63–87.

Shany, Y. 2014. Does International Law Grant the People of Crimea and Donetsk a Right to Secede? Revisiting Self-Determination in Light of the 2014 Events in Ukraine. *Brown JWA* 21: 233–244.

Shaw, M.N. 1997. Peoples, Territorialism and Boundaries. *EJIL* 8: 478–507.

Shelton, D. 2011. Self-Determination in Regional Human Rights Law: From Kosovo to Cameroon. *AJIL* 105: 60–81.

Shevtsova, L. 2014. Caer en la trampa de Putin. *Política exterior* 28: 62–74.

Shukovich, O. 1964. Self-Determination as a Principle of Coexistence. *Annuaire d'anciens auditeurs de l'Academie de Droit International de La Haye* 34: 175–183.

Simma, B. 1999. NATO, the UN and the Use of Force: Legal Aspects. *EJIL* 10: 1–22.

Simon, G. 2014. Zusammenbruch und Neubeginn. Die Krise ukrainische Revolution und ihre Feinde [Collapse and a New Beginning. The Ukrainian Revolution and Its Enemies]. *Osteuropa* 64: 9–40.

Slomanson, W.R. 2015. Crimean Secession in International Law. *Hungarian Yearbook of International Law and European Law* 303–329.

Sofaer, A.D. 2000. International Law and Kosovo. *SJIL* 36: 1–21.

Soroeta Liceras, J. 2013. La opinión consultiva de la Corte Internacional de Justicia sobre Kosovo de 22 de julio de 2010: Una interpretación judicial sui generis para un caso que no lo es. Aplicabilidad de la cláusula de salvaguardia de la Resolución 2625 (XXV) o de la secesión como remedio. *REEI* 25.

Stromseth, J.E. 1992. Self-Determination, Secession and Humanitarian Intervention by the United Nations. *ASIL Proceedings* 86: 370–374.

Šturma, P. 2009. The Case of Kosovo and International Law. *Polish YIL* 29: 51–63.

Stykow, P. 2014. Innenpolitische Gründe der Ukraine-Krise. Gleichzeitige Demokratisierung und Staatsbildung als Überforderung [Domestic Origins of the Ukrainian Crisis. The Overwhelming Challenge of Simultaneous Democratisation and State-Building]. *Osteuropa* 64: 41–60.

Šuković, O. 1991. Self-Determination as a Principle of Coexistence. *Annuaire de l'Anciens Auditeurs de l'Académie de droit international de La Haye* 34: 175–183.

Sunstein, C.R. 1991. Constitutionalism and Secession. *UCLR* 58: 633–670.

Sur, S. 1999. L'affaire du Kosovo et le droit international points et contrepoints. *AFDI* 45: 280–291.

Tamayo Álvarez, R. 2014. La secesión unilateral de Crimea y el derecho internacional. *Revista Análisis Internacional* 5: 97–113.

Tancredi, A. 2006. A Normative Due Process in the Creation of States Through Secession. In *Secession. International Law Perspectives*, ed. M. Kohen, 171–207. Cambridge and New York: Cambridge University Press.

———. 2008. Neither Authorized nor Prohibited? Secession and International Law after Kosovo, South Ossetia and Abkhazia. *Italian YIL* 18: 37–62.

———. 2011. The ICJ's Kosovo Advisory Opinion as an Exercise in Pre-Understanding. In *Questions de droit international autour de l'avis consultatif de la Cour Internationale de Justice sur le Kosovo*, ed. M. Arcari and L. Balmond, 217–236. Milan: Giuffrè.

———. 2012. Some Remarks on the Relationship between Secession and General International Law in the Light of the ICJs Kosovo Advisory Opinion. In *Kosovo and International Law: The ICJ Advisory Opinion of 22 July 2010*, ed. P. Hilpold, 79–108. Leiden; Boston: Martinus Nijhoff.

———. 2014a. Secession and the Use of Force. In *Self-Determination and Secession in International Law*, ed. C. Walter et al., 68–94. Oxford: Oxford University Press.

———. 2014b. Crisi in Crimea, referéndum ed autodeterminazione dei popoli. *DUDI* 8: 480–490.

———. 2014c. The Russian Annexation of the Crimea: Questions Relating to the Use of Force. *Questions of International Law, Zoom Out* I: 5–34. www.qil-qdi.org.

Thakur, R. 2016. Rwanda, Kosovo, and the International Commission on Intervention and State Sovereignty. In *The Oxford Handbook of the Responsibility to Protect*, ed. A.J. Bellamy and T. Dunne, 94–113. Oxford: Oxford University Press.

Thürer, D. 1984. Das Selbstbestimmungsrecht der Völker. *AVR* 22: 113–137.

———. 2000. Der Kosovo-Konflikt im Lichte des Völkerrechts: Von drei-echten und scheinbaren – Dilemmata. *AVR* 38: 1–22.

Tolstykh, V. 2014. Reunification of Crimea with Russia: A Russian Perspective. *Chinese JIL* 13: 879–886.

———. 2015. Three Ideas of Self-Determination in International Law and the Reunification of Crimea with Russia. *ZaöRV/HJIL* 75: 119–139.

Tomuschat, C. 2006. Secession and Self-Determination. In *Secession. International Law Perspectives*, ed. M. Kohen, 23–45. Cambridge and New York: Cambridge University Press.

Treviño, J.M. 2014. La flota del mar Negro y la crisis de Crimea. *Política exterior* 28: 76–83.

Tricot, R., and B. Sander. 2011. The Broader Consequences of the International Court of Justices Advisory Opinion on the Unilateral Declaration of Independence in Respect of Kosovo. *Columbia JTL* 49: 321–363.

Troebst, S. 1999. Chronologie einer gescheiterten Prävention: vom Konflikt zum Krieg im Kosovo, 1989–1999. *Östeuropa* 49: 777–795.

United States Opposes Request for ICJ Advisory Opinion on Kosovo. 2009. *AJIL* 103:140–142.

Urrutia Libarona, I. 2012. Territorial Integrity and Self-Determination: The Approach of International Court of Justice in the Advisory Opinion on Kosovo. *Revista destudis autonòmics i federals* 16: 107–140.

Usov, S.A. 1996. The Status of the Republic of Crimea: History and Present-Day Problems. *Russian Politics and Law* 34: 59–72.

Van den Driest, S.F. 2015a. Crimea's Separation from Ukraine: An Analysis of the Right to Self-Determination and (Remedial) Secession in International Law. *NILR* 62: 329–363.

———. 2015b. From Kosovo to Crimea and Beyond: On Territorial Integrity, Unilateral Secession and Legal Neutrality in International Law. *IJGR* 22: 467–485.

Van Steenberghe, R., and A.Cl. Boúúaert. 2011. L'avis de la Cour internationale de Justice sur la déclaration d'indépendance du Kosovo: Audace et retenue de la Cour au sujet d'une question controversée. *Rev. dr. Int. et comp.* 88: 343–386.

Vashakmadze, M., and M. Lippold. 2010. Nothing but a Road Towards Secession? The International Court of Justices Advisory Opinion on Accordance with International Law of the Unilateral Declaration of Independence in Respect of Kosovo. *GoJIL* 2: 619–647.

Vidmar, J. 2009. International Legal Responses to Kosovo's Declaration of Independence. *Vand. J. Transnatl L.* 42: 779–851.

———. 2010. Remedial Secession in International Law: Theory and (Lack of) Practice. *St. Antony's International Review* 6: 37–56.

———. 2011a. The Kosovo Advisory Opinion Scrutinized. *LJIL* 24: 355–383.

———. 2011b. Kosovo: Unilateral Secession and Multilateral State-Making. In *Kosovo: A Precedent?: The Declaration of Independence, the Advisory Opinion and Implications for Statehood, Self-Determination and Minority Rights*, ed. J. Summers, 143–177. Leiden; Boston: Martinus Nijhoff.

———. 2012. Conceptualizing Declarations of Independence in International Law. *Oxford JLS* 32: 153–177.

———. 2015. The Annexation of Crimea and the Boundaries of the Will of the People. *German LJ* 16: 365–383.

von Carlowitz, L. 2003a. UNMIK Lawmaking between Effective Peace Support and Internal Self-Determination. *AVR* 41: 336–393.

———. 2003b. UNMIK Lawmaking between Effective Peace Support and Internal Self-Determination. *AVR* 41: 336–393.

Wall, A.E. 2020. Legal and Ethical Lessons of NATOs Kosovo Campaign. *International Law Studies* 78: 571.

Walter, C. 2014a. Postscript: Self-Determination, Secession and the Crimean Crisis 2014. In *Self-Determination and Secession in International Law*, ed. C. Walter, A. Von Ungern-Sternberg, and K. Abushov, 293–311. Oxford: Oxford University Press.

———. 2014b. The Kosovo Advisory Opinion: What It Says and What It Does Not Say. In *Self-Determination and Secession in International Law*, ed. C. Walter et al., 13–26. Oxford: Oxford University Press.

Warbrick, C. 2008. Kosovo: The Declaration of Independence. *ICLQ* 57: 675–690.

Watson, K.W. 2008. When in the Course of Human Events: Kosovo's Independence and the Law of Secession. *Tul. J. Intl & Comp. L.* 17: 267–293.

Weller, M. 2011. Modesty Can Be a Virtue – Judicial Economy in the ICJ Kosovo Opinion. *LJIL* 24: 127–147.

Wengler, W. 1957. Le droit de la libre disposition des peuples comme principe du droit international. *RHDI* 10: 26–39.

White, R.C.A. 1981. Self-Determination: Time for a Re-Assessment? *NILR* 28: 147–170.

Wilde, R. 2011. Self-Determination, Secession, and Dispute Settlement after the Kosovo Advisory Opinion. *LJIL* 24: 149–154.

Wildhaber, L. 1995. Territorial Modifications and Breakups in Federal States. *Canadian YIL* 33: 41–74.

Williams, P.R. 2003. Earned Sovereignty: The Road to Resolving the Conflict over Kosovo's Final Status. *DJILP* 31: 387–425.

Wilson, G. 2009. Self-Determination, Recognition and the Problem of Kosovo. *NILR* 56: 455–481.

———. 2015. Crimea: Some Observations on Secession and Intervention in Partial Response to Müllerson and Tolstykh. *Chinese JIL* 14: 217–223.

———. 2016. Secession and Intervention in the Former Soviet Space: The Crimean Incident and Russian Interference in Its Near Abroad. *Liverpool Law Review* 37: 153–175.

Wippman, D. 2001. Kosovo and the Limits of International Law (NATOs Bombing of Kosovo Under International Law). *Fordham Intl L.J.* 25: 129–150.

Wolczuk, K. 2002. Catching up with Europe? Constitutional Debates on the Territorial-Administrative Model in Independent Ukraine. *Regional & Federal Studies* 12: 65–88.

Wydra, D. 2004. The Crimea Conundrum: The Tug of War between Russia and Ukraine on the Questions of Autonomy and Self-Determination. *IJGR* 10: 111–130.

Yee, S. 2010. Notes on the International Court of Justice (Part 4): The Kosovo Advisory Opinion. *Chinese JIL* 9: 763–782.

Youngs, R. 2009. A Door Neither Closed nor Open: European Union Policy Towards Ukaine During and Since the Orange Revolution. *International Politics* 46: 358–375.

Zajec, O. 2014. La obsesión antirrusa: Los buenos, la bestia y Crimea. *Le Monde diplomatique en español* 222: 1–5.

Zappalà, S. 1999. Nuovi sviluppi in tema di uso della forza armata in relazione alle vicende del Kosovo. *RDI* 82: 975–1004.

The manufacturer's authorised representative in the EU is Springer
Nature Customer Service Centre GmbH, Europaplatz 3, 69115 Heidelberg,
Germany. If you have any concerns regarding our products, please
contact ProductSafety@springernature.com

Printed and bound by CPI Group (UK) Ltd, Croydon, CR0 4YY
01/10/2026
02225952-0009